¡PRESENTE!

DISSIDENT ACTS   a series edited by
Diana Taylor and Macarena Gómez-Barris

THE POLITICS
OF PRESENCE

¡PRESENTE!

DIANA TAYLOR

DUKE UNIVERSITY PRESS   DURHAM AND LONDON   2020

Designed by Aimee C. Harrison
Typeset in Minion Pro and Le Murmure
by Westchester Publishing Services

Library of Congress Cataloging-in-Publication Data
Names: Taylor, Diana, [date] author.
Title: ¡Presente! : the politics of presence / Diana Taylor.
Other titles: Dissident acts.
Description: Durham : Duke University Press, 2020. | Series: Dissident acts | Includes
bibliographical references and index.
Identifiers: LCCN 2019054634 (print)
LCCN 2019054635 (ebook)
ISBN 9781478008552 (hardcover)
ISBN 9781478009443 (paperback)
ISBN 9781478008897 (ebook)
Subjects: LCSH: Presence (Philosophy)—Political aspects. | Performative (Philosophy)—
Political aspects. | Performance art—Political aspects. | Hispanic Americans in the
performing arts. | Performing arts—Political aspects—United States. | Knowledge,
Theory of. | Social epistemology. | Eurocentrism. | Decolonization—Latin America. |
Hispanic Americans—Race identity.
Classification: LCC BD355 .T39 2020 (print) | LCC BD355 (ebook) | DDC 320.01—dc23
LC record available at https://lccn.loc.gov/2019054634
LC ebook record available at https://lccn.loc.gov/2019054635

Cover art: Frames from Francis Alÿs, "The Multiplication of Sheep," in *Cuentos
patrióticos* (Patriotic tales), in collaboration with Rafael Ortega, 1997. Single-channel video
projection, 14:40 minutes. IMAGE COURTESY OF THE ARTIST.

To my family, who have accompanied me always:
Eric, Alexei, Marina, Gladys Lowe, Jonathan Schuller

And to my grandchildren,
Mateo Taylor Lowe, Zoe Taylor Lowe,
Shoshana Schuller, and Liora Schuller

Walking hand in hand with you, into new times.

CONTENTS

Prologue
Jumping the Fence

An undisciplined student, impatient with my high school classes at the British high school in Mexico City, I used to jump over the fence a few times a week after roll call and walk home. The pounds, shillings, and pence of my math class gave way to the pesos I'd spend on jicama with lime and chile to eat on the way. I'd throw off the outward signs of colonial discipline—the tie, blazer, knee-high socks, Oxford shoes—that I'd been forced to wear since I was a nine-year-old in the Canadian boarding school and now back home in Mexico. I set about to learn in my own haphazard fashion. I loved Shakespeare, Marlowe, and the Russian novelists, but also the Mexican comic and philosopher Cantinflas, who taught me, "Ah! There's the catch: it's neither this nor that, but completely the opposite."[1] In my life, every day was opposite day. If I graduated from high school it was because *Díos es grande* (God is great), as people say in Mexico, and probably more important, because students in the British system had to pass the General Certificate of Education administered out of the University of London. The exams were devised and graded in London, where no one cared if I had jumped over the fence to escape school in Mexico. I passed. Five Ordinary levels and two Advanced levels in literature and history. Not brilliant, but not bad for someone who refused school. And it got me into college, another haphazard adventure beyond the purviews of this prologue. Yet the irony is not lost to me that it was the "neutral" and "institutional" positioning of the authorized reader in London who got me through, outweighing the years of experience my local teachers had endured with the unruly child they deemed unfit for further study.

I have spent much of my professional life finding ways to work beyond the fence. I have never really belonged to (or in) any one field or academic department, so I tried to create other spaces for thinking and interacting with others. In my earlier years at Dartmouth, historian Annelise Orleck, journalist Alexis Jetter, and I started the Institute for Women and Social Change, bringing female artists, activists, and scholars from throughout the world. What, we wondered, did people do to sustain themselves and their communities exposed to dehumanizing and oppressive conditions when it seemed that very little could be done? We invited thinkers such as Wangari Maathai, Winona LaDuke, Dorothy Allison, and Cherríe Moraga to Hanover, New Hampshire, to imagine more life-sustaining ways of making worlds, making politics. Soon after, I started the Institute of Performance and Politics with my friend and colleague Doris Sommer at Harvard to create spaces of performance interaction and activism that exceeded departmental and even university limits. We launched the Mexican political masked performer SuperBarrio for president in 1996, and in early 1997 worked with Bread and Puppet to fill the Rockefeller Center at Dartmouth with images and cardboard figures we made of people from ethnic groups from throughout the Americas who would never be asked to enter that building. After moving to NYU in 1997, I worked with two of my doctoral students—Zeca Ligiéro, a professor from UNI-RIO in Brazil, and Javier Serna, a professor in the Autonomous University of Nuevo León in Mexico—to begin the Hemispheric Institute of Performance and Politics in 1998. Hemi was conceived back then as a cultural corridor throughout the Americas, creating physical, digital, and archival spaces of interaction where scholars, artists, and activists could collaborate on performance-based transdisciplinary, transborder projects and topics. At our first Encuentro in Rio de Janeiro, entitled *Performance* (as we tried to socialize the word as a theory as well as praxis), it was hard to convince people that we had anything to talk about. What, some artists asked, did they have to say to scholars? Activists, maybe. Not sure. But scholars? I noted that many focused their work on "the body": The body as front and center in performance art. The body on the line in activism. Who, I asked, problematized thinking about the body as gendered, raced, sexed, aged, with different kinds of aptitudes and abilities? Okay, okay, you can stay. Money from the U.S.? The empire? This must be another form of cultural and artistic extractivism. Every conversation was like that, negotiating how people who lived in different countries, communities, conditions, languages, and so on could talk in spite of the brutal economic, social, and political divides that separate us. Now, twenty years later, with some sixty academic and cultural organizations as institutional members, the conversations have changed. They're certainly no easier or less painful (as chapter 6 makes clear), but the debates and points of conflict continually shift.

This book, an *amoxohtoca* or "journey of the book" in Nahuatl, traces my meandering journey through the Americas, around, back, and back again as I've engaged in an unsettled and undisciplined approach to scholarship that prioritizes relational and embodied forms of knowledge production and transmission that take us beyond the colonizing and restrictive epistemic grids that some of our Eurocentric disciplines and practices impose on us. Yet transgressing those grids also invites all sorts of tensions and misunderstandings, some more productive than others. One of the most generative for me came in a conversation with Silvia Rivera Cusicanqui, who was explaining an Aymara concept of inter-relatedness. I understood her to say that *jaqxam sar* meant "to be me, I have to walk and talk with others." To be me, someone else has to name me, acknowledge me. These words guided much of my thinking as I reexamined colonialist and decolonial notions of subjectivity. When a year or so later I checked back with her to make sure I had used *jaqxam sar* appropriately, she did not remember our conversation and, more disorienting, said that *jaqxam sar* actually meant something else altogether. The concept "to be me, I have to walk and talk with others" made sense, she said, but not the term. So I claim both the misunderstanding and the concept, with the epistemic and political demand it makes on us, as I negotiate my way through these spaces and chapters.

To be me, I've learned along the way, I have to talk and walk with others. The artists, activists, and scholars who have walked and talked beside me on this journey have taught and sustained me in ways I cannot properly credit. This book is an attempt to continue some of the conversations we've started.

My conversations with Juan López Intzin (or Xuno López) added "enhearting" to the walking and talking. The Mayan, specifically Tzeltal, worldview situates the heart at the center of knowing and being with others. He calls this "epistemologies of the heart." Sometimes, like Stefano Harney, I've come to think of myself as an "idea thief." What might pass as a conversation beyond the fence still falls under the codes governing ownership in Academia. For years, I've lived with the regret of not starting *The Archive and the Repertoire* by acknowledging that one of the initial thoughts I had about repertoires as systems contiguous but independent from archives came during a conversation with Rebecca Schneider in a gas station in Wales on the way from PSi to London. On the table, she mapped out how the archive or library had always been physically separate from the theatre in ancient Greek and Roman cities. She was interested in what falls out of the archival, the remains, and cited my example of the missing finger from Evita's corpse in *Disappearing Acts*. For years, I had worried about the "other" of the archival, what I finally came to call the "repertoire" of embodied practices that survived the erasure wrought by the colonial archive. My interests came not from ancient Greece but out of recognition of the colonial dispossession created by the privileging of archival knowledge. So who owns what? I'd rather think of it as owing instead of owning. I owe Rebecca. I owe Xuno. I owe Silvia, I owe many people many things, even, as Moten and Harney put it, everything. I am deeply in debt. Encumbered. It makes me happy to know it and acknowledge it.

Some people, like Jesusa Rodríguez, have participated directly in much of my meandering. She is a companion and protagonist in much of this *amoxohtoca*. Lorie Novak, as many photographs in this volume attest, has often been a cotraveler, extending vision to places where my eyes could not see. Marianne Hirsch, Richard Schechner, Fred Moten, Marcial Godoy-Anativia, Toby Volkman, Juan López Intzin, Rebecca Schneider, Faye Ginsburg, Leda Martins, and Jacques Servin have been essential to my way of thinking and acting in the world. David Brooks of *La Jornada*, Diana Raznovich, Catherine Lord, Kim Tomsen, Julio Pantoja, Ricardo Dominguez, Benjamin Arditi, Peter Kulchyski, Reverend Billy, and Savitri D. have accompanied and inspired me, each in their own way. Some thinkers, such as Silvia Rivera Cusicanqui, Judith Butler, and Greg Grandin, come up again and again in my travels. Thanks to Manuel R. Cuellar and David Jesus Arreola Gutiérrez for their help with Nahuatl! And to Alexei Taylor, who can draw what I can only imagine. I have learned a considerable amount from Grace McLaughlin and Anthony Sansonetti, the two best research assistants imaginable. I thank you all. The voices of many of my colleagues, students, and Hemi collaborators and co-conspirators accompany me wherever I go. ¡Presentes! ¡Gracias!

Thanks to the Institut D'Etudes Avancée de Paris, which offered me a research fellowship in spring 2017, allowing me to find time to start putting this book together.

Thanks always to Ken Wissoker of Duke University Press, who has stewarded almost all my books, to Liz Smith, the senior project editor who worked on this book, and Macarena Gómez-Barris, coeditor of our series Dissident Acts.

As always, Susanne Zantop, I wish I could walk and talk with you.

ONE

¡Presente!

There can be no discourse of decolonization, no theory of decolonization, without a decolonizing practice.—SILVIA RIVERA CUSICANQUI, "Ch'ixinakax utxiwa"

Not long ago, I received a mass email from Juan Carlos Ruiz, then codirector of the New Sanctuary Movement in New York, asking us to be ¡Presente!, to show up and stand up to U.S. policies of deportation that are currently tearing families apart. I've known and admired Ruiz since we met in 2014, and he invited me to serve as a judge on the Permanent People's Tribunal (PPT), a nonbinding court of opinion that hears and responds to the plight of persecuted peoples whose claims will never be taken up by a court of law. That was the third hearing, this one held in New York City, that accused the Mexican and U.S. governments of crimes against humanity.[1] Several eminent human rights advocates were part of that tribunal—Raúl Vera, bishop of Saltillo; Father Alejandro Solalinde, nominated for a Nobel Peace Prize for his defense of migrants; and other luminaries deeply committed to the defense of human rights.

During those three days, we listened to migrants tell us of murders, forced disappearances, rapes, kidnappings, and robberies they faced as they headed north to the U.S. through Mexico. We heard from Deferred Action for Childhood Arrivals students whose families were threatened with deportation, not knowing then that they too would soon be at risk. Undocumented domestic workers spoke of the violent and degrading conditions in the unregulated labor market. Afro Garifuna women from Honduras said they'd been tricked with rumors that they could safely cross into the U.S. if they came alone with their small children. Instead they were shackled and released to relatives. They had to sit near an outlet during our hearings to keep their ankle monitors charged—a modern instantiation of black Latinx women in chains. For a moment, the ongoing, state-sponsored or sanctioned brutality made itself painfully visible. I knew of these dehumanizing politics, of course, but seldom so directly and intimately. As each person confided in us, looking us in the eye, she or he trusted us to do something about the cruel injustice. Courts adjudicate, after all. There are supposed to be consequences for criminal acts. While the jury declared the governments guilty of crimes against humanity, as charged, the tribunal's main contribution was more symbolic and informative than juridical. It was, in a sense, "just" a performance, an enacted aspiration for justice. Although the PPT has major standing in human rights circles, we knew that nothing concrete would come of it. These stories too would sink back into invisibility, part of the normalized cruelty in which we carry on our everyday lives. Never have I felt more powerless and responsible to and for people I did not know.

What can we do when apparently nothing can be done, and doing nothing is not an option?

For many involved in the tribunal, however, the performance of listening and fighting for justice was morally and ethically binding. We had to be ¡presentes! Everyone on the jury had a history of sustained, at times life-threatening, activism. Solalinde's early work creating shelters for migrants was inspirational. He would accompany them on occasion as they traveled deadly routes, arguing that his priest's collar offered a modicum of protection. Juan Carlos Ruiz helps organize a sanctuary movement to shield migrants from deportation, often getting arrested in the process. Someone else on the jury was a lawyer who worked tirelessly for migrant rights. I am an academic, a performance studies Latin Americanist—so I decided to do what I do best: research and document and transmit—link my knowing to a doing, to thoughtful and sustained action.

With several colleagues at the Hemispheric Institute (Hemi), we agreed to spend a good deal of time on the road through Central America, Mexico, and the Mexico-U.S. border region interviewing and working with migrants and those who care and advocate for them.[2] This was an act of *acuerpamiento*, learning of a situation by living it in the flesh. We had to walk the walk. We also needed to *hermanarnos* (become brothers/sisters) to build trust, to listen, and to care. We could then create a record of the testimonies of those we encountered in our path. We moved through Honduras, El Salvador, Guatemala, crossed the Suchate (the border river between Mexico and Guatemala), followed the migrant trails on and off, back and forth, for months that became years. We spoke with migrants and their defenders in shelters, the volunteers who provided care for amputees who had lost limbs on the train (La Bestia), sought out the unmarked graves of those who died on the way, and met with families of those who have disappeared.[3] At times, the local military kept us in their scopes, threatening anyone who spoke with us. The activists in the region shrugged the hazard off—the government already knew who they were and would eliminate them as they saw fit. The murder of environmental activist Berta Cáceres in Honduras just before we arrived proved that. Things were terrible under Obama, but now under the Trump administration everyone we spoke to knew it would get much worse. How's this going to end? we'd all ask each other.

Marcial Godoy-Anativia, the managing director of Hemi, and I got so tired and heartsick at times on those routes that we noted we were losing our capacity to speak, to form coherent sentences in either Spanish or English. We traced the hemisphere's "vertical border," joined activists and scholars on the border in Arizona and later in New York City to protest against Immigration and Customs Enforcement (ICE) and call for the release of those detained. We have participated as international observers on human rights missions and brought dozens of graduate students from throughout the Americas to walk the trail with us.[4] At one shelter, the students and migrants—some roughly the same age and a few even from the same countries—started dancing together. It was hard to distinguish between them. At the end of the afternoon, we got back on our air-conditioned bus and they were left to fend for themselves on their dangerous trek north. If they were to ride with us, they would be immediately jailed and deported by the federal and local agents who stopped our bus multiple times a day. We all felt sickened by the wild disparities in terms not just of privilege but of life expectancy. Acuerpamiento only goes so far. Why would they even talk to us? What could they conceivably get out of the exchange? One migrant articulated a powerful stipulation—I will talk to you all, he said, but you promise me you will do something about this. We all agreed, and many of us have worked in various ways to make good on that promise. One of the trans students started working with trans migrants on that journey and never stopped. Others are now lawyers and rights activists. Some devised artistic interventions. At Hemi, we created Ecologies of Migrant Care (https://migration.hemi.press/), a bilingual digital repository of more than one hundred accounts/testimonials by migrants and those who care for them. The videos, allow them to tell their own stories, in their own words. Our project shares the vision articulated by Fray Tomás, who started and runs the "72," the shelter for migrants in Tenosique, Mexico: "We aren't the voice of anyone. They have their own voice; they're subjects in their own right. They are very brave people."[5] A "human library," as Óscar Martínez, author of *The Beast* called it.[6] We continue to add more interviews, artistic interventions, and teaching resources to extend access to the materials now and into perpetuity (in library terms) in collaboration with NYU Libraries. This, we hope, is one way of protecting the stories from sinking into permanent invisibility. Someone will find them. Some will care.

Being here/there, physically on the route, talking and walking with others makes physical, political, and ethical demands on us. It was painfully clear that we do not know what they know, or experience or share their struggles and fate, but these interactions offered us another powerful way of knowing and acting on what we knew. Since 2014, I have participated as an activist, a professor, and a researcher in a series of interventions concerning the migrant crisis.[7] It's hard to know that we can only do what we can do; harder still to accept that we must to do what we can do. Despair and cynicism are not options.

This study revisits and reperforms the history of state violence born of conquest, colonial histories, imperialist interventions, and neoliberal extractivist practice, reborn continually with new unfolding projects of violence and disappearance. My question: How do we live and respond ethically to this systemic brutality, knowing full well that many of us are embedded in it and benefit from the economic inequalities it produces? While the migration catastrophe is only part of the problem I examine, Ruiz's email asking us/me to be ¡presente! precipitated a political as well as personal reflection—what does it mean to be presente to others and to oneself?

¡Presente!, with and without exclamation marks, depends on context. As much an act, a word, and an attitude, ¡presente! can be understood as a war cry in the face of nullification; an act of solidarity as in responding, showing up, and standing with; a commitment to witnessing; a joyous accompaniment; present among, with, and to, walking and talking with others; an ontological and epistemic reflection on presence and subjectivity as process; an ongoing *becoming* as opposed to a static *being*, as participatory and relational, founded on mutual recognition; a showing or display before others; a militant attitude, gesture, or declaration of presence; the "ethical imperative," as Gayatri Spivak calls it, to stand up to and speak against injustice.[8] ¡Presente! always engages more than one. Sometimes it expresses political movement, sometimes a being together, walking down the street or celebrating and enacting our response, position, and attitude in our encounter with others, even when the other has been disappeared, or hides its face.

While these examples focus on presente as interactive and political, it also has a more self-reflexive dimension—how present am I in my own body, in the dailiness of my own life? Jesusa Rodríguez, one of Mexico's major artists, activists, and now senators, and I have led an exercise in performance pedagogy (which I discuss at length in chapter 3) that makes one critical point: The way you do *this* is the way you do everything. It doesn't matter what the *this* is. The way I decide to meet up with a friend, advocate for justice, look away when I see a homeless person, make a meal, or teach a class is how I do everything. Am I in a hurry? Multitasking? Thoughtful? Thinking of something else? A perfectionist? Good enough is good enough, and almost good enough, I reassure myself, is sometimes fine too? Ruiz's call to be presente suddenly made me reflect on the ways in which I am/not presente in everything I do. Presente to whom? Where? Why? What does it mean ethically and politically? In scholarly and pedagogical terms? Presence, as ¡presente!, as embodied engagement, as political attitude, asks us to reexamine what we (think) we know, how we know, and the obligations and responsibilities that accompany such knowledge.

¡Presente! as an organizing concept informs my project in several key ways: epistemically, politically, artistically, and pedagogically. ¡Presente! performs the methodology (walking), the attitude, and the existential urgency of the argument. It is the argument. We need to be ¡presentes!

These various aspects of ¡presente! mutually reinforce each other to provide the pathways through the chapters, connected through my personal experience in ever-extending networks of activist commitment. No word in English captures the force or the multivalence of this term. The gesture of the raised fist enacts the militancy. The declaration "We're here, we're queer, get used to it" reflects the solidarity and defiance. Shared moments of silence allow us to accompany others. "Say her name" conveys its recuperative gesture. Singing and dancing in a rally capture its joyful, animating quality. Yet it's important to cluster these many meanings in a name and think them through together in this word/act. ¡Presente! allows for that; the chapters here remind us that no one aspect is enough; refusal is not enough, defiance is not enough, critique is not enough, joy—alas—is not enough.[9] Political interventions require a complex play of dispositions, moves, and gestures.

¡Presente!, moreover, immediately conjures up the bilinguality of this project that I have thought through concurrently in Spanish and English. The English lies nested in the Spanish, just one *e* short. The Spanish exceeds the English, especially with the emphatic exclamation marks that reflects attitude and, more often, commitment and determination. If the study moves between present and presente, it's because I do. As I was born to Canadian parents who relocated to Mexico after living in Cuba, my process of becoming moves between languages. I realize that certain ideas and attitudes take shape in one language or the other, but rarely in both in the same way. Thinking, feeling, gesturing, or acting on them in the (momentarily) "other" language requires an act of embodied, linguistic, epistemic, and emotional translation, estrangement, approximation, or accommodation. Neither language is enough, and even both together fall short. To be clear: there is nothing inherently illuminating or liberating about bi- or multilinguality. We all live simultaneously within various linguistic codes—be they regional linguistic variations, slang, jargon, or other group-specific forms of communication. But becoming between languages, living between here and there, has helped me to understand between-ness, beside-ness, entanglement, and negotiation as integral components of thought and presence itself, not simply instantiations of geographical or methodological located-ness.

Mexican Spanish, for example, has indigenous languages living alongside and within it, pushing the frames of intelligibility to allow native worldviews to express themselves. In Mexico, for example, I live in Tepoztlán, a small indigenous town in the Tepozteco range of sacred mountains and home to Tepoztecatl, the lord of the mountains and the wind. My house is on Cuauhtemotzin, a street named after the last Aztec ruler ("one who has descended like an eagle"), executed by the Spanish conqueror Hernán Cortés. My house too retains its Aztec name, Cuatzonco, meaning "head of the barrio"—and a long, turbulent history. Without speaking Nahuatl, I say these words every day. That constant invocation reanimates a history of conquest and settler colonialism of which I am a part. The same thing happens in English—Spanglish and Black English remind us of the multiple cultures, epistemes, and attitudes that flourish within supposed monolinguality. Ay te watcho. Mucho be careful. Ailóbit.[10] The unsettled, constant back and forth of code-switching, for example, conjures a sense of proximity. Certain words and homonyms bridge languages, allow them to touch (at times infelicitously), and open up multiple interpretations. A well-known example from my youth: Ford Motor Company could not understand why its popular Nova model did not sell in Mexico until someone pointed out that "no va" means "doesn't go" in Spanish. The points of proximity and rupture, the iterations and multilayeredness of language, form part of the dis- re- mis-placements and movement that I mark throughout this study. The constant traversing of historical, national, temporal, and linguistic frames is a thinking/touching/becoming in motion that cannot be thought of as translation proper; it does not try to reproduce or represent stated ideas faithfully. Translation, in this sense, seems more like an evolving dialogic, citational, and performatic movement that builds on meanings and gestures, highlights the slippages and gaps, and exhausts the potentialities of silences and the unspoken to understand why some concepts, possibilities, and realities come into or fall out of awareness.

My bilinguality and biculturality, moreover, underline another aspect of presente. Traveling back and forth from Mexico to Canada to boarding school ("to learna di inglish") from ages nine to fourteen and then much later to the U.S. for my PhD and now for work, I began to think of myself as a cultural broker, a trafficker in ideas with the privilege, access, and betrayal that implies.[11] Some concepts traveled; others were left behind. Much of what I bring into the discussion is not mine to tell, but the people who should be in the room have been denied entry. The theoretical contributions from indigenous scholars in Latin America often find themselves filtered, not to say pilfered, by Latin Americanists trained and working in the U.S. who use those ideas for their/our own ends. Indigenous scholars have often accused U.S.-based academics of extractivist practices, producing unengaged and ungrounded work that does not reflect their context.[12] But too often I have been the only person in a room to ask, "What about Latin America?" When I speak, I do so as a Latin Americanist trained in Mexico and the United States, not as a Latin American. How can I represent the systemically absented? Or speak for others? I cannot participate in the colonialist gesture of assuming a field absent other voices and perspectives—hence the continuing political urgency of insisting on presence.

By moments I've come to identify with Malinche, the multilingual indigenous woman who was Cortez's translator and lover. She is often depicted as a bridge figure in the chronicles. Mexicans have long hated her, accusing her of giving Europeans entry to Aztec practices and ideologies, thus precipitating the destruction of their empire.[13] If being presente demands an ethical engagement, it seems that the terms of my presentness—racially, through social status, disciplinary training, and institutional location—calls attention to its many complexities. I am simultaneously a Mexican in Canada and the U.S. and a *guerita* (light-skinned, epidermically white) in Mexico. I have a slight Spanish accent in English, which nonetheless has become my dominant language. I am a scholar at a major U.S. university inaccessible to all who cannot afford the high cost of tuition. My retirement funds are invested in the exploitative forces that I work against. I'm an activist of human rights, and a person of a privilege. Present/e, for me, means owning my mis-fit, mis-translations, and mis-appropriations in a series of interventions and dialogues across disciplinary, linguistic, and cultural/national border crossings.

Mis-fitting has its advantages. Returning recently from Bolivia to Mexico, I forgot that I had a large bag of coca leaves in a jacket I had worn inside the Potosí silver mines—the economic engine that produced the Spanish empire in the sixteenth century and positioned Europe at the center of the known universe, as I argue later. Coca was an obligatory gift for the miners and for the terrifying statue of the guardian figure, El Tio (uncle), who protects the mine. Having offered copious quantities of coca leaves to all, I had slipped the bag of remaining leaves in my jacket pocket and forgotten about it. Claiming my suitcase in Mexico City, I remembered with alarm the jacket and the coca leaves. Passengers exiting customs were divided into two lines—the X-ray machine for luggage, and the line that went past the customs officer and the sniffer dog. I got the dog, who immediately jumped on the suitcase holding my jacket and started barking enthusiastically. The customs officer was bewildered: a well-dressed white lady of a certain age was hardly his idea of a trafficker. The dog kept jumping on my bag. I stood frozen by images of spending the night in a jail or in custody someplace. The customs officer asked if I was carrying food in the bag. No. He looked at me some more, then asked if I owned a dog. Yes. "That must be it," he said, relieved. "Go ahead." I could only imagine the dog's reaction as it saw me wheel my bag out the exit. "Why do you train me if you're not going to take my skills seriously?" I was the grateful beneficiary of the difficulty in overriding assumptions and stereotypes related to race, class, age, and privilege.

But my mis-fits also oblige me to use my scholarly training and access as well as my racial, class, and professional privilege to intervene in every way that I can. We—scholars, artists, and activists—often coemerge from and inadvertently continue to coproduce these colonial scenarios. It's not just a decolonial theory about "it" (be it oppression, inequality, subalternity, and so forth) addressed to "them," it's about a decolonial practice (as Silvia Rivera Cusicanqui says) that implicates me and the way I teach, research, write—remembering that the way I do this is the way I do everything. Part of my responsibility is to learn, unlearn, listen, engage, challenge, and if possible change the scenario. Here, then, I venture out and bring back my personal, at times truncated and one-sided, reflections from those interactions.

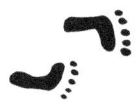

This book is a product of many encounters that respond to one, under-lying question: How to be present ethically and politically as a scholar, an activist, and a human being—with/to/among the many people struggling against a virulent brew of colonial-imperialist-capitalist-authoritarian-environmental-epistemic violence throughout the hemisphere? What makes this a book rather than a collection of essays is that presencing works as a practice, a methodological as well as theoretical thread. I came to see this inquiry as a form of walking theory, thinking in and through the embodied and discursive acts of transfer. The ideas were generated by the encounters, the predicaments, the physical motion, challenges, and expenditure that I describe. The personal entanglements that arise in each section elucidate different aspects of present/e, ways in which social actors intervene in the violent historical scenarios that constitute our hemispheric Americas.

The chapters and pathways draw on conversations in performance studies, Latin American and hemispheric studies, Native studies, Latinx, Chicana/o studies, de- and anticolonial studies, affect, memory, gender, queer, and trans studies, trauma studies, and other postdisciplines, the overlapping configu-rations that emerge beyond the fence, to think through the embodied and political aspects of ¡presente! as protest, as witnessing, as solidarity, as the reciprocal process of becoming in place and with others. The presentness and embodied dimensions of presente enable a set of practices developed in performance studies that recognize scholars as coparticipants in the strug-gles, scenarios, and encounters we engage in. Dwight Conquergood put it succinctly: "Proximity, not objectivity, becomes an epistemological point of departure and return."[14] What we know, in part, depends on our being there, interacting with others, unsettled from our assumptions and certainties, forging at times the conditions for mutual recognition, trust, and solidarity. It's impossible to pretend to be objective or disembodied. The performance itself, as a framework and as a doing, contributes to the meaning.

Instead of further cementing demarcated disciplines and institutions, this study brings together work by people from diverse locations, backgrounds, and disciplines who contest colonialist theories and practices that produce isolated silos of knowledge. The chapters evolve from the point of view of the relational "I" that accompanies others, participates, experiences, responds, analyzes, and writes down the tentative lessons and conclusions drawn from these interactions. "I" am present to various degrees in each one of the scenarios I lay before you. The "I," however, is not autobiographical. I don't ask that you get to know "me." Rather, it calls attention to the necessary situatedness of knowledge that always emanates from the embodied practices of historically, socially, gendered, racially codified bodies. The located "I," in dialogue with other "I"s, serves as a medium for transmission for the acts, ideas, struggles, and possibilities outlined in the various chapters. Nonetheless, to use Richard Schechner's formulation, the "I" is not *not* autobiographical.[15] My situatedness in both space and professional status, my physical appearance and abilities, my linguistic and experiential limitations present me, affect how others interact with me, and frame what I can and cannot see, can/cannot register, participate in, or transmit. The "I" is, as Michel de Certeau posited, "a locus in which an incoherent (and often contradictory) plurality of such relational determinations interact."[16] "I" embody and represent all sorts of social forces that exceed my capacity to grasp or control.

Present/e, simultaneously singular and plural in both languages, conveys the ontological condition that one is/we are never fully present alone, and plurality always entails singularity. This "I" is part of a "we," or various "we"s, inextricable from them, yet remembering, again, as Jean-Luc Nancy makes clear, that we are *with*, yet separate.[17] "We" exists in states of besideness and betweenness. We all appear to others, and others appear to us. Yet there is nothing transparent about this process of appearance. We do not just recognize and acknowledge each other in a neutral "space of appearance."[18] The I/we entails complex rituals and politics of recognition. If, as Hannah Arendt argues, "in acting and speaking, men [*sic*] show who they are, reveal actively their unique personal identities and thus make their appearance in the human world,"[19] we need to ask what happens to those non-Enlightenment, nonliberal subjects—the slaves, the poor, the migrants who will always be a "what" rather than a "who" in certain spaces. Who gets to speak and reveal their "unique personal identities"? Who gets to speak for whom? Do "I" even recognize you as human? As part of my "we"? Do you acknowledge me? How many "we"s do we all belong to? Who is being presented, presenced?

These positions, always negotiated, at times transitory, are never given. Subcomandante Marcos, now known as Subcomandante Galeano, for example, identifies with all struggles and locates himself strategically: "Marcos is gay in San Francisco, Black in South Africa, Asian in Europe, Chicano in San Isidro."[20] In *I AM*, Guillermo Gómez-Peña says that the Sup reperformed his 1992 piece, "Spanglish Lesson" ("an Aztec in Nova Hispania/a Mexican in San Diego/a Puertorrican in New York") to counter the Mexican government's taunts that Marcos was gay, thinking that might discredit him.[21] Performances of identity are always reperformances—sometimes enactments handed down from above, sometimes oppositional forms of being articulated from below. Who gets to set or redefine the terms? Marcos, always, is and is not Marcos.[22] These performances function as repertoires transmitting genealogies, gestures, acts that allow for multiple identifications, affinities, allegiances, and *saberes* (both "ways of knowing" and "what is known"). I like Schechner's formulation of the not/not. I am not Mexican, but I am not/not Mexican. I am not a Gringa but I am not/not a Gringa. I am not a traitor, but I am not/not a traitor. Mine too is always a reperformance of negotiation and betrayal. I have chosen to live my Malinchismo as a gift, as a form of freedom from nationalisms and imperatives to self-identify in specific ways. I can affiliate, empathize, advocate, and accept responsibility, but I do not identify or belong in any one way. Who we are depends in part on our way of being presente.

Coming into Presence

We have to work towards [a] political identity [for] migrants as collective subjects and bearers of rights capable of revolutionizing the world—wherever they come from, wherever they pass through, and wherever they are going. A new economic identity for migrants . . . a new social identity from a social fabric that has been destroyed, overtaken by violence. They move from one country overtaken by corruption and impunity to another full of discrimination and humiliation. We must create this new identity by weaving together many cultures, many identities. . . . We describe this small project called La 72 with some irony as a "liberated territory." We are part of a new collective with a powerful identity.—FRAY TOMÁS, founder of the migrant shelter in Tenosique, Mexico, La 72

By what means of subjectification do we come into presence?[23] How does de-subjectification produce absence? How do men, women, and children become stateless "migrants," people without rights, expendable, disposable? How do we come to be Mexican or black or Indian or female, straight, queer, trans, or whatever it is we are? ¡Presente! explores the violent implications of the Western notion of self-reflective subjectivity through a series of scenarios of conquest, colonization, extraction, imperialism, and ongoing state violence in the Americas resonating from colonial histories. The conquest of the Americas in the fifteenth and sixteenth centuries inaugurated the global project of capitalism and, powered by the silver coming out of Potosí, established Europe as the center of the modern world. The conquest, too, ushered in notions of subjectivity and race that objectified both Amerindian and the African slave populations. The major political and economic recentering that placed Europeans as the powerful, defining, and conquering "I," Enrique Dussel argues, was "essential to the constitution of the modern ego . . . as subjectivity that takes itself to be the center or end of history."[24] Dussel traces how Descartes's 1636 "cogito" articulates and sustains the Enlightenment view of subjectivity through Kant's "culpable immaturity" of lazy others, through Hegel's dismissal of the New World as "immature and recently formed," through to Habermas's failure to understand the conquest as constitutive of modern subjectivity. Hegel's contempt for inhabitants of the Americas ("the inferiority of these individuals in every respect is entirely evident") and Africa (a "human being in the rough") are the other side of the same coin of the self-defined, self-referential "I." The Europeans alone are bearers of "the Spirit," the Hegelian notion of "the transcendental (interior or temporal) 'I,'" as Denise Ferreira da Silva defines it, and enjoy "the absolute right" over others who have no rights.[25]

The non-"I" is constantly subjected to all forms of racist, sexist, homophobic, and xenophobic assaults and microaggressions that become internalized and accumulate in bodies. We know now of the long-term effects of the ongoing process of subjugation that manifest not only in issues related to self-esteem but also as physical illness. The exterminating "I," however, needs its "not I" to define itself against, obfuscating the fact that the "other" is always also the "not not I" constitutive of the self-defining "I."[26] The "I" co-emerges, becomes copresence with the "not I," product of the same violence, embodying the self-blinding and brutality needed to make the "not I" into soulless brutes and "natural slaves."[27] Conqueror/conquered. Victimizer/victim. Slave master/slave. Murderer/corpse. These subjectivities are coextensional. The enactment of current practices of violence, dispossession, and disappearance, I argue in chapter 4, stems from these colonial and imperialist self-definitions and projects that enrich the haves and nullify the have-nots, rationalized in the name of capitalism and modernity.

Presente and present share an etymological root from Latin: *praestāre* (to give, show, present for approval) and *praesēns* (being there).[28] It entails the display or presentation of self and others. In the fifteenth century, this meant the coming into presence of indigenous and African peoples as things in preexisting European regulatory systems. Columbus took nine or ten misnamed Amerindians to Europe as a present or gift to present them to the Spanish court in 1493 as proof that he had discovered the sea route to Asia.[29] Did the captives' being there, present in their humanity, misrepresented in terms of their origins, override the stunned wonder of those in court? Present, yes, but present as strange, inhuman, found objects. How many survived? Nobody knows.

So began centuries of turning presence into absence for indigenous and African peoples in the Americas, somebodies into nobodies in what Frantz Fanon calls "a zone of nonbeing."[30] Humans mutated into exploitable and disposable property.[31] So began the hemispheric colonial history of being in transit, from the forced transportation of these Amerindians to the Spanish court, to the brutal shipping of Africans through the circum-Atlantic, from the Trail of Tears endured by Native Americans, to the current forced migration of Central Americans escaping violence in their home countries, ravaged in the 1970s by U.S. Cold War practices.[32]

On display, then, from the inaugural scenario of conquest was a new and yet reiterative domain of New Spain, the geopolitical formation of the so-called Americas populated by creatures rendered strange. "New" ushers in a linear, fractured temporality, a before-after, that separates peoples and practices from themselves and allows invaders to conquer and destroy existing worlds, including their notions of time.[33] This violent dis-encounter, rather than "encounter," as scholars have long liked to call the age of conquest,[34] ushered in what Achille Mbembe calls "the ever-presence and phantom-like world of race."[35] Racial categories such as "Indian," "mulato," "mestizo," "creole," and "criollo" came into the world. Racialization proved the "most efficient instrument of social domination in 500 years," according to Aníbal Quijano.[36] As a category of thought and policy, the concept of race emerged earlier than previously recognized by European theorists with little knowledge of the Americas. Even the brilliant Hannah Arendt erroneously argues that race became operationalized as "a principle of the body politic" on the "Dark Continent."[37] Anyone who maintains that "race was the Boers' answer to the overwhelming monstrosity of Africa—a whole continent populated and overpopulated by savages" has not read Columbus's letters or looked at Theodor de Bry's sixteenth-century engravings of America.[38]

If, as Alexander G. Weheliye suggests, we need to think of "racializing assemblages . . . as a set of sociopolitical processes that discipline humanity into full humans, not-quite-humans, and nonhumans" rather than race "as a biological or cultural classification," then we need to think how these assemblages were developed in tandem at the time of the conquest.[39] Dozens of Mesoamerican groups collapsed into "Indians." Iberians, accompanied by

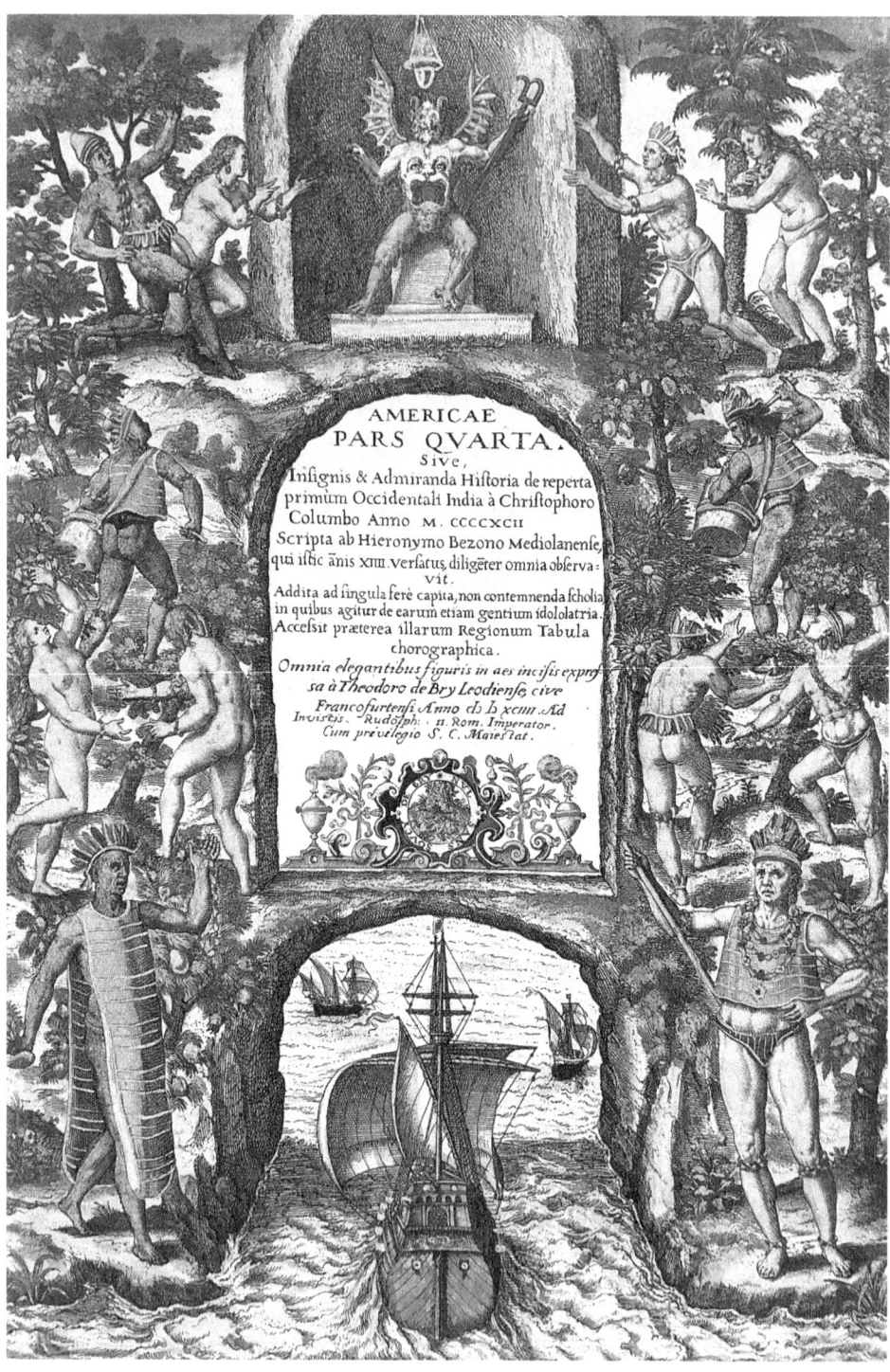

1.2 Theodor de Bry, *Americae* (sixteenth century).

African soldiers and slaves, produced new racial categories later codified as *castas*. As Amerindians perished at an extraordinary rate—95 percent of the population died in the first fifty years of contact—more than 110,000 African slaves were brought to Mexico between 1521 and 1624 to do the back-breaking work that, according to Friar Bartolomé de Las Casas, the indigenous peoples were too weak to do.[40] From the beginning, and some argue for the first time in human history, racial difference was created, depicted, and naturalized as a biological fact and economic necessity.[41]

The indigenous and African populations were conceived as necessary in providing the "free" labor for imperial capitalist expansion but expendable in terms of all else. Because they vastly overwhelmed the Europeans demographically, the colonizers mandated the absolute subjugation and management of both groups.[42] The newly imposed legal structures cemented the social barriers between conquerors and conquered.[43] Zoning laws along ethnic divides, the strict distribution of labor, and castes kept people separated even though the racializing assemblages created them as expendable others.[44] Instead of the hundreds of ethnic civilizations living in the Americas at the time of the conquest, the indigenous peoples were identified as *indios*, mestizos, *castizos*, *cholos*, and *pardos* depending on reproductive practices and social rank. The caste system similarly stripped Africans and their descendants of their ethnic, linguistic, and regional backgrounds. Thirty-six categories of the castas denoted blacks as *lobos* (wolves), *zambos* (bowlegged), *saltatrás* (a step backward), *tente en el aire* (suspended in the air), and *no te entiendo* (I don't understand you).[45] These words, along with the images that illustrated them, showed Africans and Afro-descendants conjured into presence as dark, brutal, backward, incomprehensible. While many of these terms were not in common use, words such as *negros*, *morenos* (dark), *mulatos*, and *pardos* were used, the last two reserved for mixed-race peoples.

While the intertwined histories of Amerindians, Africans, and their descendants exceed my study, they came into presence as things, property to be exploited. Colonists circumvented existing prohibitions against enslaving indigenous peoples.[46] In some cases, they argued that as pagans, indigenous peoples were not protected by existing laws. Others, like Ginés de Sepúlveda, held the opinion that it was legitimate to enslave indigenous people because they were by nature slaves of "inferior intelligence along with inhuman and barbarous customs. . . . They have established their nation in such a way that no one possesses anything individually, neither a house nor a field, which he can leave to his heirs in his will."[47] Capitalism served as both an instrument and ideology of conquest. Whether they were designated as slaves or peons, indigenous workers were often placed in conditions of servitude that have continued into the present.

This structural coming into presence of Afro and indigenous peoples, not as subjects but as subjugated and expendable labor, as racialized things, then, needs to be thought together. Like Mbembe, I understand Foucault's definition of racism as being "above all a technology aimed at permitting the exercise of biopower," defined by Foucault as "the set of mechanisms through which the basic biological features of the human species became the object of a political strategy."[48] We would do well, however, to push the date of the rise of capitalism and the various manifestations of modernity linked to biopower back to the conquest, colonization, and slavery of the fifteenth and sixteenth centuries rather than to the eighteenth century as Foucault posits. "The modern world-system was born in the sixteenth century," as Aníbal Quijano, Immanuel Wallerstein, Enrique Dussel, Ramón Grosfoguel, and others have shown, with the geosocial construction of the "Americas."[49] The exercise of biopower to control and annihilate populations during this period remains linked to the rise of capitalism, as Foucault noted. But the rise of "global networks" and alliances, "European capitalists," "armed trade," "a military-fiscal state," "the invention of financial instruments," "the expropriation of land," slavery, and a legal system defending these practices were all put in motion with Columbus's arrival in the Americas.[50]

We also need to extend the paradigm to consider the continuous (and changing) coming into presence of the "Indian" from the fifteenth century throughout what is now Latin America, and a century or so later after the British and French colonists arrived in what is now the U.S. and Canada, to the present.[51] As Linda Tuhiwai Smith states, "Imperialism frames the Indigenous experience."[52] For all their differences, such as indigenous peoples who had city-state polities (Aztec, Inca, Maya) versus the northern "Bush people," gatherers and hunters,[53] many Native American nations and communities (in the hemispheric sense) still share important commonalities: from recognizing "the presence of energy and power [as] the starting point [and cornerstone] of their analyses and understanding of the world,"[54] to an emphasis on communal and relational subjectivity; oneness with the land (or *mapu* for the Mapuche), the cosmos, and everything in it; notions of *mino bimaadiziwin* or the "good life" for the Nishnaabeg that Leanne Betasamosake Simpson writes about;[55] to the fight for the *dignidad rebelde* (rebellious dignity) of the Zatapistas and the Sioux activists at Standing Rock. As colonizers and settlers imposed different languages, religions, labor and living conditions, and practices and policies dispossessing native communities of their land for over five hundred years, the nations and groups have found various ways of coming into presence through "resurgence" that reasserts their names, languages, and traditions through protest and at times armed struggle.[56] This ongoing becoming is best thought through a hemispheric and performance lens. As Simpson notes, "performance art" (and I would argue performance more broadly) proves invaluable to understanding "Indigenous thought . . . obtained through collective truths that are derived from the experience of individuals, relationships and connections (to the non-human world, the land and each other) through action or 'presencing,' and through creative process."[57]

Afro-descendants have also been variously figured in and out of social existence—in the fifteenth and sixteenth centuries by the loss of their names and places of origin enabled by the castas system and again in the eighteenth century with its dismantling. In Mexico, with the largest number of free blacks and the second largest of slaves in the seventeenth century, the Afro and indigenous populations continued to mix. Ben Vinson III argues that Mexico's attempts to eliminate the caste system upon achieving independence in 1821 led to the "'historical forgetting' of the black population" until about 1940.[58] They fell out of presence officially, if not literally. The vast majority of the population that included Afro-descendants and indigenous peoples were designated mestizos, their individual histories buried once again under nomenclature. Who knew until recently that there even were Afro-Mexicans? Nobody asked.[59] The first time that Afro-descendants could identify as such in Mexico was on the 2015 Intercensus, where 64.9 percent also identified themselves as indigenous.[60] An estimated 15 percent of the Mexican population is indigenous, though a far greater number is of indigenous descent. The names have changed, but the discriminatory logics remain the same. This example of race as a system of desubjectification shows the complex operations and interconnections of coming into and falling out of presence as part of a transpersonal, historical continuum.

Major theorizations of race in the Americas also come in and out of presence in odd ways. Many key anticolonial scholars born in the Americas, people such as Frantz Fanon, Aimé Césaire, Stuart Hall, and others who identify as Afro-descendants have mostly left the extermination and domination of indigenous peoples out of their thinking about race. Césaire's *A Tempest*, for example, depicts the submissive Ariel as a "mulatto slave" (Afro-European) and the rebellious Caliban as a "black slave."[61] The indigenous presence completely disappears in this version of conquest and coloniality, just as the Taíno and Guanahatabey have almost been erased from the islands now known as the Caribbean and Antilles. Even the memory of the erasure is erased. Caliban, Shakespeare's "savage and deformed slave," I always assumed, was indigenous. Columbus's reports in his 'First Letter" (1492) of an island named Carabis inhabited by people who are "extremely fierce" and "eat human flesh" inspired Montaigne's essay, *Of Cannibals* (c. 1580), which scholars assume was the basis for Shakespeare's Caliban.[62] Columbus in that letter specifically stated, "They are not Negroes, as in Guinea, and their hair is straight." But then, Columbus thought he had reached Asia. Cuban theorist Roberto Fernández Retamar, in his *Calibán*, sees him as the symbol of mestizo (indigenous/European) America.[63] Theories of race in Latin America and the Caribbean have developed in parallel linguistic and political tracks. Studies of race tend to focus on Afro-descendant populations, primarily in Brazil, while studies of indigenous and mestizo Americas often ignore race.[64] Each assigns different aspects of the same history to oblivion. Colonialism imposes its own geographies of knowledge.

While many reasons contribute to the disconnect, here I will simply point to four. First, colonial metropoles in Britain and France played central roles in training intellectuals from their former colonies and disseminating their findings. Spain played no such role. If anything, it turned its back on the new racial categories and peoples that were produced by its conquest and colonialism of the Americas. The words "mestizo" and *mestizaje* did not enter the official dictionary of the Real Academia until 1992. *Mestizar* appears in the *Diccionario del uso del español* as "adulterating the purity of a race by its cross with others."[65] Not a word about the centuries of Spanish mixing with the indigenous and African peoples they named and dominated. Dictionaries, like histories, perpetuate erasures.

Second, Spain was not a center of philosophical or scientific thought even before its sharp economic decline in the seventeenth century. Secular universities in the late eighteenth century, as Ramón Grosfoguel points out, "used the Kantian anthropological idea that rationality was embodied by the White man north of the Pyrenees mountains."[66] In part, Spain's lack of prestige stemmed from European perception that the Spanish language, suited to emotions and literary expression, was inadequate to the task of rigorous rational inquiry, as Walter Mignolo argues.[67]

Third, colonial spheres of interest and ideology expanded along linguistic, not geographical, lines. Fanon's Martinique, for example, was part of France; Jamaica, where Hall was born and trained, part of Britain. Their positioning as Francophone and Anglophone (as opposed to American in its hemispheric sense) post- and anticolonial scholars accounted for the ways in which they thought about race and coloniality from the perspective of other, fundamentally different, instances of colonialism developed in relationship to India, Africa, and Algeria.

Fourth, the Americas, including the complexities inherent in the production of "race," do not figure into the ways in which major European theorists such as Arendt and Foucault thought about race as the ideological driver of capitalism. Therefore, the Americas drop out of most reflections on race, coloniality, and biopower when critical discussions of postcolonial theories do not neatly apply. Hannah Arendt excludes the Americas and Australia from her thinking as "the two continents that, without a culture and history of their own, had fallen into the hands of Europeans."[68]

Generalized lack of understanding about the impact of colonialism on both Afro-descendants in Latin America and Amerindians continues to be understood as a deficiency on the part of the ignored.[69] Juan López Intzín (Xuno López), a Mayan Tzeltal speaker, whose work I engage throughout, recently pointed out that in the sixteenth century the Spaniards were arguing about whether Amerindians had souls. Now people argue about whether they're intelligent.[70] My turn to necropolitics and other theories developed in relation to blackness and the slave trade attempts to place the colonial European paradigms in conversation with indigenous perspectives, when possible, to call attention to the historical and theoretical lacuna in the study of ongoing coloniality in Latin America.

Para-presente

What if we considered these overlapping histories and theories of subjectification together, as copresent, coemergent? While annihilating systems of power have systemically denied subjectivity to women and indigenous, black, trans, migrant (and many other) communities for centuries, these histories tend to splinter off into isolated, parallel events and instances. Linguistic and regional separations, spheres of influence, temporal divides, and other factors make it difficult to see this violence as always, already, and everywhere connected. Western linear temporalities and spatial boundaries delimit our understanding.

While ¡presente!, as in present tense, screams out the urgency of the now, its reiterative power points to its ongoing demands, the constant shuffle between the past, present, and future configured differently in different epistemes. In indigenous and African cultures, long considered anachronistic or backward by some commentators, time is plural, multilayered, and coexists alongside other times—the times of the gods, the natural elements, the ancestors, human time, and so on. Leda Martins writes of "spiral time" in the worldview of Yoruba and Congo descendants in Brazil, in which the "past" lies ahead, in view, and the future sneaks up from behind.[71] Silvia Rivera Cusicanqui notes the simultaneity of past and futurity in the Aymara worldview: "There is no *post* or *pre* in this vision of history that is not linear or teleological but rather moves in cycles and spirals and sets out on a course without neglecting to return to the same point."[72] For the Aztecs, according to James Maffie, "time's passing . . . consists of the successive comings and goings—accompanying and abandoning—of *qualitatively* different kinds of tonally-energy burdens . . . each kind if time has its own kind of energy, character, or personality."[73] The Zapatistas, according to Marcos aka Galeano, think of temporality as an hourglass, "through which one can see time going by and try to understand that, but see the time that's coming at the same time."[74] The particular mix of anachronism, futurity, and existential/political emergency invites us to think of para-times. "Para," as a prefix, attaches itself to other words to denote proximity; para stands along with, by, besides.[75] Paranormal exceeds scientific explanation but remains attached and defined by the normal. Paraphrase signals another way of saying something—not the same words, but closely attached to their meaning. Paramilitary, as auxiliary or unofficial armed forces, might not be military, but they're not not military. Para-times encourage us to think of geological time, historical time, environmental, human, and animal time alongside, within, and with each other rather than as sequential. One time frame does not necessarily account for another. At times the various moments appear together, a palimpsestic layering. At others, they loop as a reiterative, seemingly endless again-ness. Even in the human experience of time, certain phenomena can never be analyzed in and through their own moment. History, tradition, religion, trauma, for example, are not coterminous with the events that gave them rise, whether it be the birth of a savior or a blow or a defining event. The effects and affects come later. In other ways, too, we do not all live in the same moment, and this is not just because we inhabit different time zones. The street vendor in Bogotá selling indigenous food lives in a para-time and space, alongside the one inhabited by her customer, the affluent corporate businessman who drives by in his new car.

Para-times strain the more expansive Western notions of temporality. Even queer and trans temporalities, which I explore in chapter 6, can fracture along racial and ethnic lines as the anachronistic or para-temporal nature of native queer thought crashes into the exigencies of identitarian politics.[76] Coming into presence for queer Cree artist Tomson Highway means conjuring up a vanishing world of possibilities in front of our Western eyes.[77] The *now*, for Cree speakers like him from northern Manitoba and the Northwest Territories, rehearses its own demise.

In Western cultures, capitalism has reduced the non-Western experiences of time into productive/nonproductive time, work time and time off. From a topological perspective, time is usually represented as linear, a line that ties past to present, to future, though at times the line might be depicted as thoroughly knotted. In addition to the existential condition of "time present and time past . . . both perhaps present in time future" of T. S. Eliot's *Four Quartets*, we now have the temporalities of surveillance systems and political preemptive strategies where, quite literally, "What might have been and what has been / Point to one end, which is always present."[78] Present danger, unlocatable threat, but still linear.[79] By the mid-2010s, preemption becomes the dominant tactical, existential, and ontological regime that Brian Massumi labels *ontopower*: "For a future cause to have any palpable effect it must somehow be able to act on the present."[80]

The colonization of the future hijacks the present and obscures other epistemic conditions, other ontologies: the decimation of past and present to preclude a future. Preemptive strikes simultaneously perpetuate the racist, colonialist, imperialist, and extractivist violence of the past, ensuring that nothing will grow there but more violence. These are the "ruins yet to come" that Ricardo Dominguez speaks of.[81] In other words, empire has colonized the future; capitalists can defy limits by sending Teslas into space even as their border officials reinforce boundaries by building walls and placing migrant children in cages. The long- and short-term health effects of traumatic loss ensure that the newly recolonized don't have a future.[82] The Guaraní, Dussel tell us, "understood the end of the world in terms of the end of the forest and the elimination of any future time."[83]

Yet, in the expandable now and porous present of performance, we might find fragments of other ways of being present.[84] Rebecca Schneider builds on historian Howard Zinn's notion of "fugitive moments," moments salvaged from the past to "present us with its own alternative futures—futures we might choose to realize differently." In performance, she argues, reenactment and other forms of repeat show the potential for time to be "malleable political material."[85] Performance, as we shall see, serves a vital role in opening spaces to breathe and come into presence as a strategic "we" to reimagine other ways of acting and thinking in the world.

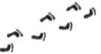

Presente, but where? Two enormous housing projects in the southern part of Mexico share the same name. The Siglo XXI Migratory Station, a large and forbidding detention and deportation center, "lodges" and "repatriates" (in the language of the Mexican government) about 250,000 Central American migrants a year who escape the violence in their countries to seek refuge, safety, and work elsewhere.[86] The U.S. has outsourced its militarized policies to keep migrants away from its own southern border. Near that Siglo XXI, the familiar logo for the Century 21 real estate agency reminds the better-off that they can live anywhere. "More Americans have been added to the population of Mexico over the past few years than Mexicans have been added to the population of the United States, according to government data in both nations."[87] Many U.S. citizens in fact move to Mexico precisely not to work. They want to retire with a higher standard of living, cheaper services, and a better climate than they would have back home.

The two projects/discourses exist in an interwoven relationship, and not just because their names mirror each other. Each, representing a different migratory population, points to deep blind spots in our discussions about who gets to be where. Century 21 ads feature images of open spaces and pristine nature to encourage what it calls "relentless moves" to unexplored frontiers.[88] Relentless? As in "constant, continual, continuous, non-stop" expansionism?[89] Anything is possible for their clients; it's all about choice, comfort, safety, and a sense of adventure. Wealthier migrants, part of what a recent *New York Times* piece called "millionaire migration," might own multiple houses around the world in case things get tough back home or they need to park their money and avoid paying taxes.[90] The same online dictionary spells out the second meaning for relentless: harsh, grim, fierce, cruel . . . remorseless, merciless. Siglo XXI offers its inhabitants enclosure, walls, surveillance, abuse, and deportation back to the violence they have risked their lives to leave behind. Migrants have no choice. Everything is impossible.

Here we have it: the seeming contradiction of capitalism's newest frontiers coexisting with the U.S. as a walled state;[91] mobility and immobility; access granted and denied—in short, the world of the liberal individual subject and the nobodies who can be used and discarded. Mirror images; each depends on the other for its existence.

Instead of a contradictory embroilment, however, I would call it para-doxical. Para-, beside, but also "beyond, wrongfully, harmfully, unfavorably, and among."[92] We live in para-worlds, para-spaces, in which the Derridian lament of "crimes of hospitality" have turned a guest, a "person eating at another's table" into a "parasite" (the original meaning of parasite as guest), a criminal, an inmate at Siglo XXI.[93] Even the biological understanding of parasites as only invasive and dangerous has undergone radical change in the last twenty-five or so years. Humans have more bacteria than cells in their bodies—we need them to live—and both bacteria and parasites can be symbiotic and/or pathogenic. Migrants and refugees, according to conservatives, live off the wealth and goodness of all the hardworking Americans.[94] Conversely, the retirees and the wealthy migrants, we might argue, live off the labor of others who help them amass their disposable incomes and who look after them, their children, and their houses, food, and dirty laundry.

In our twenty-first century, neocolonial patterns of settlement, occupation, tourism, and migration are once again being reshuffled, creating ever new para-spaces, times, and worlds nested in and alongside others hidden from view. The getaway, the lockup. Migrants and refugees have often been pushed off their lands as multinational corporations take them over for hydro, mining, agro, and tourist industries, often with the help of paramilitary soldiers. The "para," here, points to the privatization of violence, paid for by industry, needed to maintain both its relentless lateral expansion and its walled enclosures. The bodies of murdered migrants end up in mass pits and unmarked graves.

The understanding of what present/e means unfolds as does the list of who can be present where, when, and how. The material supports for the political space of appearance and, as important, the space of disappearance are the often-ignored aspect of being (not) present. The various elements of presente can override and annihilate the others now and for a very long time. Yet even within necropolitics, this politics of death, we find necro-resistance and necro-art, the politics of life fought in and from the space of death itself, affirming the continuing presence of all those whom biopower has deemed expendable, the "resurgence" of cultural practices Leanne Betasamosake Simpson writes of, long ago declared dead.[95]

Epistemicide

Here, I advocate for an embodied form of engagement with others that takes us beyond the disciplined and restrictive ways of knowing and acting that our Eurocentric traditions offer us. I join fellow travelers working to undiscipline disciplines, to move from the university to the multiversity, as well as those who search for alternative epistemic practices in their academic fields and elsewhere—in art, performance, and other forms of world-making. Performance itself, as Guillermo Gómez-Peña notes, offers "a conceptual 'territory' with fluctuating weather and borders, a place where contradiction, ambiguity, and paradox are not only tolerated but encouraged. . . . Our performance country is a temporary sanctuary for other rebel artists and theorists expelled from monodisciplinary fields and separatist communities."[96] This territory is full of fugitives, artists, scholars, and activists who resist colonialist limitations.

¡Presente! enacts not just an attitude and a defiant stance but also a way of knowing and being in the world that asks us to rethink and unlearn some of the limitations imposed by Western thought and education. Our epistemic, political, and economic institutions were built on the backs of the conquered, the enslaved, the indebted, and the excluded, and not simply because black slaves and indigenous peons built the universities in the Americas that would deny them entrance. The colonialist project coproduced systems of rational thought in which the isolated, individuated subject came into being as a product of his own self-recognition, turning all else into an object of knowledge to be mastered and controlled.[97] This epistemic move annuls reciprocity and relationality. It facilitates the extermination and enslavement of those others, the "not I." The repercussions on the subjugated peoples not included in the defining "I" have been devastating. The coemergence has produced a class of the annihilating or killer "I"s.

Not only were the colonized peoples excluded as subjects and producers of knowledge, but Western educational systems organized knowledge into what Boaventura de Sousa Santos calls "monocultures." He coined the term "epistemicide" to signal the damages to ways of knowing that fall outside neat divisions and classifications.[98] Aníbal Quijano makes a similar point, as does Grosfoguel, who links the attack on indigenous systems of knowledge to the expulsion of Jewish and Muslim populations from Spain, the enslavement of Africans, and the burning of women as witches to establish "racial/patriarchal power and epistemic structures at a world scale entangled with processes of global capitalist accumulation."[99] Written documents, beginning with the *Requerimiento*, declared the invaders the rightful owners of the lands.[100] In God's name, the pope bequeathed them to the Catholic king and queen of Spain. The archive, as I argued in *The Archive and the Repertoire*, became an instrument of conquest.

Before the conquest, the indigenous empires (Aztec, Maya, Inca) valued education. The Aztecs, for example, had a formal educational system for both noble and common boys and girls. In the schools or *calmécac*, young nobles were taught by the wise ones, the *tlamatinime*, those of "the transmitted knowledge" who "taught and followed the truth."[101] The youths were expected to dedicate themselves to the priesthood, war, or the arts.[102] The wise, in turn, transmitted the way/road through song and painting (writing in glyphs): "They were in charge of painting all the sciences they knew and had achieved and of teaching by means of memory all the songs that conserved their sciences and histories."[103]

Knowledge, as in painting, memorizing, learning, and practicing skills, is not a thing out there in the world, ready to be found or measured or ingested. Knowing, like memory, like identity, is relational. It's a doing, a learning, hard work that we do with others, a passing on carried out in the present. In Quechua, the word for learning, *yachasun*, exists only in present progressive form because learning always takes place in the present.[104] What counts as knowledge, and who participates in knowledge production, however, has almost always been defined by issues of class, gender, and other ideological factors. Colonization dismissed the noncanonical forms of knowledge of the conquered as well as the people who practiced them as *gente sin razón* (those without reason). The Huarochirí Manuscript, written in Quechua at the end of the sixteenth century by Francisco de Avila, announced, "If the ancestors of the people called Indians had known writing in early times, then the lives they lived would not have faded from view."[105] That he could not see or understand their cultural productions did not mean they ceased to exist or to have lasting value. Many indigenous languages, rituals, fiestas, songs, architectures, embroideries, and culinary, medical, and agricultural practices remain visible today.

Epistemicide produces what Leanne Betasamosake Simpson calls "cognitive imperialism that was aimed at convincing us we were weak and defeated people."[106] The pain and costs of epistemicide continue, excluding many forms of knowledge and knowledge producers, wrecking humans, animals, ecosystems, and cultural systems. Our disciplines often unwittingly sustain the very inequalities some of them purport to address because they have been shaped by that same system of compartmentalization and separation. How much do we need to unlearn so that we can learn again, differently? ¡Presente! envisions knowledge as a relational act, an engaged and located knowing, as a process of being with, literally walking and talking with others with all the theoretical pitfalls and ethical and moral complications and contradictions in terms of access and power that entails. Not engaging does not solve any of the existing difficulties; it simply avoids them. Being with, in motion, accepts knowledge as a practice developed in transit with others, not knowing what lies around the bend, always developing, never arriving.

This study, in its own way, joins others written in the last decades that have attempted to challenge these self-induced and self-serving blinders that now, many agree, threaten to exterminate us and all else on earth. Knowledge (what it means, who makes it, for whom, toward what end, and so on) in Western thought, it seems, is beginning to emerge from the epistemic lockdown mode that narrows our understanding of subjectivity, agency, even life to everything surrounding "us," meaning not just humans but rather *some* humans. As Critical Art Ensemble declared in 2000, "there is no paradigm, model, or application that is not in some kind of critical trouble."[107] Foucault in 1975 had already noted a shift in theoretical thinking from "the all-encompassing and global theories" to "something resembling a sort of autonomous and non-centralized theoretical production that does not need a visa from some common regime to establish its validity."[108] He recognizes the "insurrection of subjugated knowledges" that had previously been "masked" and "disqualified." These "knowledges from below" have always been in evidence for the communities that produced and animated them.[109] Although I would in principle prefer the use of the plural, knowledges, or *saberes* (ways of knowing), Foucault's use of the plural here inadvertently suggests that the all-encompassing, traditional Western knowledge (singular) is being challenged by all these little knowledges. This risks reaffirming the imperial "I"/subjugated "not I" binary that I critiqued earlier, although now the "I" has come under attack. My point here is simple: instead of using singular knowledge for the powerful and plural knowledges for the subjugated, recognize that we all produce knowledge, or knowledges. What's becoming clearer to many of us, however, is that we (the people I walk and talk with) are among those who bear the violence of monocultural thinking. These insurgent knowledges, as Foucault noted, are the product of struggle. They/we form part of the undercommons that Fred Moten and Stefano Harney describe.[110] The recent naming and critiques of the Anthropocene reflect the heightened awareness of the many costs of this patriarchal, capitalist, colonial-centeredness and push for more humane and environmentally sound policies. The new Copernicanesque revolution that situates humans as part of (rather than at the center of) life, obliging us to factor in the externalities of all our actions, requires us to decenter our inherited epistemic systems.

Native studies, critical race theories, feminist, queer, and trans theories, and disability studies, among others, envision knowledge as inseparable from struggle, and they push to decenter the white, masculinist discourse that authorizes a specific type of knower and determines what counts as knowledge. Anti- and decolonial struggles have been all about challenging the centeredness of the West and the Western subject that has relegated all else to the periphery.[111] As Ngũgĩ wa Thiong'o has been arguing for decades, decolonization includes revalorizing the autochthonous languages that allow us to know, think, communicate, and be outside the colonial framework.

Scholars and scientists from a broad spectrum of traditional disciplines have also joined the struggle to expand what we consider knowledge and whom we deem animate beings. Many entities, we're learning, are alive and interact with everything else. Biological studies in quorum sensing discovered that bacteria—among the oldest known life forms—do not function as a singular organism but communicate, coordinate, and adapt to their environment. The realization that animals, trees, the earth, and all else have agency that exceeds human comprehension has made it into popular culture—trade books, talk radio, television shows, cartoons, podcasts, and blogs teem with findings. Some scholars object to what they see as the overly broad, vitalist form of materialism, objecting that it "is out to decenter the all-sovereign subject into the mesh of material forces that constitute it."[112] Well, yes, as I argue in chapter 8. Exactly.

Various strategies of separation and containment continue. Some are obvious: we continue to separate knowledges into parts, divisions, fields, and subfields of specializations unintelligent to those in contiguous areas, making it difficult if not impossible for people to speak and think beyond these divides. Others less so: our emergent technologies and forms of transmission, such as media culture and digital platforms, further tighten our epistemic grids. Programming and code, Tara McPherson argues, are "lenticular . . . a structural device that makes simultaneously viewing the various images . . . nearly impossible." The lenticular, she continues, "is a way of organizing the world. It structures representations as well as epistemologies. It also serves to secure our understandings . . . in very narrow registers, fixating on sameness or difference while forestalling connection and interrelation."[113] So while we may program inter- and postdisciplinary courses and seminars, the ways in which we conceptualize, organize, and learn knowledge further cements the boundaries.

Indigenous communities learned long ago that the positioning of the colonial patriarchal knowing, thinking subject (*gente de razón*—the people of reason) over them, the *gente sin razón*, has cost them not only their territory, their livelihood, but also their capacity to self-identify, and even at times their lives. Gradually many others on earth are feeling the impact of the rapacious policies that align self-refereniality and self-interest with control and profit. While I will expand on this later, ¡Presente! allows me to explore how some indigenous thought dovetails alongside (not against, or under) current findings in the humanities, social sciences, and sciences, enabling a rearticulation and reanimation of a politics of presence that draws from various epistemological systems but does not claim the knowledge of any one disciplinary base. The move toward postdisciplinarity invites us to meet and have a conversation on the other side of disciplines, beyond the fence and the academic formations and divisions that have created many of the epistemic black boxes that make certain kinds of knowing possible and others impossible or difficult to apprehend.

Here, then, I join Santos in the practice of a rearguard theory. "Our knowledge," he writes, "flies at low altitude . . . stuck to the body." Rearguard theory, "based on the experiences of large, marginalized minorities and majorities that struggle against unjustly imposed marginality and inferiority," pertains to the pre- and postdisciplinary realms.[114] Many of us are strangers here, having learned certain important skills but forgotten others. Younger physicians in the United States, for example, have been trained and socialized to use increasingly sophisticated diagnostic equipment. The reimbursement incentives and liability environment further enable this trend. This results in a general degradation of history taking and the physical examination of patients. The cornerstones of the doctor-patient relationship, the human interaction skills, are being forgotten. Many economic, social, and political forces across the board shape what we know, what we are taught not to know or value.

Here, jumping the fence beyond our designated, disciplinary area, we've left our expertise at the gate. There are no clear paths or reading lists. Rearguard theory resonates with J. Halberstam's "low theory," a way to think and "locate all the in-between spaces" and negotiate and push through "the divisions between life and art, practice and theory, thinking and doing, and into a more chaotic realm of knowing and unknowing."[115] Not everyone agrees on what these alternative spaces should look like. For Harney and Moten, the undercommons offer a space where no one is correct or corrected. For them, it is a refuge, "'no questions asked.' It is unconditional—the door swings open for the refuge even though it may let in police agents."[116] The Zapatistas, whose communities are under constant threat of extermination, literally require that people show passports or papers for entry to their territories. They fight to keep the police and military out, even as they forge a utopian, capacious, alternative world: "a world that holds many worlds." For them, it's all about the question—how to live in a dangerous world defined by lack of equality, respect, and care. We all need to answer that in our own ways. So rearguard theory can never operate in the same way everywhere and always. Nonetheless, it needs to include the broader ecosystem of which we are only one part. And in addition to Halberstam's "unknowing," it would demand an active unlearning of some of the training that we've internalized about what matters, and what constitutes acceptable objects of analysis and forums for debate and dissemination.

Time to slow down.

Pause.

Stop in our tracks.

Acknowledge that it's hard to unlearn.

Like learning, it takes practice, and constant repetition.

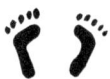

1.3 Alexei Taylor, *Footprints Standing*, 2019.

Linking Knowing to Acting

Plato, Arendt reminds us, "was the first to introduce the division between those who know and do not act and those who act and do not know . . . so that knowing what to do and doing it became two altogether different performances."[117] What might a performance that links knowing and acting look like? Taking a lead from performance theorists and artists, ¡Presente! enacts ways of learning and transmitting knowledge by moving through scenarios, dialogues, long table discussions, and various exercises and pedagogies that stage research as performance as well as performance research. If, as I argue, knowledge production is a relational practice, involving action, then how do we perform and exercise these acts of knowing? The separation of knowledge production (authorized educators) and consumption (students) in today's capitalist culture builds on centuries of separating knowing from doing. Knowledge production, as a cohesive performance, entails elements of interrelationality, of choice, of agency, reflection, and follow-through.

When I asked Silvia Rivera Cusicanqui, a feminist sociologist and activist from Bolivia, how to say "I" and "me" in Ayamara, she looked perplexed. Aymara, like many other native languages, does not have a word for "me." There is no "I" but rather *ch'ixi*, a collective subject forged through the negotiation of the individual "I" and the collective "we."[118] To exist as me, I need someone else to point to me, to recognize and acknowledge me. In other words, to be me, I have to walk and talk with others. This is not the self-defining, self-reflexive "I" of the cogito. Indigenous groups, for their differences and specificities, share a sense of a communal subjectivity. The "I" or "me" is always relational, transitive, a being with. In the language of Pangnirtung, spoken in the Arctic, my colleague Peter Kulchyski says that "I" exists as "a suffix, -tunga or -junga (depending on whether it follows a consonant or vowel). Quviasuktunga (I am happy). Uqalimajunga (I am reading)."[119]

The "I" that initiated the conversation is not the "I" that emerges. But we need to be in the conversation. As Rivera Cusicanqui makes clear, there is no anticolonial discourse without an anticolonial practice.[120] The way we do this is the way we do everything.

For me, that means going to meet people in their own spaces, on their own terms, not to study or observe them but to listen and learn from their actions, words, and epistemic systems. This is a stretch for me intellectually and physically, but also affectively, ethically, and politically. The contradictions and ambiguities abound. It is impossible, I agree with my friend Jacques Servin of The Yes Men (chapter 9), to really lead an ethical life. I fly in a plane that burns fuel and enter Mexico with a passport to meet with migrants who hide from the deportation police, their feet blistered from walking. I keenly feel the contradictions and discuss them with the people I encounter. Why, we ask ourselves, do we even want to talk and walk together? What are the stakes? The relative advantages? The answer is not obvious, or a given I can take for granted.

What I/we means, what it can and cannot know, is necessarily linked to those others with whom we walk and talk. Colonial and neoliberal conditions (including of course language, skin tone, educational systems, migratory status, income inequalities, and cultural practices) continue to delimit many of those exchanges. "Ch'ixi" and "Quviasuktunga" can only ever exist in quotations for me. I haven't learned to pronounce these words—my vocal cords, tongue, lips, brain, and even heart would have to undergo training.

If I sense their existential, epistemic, and ontological dimensions and potentiality, it's only because Rivera Cusicanqui and Kulchyski took the time to explain the concepts to me. The forms of rationality these words conjure might, in the final analysis, sound like Nancy's *being with*, but their genealogy differs profoundly. It has nothing to do with the Hegelian notion of "I" as a "pure self-contained unity," as "the philosophical subject" that grounds Western thought and that Nancy parts from, and parts with.[121] This "I" does not "presuppose [. . . the] self-contained Ego" based on differentiation from all other/s: "Relating itself to itself, it relegates the other to a self (or an absence of self) that is different."[122] This is not Heidegger's something that comes from nothing, the self-conscious and self-referential being or *Da-sein*.[123]

What am "I" left with, and where to start, in the search for alternate epistemologies, understandings, genealogies, and practices of rationality, of *hacer presencia*?

Epistemologies of the Heart

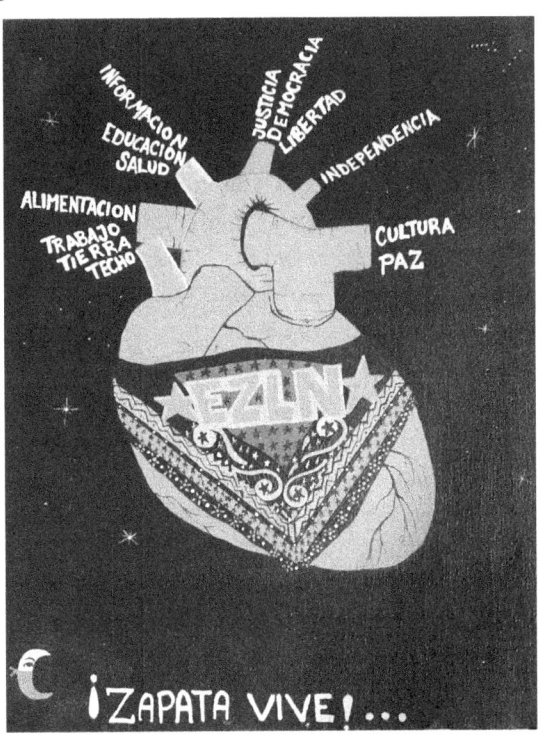

1.4 Artist unknown, *Zapatista Heart*. Date unknown. COLLECTION OF DIANA TAYLOR.

The question for me, an academic trained in the Western tradition, is how even to imagine that "I" can begin to unlearn some of the concepts that blind me. How to think from another place that is not only the highly differentiated and isolating "I" of Western thought, reflected in the *Oxford English Dictionary*'s definition of "present": "The state or fact of existing, occurring, or being present." Being present to what? To whom? To what end? I am counting on my bilinguality and biculturality to help me get started on this road.

The Mayan Tzeltal-speaking scholar Juan López Intzín, known to me by his indigenous name, Xuno, has also inspired me, embarked as he is on his own journey to try to think differently, from a different place, through different linguistic possibilities.[124] Inevitably schooled in a colonial system, and given the colonial name Juan López, he turned to his native Tzeltal as a starting point to think other, decolonial ways of being in the world. Sacred texts such as Popol Wuj (or Vuh) offer alternative cosmologies from which he develops his theory of "epistemologies of the heart."[125] This creation story initiates with discussions among various creators, not a singular god. Involved were the Framer, Shaper, She Who Has Borne Children, He Who Has Begotten Sons, Hunahpu Possum and Hunahpu Coyote, Great White Peccary and Coati, Sovereign and Quetzal Serpent, Heart of Lake and Heart of Sea, Creator of the Green Earth and Creator of the Blue Sky.[126]

The multiplicity of gods reflecting cosmic, animal, and personified dimensions of existence avoids the concentration of power in a singular God the Father. At the same time, however, the multiple forces create the deep underlying instability and precarity of the Mesoamerican experience of the cosmos as always on the verge of extinction. The Framers had experimented with earlier worlds, other forms of life that they hoped would invoke their names and sing their praises. As each creation failed, the Framers destroyed their creatures, their world, and their universes. Four suns had already perished amid environmental devastation (flood, fire, hurricane). Everyone expects the fifth to meet a similar catastrophic end. López Intzín goes back to the section in the Popol Vuh, for example, in which the people or effigies made of wood (the second of the Framers' creations) were found wanting and destroyed:

> The small and the great animals came in upon them. Their faces [of the effigies] were crushed by the trees and the stones. They were spoken to by all their maize grinders and their cooking griddles, their plates and their

pots, their dogs and their grinding stones. However many things they had, all of them crushed their faces.

Their dogs and their turkeys said to them:

"Pain you have caused us. You ate us. Therefore it will be you that we will eat now."[127]

The destruction of these wooden people resulted from their lack of *ch'ulel*, the life force that resides in everything. The effigies' inability to honor everything around them—the animals, the trees and stones, their cooking utensils—prompts the uprising against them. They are destroyed by those whom they abused.[128] This is one of the many examples that López takes from the Popol Vuh to argue for the current vitality among contemporary Mayans of an epistemic system reflected in their ancient texts.

Even for him, using ancient texts to sustain his inquiry is a daunting undertaking. The conquest, he says, colonized and domesticated almost all the indigenous peoples of the Americas.[129] How, five hundred years later, can he de-domesticate himself and others? He begins by unthinking (*in-pensar*) and feel-thinking (*sentipensar*) what "respect" and the "good dignified life" or "life with dignity" (*vida digna*) might mean from an indigenous epistemic system. This system assumes the heart, not the head, as the starting point for reflection, knowledge, and understanding. Heart is a noun and a verb— much like the popular logo, x hearts y. The process of decolonization entails "yo'taninel sbentayel snopel sp'ijil jolo'tan[il]," the walking and enhearting reflection toward knowledge of the mind-heart, which bears resemblance to ch'ixi as "parallel co-existence."[130] López calls this the "stalel, ways of being-being-here, think-feel, act and know the world."[131] He credits his bilinguality, as does Rivera Cusicanqui in the *Potosi Principle*, with the expansive dialogic character I alluded to earlier, allowing him to study and build on meanings and gestures to explore other epistemic potentialities.

While being and knowledge can be expressed in multiple ways, English regularly uses one verb each, "to be" and "to know," to express a broad range of emotional, physical, and mental states and identities. In English I/we can be alive, dead, happy, sad, depressed, straight, trans, black, white, brown, strong, weak, sick, slim, or just about anything. Not so in Spanish. Spanish differentiates both being and knowing into two main concepts. *Ser* (to be) transmits a sense of permanence. Certain traits—like gender, sexual orientation, national status and racial identity, height, and religious affiliation— supposedly endure. Others that refer to location (I am here/*estoy aquí*), mood (we are happy/*estamos felices*), and existential conditions such as alive or dead (*estamos vivos o muertos*), use *estar* (to be) to signal a transitory state. I would love to study some of these designations. Nationality is permanent? So is gender and sexual orientation? I'd especially like to think of how death comes to be a transitory condition in this language, but that is a project for another day.

Spanish also has two words for "to know." *Conocer*, related to cognition, means to be familiar with someone or something, while *saber* is related to wisdom (*sabiduría*), facts, and taste (*sabor*). *Saberes*, plural, captures the multiplicity of knowledges, the many ways of knowing. These differentiations also have far richer epistemic possibilities than I can explore here, and the nuances between the words are endlessly frustrating for English speakers—who can simply be and know everything. While this sounds flippant, this is an example of how the words and grammatical structures we have available to us shape our sense of being in the world. Yet both of these colonial languages clearly fall short of the Maya-Tzeltal quoted above in which *stalel* suggests a broader understanding of the constellation "being-being-here, think-feel, act and know the world" that make knowing/acting/being/feeling/inseparable. But even for Xuno López these Mayan Tzeltal words only approximate the "original" words found in the Popol Vuh in the language of the Maya K'iche. No one, clearly, is exempt from the burden of learning and trying to work things through. So instead of a search for origins, Xuno López seeks approximations, insights, and pathways into alternative ways of being in the world.

Two key elements of the epistemology of the heart, according to Xuno López, are the Tzeltal notions of the ch'ulel and *ich'el ta muk*. Ch'ulel, in play throughout this book, recognizes that everything has a life—humans, animals, plants, mountains, and so forth—and thereby allows for intersubjectivity: "The ch'ulel is what turns everything that exists into a subject, allowing us to interact as subject to subject."[132] The "ich'el ta muk is the recognition of the value, grandeur, and dignity of all that exists, including humans, animals, and the ecosystem." That concept interpolates all living beings as subjects—not the Althusserian state subject, not subjects reduced to commercial or inanimate objects as in my chapter 8, "Dead Capital." The combination of the two elements opens several world-remaking possibilities—anticolonial, communal, and ecologically sustainable. "It is necessary," Xuno López believes, "for us to deconstruct the vision of the world, the mentality, and the subjectivity that have been imposed upon us since the conquest, and instead look at the world from that situated heart that is at the center of our communities and collective processes. This is what we call epistemologies of the heart. The heart is a key element in our Indigenous thought."[133] Knowledge qualifies as organic, a product not just of our brains but of our entire body in relation to other living things. As opposed to the thingification of people, animals, and all else in rapacious capitalism, López's situated heart (he credits Donna Haraway's "situated knowledge") enables the "humanization" of things that animate our world.[134] Sharing this epistemology would require a radical unlearning of much that Westerners know, including the notion of the differentiated I.

Underlying both Rivera Cusicanqui's explanation of ch'ixi and Xuno López's ch'ulel and ich'el ta muk rests the notion of mutual recognition, valorization, and respect among far greater numbers of animate beings or subjects. Becoming itself requires this act of mutual recognition, this being presente, talking, walking, and enhearting with others. The epistemic systems one can glean in these words and practices might allow me/us to envision a more capacious understanding of "present" as "presente," as an ethical and political practice, a way that strengthens intersubjective generosity and mutual recognition. We might end up talking to each other in the undercommons. "We owe each other everything," Moten and Harney acknowledge. This reminds me of the Zapatista saying, "Para todos, todo. Para nosotros, nada." (Everything for everybody. For us, nothing.) It's not about "us" in a narrowly defined way anymore than the "I" is about me. Bruno Latour's recent work expresses his conviction that Western epistemic tools are not up to the task of generative world-making: "To put it as starkly as possible, I would claim that those who intend to survive the coming cataclysms of climate on hope and faith, or who square off against it armed only with the results of externalized and universal knowledge are doomed."[135] It's, as Jack Halberstam acknowledges in the preface to *The Undercommons*, another way of being together, a realization that "we must change things or die. . . . If there is an undercommons, then we must all find our way to it."

For Xuno López (and Rivera Cusicanqui in her way), the ontological exploration is practical and political as well as epistemic. The various dimensions animate each other. The situated heart, nurtured in an expanded environment of recognition (that includes trees, rivers, and mountains that others might consider inanimate objects), cannot tolerate domination, exploitation, and domestication. It becomes *el corazón rebelde*, the rebellious heart of the Zapatista movement. That movement, as I discuss in chapter 3, draws from ancient Mayan teachings and from contemporary research and practice. Scholars such as John Holloway, Noam Chomsky, and Donna Haraway inform contemporary Zapatista thought. "[Zapatistas] adapt, they say, *'para no dejar de ser'* (so as not to cease being) historical beings."[136] Xuno López, with the Zapatistas, does not subscribe to identity politics or to theories of authenticity. One doesn't have to be indigenous to be a Zapatista any more than one has to be a woman to be a feminist. Nor does he sequester indigenous knowledge; he prioritizes ideas in dialogue and exchange. Traditions inspire, but they need to be revisited and updated by all sides. Xuno López, for example, is a feminist who advocates for greater rights for women even in the Zapatista communities founded on the 1994 Women's Revolutionary Law. Communities adapt in order to survive.

While seemingly occupying a different epistemic universe altogether, N. Katherine Hayles offers a surprisingly congruent notion of an expanded understanding of cognition through cognitive biology. On the other side of disciplinary divides, different conversations become possible. Without alluding to ch'ulel, cognitive biology understands that cognition is more generalized than what we're used to believing.[137] Hayles, following Ladislav Kováč, agrees that "cognition is not limited to humans or organisms with consciousness; it extends to all life forms, including those lacking central nervous systems such as plants and microorganisms."[138] Hayles too divides knowing into two types, though her terms do not map onto the distinctions between "saber" and "conocer." Hayles distinguishes between thinking and cognition: "Thinking, as I use the term, refers to high-level mental operations such as reasoning abstractly, creating and using verbal languages, constructing mathematical theorems, composing music, and the like, operations associated with higher consciousness. Although Homo sapiens may not be unique in these abilities, humans possess them in greater degree and with more extensive development than other species."

"Cognition," for Hayles, "is a much broader faculty present to some degree in all biological life forms and many technical systems."[139] The distinction, for her, is the one she develops to "replace human/nonhuman: cognizers versus noncognizers. On one side are humans and all other biological life forms, as well as many technical systems; on the other, material processes and inanimate objects."[140] Cognizers, she goes on to explain, have choice; they are actors. The word "agents" she reserves "for material forces and objects" in recognition that "noncognizers may possess agential powers that dwarf anything humans can produce; think of the awesome powers of an avalanche, tsunami, tornado, blizzard, sandstorm, hurricane" even though they do not exercise choice.[141] The universe, then, is animated by actors and agents rather than objects and things, each trying to find ways to adapt and thrive. All life, Kováč argues, "incessantly, at all levels, by millions of species, is 'testing' all the possibilities of how to advance ahead. . . . At all levels, from the simplest to the most complex, the overall construction of the subject, the embodiment of the achieved knowledge, represents its epistemic complexity."[142]

Hayles's inclusion of "technical systems" within the realm of cognition might seem out of line with the indigenous epistemic systems I cited earlier. But I think that technical systems form a vital part of indigenous cognitive universes. The Huichol or more correctly the Wixáritar people of central Mexico make sacred paintings by pressing yarn, beads, or fine thread into wax as they take peyote. The art communicates the pathways, visions, and interactions with the gods and thus becomes a way of knowing, thinking with, and being with in motion, in transit. If, as Hayles suggests, "cognition is a process that interprets information within contexts that connect it with meaning," then the art might well unveil a truth unknown to the Wixáritar and inform other meaning-making practices.[143] The sacred drums, in other communities, speak; they are actors in their contexts. My aim is not to push comparisons, but rather to think of connectivity across these various epistemic frames and beyond disciplinary divides where people are grappling with similar phenomena and asking similar questions. I can imagine a discussion between someone trained in cognitive biology and someone versed in indigenous epistemologies (among many others) to develop strategies for expanding our conversations. The languages may all be different—from computer code to Wixáritar wax paintings to theories of "participatory sense-making" and "distributive cognition"—but the impetus is a common one.[144] All species continually test ways to survive and thrive, as Kováč puts it. The Zapatistas adapt, they say, "para no dejar de ser" (so as not to cease being) historical beings. Western academics like myself attempt to break out of our epistemic lockdown by envisioning other ways of being and becoming in the world. The goals may vary—for me, I strive to know differently, not just to survive but to be less complicit in the colonialist production and practice of knowledge.

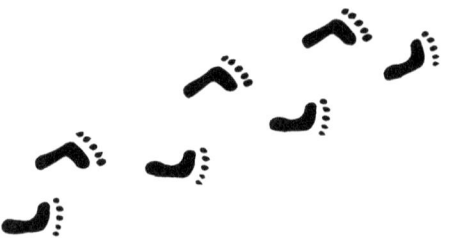

1.5 Alexei Taylor, *Walking*, 2019.

Versions of the chapters in this book were written over a period of ten or so years, and I noticed that I was developing a peripatetic strategy for staging the work. My observations and theorizations sprang from my walking and talking with others. In some cases, this practice resembled Aristotle's walking in circles around the outside edge of the grove as he spoke with his students, who literally followed him. The term "peripatetic," from the ancient Greek word περιπατητικός (*peripatêtikos*), which means "of walking" or "given to walking about," points to three distinct but related aspects of how I understand walking theory.[145] The first, and most obvious, emphasizes the role of movement in learning as practice that I stress throughout. Second, as Aristotle was not a citizen of Athens and therefore could not own property there, the Lyceum where he gathered with students was a more improvised, less institutional setting for scholarly discussions. And third, the discussions were consequently more informal, though no less deep or challenging. There's an outside quality to this model that interests me and that (without making the connection) I have reproduced in my own itinerant practice—outside the formal boundaries of the Academy, physically outside in an improvised or mobile space, decentering the periphery of the grove, outside the nation-state or not wholly identifying or belonging to it, and beyond the lecture format toward more informal yet challenging conversations.

Walking and talking, or the peripatetic method, underlines the notion of knowledge production as doing—seeing, listening, reading, thinking, talking are all actions that we undertake together. We interact with people and the world around us. Even reading alone, we are in the company of the author. Books, insights, songs, and much else accompany us everywhere we go. But in this study, and in the practices I describe here, we meander through various places for short periods of time—Mexico City, Chiapas,

Guatemala, São Paulo, Santiago de Chile, back through Central America to Chiapas, New York, Montreal. The questions link and cut through all these spaces, including the politics of movement itself. Additionally, several of these pieces developed in dialogue with my students, and often I followed them. Sometimes they led me through fields and issues I wasn't familiar with. At others, we literally moved in zigzag fashion through the south of Mexico, thinking with and through the people and situations we experienced.

Some chapters, such as chapter 7, "Tortuous Routes: Four Walks through Villa Grimaldi," think about walking through multiple acts. "I" walk through the former detention and torture center in Chile at various times over a period of a decade, with different survivors, colleagues, students, and sometimes alone with an audio tour. Each time I see/experience something different. My walks through the space have led me to question who it is for (survivors, visitors?) and what it does. Is the "peace park" a memorial for the thousands who were tortured and hundreds who died there, or has it morphed beyond recognition into a cultural center to draw and instruct the general population? The movement, then, is not necessarily or even usually linear, and even the same space changes over time. Chapter 3, focused on the Zapatistas, unfolds in a slow, spiraling motion. Life is a struggle, as much for contemporary Mesoamericans as for their ancestors. The migrant trails from Central America through Mexico on the way to the United States (chapter 5) are often *caminos de la muerte* or roads of death. In chapter 8, I follow Teatro de Vertigem's disjointed, inside/out performance route for 958 meters, through the underbelly of São Paulo, immersed in an enactment of capitalism that I have long understood but never truly experienced. Some stops, as in chapter 9, exist at the intersection of many spatial practices. Chiapas, Mexico, becomes one more site where the Monsanto Corporation (legally a person) exists and pushes its genetically modified corn even as it practices similar operations throughout the world. Monsanto is simultaneously there and everywhere, a person and disembodied. The intervention we performed there with Jacques Servin of The Yes Men and Jesusa Rodríguez aligned digital space with national activist, legal, and educational organizations in Mexico and the United States. And so, through the movement and tempo that make up this book, the connections among several previously invisible spaces and practices suddenly light up. After writing two or three of these pieces, I began to think of them as walk-throughs, though I hope the term might be repurposed as a move-through. Along with my friends and colleagues with disabilities, I know that walking is no one thing.

My experience of walking, like all else, is shaped by who "I" am and have become: as a baby in northern Mexico, I contracted polio. After years of braces and operations, I eventually assumed my status as the upright mammal Bataille and others take for granted.[146] I continue to live and deal with the sequelae. So walking can never be an abstraction for me, a thinking and being that ignores bodily exertion and situatedness. I'm aware of almost every step I take, even as I walk and talk with others. I measure feasibility in meters and kilometers. Thus, walking for me is not about freedom, leisure, or domination as for eighteenth-century English gentlemen, the embodiment of the individual and differentiated Enlightenment subject: "I cannot see the wit of walking and talking at the same time. . . . The soul of a journey is liberty, perfect liberty, to think, feel, do, just as one pleases."[147] Walking reminds me not only of my physical limitations and dependency at times on those who walk with me, but on how small I am compared to everything around me—the city, the Mayan highlands, the Sonoran Desert. In the desert, with its weaponized nature, a rattlesnake can be more powerful than a mere human.

Walking is a thinking/becoming in motion, a pedagogy and training (peripatetic). Walking is one of those acts that form, rather than result from, thought.[148] The act of walking produces its own way of thinking, unthinking, and thinking-feeling negotiating assuredness and vulnerability, motion along with uncertainty. It demands we pay attention to terrain, to time, to the conditions on and of the ground under our feet, to the limits of our own physical bodies, to our balance and fear of falling, to the politics of access and characteristics of a specific location, to the direction of our movement, to distance and reduced visibility. What lies around that corner, or over that mountain? We need to face, negotiate, and resolve challenges. Decisions need to be made. Walking, for some, can enact possession, a visual control and domination that suggest that everything I see is mine. At times walking confirms and transcends distance, and even our own limitations.

Walking can lead to new insights: "A schizophrenic out for a walk is a better model than a neurotic lying on the analyst's couch."[149] Deleuze and Guattari take us on a "stroll of a schizo," beyond the repressive boundaries of "the self and the non-self, outside and inside, [that] no longer have any meaning whatsoever."[150]

Walking is also a political practice. The way we do this is the way we do everything.

1.6 Wall mural depicting Central American migrants in Ciudad Hidalgo, Mexico, on the border with Guatemala, 2015. Artist unknown. PHOTO: DIANA TAYLOR.

For Gandhi, coming from a non-Western epistemic system and an anticolonial struggle, walking referred to a specific personal and political practice. As opposed to the leisure and freedom assured by wealth, his walk was a poor practice, one identified with poverty insofar as the poor can afford no other means of transportation.[151] A simple practice (place "one foot in front of the other") also enacted his philosophy of a simple life, one that attempted not to exploit others and their labor.[152] Gandhi's walking entailed determination, endurance, and commitment, an understanding that enabled his political commitment to the slow and steady quality of the walks and marches in the pursuit of independence.[153]

There are so many ways to think about walking, so many places that walking leads us.[154]

For Central American migrants, scurrying and hiding in their attempts to cross the border into southern Mexico to reach its northern border into the United States, walking is a terrifying, lonely, and seemingly endless enterprise. Gaunt from dehydration and exhaustion, their feet blistered and bleeding, they tell of being caught by federal and local agents and shipped back to their home countries, only to depart again, on foot, in search of a safer life.[155] Their children, if they travel with them, refer to themselves as migrants, beings in motion who come into presence with no location or national identity.[156]

"To walk" (NEHNEM(I) for the Mexica (Aztecs) shares a linguistic root with "to live" (NEM(I).[157] Neltiliztli, from nelhuáyotl (meaning cement or foundation) is related to "foot" (néhuatl). The concept of truth is based on standing, on having a foundation, on being well grounded.[158] The glyph of the footprint for Mesoamericans represented movement, identity, location, relationality, and history. Mexica maps and writings are dotted with footprints to indicate where people were coming from and where they were headed. Four footprints in a circle signaled the marketplace.[159] The long road signified historical process and struggle.

Tira de Peregrinación, one of the earliest migration documents we have in the Americas, tells of the slow migration over two hundred years of the Chichimeca and the Mexica from Aztlán toward Tenochtitlan, where they would establish the center of their emerging empire. The walkers carried their gods on their backs as they made their way south. The map, like other Mesoamerican maps, does not show the contours of the geographical territory but rather the events, motion, and internal relations between and among beings: divine, natural, human, animal. The footprints condition the

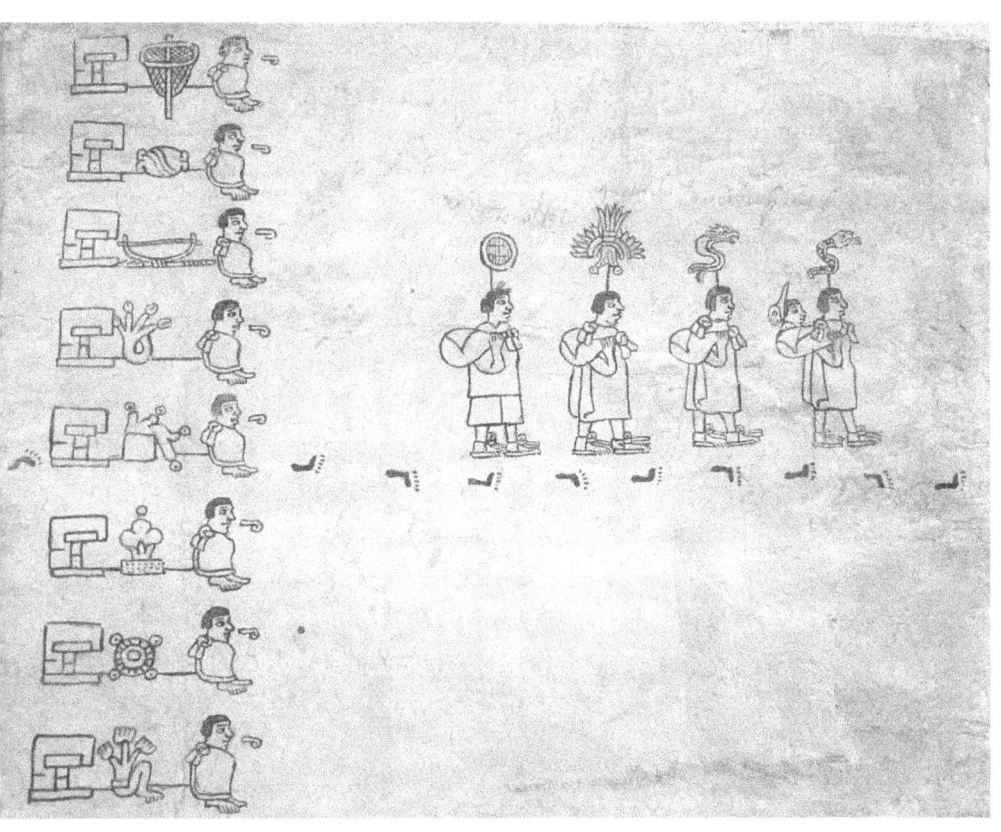

1.7 The *Tira de Peregrinación*, also known as *Codex Boturini* (sixteenth century).

map: "an action permits one to see something," the events and their telling.[160] Presence structures space and the other way around. Practice on the ground creates the contours, from the body's vantage point, as opposed to the bird's-eye view of geographic formations in European maps of the same period. The walkers do not see the goal clearly ahead of them. They follow the promise that they will recognize the place when they come to it. And, as the walkers' bundles make clear, we never walk alone, even when solitary. The Mexica carry their gods, ideologies, supplies, and weapons on their backs; they accompany them everywhere. Their bodies, like ours, transmit traces of familial, group, and territorial affinities, obligations, and belongings. Their clothes signal gender and status; the signs attached to their heads are place markers. They, like us, carry their worlds with them even as they venture into the unknown. In short, walking, as one way of becoming in motion, is utterly culturally coded. It's never a simple practice, never "one foot in front of the other."

Here I take up Juan Carlos Ruiz's invitation to "join us: say ¡presente!" This writing is a journey, an *amoxohtoca*, a moving from one event and location to another, a bringing into focus, a way of making sense. As I set forth, I hope you'll talk and walk with me.

TWO

Enacting Refusal
Political Animatives

On August 28, 1968, at the height of the explosive student protests in Mexico, government officials forced civil servants to *hacer presencia* (literally, "make presence") in the massive Zócalo, Mexico City's central square in front of the National Palace. This was the site of the *cue* or holy temple (Templo Mayor) at the center of the Aztec empire. After the conquest, the Spaniards forced the conquered to tear down their cue to build the cathedral. In 1968, the government choreographed the counterprotest as a response to the take-over of the Zócalo a day earlier by hundreds of thousands of students who had raised a black-and-red strike flag on the central flagpole and made a series of demands: the release of their fellow protesters from jail, an end to police violence, and a face-to-face meeting with President Díaz Ordaz. The president refused, staging instead a performance of party loyalty labeled a *ceremonia de desagravio* (act of redress) to atone for the desecration of the flag. Officials once again raised the enormous Mexican flag that dominates the square. Due to technical difficulties, the flag got stuck at half-mast, fore-shadowing perhaps the tragedy to come. The thousands of workers forced to attended this oversize show of national unity and purpose faced the speaker. All at once, without apparent prompting or preparation, they turned around and literally started bleating like sheep and yelling, "Somos borregos! Nos llevan!" "We're sheep of the administration. We're being herded."[1]

The civil servants are present, but they present themselves as sheep, not as subjects but as subjugated political animals. They perform their agency by becoming nonagents. Yet they, not the government, remind us that they control their representation. The government refuses the students' demands, but workers too can refuse to play authority's game, to pretend to be loyal workers in the fake revolutionary party that is the PRI—the oxymoronically named Institutional Revolutionary Party that ruled Mexico from 1929 to 2000 and was in power again from 2012 to 2018. Their "baaa" attests to the degraded condition, even ontological deformation, of workers in the country's crony capitalist economy of the 1960s. They are ¡presente! in their refusal. They turn their back on the state's representation of itself as a thriving democracy of free subjects and re-present themselves as absurd figures in a ridiculous sham government. The workers seem to enter into what Hannah Arendt calls the "space of appearance": "the organization of the people as it arises out of acting and speaking together . . . [whose] true space lies between people living together for this purpose."[2] The government assumes it controls the space of appearance, demanding a show of loyalty from its vulnerable subjects. But with one turn of the collected bodies, one unified "baaa," one ¡presente!, they call into question the space of appearance itself. Who can appear and how? In this simulated space of political representation, the workers cannot appear as a "who," a "somebody [with] qualities, talents" but as a "what."[3] Herded into the Zócalo, they're expected to comply with the party script that casts them as docile, faceless workers. By performing as sheep, stripped of humanness and agency, the workers show the degraded political subjectivity for what it is, subverting the state's staged image of shared space and collective purpose. A defiant, contingent "we" emerges through this simple act of defiance. The spontaneous and unpremeditated bleating at and turning one's back on authority illuminates much of what I want to get at in ¡Presente! as an act of political defiance.

As I wrote in chapter 1, presente is simultaneously an act, a word, a gesture, an attitude, an acknowledgment and response to authority's hail, a war cry in the face of nullification. The reaction turns on a dime. There are many ways of being ¡presente!, and each enactment has its own logic (with significant overlaps at times), which I explore throughout this book. ¡Presente! in the case of the civil servants stages defiance and solidarity, a literal standing with and for others also contesting authority. At times, however, ¡presente! means showing up with others to fight for those who are not, cannot be, there to fight for themselves. Taking note, recording, witnessing, remembering, studying, and scholarly writing might at times also constitute acts undertaken in defiance of or solidarity with others. These actions entail different performance modalities, as I explore throughout these chapters, but they too are political attitudes and projects. When the Mothers of Plaza de Mayo walk around the plaza, demanding "¡Aparición con vida!," that their children be "brought back alive!," their disappeared are once again

¡presentes! Coming into presence, into ¡presente!, means becoming a "who" to one another in spaces that withhold recognition, and forging spaces of appearance out of spaces of disappearance. ¡Presente! makes political interventions that require a complex play of dispositions, moves, and gestures.

How?

The government's command that the civil servants be present, that they make presence, clearly exemplifies Louis Althusser's hail, the "hey there" of those in authority that interpellates their addressees as state subjects.[4] Yet the event also affirms that what Félix Guattari calls "subjective pluralism" and the "group subject" is both singular and plural.[5] The term "collective," referring not just to a bunch of sheep that supposedly are easily led, "should be understood in the sense of a multiplicity that *deploys itself*."[6] Much like the civil servants, whose rebuff gives a meaning to the term "collective" different from the one the government had in mind, the collective is both singular and multiple, both the object of the government's performative utterance and the subject of the act of refusal.

The mechanism of enacting refusal (baaa) in response to a command to *hacer presencia* can productively be thought through J. L. Austin's theory of the performative, as a specific category of action. A performative is successful, Austin argued, when certain circumstances or conventions are in place. Words then can act, do something, or make something happen.[7] Those in authority—the priest, or judge, or official—utter the words. Those in attendance—at the wedding, in the courtroom—follow conventions and validate the proceedings. The structuring of the act of redress in front of the Zócalo certainly set up the circumstances for the performative to succeed. Look at them all, present by our orders. On this performance, however, rests the legitimacy of the state itself.

Performatives are not "true" or "false," Austin notes, but rather "happy" (successful) or "unhappy" (unsuccessful), depending on the "uptake."[8] Andrew Parker and Eve Sedgwick note that the performative "invokes the presumption, but only the presumption of a consensus between speaker and witnesses."[9] The civil servants refuse to perform the consensus that the state demands. Parker and Sedgwick might call this act of refusal a "negative performative" insofar as it signals a "disavowal, renunciation, repudiation, 'count me out.'"[10]

To refer to the civil servants' rebuff to the performative command to be presente, however, I use the term "animative" to name the unspoken resistance that exists as and through enacted refusal. Athletes take a knee during the national anthem. The teacher speaks; the student looks out the window or talks to a neighbor. The Zapatistas cover their faces and turn their backs on the government. Not present, really, but not *not* present. What happened? These acts require interpretation—Did the athlete get an itch? Did the student get summoned? Did the Zapatistas stumble onto the wrong set? No—the animative is not a physical symptom or reaction to a stimulus but a codified act of noncompliance.[11] Not a performative, but not a negative performative. This kind of refusal is not a "You're fired" reply to power, an enunciation that qualifies as a negative performative, but an act or gesture that interrupts the conventions on which the performative relies.

Animatives, as I define them, are embodied, communicative acts that refuse the performative utterance that tries to interpellate and frame them. Animatives, thus, are necessarily relational and responsive. Taking a knee and looking out the window only enact refusal within their specific contexts, the codes within which they function. Their efficacy relies on the extent to which they can upend or derail the performative utterance through expressive and affective body-to-body transmission. Like performatives, they are not true or false—their power lies elsewhere: Can they disrupt? Is the onlooker affected? Animatives can take shape as micro rejections (I look out the window when my teacher calls on me) or macro resistance (the Zapatistas refuse to participate in the state's political project). Animatives are part movement, as in animation, part identity, being, soul, or life, as in the Latin *anima*. The term captures the fundamental movement that enlivens embodied practice and emotion. The Spanish *animo* (cheer up) emphasizes another set of meanings, this time from the Latin *animatus*: courage, resolve, and perseverance. It enacts affects and dispositions: fears, hopes, outrage, and, of course, animus and animosity. Mel Y. Chen's concept of "animacy" captures the affective qualities underlying animatives, as "agency, awareness, mobility, and liveness."[12] Animatives, however, refer specifically to acts that convey the affect. In other words, we know affect through acts (animatives, gestures) and not the other way around. Animatives, as acts, are the key to political life. But affect, clearly, goads action. As Manuel Castells reminds us, "emotions are the drivers of collective action."[13] Political animacies and animatives (some faith based, some hate based, some fact based, among others) flourish on all sides of the ideological divides. Animatives encompass defiant, boisterous, contradictory, hostile, and vexed behaviors. They exist in the realm of the potentially chaotic, liberatory, fascist, anarchist, and revolutionary.

If performatives, as language that acts, require certain conventions to be in place for their efficacy, animatives defy those specific conventions taking place in the messy, sometimes ugly, and often unstructured and unconventional gatherings among those who refuse interpellation. But that doesn't mean animatives defy all conventions. Raising a fist in resistance, for example, is a coded gesture within a convention that has a recognizable history and is understood by protesters and power figures alike. Other large-scale acts such as protests and social movements might also defy some mandates while observing others. The civil rights March on Washington in 1963, as L. A. Kauffman notes, seen "as a pinnacle moment of social struggle" against which other protests are measured, performed defiance on one level while being "completely controlled by the organizers. . . . The protest march that's come to epitomize peaceful popular dissent in America was an event where all but authorized messages were silenced."[14] The battle to win communal or national consensus takes place on the complicated, at times seemingly contradictory, terrain on the ground.

Because performatives, in the Austinean understanding of the term, always rely on authorized frameworks and consensus for their success, the threat of disruption always hovers over them. One of the many things I love about Austin's writing on performatives is his elaboration of the ways they can go wrong. Trump's swearing the oath of office in January 2017 could function as a primer of the misfires, misinvocations, misapplications, infelicities, and unhappiness that Austin identifies in his "unhappy performatives." The performative was not false—the oath was taken—but the utterance-act "was void, or given in bad faith."[15] Not everyone was following the same playbook.

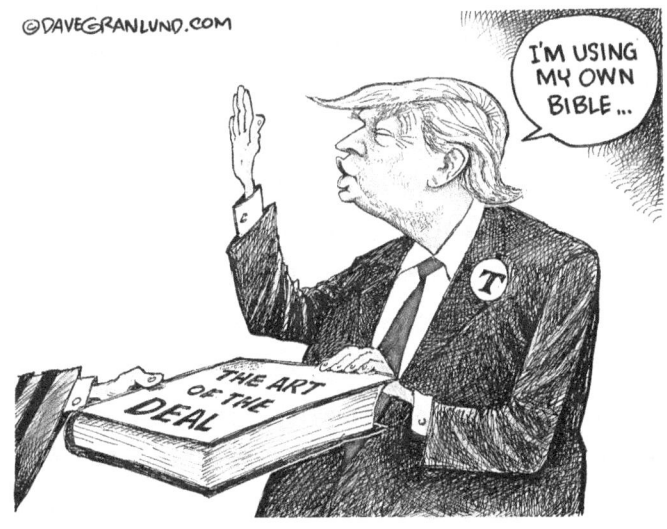

2.1 Dave Granlund, "Trump Oath of Office," 2017. © Dave Granlund.

Performatives that fail, as Trump's mode of operation makes clear, can still succeed on some level for certain audiences. "Lock her up!" did not result in the incarceration of his political opponent Hillary Clinton, but it certainly rallied his followers to ensure his electoral victory. Examples of performatives that fail can also reveal strategies of resistance against the conventions and codes within which performatives attempt to claim enunciatory power.[16]

While animatives are one example of acts that can disrupt a performative, the theatrical aside counts as another, as does the idea of *obedezco pero no cumplo* (I obey, but I won't follow through) and Michel de Certeau's foot-dragging or "la perruque."[17] These lateral moves avoid direct confrontation even as they seek to subvert the success of the undertaking. *Relajo* in Mexico, translated into English as both "commotion, ruckus" and "joke, laugh," only ever works to upset conventions. Relajo is an act of devalorization, or what Jorge Portilla calls "desolidarization" with dominant norms in order to create a different, joyously rebellious solidarity—that of the underdog.[18] Without authority to be defied and codes of conduct to be upended, there would be no relajo. Other words such as *choteo* in the Spanish-speaking Caribbean name acts of spontaneous disruption and at times laughter that defy authority, that rupture (even for a moment) the configuration and limits of a certain group or community. Purposeful misunderstandings might also qualify as animatives. In becoming a U.S. citizen, a pacifist might roll up her sleeves when asked to swear to "bear arms" for her country. Homonyms to the rescue. Presente, yes, but not in the way that authority demands.

Performatives command or promise, but they are not necessarily generative—demanding "freedom" or "justice for all" or "Make America Great Again" does not automatically bring those aspirations into existence. The utterance needs to be carried through with the acknowledgment or agreement of those attending to produce a new legally binding real—a marriage, a verdict. Benjamin Arditi, in "Insurgencies Don't Have a Plan—They Are the Plan," argues that protests themselves enact "the promise of something other to come."[19] The enactment, the uptake, the bodies on the street or activating for change, need to be presente to complete the act. "You have to act to make it come about."[20] The promise might be there, the enactment is crucial, but it might not produce the "yet to come." The fact that the performative fails, that the promise or aspiration might not produce a new real does not mean, as we saw, that it accomplishes nothing. The performance, the *as if*, opens a space toward something (justice for all, or a white segregated America) that has not yet arrived and that might never be achieved.

Political *as ifs* express the desire and demand for change; they leave traces that reanimate future scenarios. In Mexico, for the protesters this meant imagining the political as an arena of convergence, contestation, and potentiality rather than (as we've known it to be) a done deal, brokered behind closed doors by those in control. The *as ifs* and *what ifs*, often dismissed as posturing or only pretending, can open liberating or repressive pathways to social reinventions, amplifying the limits of the political imagination. The pushback might come in the form of other performatives, competing scenarios, and animatives. These aspirational utterances do not constitute successful performatives. At times, the reiterative calls for justice or the invocation of freedom might be lip service to replace meaningful action. Similarly, some gestures are empty. At other times, the invocations against migrants, blacks, Mexicans, Jews, et cetera, show that deep-seated racism is always there, ready to be tapped and operationalized at any moment to build walls, attack synagogues, and ban Muslims.

The reason for teasing out the ways in which these various dimensions of ¡presente! work is not to cement distinctions but rather (in the spirit of Austin) to expand the range of political possibilities and methodologies within the broader rubric of performance. There are, as I've insisted throughout, many ways of being ¡presente! I use these terms, then, not to privilege clear-cut understandings of political dynamics, such as high/low, bad/good, efficacious/failed, populist/elitist, or real/pretend. It is urgent to remember that performance is always unstable. All the more reason to understand the degree to which various forms of presente (including performatives and animatives) can disturb and upend political hierarchies and structures, and their legitimating discourses, by interruptions enacted from and on the ground.

So back to the sheep.

Word of the civil servants' defiance electrified the Zócalo. The students, many as young as fifteen, remained near the plaza after their forced removal the night before and tried to push their way back into the space. Carlos Monsiváis wrote at the time of the feelings of optimism and "ecstasy of the multitude" as the students pushed on in the face of intimidation.[21] The collective longing and commitment for social justice were palpable, not just to the student protesters themselves but to the population at large, as the civil servants' bleating attested. Bodies of all kinds, including the human body, make their own demands in ways that cannot be adequately understood by looking primarily at language. The students pumped energy into the sclerotic system. It was electrified. Political bodies are amplified and expanded by the mission, emotions, and hopes that animate them. As bodies, we are networked—connected, extended into the surrounding environment. Wired through neurological and hormonal pathways, our bodies sense and communicate the frustrations in and around us. Standing close together, people's unrest becomes palpable. One person lowers the flag, another bleats, others follow. Politics takes place in the space between, beside, and around us, the productive gaps across which we struggle to recognize each other.

Political subjectivity and space undergo change and mutually produce each other anew. As the students jostled one another marching down streets, they knew they were protagonists in a historic struggle for social justice. Denied a face-to-face dialogue with the president and shut out of the Zócalo, they demanded a space of recognition. The crowded space around the Zócalo became once again the scene of political reimagining, though as Rebecca Schneider cautions, it is necessary to "both question and critique, deploy and resist . . . the norms of appearance that make a space 'public.'"[22] It forced 300,000 to 400,000 people to communicate, protect, and rely on one another. These bodies, ignored by the corporate media, served as their own form of mediation. They acted on their own outrage and desires.

Animatives often terrify governments whose main goal is to control bodies through the mobilization or threat of force, or through the use of performative edicts, decrees, and official utterances with the force of law. Bodies and embodied actions coming into presence in less containable ways. Instead of the obedient ¡presente! response to authority's roll call, there is the potential for ¡presente! as political contestation. Even the docile sheep act up. The acts challenge onlookers to interrogate and interpret spectacles of defiance and resistance. Is the act persuasive? Do we want to join in? Who participates in the action? Who controls it? For better and for worse, animatives lack the legitimating structures, authority, and hierarchies that empower performatives. Animatives—linguistically so close to animation, to what Sianne Ngai calls the "non-stop technology" of cartoons—also raise serious questions of agency. "Animatedness," she cautions, is "unusually receptive to outside control."[23] The inanimate body usurps the "human speaker's voice" and agency.[24] The ruckus may well be joyous and liberating, but it's not always clear who controls it and what it's really about.

The command performance of civil obedience turned out badly for the government. The act of redress backfired and went down, in Austinean terms, as an unhappy performative. The failure or infelicity of the act, however, had grave political consequences for the students and for the country as well: the gates of the presidential palace opened and tanks charged at the bodies in the square.

On October 2, 1968, less than five weeks after the workers-as-sheep event, several hundred students involved in the protests were massacred in the Plaza of Tlatelolco, a housing complex adjacent to the Zócalo. Their bodies were incinerated and disappeared. No one knows exactly how many were killed that night. The time for pretending that Mexico was a democracy that offered a space for political antagonism, pluralism, conflict, and negotiation was over. The Zócalo, designed as Mexico's most public square, proved to be yet again a space of disappearance.

Why such a violent response from the government? The 1968 Olympics, scheduled to take place in Mexico City, were less than two weeks off. The unrest in the country made the organizers queasy. The protests had to stop. The games must go on. Sport stadiums had been built, airline tickets bought, hotels reserved, and athletes had trained for the high altitude. When athletes Tommie Smith and John Carlos raised their fists on the podium to protest the treatment of black Americans, their defiant gesture linked the protest inside the stadium to the one outside. Several kinds of silence converged: the silence (or quiet) of the powerful gesture that Kevin Quashi calls attention to, the "sense of inwardness" and "intimacy" conveyed by the silent protest, and the brutal silencing of protest outside.[25] Silenced, too, were the various histories of oppression that collided in that moment, foreclosing hopes for solidarity. Even though the international news largely ignored the massacre and no one speculated that the causes of oppression were related, the acts of refusal nonetheless called attention to the many who were willing to turn their backs or bleat or raise their fists in the face of violent authority.

Erica Chenoweth and Maria J. Stephan, authors of *Why Civil Resistance Works*, would classify the 1968 student movement in Mexico as a failure because it did not achieve its stated goals.[26] And yet there is an enormous amount to be learned from "unhappiness." Faced with a Mexican state that brutally curtailed the rights of its citizens, the young students had led a powerful, nonviolent resistance movement. As in other youth movements before and after, such as those organized around economic inequality, gun violence, climate change, gender and racial violence, and so on, children and young adults risked their lives to claim their right to a present as well as a future. They succeeded in activating a broad sector of the population—including professors, teachers, artists, and, as we saw, Mexico's civil servants—in support of social justice. Even the church bells of the National Cathedral in the Zócalo pealed to endorse their aims.[27] They were clear in their goals and maintained the moral high ground. Nonetheless, faced with a murderous, repressive military force, the movement crashed, and supporters returned to their political subjugation. The country went quiet; all open dissent ceased. Mexico's "Dirty War," backed by the United States, continued to disappear students and other dissidents and silence journalists throughout the 1970s and, one could argue, into the present.[28] At the same time, intellectuals, artists, journalists, and activists dedicated themselves to a transformation that can also be felt into the present. From the quiet struggle for human rights, freedom of expression, and gender and sexual equality to the Zapatistas' armed declaration of war on Mexico's "bad government," Mexico's progressives have continued to move toward the vision of social justice articulated in 1968. The Zapatistas' experimentation with other ways of being presente both politically and ontologically, as I explore in chapter 3, has in turn inspired hundreds of other community and collective organizations throughout Mexico and beyond.[29]

So what would efficacy or happiness mean for social movements faced with this level of brutality? If we define success only in terms of achieving specific goals, then we inevitably fail. While the students failed to achieve their stated goals, their relentless activism brought alternative, more-democratic power structures into focus in the political realm. Their movement moreover made visible the failure of the state, rendered illegitimate through its criminal abuse of power. The '68 massacre lives. It has shaped the Mexican social and political imaginary. Many believe that "another world is possible," as the Zapatistas say. Still today, every October 2 people throughout Mexico hold events to honor and accompany the students, who are always ¡presente! "El dos de octubre no se olvida" (We do not forget October 2).

For me, going back to 1968 is like revisiting the ur-moment in Mexico when everything changed for those of us who had not really understood that the government would kill students en masse and in full public view rather than negotiate a more open public sphere. I was finishing high school in a British school in Mexico City, still following the path of domestication and discipline that my parents had chosen for me as a young child in Parral, Chihuahua. I was still wearing the outfit—the blazer, tie, pleated skirt, and oxford shoes—that recalled my boarding school years in Canada. While I had friends in the movement, the private school insulated me somewhat from the violence erupting in the city. In school, I remember, we'd debate whether Mexico would become a more egalitarian, democratic country, like the United States, maybe, where those in power were not corrupt and actually obeyed the law. No one mentioned the war in Vietnam or the systemic violence in the United States against Native, black, and Latinx Americans and other marginalized populations.

When I heard about the sheep event, it immediately struck me as an act of genius. It reaffirmed my own attitude toward authority, which I manifested by jumping over the school fence after roll call whenever possible and walking home. ¡Presente! But not really. This partial compliance exemplifies one of my favorite Mexican expressions and worldviews, "Sí, pero no." Democracy? Here? There? Where? Yes, well, maybe, no?

So I never forgot the story of the sheep. The more I researched the 1968 incident, however, the more questions I had. What actually happened? Did the workers actually turn their backs? Some people say yes; others don't mention it.

A government report describes the upheaval caused by the student movement on August 27 during which some 300,000 to 400,000 people marched toward the Zócalo threatening a strike. They had their black-and-red strike flag, sang the national anthem, demanded the release of students jailed in the Lecumberri prison, and waited for the promised meeting with President Díaz Ordaz. The students lowered the Mexican flag and raised the black-and-red flag up the central flagpole. The bells of the cathedral rang incessantly to support their cause. The government interpreted these acts as a provocation and mobilized its tanks, heavy weaponry, bayonets, and tear gas, and finally removed the students from the Zócalo early in the morning of August 28. They lowered the black-and-red flag. Young people, pursued by members of the armed forces, fled from the Zócalo, through Mexico's so-called Historic Center.

On August 28, the aggrieved government sent an announcement through the press and its agencies that it would perform an Act of Redress (Ceremonia de Desagravio) for the desecration of the flag.[30] Civil servants from throughout the Federal District were called in to perform their loyalty. As we know, things did not go as planned: "Bureaucrats from the Federal District, that had been hauled in to make amends in the face of the ominous event, began to shout in unison: 'We're sheep!! We're penned in!' The students managed to burst their way into the ceremony. The act finished with intervention by police and army forces and new persecutions through the Historic Center."[31]

The well-known historian and novelist Paco Ignacio Taibo II, also a student at the time, tells of being part of a large group of students in the movement trying to get into the Zócalo when the sheep disturbance took place. In his book *68*, he writes, "They called a meeting of public servants working for the State and obliged them to leave their offices in a straight line. The act went badly for them. Many bureaucrats started to shout: 'We're being herded; we're [President] Díaz Ordaz's sheep.'"[32]

Writer Elena Poniatowska offers a testimony by another witness: "Government workers were already quite unhappy about being forced either to attend official ceremonies or lose their job. . . . The government employees attended this civic purification ceremony all right, but not in the spirit the government had expected. They flocked out of the ministries and public offices shouting 'We're sheep, they're herding us around . . . baaa, baaa, baaa.'"[33] So did they baaa before getting to the Zócalo?

One art review notes that the state workers rebelled by walking around the flagpole in a circle.[34] Only a few descriptions mention them turning their backs on the speaker. Art critic Katrin Wittneven does, noting that the sheep episode remains fixed (though with differences) in the Mexican imaginary: "In Mexico, people still remember that thousands of civil servants expressed their protest in the late sixties by rebelliously turning their backs to the government tribunes and bleating."[35]

The divergent ways the sheep event has been recounted, and even the reports and documentation that mention it, offer only partial accounts. So my description is limited in terms of its truth value. The incident happened—we have documentation to prove it—but did it happen the way it was reported or the way I remember it?

Studying acts that took place in the past without an archival record is challenging not only for performance studies scholars but also for historians, ethnographers, and others who take a humanistic approach to cultural practices and meanings. Because the live, the behavioral, the experiential are our primary domain, even when the live is mediated though the digital, the literary, the medical, and so forth, I cannot always refer the reader to a text, website, painting, photograph or film, set of statistics, X-rays, or lab reports (the things pertaining to the archive, as I've argued earlier) to confirm or challenge my recounting of the situation.[36] Sometimes, as with the video that I discuss shortly, "The Multiplication of Sheep," part of *Patriotic Tales*, by the Belgian-Mexican artist Francis Alÿs, I can link to the video that I take as one of my sources. Our interpretations of what we see in it might differ, but the incident itself is well documented, and the video itself may degrade but won't change. My interpretation might differ from others' and, as is often the case, may change over time. Each new encounter with the material might add a dimension, but the video is a relatively stable referent.

Other times, when I have no recourse to the archival register, I need to transmit the scene in part through my observations, experiential engagement with others, and the knowledge that I bring to the context. The "I"—the situated I, the observing and narrating I, the I as coparticipant in the drama, and at times the autobiographical I—then, becomes central to the degree that it transmits an accurate portrayal, or the experiential or affective quality, or the ethical and political complications of the subject of discussion. How else can a reader know what to make of the analysis? Performance studies scholars, ethnographers, and historians share some of the challenges and methods for examining the partially or even unrecorded past—speaking with people who were there or remember the events, studying the sites where they took place, reading all available materials, and so on. What varies among these disciplinary practices, and also among practitioners within these fields as well, are the objectives, methods, assumptions, and the ways of engaging with others.

Historians, rarely writing in the first person, rely on documentation that records change over time to establish facts and maybe even some kind of truth. Did the events happen? When, why, how? The framework of change over time requires a distanced, expansive overview perspective. While seemingly objective and disembodied, their writings too are challenged by the indeterminacy of reports and documents. These, as written artifacts, are also made, the product of certain perspectives and interests. Some details may be included, others left out. Those who created the reports worked from assumptions and value systems, which today's scholars, working from their own assumptions and values, need to interpret. Explorations into the past can only be made from the present and always involve conjecture and interpretation. Hayden White put it well when he said that "the 'present' . . . must serve as a solid ground from which a bridge can be projected into a past incompletely mapped and inhabited by ghosts and marked by graves."[37] We can only ever analyze from this bridge, from this place on which we stand and that grounds our perspective.

Performance ethnographers with methodological ties to anthropology, such as Dwight Conquergood, focus more on the relational nature of scholar/informant, and the ethical issues they raise, than ascertaining the accuracy of the situation: "The performative view brings ethnographer and native together as co-actors, mutually engaged collaborators in a fragile fiction."[38] While the "ethnographer and native" language smacks of a colonialist vein in anthropology, Conquergood's work unwaveringly stresses the embodied interactions and ethical entanglements between interlocutors and "the inescapable moral tensions of ethnographic praxis."[39] Whatever we come to will be a "fragile fiction" that induces a personal and cultural "self-knowledge, self-awareness, plural reflexivity, that makes it political."[40]

While I share some of the methods of those who describe themselves performance ethnographers or autoethnographers, I would not use the language of fieldwork, field notes, data, and other terms from anthropology to describe what I do.[41] Closer to theatre practitioners perhaps, I focus here on performance scenarios and events that keep reappearing—always in different shapes, with different actors, and modified contexts—to reveal the ways in which communities imagine and rehearse meaning, conflict, and possible resolutions.[42] The overarching structuring power of the scenarios, the explanatory force of event, rather than the historic truth or accuracy of the details, speak to me. We act, we make and transmit meaning, through the events in these scenarios. "El 68" became an Event with a capital E. Events (unlike facts) are not out there in the world; they are constructed from incidents and occurrences and take on different meanings over time—here the student movement, the civil servants' bleating, the massacre. If anything, as the historian Pierre Nora suggests, events depend on the awareness of the beholder as much as the other way around: "What is the event and for whom? For if there is no event without critical consciousness, there is an event only when, offered to everybody, it is not the same for all."[43] We were all present/e, but not in the same way.

So the events of August 28, 1968, took place, even though the facts remain blurry. For my purposes, it really does not matter if the workers-as-sheep turned their backs or simply bleated (although I certainly wish I knew). Both acts constitute animatives that disrupt and delegitimate the government's performative. The point remains the same—state workers explicitly acknowledged, and contested, their role as sheep in an authoritarian government. Taibo, the historian, concludes, "The only thing that works is memory. Collective memory. Even the smallest and saddest individual memory."[44] And that too is highly variable. But the telling, retelling, and reenactment of the sheep event contribute to it staying alive in one form or another, making visible the structuring scenario of continuing oppression that underwrites the history of Mexico pre- and postconquest. Making memory, keeping it alive, ¡presente! is another aspect of making history. And here is where studying the event, as opposed to all the specific facts, becomes meaningful for me as a performance studies scholar. My question is not what happened exactly, but why does the event continue to resonate? Performed action makes its own heuristic interventions and claims.

The Sheep, Again

How do iconic events stay presente, alive, re-presented and animated again and again in various forms? Thirty years after the massacre of the students, the performance artist Francis Alÿs staged a video performance, *Cuentos patrióticos* (Patriotic tales), based in part on the defiance of the bureaucrats, called "La multiplicación de los borregos" (The multiplication of sheep) (figs. 2.2–2.5).[45] He walks around the same flagpole with the oversize, undulating Mexican flag in the Zócalo leading a sheep on a leash. The performance video begins with a close-up of a sheep against the backdrop of the National Cathedral. Slightly off to the side, we catch a glimpse of banners with the word *causa* or "cause" on it, suggesting the performance took place in the context of one of the many protests held in the Zócalo. The title, "La multiplicación de los borregos" (in pink script) announces the work. The pink might signal that rather than the red-hot act of 1968, this is a lighter but still politically (pinko?) inflected re-vision of the same. A wide-angle shot of the massive square, with people milling around it, sets the scene. When Alÿs walks on, leading a sheep on a leash, the lens focuses tightly on them. Nothing else is visible except shadows on the stone ground—the imposing linear slashes caused by the flagpole and its silhouette, and the moving shapes of Alÿs and the sheep that walks behind him in a circular direction. One by one, more sheep (not on leashes) join the circle, altering their pace to keep equidistant from each other and maintain the circular formation. The bells of the cathedral ring incessantly, reminiscent of the same bells that pealed nonstop in a show of support of the students back on August 27, 1968. Methodically, Alÿs continues to walk clockwise around the pole. He stands erect, walking in a relaxed yet deliberate manner. Soon, twenty-one sheep have joined the walk. Magically, it seems, one follows the one ahead in perfect formation. Then Alÿs drops the leash and the first sheep walks away from the circle in an orderly fashion. After every rotation of the flagpole, another sheep peels off. At the beginning of the performance, each new sheep had joined the end of the line. At the end, the sheep that leave the circle are the ones at the head of line, those walking right behind Alÿs. He does not signal to them in any way. They just seem to know when it's their turn. How do they know that? Gradually, as more sheep walk away, the circle looks more like a semicircle. The distance grows between Alÿs and the sheep. Before long, Alÿs walks at

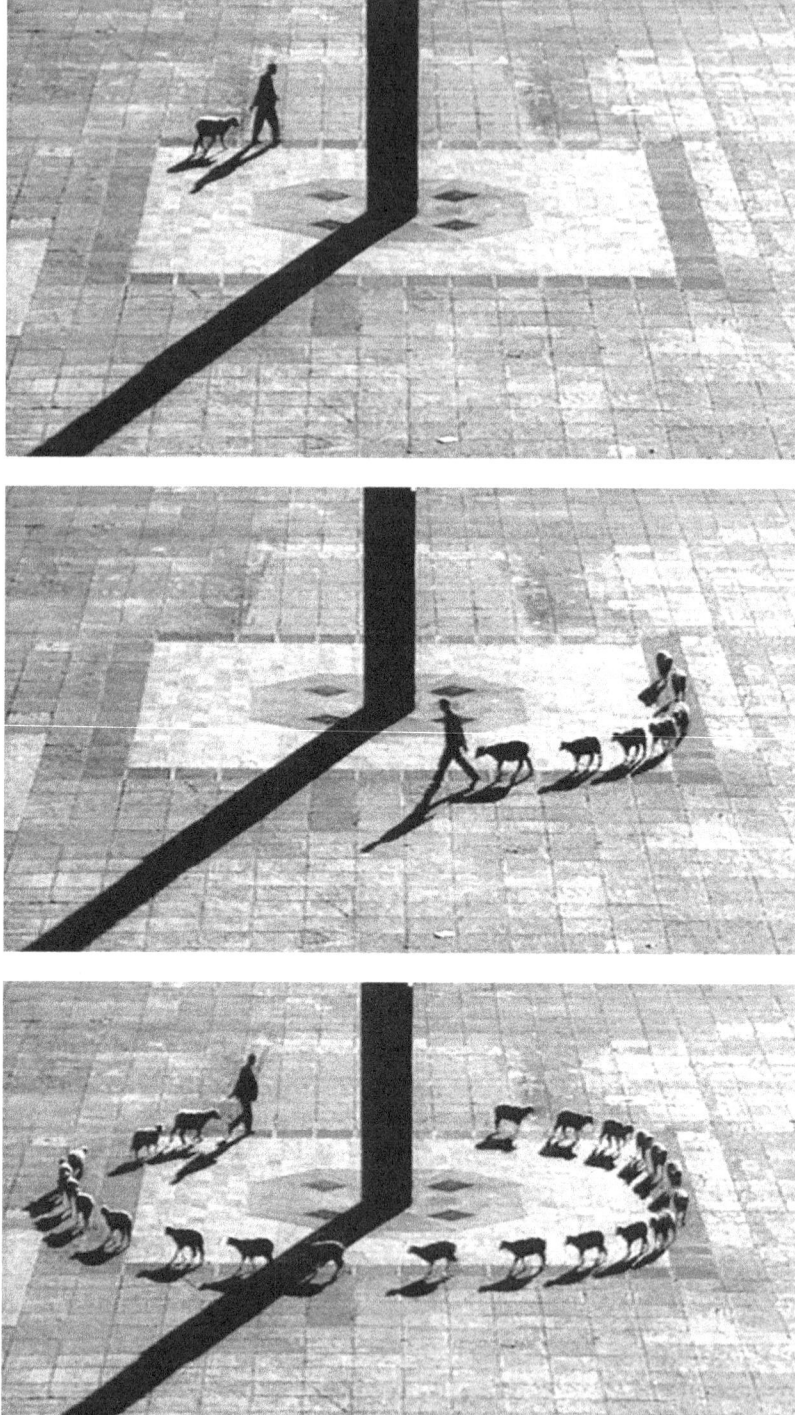

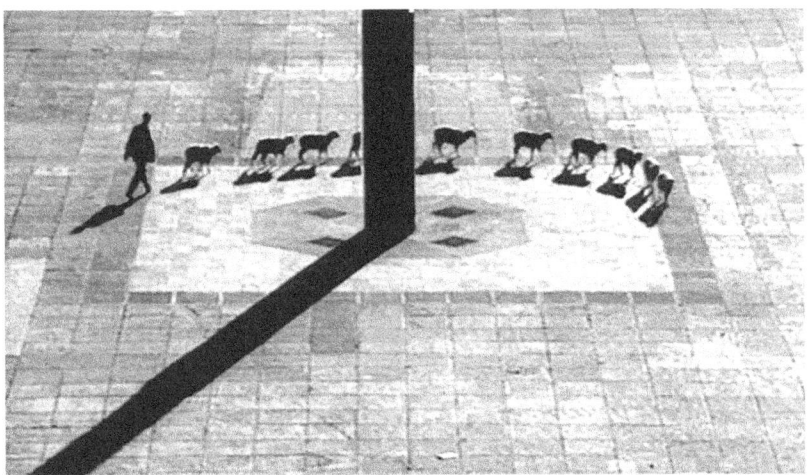

2.2–2.5 Frames from Francis Alÿs, "The Multiplication of Sheep," in *Cuentos patrióticos* (Patriotic tales), in collaboration with Rafael Ortega, 1997. Single-channel video projection, 14:40 minutes. IMAGES COURTESY OF THE ARTIST.

the end of the line, following them. Who leads whom? The sheep behave as if a thread united them. The connectivity exceeds the naked eye. Alÿs walks off after the last sheep exits. For a moment, the small area remains empty. The video ends with a close-up of a sheep's face. No baaa necessary.

Alÿs's body, his walk around the flagpole, conjures up the civil servants. Still ¡presentes! These sheep have transformed from followers into a collective, Guattari's "multiplicity that *deploys itself.*"

The performance, as shown in the video on the artist's website, lasts a little over twenty-five minutes.[46] No spectators or bystanders appear in the video once the performance starts. The video accentuates the bracketing of the event that I have argued elsewhere defines performance.[47] The focus fixes the time, space, and dimensions of what I can only think of as a stage, an area reconverted for a short time into an acting area, a different space of appearance or, better, a space where people/sheep can appear differently. When Alÿs and the sheep leave, the Zócalo looks empty, emptied, drained for a second of the many dramas fought there over the past six hundred years. The space, like a stage, is the same and not the same. The bracketing gives the illusion of fixity in terms of space and time, and yet reminds us that it exists only in relation to, and alongside, other spaces and other times. The para-space/time of performance, of politics. The performance space and/as political space is the arena of potentiality, hinting perhaps at other, better futures. Located in the Zócalo, the same geographical spot that has been the site of so many struggles and transformations, the performance highlights the constant refiguration over time of the scenario itself. The shadow of the flagpole marks the space like the hand of a sundial. The time? Now. But the sharp shadow also cuts into and across Mexican historical practice. Always.

The curator Natasha Marie Llorens writes: "Alÿs brings the memory of humans acting like sheep together with the spectacle of sheep re-enacting human protest, demonstrating that how bodies appear in public is as important as the fact that they gather. And it is their gathering that creates the space of protest, of politics. Protest—a set of relations between people—thus produces the square anew in each instance."[48] But Alÿs does more. His sheep indicate that protesters will not appear as people, never be presente as "men" in Arendt's words, "who show who they are, reveal actively their unique personal identities and thus make their appearance in the human world."[49] Those in power will withhold recognition from those who refuse official interpellation. Denied subjectivity, protesters (like migrants, like slaves) need to fight precisely for how their bodies appear in public. The space of appearance, as Arendt insisted, is not a material space but, rather, the mechanic of intersubjective recognition whereby people acknowledge one another as they reveal who they are. However, the material conditions and places where these acts and rituals of mutual and relational recognition happen also need to be fought for and won, albeit momentarily. As Judith Butler points out, "It is not only that we need to live in order to act, but that we have to act, and act politically, in order to secure the conditions of existence."[50] ¡Presente! signals the determination to appear otherwise.

On September 26, 2014, indigenous and mestizo male students from the Ayotzinapa rural college commandeered five buses to take them to Mexico City for the October 2 commemoration of the massacred students. They did that every year and always brought the buses back. That night, a mix of local, military, and federal police joined with members of drug cartels to kill six people outright, including some students. They kidnapped and tortured dozens of other students, and permanently disappeared an additional forty-three of them, as I will examine in chapter 5. State violence against students continues, unabated. Now, back in the Zócalo, we recite their names and say, yet again, ¡Presente!

The number 43 and the phrase "el dos de octubre no se olvida" resonate throughout Mexico. ¡Presente! signals the now, again, and seemingly always of political violence. It has an enduring quality that invokes the dead that don't die, the past that remains. We live in para-times and spaces, as I argue

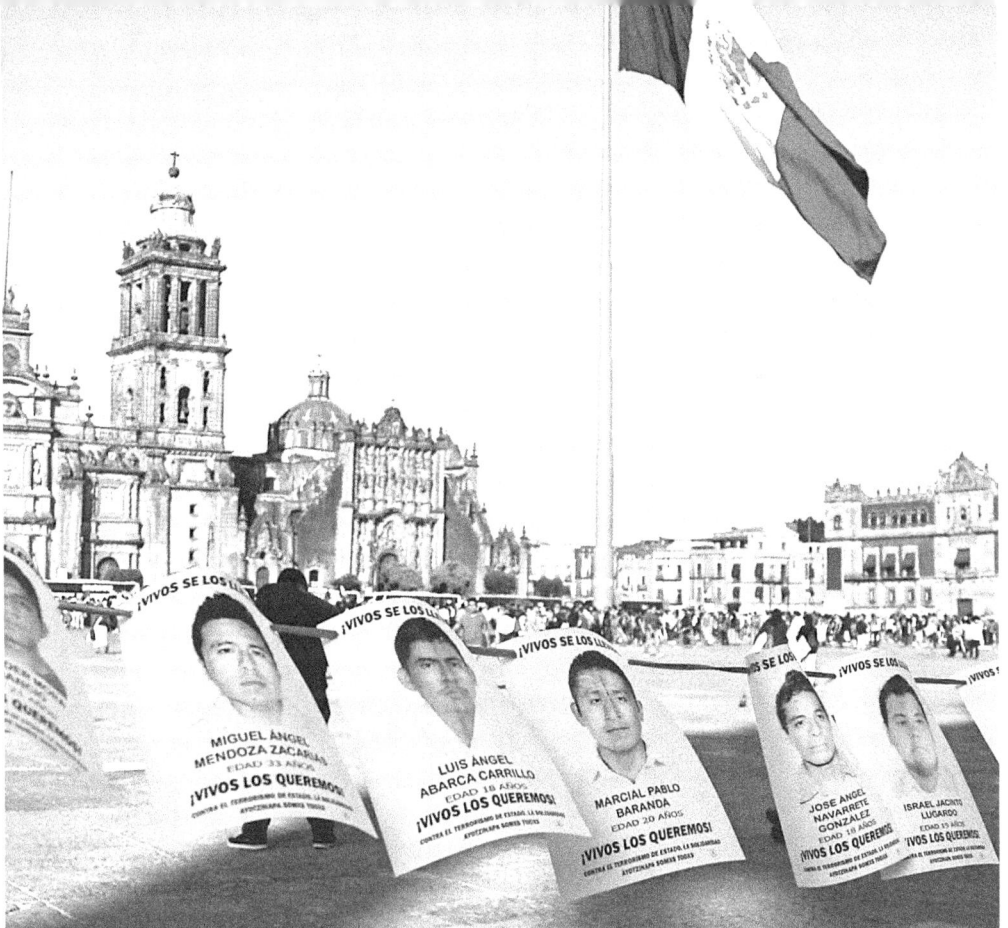

2.6 "Los 43." Date unknown.

in chapter 1, para-worlds nested in, beside, and alongside others that are always there—'68, '98, 2014. Once we see how presence is shaped, contested, destroyed, performed, and reperformed through these scenarios of (mis)recognition, we can never not see it again. Each return to the Zócalo reminds us of the unhappy performatives, the powerful animatives, the ethical imperative to witness and accompany, and the refusal to legitimate acts of brutality. Each repeat performance accumulates affective, symbolic, and explanatory power.

Each repeat, however, involves difference. This time ¡presente! took on a decidedly militant attitude. The massive resistance to the state's criminal politics threatened to overturn the government. Hundreds of thousands of protesters took to the streets, claiming once again an alternative space of appearance that acknowledged the centrality of the disappeared.

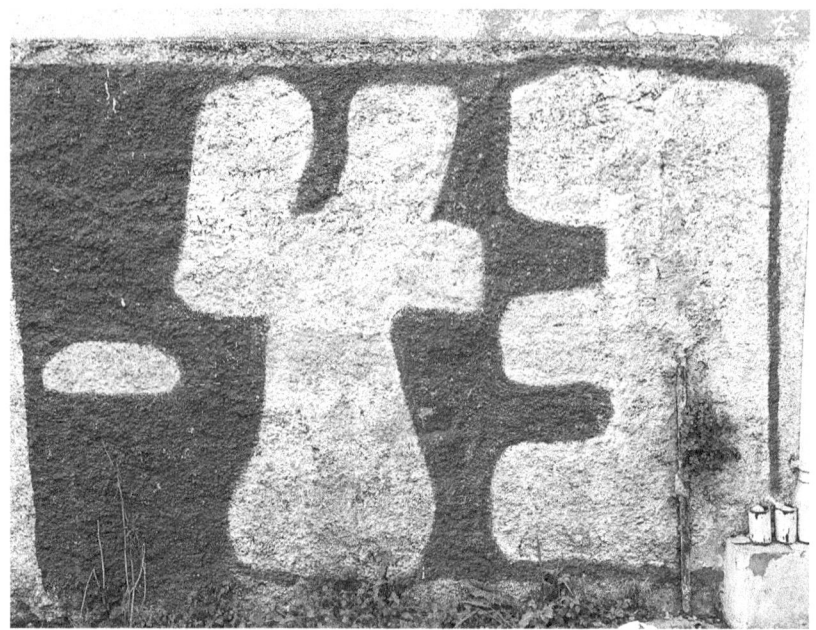

2.7 "−43," Mexico City, 2017. PHOTO: DIANA TAYLOR.

The defiant sheep showed up in multitudes—they seemed to have indeed multiplied. "Quisieron desaparecernos y aparecimos en todo el mundo" (They wanted to disappear us and we appeared throughout the world). "−43" appeared everywhere—on the sidewalks, bumper stickers, and walls (fig. 2.7).

Memes flooded social media throughout the country: #NosFaltan43 (We are missing 43) and #FueelEstado (The state did it) among others. A large installation, *43: The Antihistorical Monument* was embedded in the central avenue of Mexico City (fig. 2.8).

The former president Vicente Fox had words of advice for the families of the forty-three disappeared students, and for the rest of the population: "Get over it."[51] State violence continues, and so does the opposition of those who choose every single day—sometimes against all odds—not to side with injustice. An anti-imperial, antinationalist, post-Cartesian, and even post-human "we" is shaped through these performances. The "we" acts, through protest, art, and here through scholarship, both product and agent of the negotiation of political life. Who leads whom? Who turns their back or follows along? We continue to crash the space of appearance, producing it again, and always, anew.

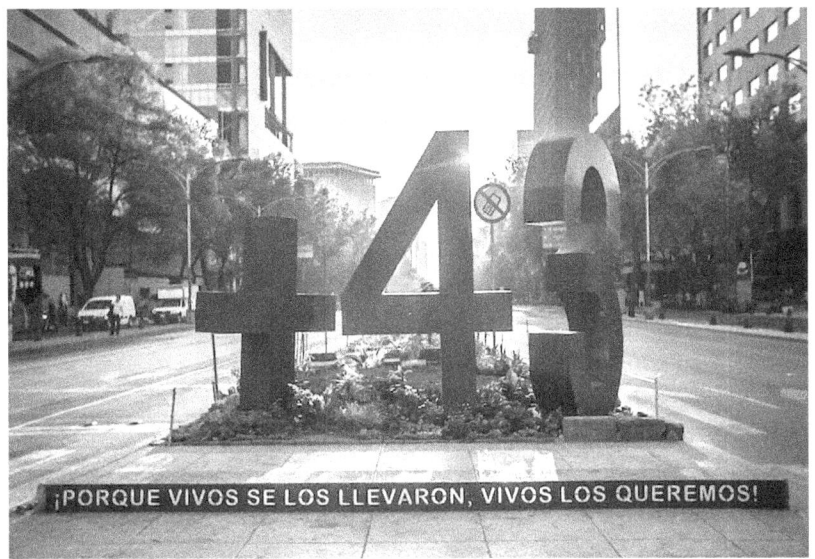

¡PORQUE VIVOS SE LOS LLEVARON, VIVOS LOS QUEREMOS!

2.8 43: *Anti-monumento Historico*, Mexico City, 2017. PHOTO: RAY MARMOLEJO LE GARREC.

Postscript

In summer 2018, Mexico prepared for the fiftieth anniversary of the Tlatelolco massacre in 1968. Artist Yael Bartana, the National University of Mexico, and the Comisión Ejecutiva de Atención a Víctimas, a commission formed to help victims, invited survivors of the massacre to leave their footprints in the 400-meter concrete slab laid down in Tlatelolco. The footprints remind us it's not over; it's never over. ¡Presente! Here rests the force of the performance of resistance that can stand up to the performative command to move on. Performance, as Richard Schechner defines it, is "never for the first time."[52] The repeats take on a life and animate the political: making presence, making memory, making space for alternative visions of livable lives.

At the same time, I met with intellectuals and activists shaped by '68. How to commemorate October 2, especially now that Mexico's progressive candidate, André Manuel López Obrador (AMLO) won the presidency by a landslide? I think of one act that makes sense: AMLO should answer the demand that students made fifty years ago and invite their leaders to an open dialogue. The students' march was accompanied by a call for a meeting, a gesture, "a call to make a response," an opening toward communication,

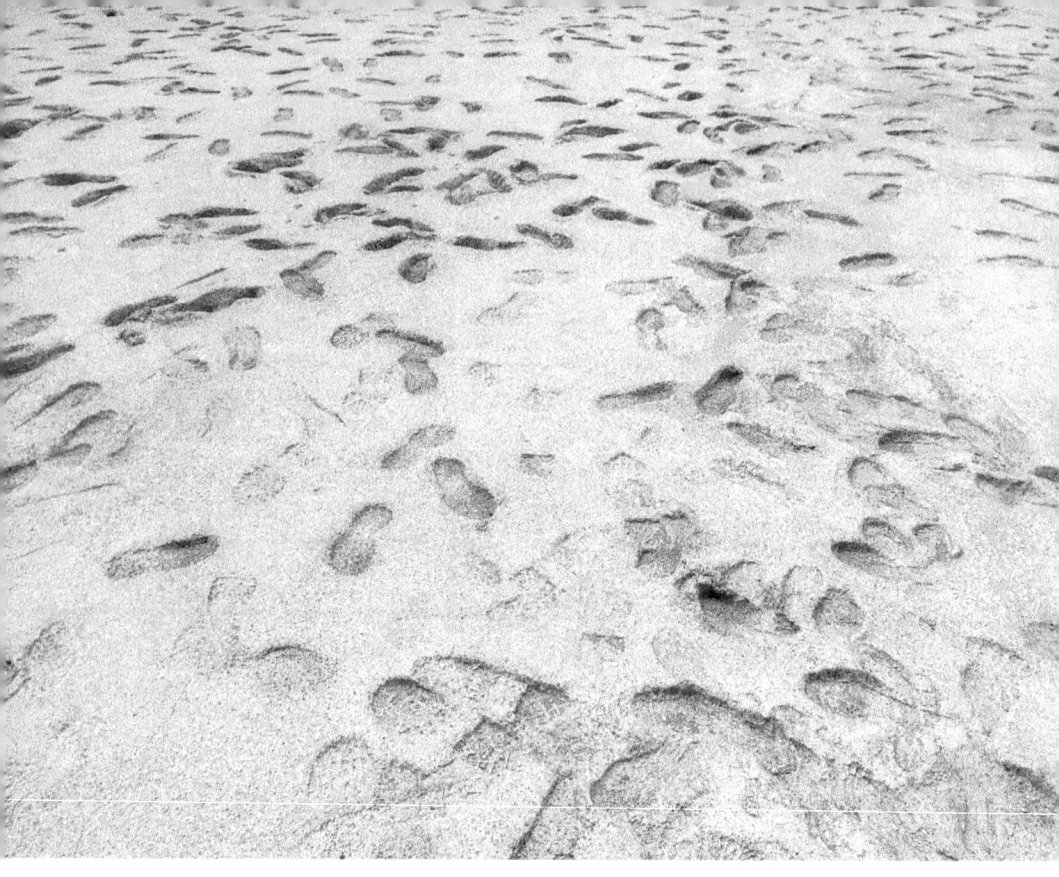

2.9 *Monumento de la Ausencia*, 2019. PHOTO: JULIO PANTOJA.

a move toward a negotiated public space.[53] That's what they were marching/asking for. Sometimes it takes decades to respond to a call. Now we see the footprints. It was past time to acknowledge the call and reciprocate the gesture.

THREE

Camino Largo
*The Zapatistas' Long
Road toward Autonomy*

We wait, we resist, we are experts at this.

Speaking and listening is how true men and women learn to walk.

—SUBCOMANDANTE MARCOS, *Our Word Is Our Weapon*

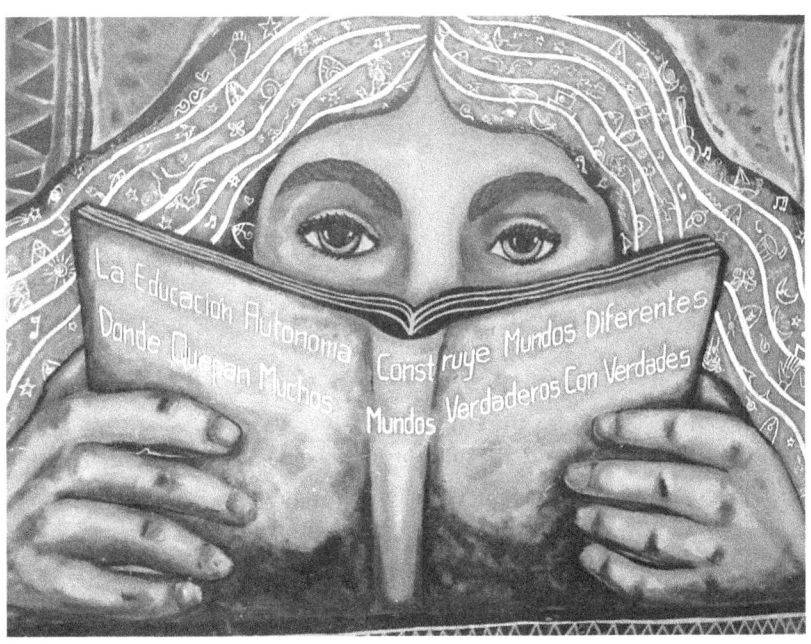

3.1 Autonomous education constructs different worlds where many worlds fit, true worlds with truths. Painting on the school at Oventic, 2013. PHOTO: LORIE NOVAK.

In August 2013, the Zapatistas decided to throw a party. A few months before the twentieth anniversary of their uprising against the Mexican government on January 1, 1994, the Subcomandante Insurgente Moisés sent out word via the internet to "quienes se hayan sentido convocados" (those who feel summoned) to celebrate the ten-year anniversary of the creation of the five Zapatista *caracoles* (autonomous municipalities; literally, "snails"), each with its own governing structure or Council of Good Government (Junta del Buen Gobierno, or JBG).[1] The caracoles were set up to organize and provide health care, education, and basic services to the various autonomous communities who receive nothing but trouble from the Mexican government. As opposed to that *mal* or bad government, the five or so men and women of the JBG who serve on a rotating basis are voted in by the community and have to obey community mandates.

The party was part of a major redirection in the Zapatistas' *camino largo*, or long road, toward autonomy. The camino largo stretches across time and space, five-hundred-plus years and counting. Their map shows a zigzag movement toward freedom, a series of complex operations through tricky territory in many senses, physical, political, and digital. What began as an act of armed uprising in 1994—a violent refusal, a *¡Basta ya!* (Enough!), an animative that resounded globally—developed into a sustained enactment of possibility. Another world is possible, the Zapatistas declared, and they set about building it. The disruptive animative evolved into the new norm, a way of life.

The Zapatistas had been very actively on the move, in their quiet way, before and after the uprising, trying to build civil support for their claims through meetings, marches, and a very active presence online, mainly through email and communiqués. They hosted a national democratic convention in Aguascalientes (August 1994) to urge people of good will of all nationalities, races, sexualities, and religions to focus on "the common enemy."[2] In 1994, Marcos rejected attempts by Mexico's incoming president, Ernesto Zedillo, to buy him off.[3] The Zapatistas entered into negotiations with the "bad" government that produced the San Andrés Accords (1996) guaranteeing autonomy and rights to indigenous peoples.[4] After losing faith in the Mexican government for failing to honor the agreements, they hosted more forums such as the First International Encuentro for Humanity and against Neoliberalism, asking all those exploited by the system to join them in the Mayan highlands to share their struggles for recognition: "We invited you all for all of us to hear ourselves and speak to ourselves. To see all that we are."[5] On May 7, 2011, and December 21, 2012, fifty thousand

Zapatistas marched in total silence through San Cristóbal and other towns in Chiapas—they didn't say why. At the end of the day in 2012, they issued a declaration, a poem: "¿Escucharon? / Es el sonido de su mundo derrumbándose. Es el del nuestro resurgiendo." (Did you hear? / That is the sound of your world crumbling. It is the sound of ours reemerging.)[6] What started as an act of refusal grew into an alternative way of living politics that few had thought possible or sustainable.

The celebration in Oventic marked one more milestone on the map. Now, after a reclusive period, the Zapatistas were beginning to open themselves up, once again, to civil society. Those who felt called, interpellated, could respond by attending. We too could be ¡presentes! In addition to the party, the Zapatistas had organized the first session of the *escuelita*, or little school, for those who wanted to live with the Zapatistas for a week and learn about their ways of living politics. As then Subcomandante Marcos (or Sup) made clear, the Zapatistas did not need us to come and give advice or tell them what to do. We were welcome to come learn from and accompany them.[7]

San Cristóbal de las Casas, situated in the Mayan highlands in southern Mexico, was alive with visitors and independent journalists from all over the world. Fifteen hundred people had been admitted to the escuelita this time, including major figures in human rights and education.[8] Another such number attended online via video conferencing from CIDECI (Centro indigena de capacitación integral, the Indigenous Center for Holistic Training), a local Zapatista-inspired university. For the celebration of the caracoles (the administrative centers of Zapatista territory), long lines of vans, trucks, and cars stretched far along the road that goes to Oventic, the caracol closest to San Cristóbal de las Casas, Chiapas, and thus, the most visited. Through the rain and mist that evening we could see the sign on the road said:

> ESTA USTED EN TERRITORIO
> ZAPATISTA EN REBELDIA
> "Aquí manda el pueblo
> y el gobierno obedece"
>
> [YOU ARE IN ZAPATISTA REBEL TERRITORY:
> "Here the people decide and the government obeys"]

An unimposing metal gate separates Oventic from the rest of Mexico. Though the entrance is a few meters off a federal highway, the caracol seems worlds apart in terms of ideology and political practice. It was about eight on Friday evening when we arrived. Though dark and pouring rain, people

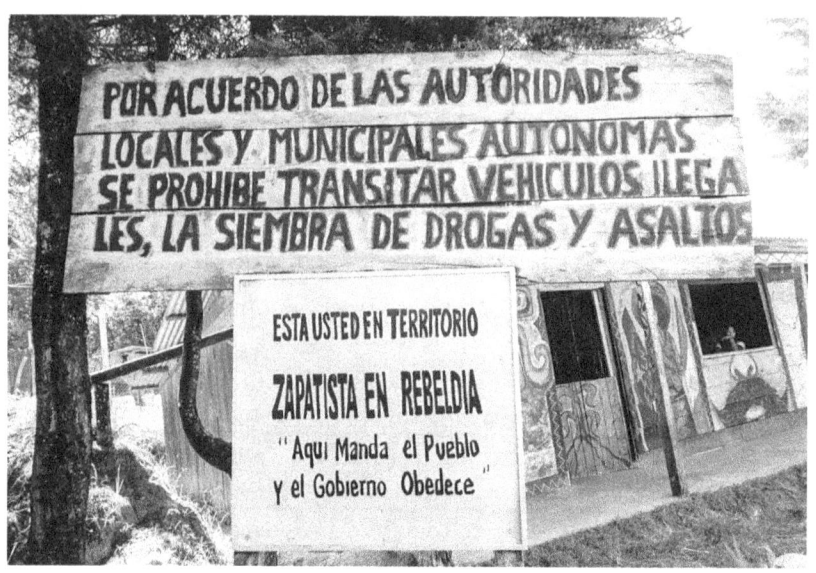

3.2 "YOU ARE IN ZAPATISTA REBEL TERRITORY," 2013. PHOTO: LORIE NOVAK.

lined up to enter through the flower-covered arch. We, all forty of us participating in the Art and Resistance course that Jesusa Rodríguez and I were coteaching for the third time in Chiapas,[9] shuffled in under the large plastic tarps just to the side of the colorful Che Guevara store that bridges the inside/outside of the caracol. The shop sells food, soft drinks, and basic supplies to the Zapatistas working in the administrative center and resistance-themed souvenirs to visitors and those passing on the road. We crowded together, waiting, as a masked Zapatista asked to see our IDs. We handed him the list with our names, places of origin, and passport numbers. We had people from throughout the Americas, Africa, Europe, Australia, and three local Mayan women who participated as artists in our group. The man looked at us. Were we a problem? Or just an oddity? He decided not to count, and went off with the list. Another came close to keep an eye on us. One of the women in our group said something to him, and he smiled through his black ski mask. He wanted to know where we were from and why we wanted to be there, a good question. "To celebrate," was all she said.

We had come to learn. Chiapas provides a remarkable arena to study art and resistance for several reasons. Here we see state repression and epistemicide at work, up close.[10] The indigenous population of Chiapas, the largest in Mexico, has long been considered an obstacle by the government, a deficit, a drag on the nation's aspirations to modernity. Three-quarters of the population lives in poverty.[11] The state has the poorest educational system in the country. According to the Zapatistas, 72 percent of children don't make it through first grade.[12] Most people have no access to clean water or an adequate sewage system. Without health care, many die of preventable or curable illness such as measles, cholera, typhus, pneumonia, parasites, and gastrointestinal diseases.[13] Ironically, Chiapas is one of the most beautiful and resource-rich states. Mexico and the ruling elites as a whole profit enormously from the petroleum, wood, electricity, coffee, honey, corn, cacao, and cattle that they extract, and they give very little back. If anything, Mexico further exploits the indigenous population and the natural resources of the land with its wooded highlands, diverse ecosystems, gorgeous lakes and waterfalls for tourism. Most visitors to Palenque or its other preconquest sites might marvel at the beauty of it all and fail to see the misery that the Mexican and local government's policies inflict on its people and the land.

An early question for our group: How much do tourists need to not know, and not see, to enjoy their travels in Chiapas? One of our several performance reflections, as I explore later in this chapter, staged the degree of "percepticide," or self-blinding, needed to not hear or see what's happening around us.[14]

Part of our shared task, through our pedagogical practice, was to interrogate why and how we were there. This meant examining not just the epistemological questions of "what" and "how" we perceive, and the limits of our perceptual habits. How can we see and know differently? The Platonic metaphysical notion of a stable "real" (a what *is*) as opposed to the shadowy world

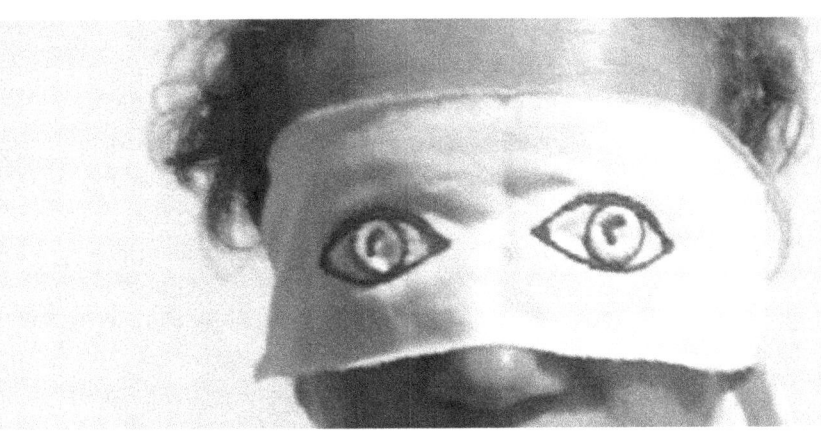

3.3 *Seeing/Unseeing Eyes*. Canadian performance artist/theorist Helene Vosters created and led the performance. 2013. COURTESY OF THE ARTIST.

of appearance (what appears to be) didn't help, as the brutal "real" hidden from the romantic tourist sell was not fixed or stable. The economic misery, rising out of conquest, was enacted anew with every subsequent change of policy and government. Instead of *being*, the exploitation and desubjectification continued as permanent *becoming*. The naturalized "reality" of the situation was produced systemically to promote a self-serving narrative of the lazy, uneducated "Indian."

We also had to examine our fantasies of being in place with others who live such different lives from our own. Later I take up the question that the Zapatista asked: What were we doing there?

The perpetually unfolding layers of violence are again aggravated by the intense activity surrounding migration in Chiapas. An estimated 500,000 migrants and refugees from Central America cross the Guatemala-Mexico border every year to reach the U.S. Because the U.S. pays the Mexican government to stop migrants in the south, the state has become increasingly militarized.[15] Violence as a whole has escalated; migrants are attacked, raped, murdered, and disappeared at times by members of organized crime groups, at times by federal or local police, and at times by ordinary delinquents trying to make a little money off of those even poorer than themselves. Human misery is the region's gross national product.

In the face of all this despair and inequality, the Zapatistas said, "No. Enough is enough." The state has become the center of indigenous thought and alternative epistemic theories and practices.

The Zapatistas have practiced resistance for a very long time, waiting, quietly, obstinately for the right moment to act. Their silence, an enactment of refusal, went unnoticed. Who, after all, would expect indigenous peoples to speak? Their quiet waiting functioned as an animative—the government wants us to actively perform our oppression, they might have said (much like the 'sheep' in 'Enacting Refusal'), and we refuse. We move when we decide to move. They signal, if only to themselves, in what Jorge Portilla might call the "solidarity . . . of the underdog."[16] They started organizing back in 1983, a full decade before they made the decision to mobilize in an armed uprising. Several theories circulate about why and when they decided to claim visibility. An archaeologist friend of Rodríguez's who works in Toniná, near Ocosingo, Chiapas, told us one version.

Toniná, a Maya ceremonial site about two thousand years old, is characterized by enormous platforms and terraces built into the mountain above the central plaza. This, he tells us, was where the Zapatistas would meet in the 1980s and develop their plans. They were waiting for the moment to act, knowing that the moment for action is never obvious. They knew not to be in a hurry. One night, as they were meeting at the sacred site, lightning from a huge electrical storm hit the side of the pyramid and sliced off a layer of overgrowth. The heavy rain that night washed off the residual brush and ash, and when they awoke in the morning they saw a gigantic staggered or stepped fretwork going up the side of the pyramid (fig. 3.4).

3.4 The stepped fret, 2019. Drawing by Jesusa Rodríguez based on an image by Jorge Enciso in Paul Westheim, *The Art of Ancient Mexico*, 116.
COURTESY OF THE ARTIST.

The stepped fretwork gives visible expression to the awareness of continuous movement and struggle that animates Mesoamerican communities. The steps, the forward push, always end up circling back in on themselves. "The constant repetition of the motif," Paul Westheim argues, does not signal harmony or resolution, nor allow pause for contemplation. The "intensity never relaxes. . . . . The powers that built the cosmos are dynamic and what sustains it is the tension by which they are mutually held in check."[17] The stepped fretwork is about moving forward and pushing back. Like the constant struggles endured by indigenous peoples, the tensions never resolve. Survival relies on pushing back, keeping in motion.

The Zapatistas, the archaeologist told us, took the revelation of the ancient fretwork as the sign they had been waiting for to push forward.

The more common version of course links the uprising to the passing of NAFTA (the North American Free Trade Agreement) on January 1, 1994. The Zapatistas considered NAFTA a "death certificate" for indigenous peoples.[18] The free trade agreement meant that local populations would lose their territorial and agricultural autonomy, such as it was. Led by the diminutive Comandanta Ramona, the Zapatista armed uprising took five important towns in the state, including the city of San Cristóbal. Why be afraid, she said: "For all intents and purposes, we were already dead. We meant absolutely nothing."[19] The indigenous rebels fully understood their colonial condition. They were fighting from the space of death. Her statement too finds echo in the stepped fretwork. I paraphrase Westheim's observation that the fretwork reflects the Mesoamericans' vision of their role: they must act to offset the danger; they must be alert, must struggle and offer their own lives.[20]

Capitán Insurgente Maribel, the fifteen-year-old woman who helped capture the town of Margaritas, replied to the commissioner who asked how old she was: "Five hundred and two . . . as old as the rebellion."[21] Time, resistance, struggle, and identity had become synonymous, all entangled in the contradictory tempo of the struggle: slow/fast, zig/zag, short/elongated, young/very old. "I Am WE," a Zapatista sign reads.

The Zapatistas have tried all sorts of approaches since the initial armed warfare of January 1994 to secure their goals: democracy, liberty, and justice—not just for them but for everyone. They have a brilliant command of performance strategies, their use of masks and silence being two of the most interesting. Anonymity characterizes the Zapatistas as a group. They have been united, as Sup writes, "by our common misery, by the collective oblivion into which we were cast 501 years ago, by the useless death we endure, by our being faceless, with our name ripped from us, by our having to bet our lives and deaths for someone else's future."[22]

What more effective performatic strategy than to claim presence by fighting from that place of anonymity of those denied the possibility of appearance, those without a face, without a name. The Zapatistas use masks every time they are with non-Zapatistas. The act of masking is an animative, refusing abjection and turning it into a show of dignity, withholding from power the identity it both obliterates and demands. The hegemonic representation of "Indian" as the forever mute, faceless, anachronistic, and illusionistic effect of colonialism crumbled as the masked indigenous fighters took over town after town. Now, suddenly, those in power thought of the mask as powerful. Not the indigenous collective masking, of course, but the default singular, individual one of the liberal subject. Who is Marcos, the government insisted? Surely his magnetism resided in his mask. When they unmasked him in 1995, their exposé failed to invalidate or weaken him.[23] Marcos, whose first nom de guerre was Zacarias, and then, post-Marcos, Galeano, was so much more than an individual. Marcos, as I write in the "Death of the Political 'I,'" was always in quotations, always a reperformance: "Marcos," like the mask, was a "persona to be acted,"[24] or as he put it a "colorful ruse," a "'hologram' born of the uprising that reflected the aspirations of those who longed to challenge the regimes of domination."[25] It was never about him as an individual. Yet even after the uprising, the press could not see or hear indigenous peoples. The mestizo in the mask became the voice and the face of the Zapatistas. Yet the mask, like the voice, is collective. The masks enact the political WE—never singular or individual. Marcos signed many of their communiqués with a collective gesture: "From the mountains of the Mexican southeast, the Indigenous Clandestine Revolutionary Committee," followed by "Planet Earth." WE are truly in this together. The mask performs both group cohesion and identity and outward anonymity. The masks enact their refusal to make their individual identities, names, faces available to us, non-Zapatistas. For decades, their animatives have withstood the government's demand that they reveal themselves.

Masks hover between the animate, the inanimate, the animative. At times, they channel the life-affirming forces and symbolic presences that are always there. As with other indigenous groups in the Americas, masking for the Zapatistas does not mean deception or disguise but rather the continual motion of becoming, of transformation and self-transformation. Masks, as James Maffie argues, for the Cherokee, the Iroquois (Seneca), the Hopi, and other peoples "disclose and present a spirit, and are better thought of as guises than disguises."[26] The ancient Mesoamerican practice of wearing animal masks and skins in battle draws on the conviction that they have shape-shifting power—the wearers draw from their and this other source of strength.

Mexico has a very strong tradition of masks stemming from before and after the invasion by the Spaniards. Mesoamerican and postconquest dances, rituals, and other performances are full of masked characters that continue into the present. Ancient ones, often made of stone or jade, are funerary masks. Many of the more recent masks appear in fiestas and dance dramas representing types—the Spaniard with the pink face, the Malinche face with the long hair, the old men with missing teeth who walk and dance precariously, the devil masks, life and death masks, and animal masks. They make visible the many forces that always accompany Mexican history—colonialism, the sense of betrayal, resistance, humor, seduction, death, and animism—always available for reanimation and mobilization. Masks signify presence as continuous transformation and surrogation. We can multiply with and as others by donning a mask. But for masks to work best, it's usually important that no one see us put them on. Actors in many performance traditions turn their backs to the public for the second of transformation. The new form that appears was not there a minute ago, as with the Zapatistas. In the blink of an eye, they were there, ¡Presentes!

At times, of course, masks hide the presence of the killers among us, especially now in Mexico when so many armed groups are masked. Masks can protect the individual identities of the killer-WE, the narcos, the *federales* or federal agents, the paramilitary, and even common delinquents. For them, clearly, the anonymity enables them to safely perform the acts of violence that might otherwise land them in trouble.

The masked Zapatistas, then, are a highly codified political body, always 'virtual,' a "'hologram' [as Marcos put it] born of the uprising that reflected the aspirations of those who longed to challenge the regimes of domination." Embodiment, as Anne Balsamo notes, is the "effect" of that aspiration, "produced by the processes through which bodies are imagined and constituted."[27] Produced as one kind of absence, the Zapatistas produce themselves as another kind of presence.

The way that the Zapatistas have used silence is also dramatic, played back against the colonial silencing. "Speaking and listening is how true men and women learn to walk," they say, but few have ever spoken or listened to them.[28] What happens when we deprive communities of the ability to speak and listen? Jacques Attali argues that noise (sound, clamor, music) "is the source of purpose and power."[29] Those in authority seek to deny indigenous people's presence, subjectivity, power. Epistemicide, the erasure of ways of knowing, to return to Santos's term, follows inevitably on conquest and domination. Much has to be silenced in order for the political colonial project to succeed. They come into presence as absent, silent, unknowable.

As the Zapatistas coalesced as a group, they choose strategically when and how to be silent. Theirs is a noisy silence that calls attention to itself. They now control the noise, and they impose conditions on those who want to speak to them. María Josefina Saldaña-Portillo writes of the Zapatistas' politics of silence by recounting her visit to Oventic in 1996 for the First International Meeting for Humanity and against Neoliberalism. She recalls Comandante David saying, "Hasta que guarden silencio, no podemos comenzar" (We can't start until you're all silent). She didn't know what silence meant, she writes, as she sat in the group of five thousand international attendees all struggling to remain quiet. Here too, the Zapatistas perform their pedagogy. Those who come to speak with them must first "experience the difficulty of attaining and maintaining silence for even a representative ten minutes. Metonymically, our ten minutes together stood in for the 'silent' ten years of Zapatista organizing: however, they also represented another kind of silence, the five hundred years of silence imposed on indigenous peoples of the Americas."[30] Yet the Zapatistas have also used the imposed silence, like the imposed anonymity, as a source of strength. As the visitors sat silently, the entire cohort of Zapatistas took their seats in the bleachers surrounding them with no one hearing them. "I was stunned," Saldaña-Portillo writes, "because even though we were sitting there being so quiet, perhaps because of the 'quiet'—the Zapatistas had been on the move and quieter still."[31]

But here, too, the Zapatistas performed their insight, accrued during centuries of struggle, for the stunned visitors. You still cannot see or hear us. We can all talk and agree about imposed anonymity, but even a physical encounter of like-minded people such as this one will reenact the centuries-old nonrecognition of indigenous peoples. The Zapatistas took their seats without anyone seeing or hearing them. That was their point. Our own inability to see or hear reflected back on us. Here. Now. Again. Seemingly always.

Throughout the decades, the Zapatistas have called on the exploited and persecuted, those inside the Olympic stadium and those outside (to go back to the protesters of enacted refusal), to become a political WE, to mutually recognize, accompany, and listen to each other. "We can continue the right path if we, the you who are us, walk together."[32] Throughout, the Zapatistas have insisted that we do not have to be Zapatistas or live like them in order to join the struggle. In fact, they don't want us to: "Fight with your weapons; don't worry about ours. We know how to resist to the end. We know how to wait."[33]

Waiting, I felt as we stood at the entrance to Oventic, is a powerful weapon. And the Zapatistas know how to wield it. In October 1996, the tensions still high after the San Andrés Treaty process, "President Ernesto Zedillo visited three military bases in Chiapas," his presence performing a threat.[34] The ailing Comandanta Ramona broke the "encirclement" imposed by government forces on the Zapatistas and went to Mexico City, along with civilian Zapatista men, women, and children, to help found the National Indigenous Congress.[35] A reporter described it this way: "Today the Zapatistas deploy a bomb that no one was expecting. . . . The bomb of patience. The bomb of overpowering tenderness."[36] This enacted a different kind of presence, the presence of those who choose when and how to become visible to the rest of us. Gradually, quietly, as the Zapatista civilians headed out, the larger group was seeking political and cultural solutions in the struggle against the bad government.

Waiting punctuated by action, the durational camino largo marked by the rapid burst of emails, communiqués, speeches, the Zapatista movement speeds it up and slows it down. Zigzagging, they try to keep danger in check. They constantly attempt to communicate, but in their own time and at their own pace, through the person-to-person digital technologies, music, and print culture. They challenge us to rethink the modalities, tempos, and temporalities of protest—the long road, the wait, mobilization, patience, silence, and "protest at the speed of dreams."[37]

In 2003, the Zapatistas formed an alternative good democratic government and autonomous administrative centers, the caracoles, now clearly emphasizing the civic over the armed nature to their struggle. During the 2006 election cycle, Marcos initiated La Otra Campaña (the other campaign), which was in fact a campaign of those others who the Zapatistas claim would never be represented by the national government. He ran as Delegate Zero, infuriating some on the left who were actively supporting Andrés Manual López Obrador against Felipe Calderón, the right-wing candidate who won what many see as a rigged election and unleashed the disastrous war against the narco that ushered in the new era of uncontrollable violence in Mexico.[38]

During moments of threat, the Zapatistas have closed off the caracoles to the world. Other times, they have opened them again to national and international supporters. The escuelitas are an extraordinary initiative to invite those of good will to learn the ways of the autonomous communities. Every participant lives with a family and has a companion to accompany her or him in the process of learning, unlearning, relearning. If a participant comes with a child, an indigenous child is also assigned to accompany them.

For all their efforts to survive, the Zapatistas' vulnerability is undeniable—not only as predominantly Indigenous peoples, but as people living in active opposition to Mexico's repressive neoliberal government. Vulnerability, here, is not a condition or state of being, but rather a doing and a relationship of power. The Zapatistas' vulnerability has been structurally imposed and economically organized from colonial times until the present. As Jean Franco makes clear in *Cruel Modernity*, Latin American countries have tried to eliminate their indigenous populations in order to be modern: "The urgency of modernization transposed racism into a different key and turned the indigenous from an exploited labor force into a negative and undesirable mass."[39] NAFTA was simply the last straw. But they adapt, the Zapatistas say, "para no dejar de ser" (so that they don't cease to be) historical beings.[40] The bottom line, using John Holloway's terminology, is that their power to live, work, and flourish has been under constant attack by the government's power over their lives, work, and well-being. How can resistance counter this making vulnerable?

And now we received the invitation to celebrate their party. What, as the Zapatista asked us, were we doing there?

Reflection One Being There (Decolonial Pedagogies)

Part of our being there, in the language of academe, had to do with practice-based research. There are academic departments dedicated to this, each with their special characteristics and foci, but we at the Hemispheric Institute call it "creative inquiry and critical practice." This entails being present, in situ, with others and using embodied experience and practice as an entry point for learning and theorizing, and not just the other way around, as in applying our theories to practices that we see or experience. The underlying concept: knowledge is not a thing, not a one-way act of communication or transfer, but an active doing we undertake with many different kinds of others. Education, as Paulo Freire argued in *Pedagogy of the Oppressed*, is "a practice of freedom."[41] Like Rivera Cusicanqui, I hold that "there can be no discourse of decolonization, no theory of decolonization, without a decolonizing practice."[42] The way we do this is the way we do everything.

First, we had to leave the classroom. Our institutions of higher learning have tended to reproduce colonialist systems of domination since the sixteenth century, denying entry to the descendants of indigenous and African laborers who built them in the first place.[43] I, like Silvia Rivera Cusicanqui, keenly experience the obligation "of the intellectuals in the domination of empire—because I believe that it is our collective responsibility not to contribute to the reproduction of this domination."[44] For us, this means learning from others, seeing/theorizing from other locations, environments, and contexts in order to establish contact between people who do not have access to our universities. In order to enter these conversations, we need to accept the conditions our interlocutors ask of us. We can assume nothing.

Jesusa Rodríguez and I admit thirty-five to forty graduate students from throughout the Americas. We choose participants from diverse backgrounds who have a broad range of interests and skills—people specializing in native studies, human rights, migration, alter-globalization, environmental justice, gender and sexuality, critical race theory, performance studies, and anthropology, but also journalists, performers, filmmakers, and photographers. Because not everyone speaks English or Spanish or Portuguese in the group, we have no shared language, theoretical discourse, skills, life experience, or default assumptions to fall back on. This in itself proves extremely productive. It forces us to challenge the colonialist imperative that others speak our language and the fantasy that we understand each other.[45] We need to actually grapple with this age-old problem in order to work together. We try to articulate what we do and why we do it to people who cannot fathom what, until then, might have seemed obvious to us. Again, assume nothing. They wait patiently as we try to make ourselves understood, just as we try to be patient as we grasp what moves them. This process slows us down and forces us be attentive. We need to find ways to make common ground.

No one in our group comes from Chiapas, except a few invited local artists and scholars. We are all outside our comfort zone. We read a significant amount of scholarly literature (in our various languages) to know why Chiapas, why colonialism and de- or anticolonialism, why the Zapatistas (necessary information that I have abbreviated drastically here), why resistance. Our pedagogic starting point is simple. We have to see and do to be able to know, but (as our percepticide performance made evident) we also need to know to be able to see and do. We hope that our presence and interactions might allow us to sense at least our role in colonialist scenarios, the problems these scenarios pose not just for others but for ourselves, and challenge our accepted ways of seeing, acting, and theorizing. Perceptual shifts occur when we alter our environment; when one (or five thousand) sits absolutely silently in the dark for ten minutes, our bodies readjust. Entering through the unknown, rather than through the known, requires an act of imagination, a willingness to accept unaccustomed bodily states, to let go of some certainties, some skills, a reassuring sense of self and the self's place in the world and yes, at times, creature comforts. Everyone in the course, simply by being there, had expressed willingness to jump over the fence to accompany the Zapatistas, who had jumped over a much higher and more hostile fence a long time ago and continue to do so every day.

Clearly, the balance between scholarly training/discipline and the more experiential realm of practice is complex and murky—we often act from a position of prior knowledge, and write about what we know, not necessarily what we experience. Our colonial archives are full of materials and sources based on evidence that no one ever experienced or saw.[46] Our post-, anti-, and decolonial theorizations often fail to engage directly with those who fight colonialism and discrimination every day, on the ground. At the same time, we understood that we too were (and are, always) masked, hiding our preconceptions and sensibilities behind a visible willingness to transcend them. The challenges abound, but not engaging, Jesusa Rodríguez and I agreed, was not an option. One goal might be to transform the mask of objective observer by engaging in a self-transforming process of participation. Our education (and our lives) depends on us developing the capacity to act and engage collaboratively, critically, and politically.

We break up into groups and distribute expertise—every group will have someone who speaks at least Spanish or English, who knows how to interview, write scholarly essays, and use digital technologies, cameras, and video. Collaboration, trustworthiness, accountability, and respect become essential, especially in the areas we will be going to. We will also have to rely on each other to reach our explicit goal—become knowledgeable about what is happening in that part of the world and transmit that knowledge (sometimes individually, sometimes collectively) into action, using our own preferred methods of communication. To do that, we need to become a WE. In a place like Chiapas, so dislocating for so many of us in so many ways, participants tend to form strong affective ties because we need each other to communicate, to accomplish our goals, to enjoy ourselves, and even, at times, to survive.

Jesusa Rodríguez starts us off with the pedagogy of stones:

> The exercise consists of asking each person to select a stone and bring it to the group. I do not specify either the size or shape; I ask for nothing more than a stone.
>
> Once the participants have gathered in a circle, I ask them to display their stones so that everyone can see them.
>
> The goal of this exercise is to stack one stone on top of another, attempting to reach the greatest height possible—one stone on top of another, and another, and another; that is all.
>
> We all work in silence.
>
> Each participant must place his or her stone on the pile at the right time, always respecting the premise of reaching the greatest possible height without knocking down what has already been built.
>
> I tell them the fate of the world depends on us building the pile.[47]

I have participated in Rodríguez's exercise many times, and have sometimes done the exercise with my own students. Both of us remark on how much you can tell about each participant by the manner in which they approach and carry out the task. The exercise allows us to evaluate if the group will be able to become a collectivity capable of accomplishing its goal. Rodríguez notes that "during the process each participant behaves in a non-premeditated manner and we'll discover that, in the end, we all approach this simple exercise the same way as we approach everything in life."[48] The way we do this is the way we do everything.

Did the person remember to bring the stone to the group? If so, what kind? Is it even a stone? Some people grab bits of concrete off the street at the last moment. How much care or thought did they put into selecting it and, later, placing it? Were they patient? Attentive to others? Showing off? The behaviors during the exercise also prove revealing. During the exercise, some people pace back and forth, trying to master all perspectives. Some want to help their classmates and bring extra stones in case someone forgot. Others

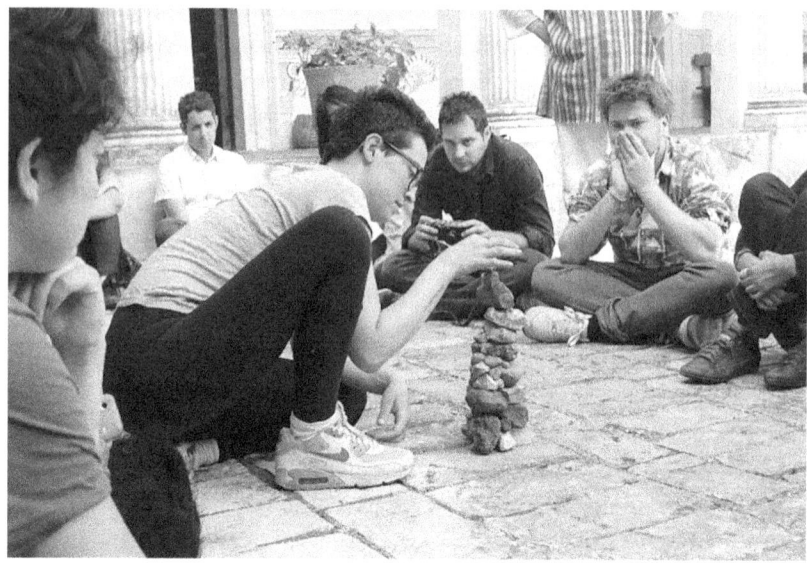

3.5 The pedagogy of stones. Olivia Gagnon balances a stone, Chiapas, 2015. PHOTO: DIANA TAYLOR.

scrutinize the process, trying to control the outcome. Did someone place a stone in such a way as to make it harder or easier for the person who comes next? Some participants rush to place their stone first while others hesitate, standing up to place their stone four and five times before actually doing it. If someone knocks some stones down by mistake, they have to build the tower back up again.

As people balance their stones, the rest of the group holds its breath, as if the fate of the world really did depend on it (fig. 3.5).

When all the stones have been placed, Rodríguez—also true to form as a theatre director—walks around the structure and examines it. Is it sturdy? Did the structure bifurcate into two or more connected columns? She makes some general remarks about what the structure says about us, as a group. If a stone does not actively fulfill its purpose (helping to reach the greatest possible height), she kicks it out of the way. No one gets away with leaning a stone against the structure or placing it in close proximity. No symbolic contributions. No free rides in a collaborative project. The chastened participant now has to balance the stone on top of the structure that, at this new height, poses a far greater challenge.

After the tower has been declared completed, we all discuss the experience. Then we proudly celebrate and protect it from mishaps for the duration of our time together.

Once while balancing my stone, I accidentally knocked down some in the pile. Rodríguez, as usual, asked me put them back up. As I sat, focused, she pointed out later during her remarks, I behaved true to form. While I held one stone very gingerly over the pile with my right hand trying to find the best way to balance it, I held all the other fallen stones close by in my left hand. As I do one thing, she noted, I always have everything else stacked up near me waiting its turn. Like landing planes at Kennedy airport. The way we do this, she reminds us, is the way we do everything.

Once, when I was leading the exercise in a major Ivy League university, the students placed four large stones on the floor and started to build on top of them. When I pointed out later that the charge had been to build the pile as high as possible, they justified their choice not to follow instructions (stone on top of stone) by saying that they needed a solid foundation. Another time, at a university in the southwest with a large Native and Latinx student population, I was stunned when one of the few white students in the class went up and purposefully took down the stones her classmates had so carefully placed and rebuilt the entire pile by herself. It didn't work. At the end she gave up, and the exercise remained unfinished. We discussed what happened. Everyone left unhappy. As Rodríguez says, how people act during the exercise is not premeditated, but it helps us see how much risk we are willing to assume, to what degree we are capable of patience and collaboration, how we facilitate or complicate the work of others, and what kinds of worlds we might be capable of building together.

The exercise of the stones, then, offers us a place to work from. The lessons learned there last throughout the course, including the theoretical discussions. How do we speak and listen to each other? Where do our comments go in the conversation? Where and when do we place them? Have they been chosen with care? Can others offer their perspectives or do individuals pretend to have mastered them all? Do our words help us achieve our collective goal? Theory is never enough. A syllabus is not enough. Practice-based research needs to be grounded in, and theorized from, practice.

The Zapatistas are of course the experts on practice-based research and knowledge learned from centuries of struggle, though they have different words to describe it. The "speaking and listening" for them "is how true men and women learn to walk." They were willing to engage with us as members of the civil society they call on to support them and their work. By "engage with us," however, I refer to the very uneven relationship I have developed with members of the Zapatista community (particularly in Oventic) over the past fifteen or so years. "Uneven" further signals their strategy of inversion—when did white nonindigenous people ever treat them as equals? Now they manage the contact. The relationship, if I can even call it that, is not personal—I know very little about them and they about me. Rather, it's between two WES—they speak from their grounding in Zapatismo, and I from my grounding in Mexico, the U.S., Canada, and academia. We both mediate between WES. I have gone to that particular caracol many times, very often with my colleagues or graduate students, and have spoken with various leaders and members of the community. Usually, they have been very reticent to talk to us except in the most formal way, structured as a meeting with the JBG where the five or so masked leaders take our questions. Nothing personal. Totally bureaucratic. You all made the rules of contact and exchange, they seem to say, now live by them.

Over the years, due to an introduction made by my colleague Julieta Paredes, an Aymara queer feminist indigenous political and cultural activist from Bolivia, I have become friendly with a few Zapatistas. We meet for coffee. Unmasked when they leave their caracoles, we can talk and walk in a less obtrusive fashion. They have helped me connect with the Zapatista communities but always anonymously and indirectly. "Go here at such and such an hour," one might tell me. "Something interesting will happen."

So here we were, waiting under the tarp outside the Che Guevara gift shop and snack bar that bridges the caracol and the highway. Families of indigenous people steadily came in and moved past us toward the party. All the adults were masked. While some people wore Western-type clothing— pants and sweatshirts—many of the Mayans were dressed in the native clothing from their various villages. The women from Chamula wore their thick black lambskin skirts and lovely embroidered tops under thin acrylic sweaters in all colors against the cold and rain. Those from Zinacantán wore the beautiful blue and purple tops with large embroidered flowers characteristic of their village, and there were many other patterns from other regions I could not identify.[49] To this day, the embroidery communicates meaning to other indigenous peoples capable of deciphering them, "hidden transcripts" as James C. Scott calls them, but in textiles.[50] Cloth transmits a history. Bodily practices and the aesthetics of the everyday, for the Zapatistas, are never removed from politics. The sartorial style, especially the *pasamontañas* (ski mask) and/or the *paleacate* (the red bandana) they wear, defines all of them as Zapatistas.

People moved through the gate beside us and proceeded briskly to buy food or soft drinks as they headed down to the large congregation area. No alcohol is allowed in any Zapatista community, as decreed by the Women's Revolutionary Law of 1993.

Our group seemed content to wait, odd for people in their twenties and thirties who had enough social mobility to be in Chiapas—odder still, given that we could not distract ourselves with any of our traditional pastimes, such as taking photographs or looking at our smartphones. The JBG prohibits visitors from taking photographs without permission, and Oventic (like the other caracoles) does not have internet access. The communiqués emanate from elsewhere. So there was nothing to do but wait. We simply waited.

Reflection Two Waiting

One reflection that came to me as we waited there was the degree to which what I see and do and feel is already the product of the social systems of which I am a part. In that sense, I seldom experience what is there in any unmediated way. Presente at that moment felt very distanced and removed from me and my experience. Part may have been the curious looks that people gave us upon entering the caracol—we were odd specimens indeed. Certainly not part of their WE. Wikipedia says the present "(or here and now) is the time that is associated with the events perceived directly and in the first time, not as a recollection (perceived more than once) or a speculation (predicted, hypothesis, uncertain)."[51] I was aware that I was not perceiving the event directly and felt, rather, full of speculation. I was being there, being with, and yet not, all at the same time. As I looked at the masked faces, I felt the weight of an invisible backpack strapped to my shoulders, bogging me down with European and Euro-American writings on and about the face—Levinas, Artaud, Deleuze and Guattari, Butler, Taussig, to name a few. Did their ideas illuminate what I was experiencing, here in the midst of hundreds of masked people going about the ordinary rituals of a communal celebration—announcing themselves as part of the community, easily identifying each other, and yet remaining anonymous to us, the outsiders? Words and phrases ring in my mind:

"The human face is an empty force, a field of death," little more than the "old revolutionary demand for form that has never corresponded to its body."[52]

"Faces are not basically individual, they define zones."[53]

Nothing clicked. I was overwhelmed by the thousands of eyes looking out of the masks, both from the Zapatistas and from the murals that cover almost all the communal structures. The eyes took us in, while withholding recognition. Who, or maybe what were we now, denied mutuality? We were present, wanting to be ¡presente!, but also always (from) elsewhere and asking for (partial) access. The idea of ¡presente! versus the reality of being present; wet, uncomfortable, wondering what would come next.

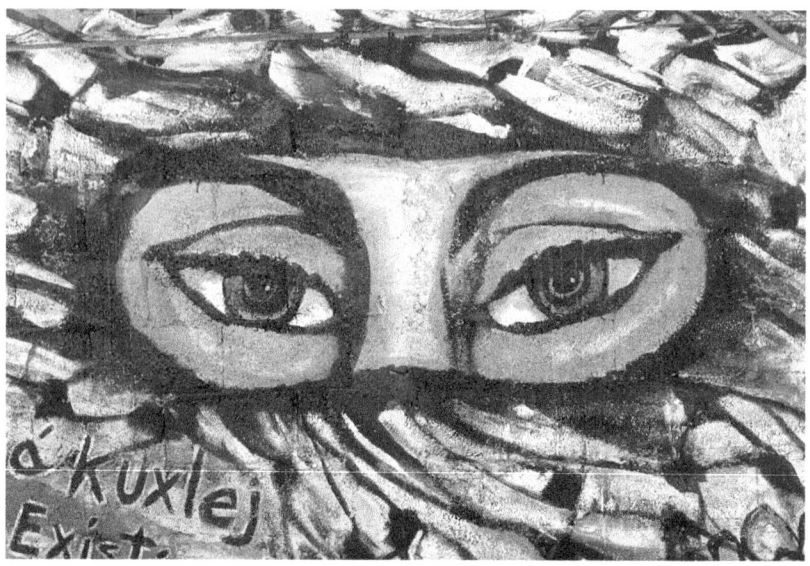

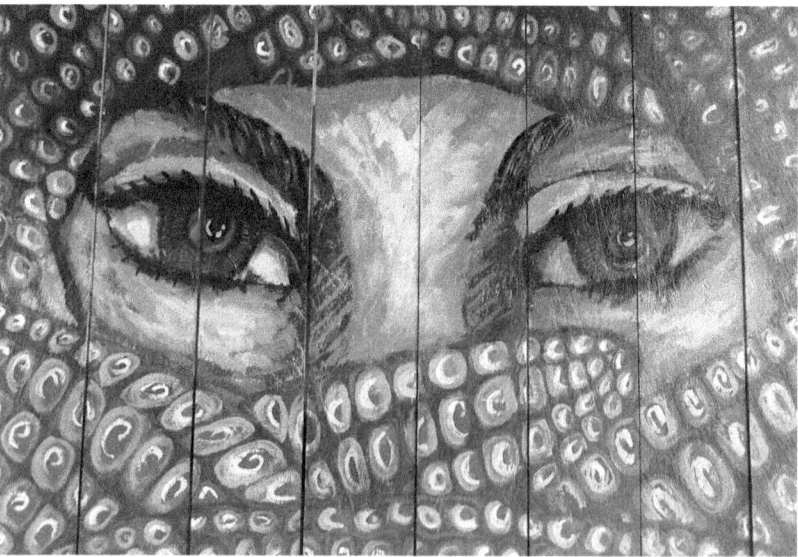

3.6–3.7. Murals in Oventic, 2013. PHOTOS: LORIE NOVAK.

This was not the first time the Zapatistas had kept our group waiting. Two days earlier we had visited Oventic during the daytime. We had asked for permission two months in advance, accompanied by Xeroxes of everyone's passports. When we arrived, two men and a woman received us at the gate. Each was wearing a ski mask on the hot August morning. "Who is in charge?" one of them asked. Taken aback, I remembered that Zapatistas regulate their interactions between proper authorities, those permitted to speak on behalf of their WE. Awkwardly, I asked for everyone's passport, photocopies, and the list with everyone's name and country of origin. I handed everything over. This was, after all, a port of entry. The woman began painstakingly writing down every name on the list, inquiring about country of origin, and about our interest in the community. "Why copy everything down when they have the list?" someone from our group asked. "Mayan technology," I thought, conjuring up Ricardo Domínguez's words.[54] Every country controls its data as well as its entrances and exits, whether it's launching the Zapatista Air Force (paper airplanes with notes flown at government soldiers) or processing intelligence through one's body.[55] The administration of information here moved through the body of this very small woman. Her inquiries were hard for me to understand, and she would repeat them patiently. Spanish was not her first language. She probably spoke Tsotzil or Tzeltal or Ch'ol or Tojolabal. What did I know? Writing, too, required concentrated bodily effort, judging from her focus in forming the words. Every so often, one of the men would run the new sheets down the hill.

We sat on the rocks or hard ground, stood, walked about, bought water from the Che Guevara snack bar, talked, and basked in the sun. We watched people go down the road on foot or in trucks, buses, on burros. From the gate, we could see the extraordinary murals painted on the schoolhouse opposite the highway from the caracol (see fig. 3.1). The girl's face is masked by an open book, scholarship as activism. The spine reads: "Autonomous education constructs different worlds where many worlds fit, true worlds with truths." Her eyes look straight at us, neither pleading nor accusatory but directly, *tú a tú* (one to one). Her hair holds Zapatista symbols such as the snail, a heart on wings, a person on a small boat, stars. We looked at the small wooden and cement buildings that line both sides of the straight long road on the steep hillside. On the left of the gate, blocked from the road by a table, a few Zapatistas standing guard, the colorful snack bar. On the right, past a small brick fortification, a blue wooden building with Diego River-

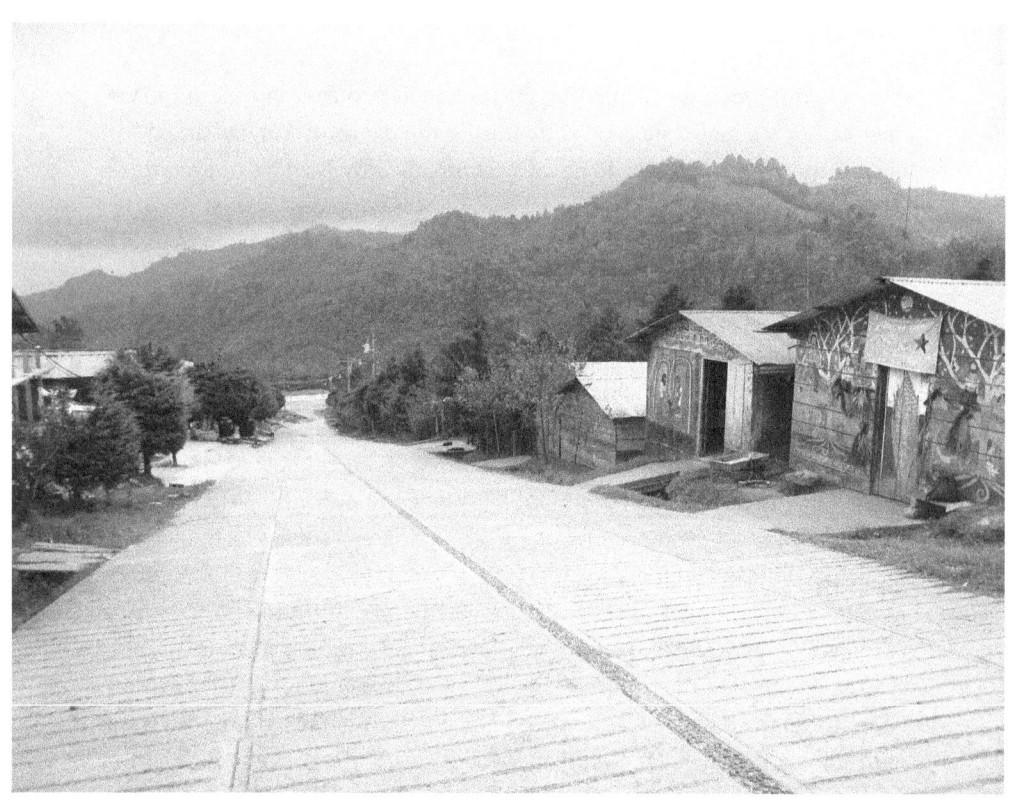

3.8 Photo of Main Street in Oventic, 2013. PHOTO: LORIE NOVAK.

aesque murals of the Mexican Revolution painted on it contained artisanal items for sale, produced by a woman's cooperative.[56] Next door, a plain concrete building housed the Oficina de Mujeres por la Dignidad (Office of women for dignity). The low heavy clouds gathering in the valley made it hard to see farther down the steep incline.

After two and a half hours, we were invited to enter. No one complained. We were there to try to understand resistance, and the Zapatistas knew all about durational performance. They have been waiting for a very long time. Patience is their bomb, as the journalist put it. Because they act collectively, not just individually, they have outlasted their individual tormentors. Presidents and state governors come and go, and the Zapatistas are still there. The authorities might fantasize about outlasting the Zapatistas, but "in spite of the hunger, the illnesses, and the exhaustion . . . every morning they discovered that the Zapatistas were still protesting."[57] While the presupposition is that resistance entails action, as importantly, we were learning, it entails patience, quietude. There is stillness in presence. For all the aspirational action-packed potential of ¡Presente!, it's actually about all its other meanings as well, accompaniment, honoring one's companions and surroundings, resistance, stubbornness, endurance, and seemingly endless labor. We, who came racing from the realm of instantaneous time and open access that characterizes globalization, stopped: we do not always control the time, space, and conditions of our actions. If we wait long enough, we might learn. Another lesson from the Zapatistas.

Stop

Pause

Reflect

It's hard to unlearn.

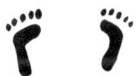

3.9 Alexei Taylor, *Footprints Standing*, 2019.

Now, on that rainy night two days later, the wait seemed longer. I began to wonder if we would be refused entrance to the party. I started feeling the heaviness of my administrative charge as group leader (faculty of record, in the language of the academy). What if they didn't let us in? What would we do? Where was my Plan B, my bag of tricks, my handful of stones at the ready? Every caracol has a "do not admit" list, but we knew from our earlier visit that no one in our group was on it. We'd get in, I reassured myself—we just had to wait. As before, we understood the politics of waiting, and we experienced, yet again, the reversal in terms of control, access, and time. The Zapatistas have the authority. This is their land; we are the visitors. We awaited permission.

For a population as subjugated as the Mayas have been in Chiapas, this was a notable reversal. Fifty years ago, indigenous people (who made up 25 percent of the state's population), were not allowed to walk on the sidewalks of San Cristóbal or enter the banks. They were treated like animals. Worse even. Women and children can still be seen carrying heavy bundles of wood on their backs, to spare the burros. Young girls can be sold or bartered away. Even now, if a young girl or woman is raped, all is excused if the rapist marries her. The woman, of course, may not agree, but she is never consulted. All of this is officially tolerated in the name of tradition. Except by the Zapatistas. Comandanta Esther, the first indigenous woman to address the Mexican legislature in 2001, said, "We know which are the good uses of 'tradition' and which the bad."[58] They reject the patriarchal and racist underpinnings of some traditions. The Zapatistas mandated equality. Even standing at the entrance to the caracol, the comportment of Zapatista women entering the space made it clear that here women were treated as equals, although they continued to bear the enormous domestic burdens of their foremothers.

After thirty minutes or so, which seemed such a long time that evening, we were granted admission and started our way down the hill.

A young Zapatista woman wearing her traditional clothing, her mask, and plastic shoes led us quickly and silently down the hill in the dark rain. The music reverberated from the loudspeakers. All the buildings that lined the road were open to serve the visitors. Plastic tarps outfitted with faint lightbulbs dotted the long road down. Wet wooden benches tottered close to the long tables covered with baskets of food. She scampered down the hill, and we all got dispersed in the rain, rushing to keep up. It was so dark I could barely see to walk. I was looking at the ground, afraid of falling, trying to follow the woman through the very dark night of the Mayan highlands. The slippery rocks of the steep hillside seemed treacherous to me with a long history of falling. My illusions of being able to be with, and to be in place, of We-making, evaporated as I turned on the flashlight on my smartphone. That moment of feeling utterly vulnerable and ridiculous never fades when thinking about ¡presente! We can never be presentes in the same way.

At last (some ten minutes later?), our guide came to a stop at the schoolhouse in the far lower field of the caracol. You'll sleep here, she indicated. Someone had told her we were having a sleepover, an idea we had discussed with a Zapatista friend and discarded because of the weather. Had he told her? Is that what had taken so long, preparing a room for us? We thanked her, knowing that most of us would probably be heading back to San Cristóbal that same night.

We all walked slowly back toward the party. If my friend were at the party, I would not have recognized him, masked now in the caracol. I would have to wait for him to come up to us. Again, recognition could never be mutual here—I would always be legible as a *guera*, *gringa*, and non-Zapatista. Here he was invisible to me.

The heavy rains had washed out the road that just two days earlier had been so nicely packed with gravel. After the rains, the Zapatistas would start, once more, to fix it. Vendors were nursing fires to heat enormous aluminum pots of water and grills to cook corn on the cob, which they sold topped with mayonnaise, grated cheese, and chili. Some sold hot corn-based *atoles* and other nourishing drinks and stews. People crowded around small stands to buy tacos and tamales. Pyramids of soft drinks lined the outer perimeters of makeshift tables. Mexico ranks top in per capita consumption of sugary soft drinks in the world. Not surprisingly, diabetes is the leading cause of death.[59] The caracol, so empty two days before, now had thousands of people milling around in the dark and pouring rain. Children—the second or third generation born into Zapatismo—played in puddles, laughing and running around chasing each other among all the people waiting for the ceremony to start. Only a few people looked as if they could be the foreign visitors who had come to the escuelita.

Our feet soaked with water and mud, we made our way toward the main basketball court, the scene of the assembly. I looked down, worried about my shoes. Vicki Patishtan, a Chamulan friend and colleague of many years, was wearing her small black plastic sandals. "Aren't your feet getting soaked?" I asked her, peering down past her broad black lambskin skirt. "It doesn't matter." She smiled. "I wear these all the time." I understood, again for the first time, how different her sense of the rain was from mine. Rain was not a bother, just a natural part of life. Her feet had no problem getting wet. Her shoes would not even have to dry out—she could just wipe them with a cloth. This was simply part of her environment. Nothing to talk about. The rain muted the sound. Over the loudspeakers we could hear a soft male voice making announcements in the various indigenous languages. Some words, *bases de apoyo* (grassroots supporters) and *bueno*, kept cropping up in all languages. When it was time to speak in Spanish, I realized he was inviting us all to gather in the *cancha*—the basketball court. The official part of the celebration was about to begin.

The cancha was lined on one side with a covered platform and an enormous Mexican flag tacked to the wall. Beside it hung a much smaller black flag with EZLN in red letters around a central five-pointed red star. The flag of the Ejército Zapatista de Liberación Nacional, like its real-life counterpart, stood proudly and defiantly next to its mammoth neighbor. The wide expanse of space around the cancha was all water and mud as the rain continued to pour down. Everyone gathered quietly, expectantly. One of the first speakers to take the microphone joked, "We Zapatistas have to resist everything, even the weather." But no one was leaving. Families shifted together under large colored tarps to get a better view.

The official ceremony began when a long line of civic representatives from the various Zapatista communities walked briskly and silently down the hill and onto the platform—about thirty or forty men and women dressed in traditional indigenous dress. White and black sheepskin tunics for men, depending on their place or origin and status; they wore their straw hats with colorful ribbons hanging from them over their ski masks. On their feet, huaraches, the leather, open-toed sandals with rubber bottoms made from worn-out tires. Women wore the skirts and embroidered blouses of their region, and the black plastic sandals. Then several Zapatistas marched with the Mexican and EZLN flags around the courtyard and stood firmly in place. The opening ceremony emphasized the armed-struggle nature of the movement, though it had been nearly twenty years since the Zapatistas had taken up weapons. Yet the E of EZLN stands for *ejercito*, or army. The L and N defined it as a national liberation movement—not just indigenous. The EZLN wanted to provide an example of democratic process and good government for Mexico as a whole, but the E reminded us of the stakes. Those who refuse to recognize the power of the state need to be prepared to fight and even die. Following that, the national anthem came over the loudspeakers, and young Zapatistas raised their arms in military salute. They too are *mexicanos al grito de guerra* (Mexicans at the cry of war—Mexico's belligerent national anthem). The open ceremony was all about military gestures as someone ordered them to stand at attention, *firmes*. The military music was as loud and grating here as anywhere. But clearly, the battle wasn't with Mexico—every act repeated their love for their country. Their fight was against the national bad government and political parties that had once and again broken treaties and betrayed indigenous rights.

Reflection Three Good and Bad Governments

The entrance to the rebel territory marks the line between two interconnected political systems; both performative, both masked. The Zapatistas' political project, I saw for the first time, was not indigenous in form or content—it was the age-old struggle for good government. On one side was the bad, neoliberal government characterized by violence, corruption, and greed. The other was good in that it examined the basic mechanisms of existing power (not as a thing one has but a practice of social relations, i.e., power over) and asked: Who exerts it? Who decides? Who gets left out? They then transformed those practices and relationships into their core principles:

1   Participatory assemblies ("the people decide")
2   Nondiscrimination (Zapatismo is nonnormative. While long exploited as Indígenas, their strategy refuses identity politics—be it ethnic, racial,

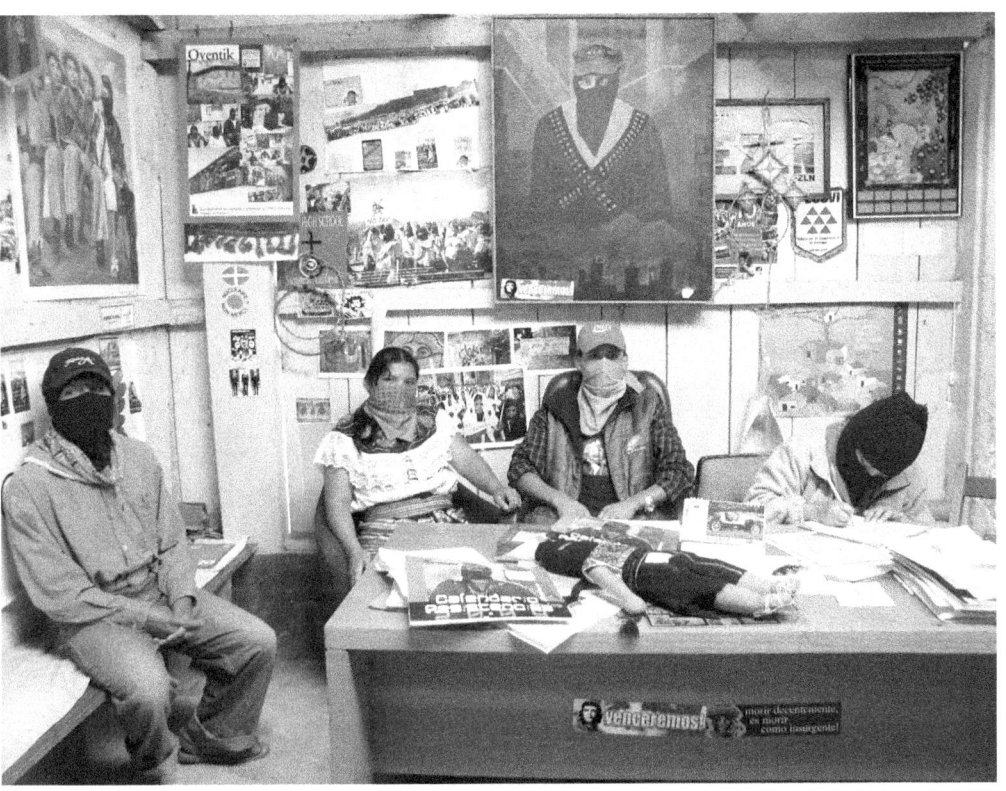

3.10 Junta del Buen Gobierno, Oventic, 2013. PHOTO: LORIE NOVAK.

religious, gender, sexual, class, linguistic.[60] This is not about being but, again, about doing, joining the struggle for indigenous rights.)

3 Collaboration ("Para Todos, Todo. Para Nosotros, Nada." Zapatismo acknowledges that individuals cannot do it alone; they exist as part of a collective: SOLOS NO PODEMOS.)

But both are governments. Both love the pomp and ceremony and rites of passage. Resistance here does not mean a rejection of government or a proposed outside to the political. If anything, as Marcos told the newly elected president Ernesto Zedillo in the mid-1990s, "We [the Zapatistas] are your other; your Siamese opposite. In order for us to disappear, you must disappear as well."[61] Zapatismo and armed resistance are the inevitable response to centuries of bad government. They refuse to cede the notion of government to the self-serving political parties. They will not be othered. They do not accept that they, as the government sees them, are the problem.

They acknowledge the historical/political causes of their marginalization while managing the effects and affects. They directly confront the violence of nonrecognition shown them for centuries. The enforced silencing gets enacted through their massive silent marches. In contrast to the stereotype of the immobile Indian, static in time and place, the Zapatistas are on the move, silently, tenaciously. Their imposed anonymity is performed through their powerful masks. They call attention to the mask as one more in a complex system of masking. Politicians disguise themselves and their deeds behind imperatives of the state.[62] When delegates from the Mexican government refused to negotiate with the Zapatistas unless they removed their masks, the Zapatistas answered, "But the state is always masked."[63] At least, the Zapatistas said, they knew they were masked.[64] Official recognition is based on a politics of faciality that produces, rather than represents, its interlocutors: Indians. This forcing into presence as faceless others annuls the possibility for human interaction. The face, Levinas insists, signals human vulnerability and makes moral demands on others.[65] The Mexican state, however, came into being ignoring the humanity and moral demands of the indigenous peoples. The Zapatistas are beyond demanding; they refuse to show their faces.

The animative and performatic force of these gestures resonates nationally and internationally—the only reason most of them are alive today. Having refused interpolation into the Mexican state, the Zapatistas have taken over the functions associated with state systems—health care, education, management of resources, the self-defense and control of its territory. To hell with the tactics of the weak! They claim the strategy, the *propre*, the proper, the space and time that belong to them, which, as de Certeau puts it, "serves as the basis for generating relations with an exterior distinct from it."[66] They command and utter the performatives, and control the convention within which they function happily. They decide who enters their territory, when, and under what circumstances. Having handed over our papers and been granted permission to proceed, we entered into their time zone.

Reflection Four Ethos

While the struggle to form a good government is not indigenous, the value system through which that struggle generates strength most certainly is. One fundamental part of the Mayan (and Mesoamerican more broadly) worldview rests on the constant anticipation of extinction. As opposed to Brian Massumi's ontopower that compellingly maps out the military logic of preemption—act now to ward off future hostile action—that he claims defines Western ontologies, ancient Mesoamericans subscribed to the cosmology that located them in the fifth sun, the four previous ones having been destroyed. Thus, they live with the memory of past annihilation and the anticipation that the fifth, like previous suns, will come to an unhappy end. The struggle for survival will never be over. As Comandanta Ramona put it, "For all intents and purposes, we were already dead," but now with colonialist and neocolonialist violence overlaid on a cosmological order. Instead of a preemptive vision, this might be called a reactive version of necropolitics now waged by the victims themselves, an ethnic group condemned to death and fighting on from the grave.[67] What to do when there is nothing to be done, and doing nothing is not an option? Keep death in check. Zigzag. Fight to the death, from the place of death, for justice, dignity, and a life worth living.

Additionally, the Zapatistas inhabit the age-old Mesoamerican system of equivalences, deep-rooted connectivity, and mutual recognition. Nature, humans and animals, and the universe are united by a cosmic lifeblood that pumps energies throughout the entire system. Movement (Y-olli), heart (Y-ollo-tl), and life (Yoliliztli) were all aspects of each other for the Aztecs.[68] For the Maya, as Juan López Intzín (Xuno López) tells us, O'tan (heart) "also becomes the space and center of incorporation of everyday experiences for people, the source and matrix of sabers and culturally situated knowledge."[69] Every aspect of existence—from biological organ, to consciousness, to cosmic movement, to life itself—deeply interconnects with the others.

The animated system eludes Deleuze and Guattari's compartmentalization of systems based on the botanical distinction between the arborescent (the tree with its roots and leaves) and the rhizomatic (that has no roots but works through networks).[70] The former is ancestral and slow, the later adaptive, flexible, and networked. For the Zapatistas, the slow, the ancestral, sustains the adaptive, flexible, and fast. The Zapatista rebellion, founded on ancient beliefs, is called the "first postmodern revolution."[71]

Humans, corn, snails, mountains, rain, and so on each have their ch'ulel, the animation and interconnectedness of all things, human and nonhuman. A Zapatista colleague of mine, inspired by Juan López Intzín, explains that "ch'ulel refers to the life in everything. It's the presence that constructs and completes everything that exists in the universe and that gives it its importance." Maffie adds that ch'ulel also signals "vitality" and has a dimension of the sacred.[72] "Ich'el ta muk" recognizes the greatness of the other, its dignity and grandeur. Mesoamericans started developing corn ten thousand years ago and they are, in turn, the people of corn. Monsanto (as I explore in chapter 9) will grow genetically modified corn, but it will kill corn's ch'ulel. Such corn will become one more dead thing in the capitalist production of dead things. Ya Basta! Enough! The challenge is "how to create a world based on mutual recognition of human dignity, on the formation of social relations which are not power relations," writes Holloway, an important interlocutor for the Zapatistas.[73]

There is no word for "I" in Mesoamerican languages. A Zapatista colleague told me, "The 'I' is a collective 'I.' But when we talk about the collective 'I,' we put interaction as a condition. All the elements of an interaction are the singularities, the personalities."[74] They affirm the concept of an inclusive WE, a NOSOTROS that dialogues with other NOSOTROS, other groups of peoples able to represent themselves. In our meaning-making systems we

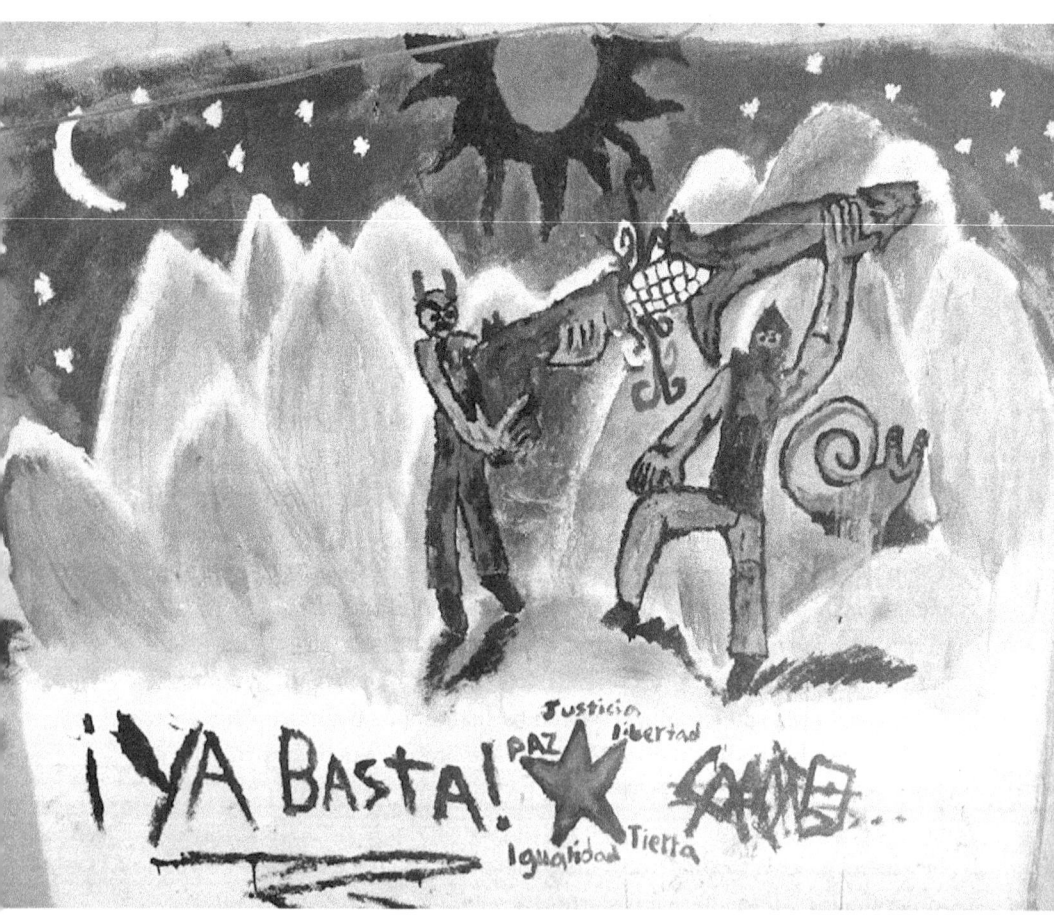

3.11 ¡Ya Basta!, 2013. PHOTO: DIANA TAYLOR.

might imagine this as one group of occupiers from, say, Occupy Wall Street in New York discussing with other Occupy groups—other WES that have been collectively and autonomously organized.

The caracol, as a social formation, enacts the system of equivalences. The snail, for the Maya, was the glyph for zero. It symbolized birth, re-birth, and fertility, as well as confinement (coming from the womb) and female sexual organs.[75] Snails move directly through the earth, epitomizing rearguard theory, the knowledge that "flies at low altitude . . . stuck to the body."[76] Zapatistas honor the slow and steady pace of the snail, the patience and expenditure required for all doing. Snails carry their homes with them; their paintings and sayings encapsulate an entire worldview. The snail shell serves as the design layout for their communal lands that spiral open from the tight administrative centers. The snail both encloses and exposes—it's a both a door and a window that enable and regulate contact with the outside world.[77]

The Zapatistas retell the oral history:

> They say here that the most ancient say that the even more ancient said that the first people on these lands appreciated the snail. They say that they said that the snail represents the entering into the heart . . . and they say that they said that it also represents a coming out of the heart to walk in the world. Not only that, they say that they said that the snail named the collective, so that the word could go from one to another giving birth to accord. They also say that they said that the snail helped the ear to hear the most distant word. That's what they say they said. I don't know. I walk holding your hand and I show you what my ear sees and what my eyes hear.[78]

Images of snails, often wearing humorous Zapatista masks, make their way into most of the murals, paintings, and textiles, just as they dominate Mesoamerican iconography (fig. 3.12). The snail, some argue, is the "proto-type of the stepped fret," a "peculiar" spiral form that "unites symmetry with asymmetry."[79]

The unassuming snail represents war in the classical Maya glyphs, the war the Mayans have long waged against colonial and imperialist masters and, now, their bankers (Chase Manhattan made the elimination of the Zapatistas precondition for a bailout after the economic disaster precipi-tated by NAFTA in 1995).[80] Here then is rearguard theory in action. The slow, steady movement, the staying close to the ground, the tenacity and humility needed for the long walk.

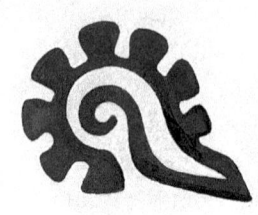

3.12 Snail. Image by Jesusa Rodríguez. COURTESY OF THE ARTIST.

Reflection Five WE

At that point in the celebration, an unnamed woman, identified only as a member of the Junta del Buen Gobierno, addressed the crowd in Spanish: "Compañeras, compañeros, hermanas y hermanos de la sociedad civil, nacional e internacional." Ever since the Zapatista uprising, as noted, gender parity has become central to the movement. This is reflected not only in all governing roles, official positions, and educational practices, but in the very language. No masculine ending word stands without its feminine counterpart, *hermanas y hermanos*. Increasingly, the gender-neutral *hermanxs* welcomes gender-nonconforming people into the fold. The compañera from the JBG spoke of the struggles the movement has endured over the years: "It hasn't been easy," she admitted, "these ten years of practice and building our autonomy. . . . It hasn't been easy for many reasons, such as the lack of experience or lack of training in governing and self-governing."[81] But the need for resistance continued, she made clear, confronted as they were by a government that continued to deny them rights and liberty and that wanted to take their lands. The Zapatistas, she said, persevere in learning how to resist and work for democracy, though the fruits of the struggle will not be visible in their lifetime. Again, a politics of life fought from a place of death for a future they will never see. The compañera asked people of good heart and good will that compose civil society to support their struggle.

Is she referring to us?

Who is being invoked and asked to support? What would supporting mean?

Most of the communications from the Zapatistas since 1994 have been addressed to "brothers and sisters" from Mexico and "people of the world." The struggle for peace, justice, democracy, and dignity, they remind us again and again, is not theirs alone. Those who aspire to the same values in civil society must resist the temptation and the "obvious comfort of doing nothing—that of sitting and waiting to observe, that of applauding or booing the actors."[82] "Brothers and sisters of other races and languages, of other colors, but with the same heart, now protect our light, and in it drink of the same fire."[83]

Supporting, then, does not mean donning a mask and going to live in the highlands of Chiapas. As Ricardo Dominguez puts it, "It wasn't 'everybody come to Chiapas, become armed and let us take over Mexico.' They were asking, 'what are the qualities of Neoliberalism in your space, how do you function in and contest that space, not by mimicking us, but by mimicking the *question*.'"[84]

Of course some Euro-Americans and mestizos have chosen to join the Zapatistas—the Sup is only the most obvious example. They live full time in Zapatista territory and follow community rules; this is the level of commitment required if one wants to be a Zapatista. There are many surrounding communities closely aligned with Zapatismo where people continue to drink alcohol or ignore other Zapatista rules. CIDESI: University of the Earth, the Zapatista-inspired university in San Cristóbal, offers political training to local youth as well as specialized programs in needed skills—sustainable agriculture, land rights, and so on. Furthermore, many Zapatista-aligned intellectuals, activists, and artists live all over the world. None of these are recognized as Zapatistas by the Zapatistas themselves, and they cannot speak in their name. Other allies go to the various communities and help out by painting murals, providing medical help, working in the educational or agricultural projects, and so on.

There is certainly work to be done, and the Zapatistas will accept help when and if it suits them. Friends of mine who have worked in the *comunidades* have felt hurt when the Zapatistas shut their doors to outsiders. They too need to wait if they choose to engage. Others accompany the Zapatistas politically, to make sure that the government does not exterminate them. They hear and honor the call: "Don't abandon us, brothers and sisters. . . . Don't leave us to ourselves. Don't let this have been in vain."[85] Others still contribute by taking up Zapatista initiatives and continuing the struggle for human and environmental rights in their own way. Their strategy, as Dominguez suggests, insists on the politics of the question: how does neoliberalism affect us and how can we fight against it? The Zapatistas eschew the politics of the answer; they will not lead, as they told us, except perhaps by example: "We do not want and cannot take the place that some want us to take, the place from where emanate all opinions, all routes, all answers, all truths; we will not do it."[86] Finding common cause means that all the WES act in their/our own way, from their/our own positions and terrains.

It's up to us. Many social justice movements have started as a result of the Zapatistas. Some of them are the hundreds of small political collectives, art groups, women's rights groups, and other initiatives that demand justice and a life with dignity that sprang up after 1994. We didn't know we had the right to demand rights before then, says one of the cofounders of Tzome Ixuk, an indigenous women's group in Las Margaritas, Chiapas.[87] Others had a global reach. The First International Meeting for Humanity and against Neoliberalism was followed by a second in Prague. Some of these activists went on to found the World Social Forum to create a global movement. And on and on from there.

The Zapatistas, I understood in one more of the temporal inversions I experienced with them, are not the past—they're our future; their disenfranchisement is an impending condition for the majority of the people living in the world today; their resistance is our lesson and our hope. It's not just our indigenous colleagues fighting neoliberalism in Standing Rock in the Dakotas, or the Zapatistas in Chiapas. Everyone who belongs to the 99.9 percent is losing rights to water, land, education, health care, and a dignified livelihood. We all need to learn how to fight for a good government. I recognize that I am ill equipped, but I understand the urgency, and I'm running as best I can to keep up with them.

After the compañera finished addressing us in Spanish, another member of the JBG from another region took the microphone and delivered the same speech in Tzeltal. When he was done, another delivered it in Tsotsil. The speeches, incomprehensible to me, seemed interminable in the downpour. I strained to recognize words and grew impatient. This is so redundant, I caught myself thinking. I knew what they were saying because I'd heard it in Spanish. Why was I standing there? The relational bonds established by language, by the sounds now in Tzeltal, now in Tsotsil, melted into zones of indecipherability; hearing did not equal meaning. Being an audience, etymologically "within hearing," did not always respect the reciprocity conveyed by its definition, the "formal hearing or reception, opportunity of being heard."[88]

I looked down at my wet feet and ruined shoes in dismay.

Stop

Pause

Reflect

I have a lot to learn about solidarity and ich'el ta muk, about patience, slowness, stillness, and about rearguard theory. Another lesson in performance pedagogy.

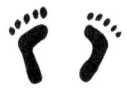

3.13 Alexei Taylor, *Standing*, 2019.

Soon the speeches were over and the flags were marched ceremoniously out of the central space. The next few minutes were all VIVAS! Long live! Viva the Escuelita Zapatista! Viva la sexta nacional e internacional! Viva la sociedad civil nacional e internacional! Viva! The vivas! got louder and louder as we reached "Viva las bases de apoyo zapatistas! Viva el subcomandante insurgente Marcos! Viva el subcomandante insurgente Moisés! Viva el comité clandestino revolucionario indígena! Viva el Ejercito Zapatista de Liberación Nacional! Viva! Viva Chiapas! Viva México!" Life, in the face of so much death. Joyous music started up to loud clapping. Soon, all the representatives marched silently off the podium, the long line of women and men walking single file, one after another, in their fine indigenous ceremonial clothing. They moved very quickly, though formally, through the pouring rain up the long road to the entrance of the caracol. The music, tinny and brassy *corridos* set to polka-type beats, was discordant. Corridos, ballads associated with popular oral cultures telling of heroic, antiauthoritarian exploits, were ironically set to the polka brought to Mexico by French invaders in the nineteenth century. Invasion and resistance, clashing chords and harmony, zigzag, all formed part of the noisy, celebratory, underdog ideology.

Then the dancing started—the music came on over the speakers and an emcee called people onto the basketball court, now the dance floor. Couples and individuals came out with black plastic tarps over their heads, ski masks covering their faces, and moved slowly, rhythmically to the music. Members from our group joined in, dancing happily in the company of Zapatistas who had opened space for them.

So, to return to the Zapatistas' question: What were we doing there? Those receptive to Moisés's summons became a WE by attending. WE did not become one WE with the Zapatistas, suddenly transformed through contact. There was curiosity and nervousness on all sides. Yet this performative gesture—the invitation and the acceptance—initiated a dialogue among these various WES, one that protects the Zapatistas from extermination, but that guides and animates us as well. They have successfully turned their backs on capitalism and the degrading and exploitative relationships among humans, animals, plants, and nature broadly that it promotes—and found another way of living. Their vision, "another world is possible," "a world

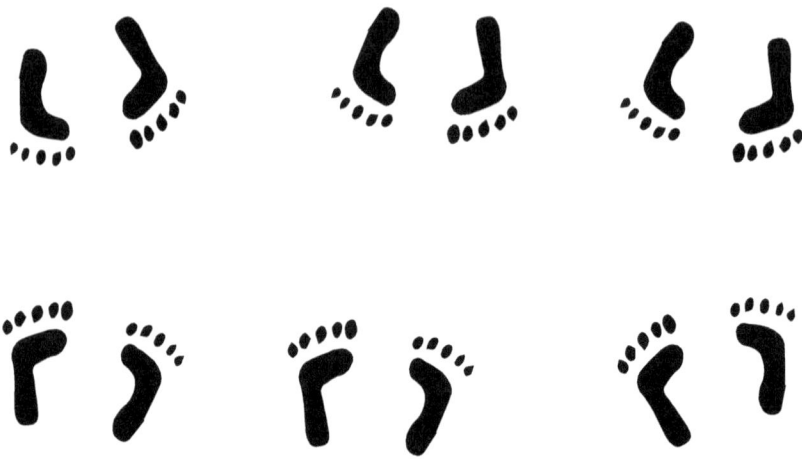

3.14 Alexei Taylor, *Dancing*, 2019.

where there is room for many worlds, a world that can be one and diverse," is performed through their commitment to communal decision making, gender equality, sexual diversity, practice-based education (that develops a critical consciousness among other topics and skills), environmentally sustainable land use, and food sovereignty. They transmit their practices through multiple venues, everything from their local schools and practices to the international escuelitas that teach and inspire activists currently involved in all sorts of environmental and food initiatives.[89] The Zapatistas invite us to align ourselves with a politics, a sustainable practice, without the extractivist impulse to appropriate their knowledges and cosmovision. As Xuno López says, it is by "continuing to learn together in a collective manner, respecting our differences, that we can create other possible routes, and other possible solutions to the disease of individualisms that capitalism has encrusted in our hearts."[90] Many of us need practice in this kind of learning.

WE also serves as the vital third part of the apparent binary established by the good and bad governments, the civil society that in part determines who lives and who dies. Systems produce vulnerability, and other systems, networks, and equivalencies can be mobilized to offset some of the debilitating effects and affects. I have come to "listen and learn," as Marcos good-naturedly asked of us, but I know too how much I have to unlearn in order to listen and learn.[91]

The rain, the mud, the poverty do not seem to quell or challenge the pride, dignity, or determination of the Zapatistas. According to accounts they cite, Zapatista communities have achieved higher standards of health and education than other indigenous communities in Mexico. But Chiapas is still, twenty years later, the poorest state in the nation. It has more inequality now than then, and higher rates of illiteracy.[92] Carlos Monsivais accompanied the Zapatistas on their 2001 March for Dignity and noted that given the discrimination in Mexico, the obvious and indisputable call for education, food, health, and land seems utopic.[93] The more the Zapatistas move forward, the farther the utopian ideals of social justice seem to get away from them. But they keep moving. My guess, sitting there with my invisible backpack stuffed with more materials, was that the Zapatistas' palpable sense of dignity offsets many hardships. They control their territory. As they had shown us, they make their own decisions and rules. Those who seek to interact with them need to abide by them. When they allow or invite us to enter their space, they are hoping for uptake. They ask us to shoulder the struggle against neoliberalism and discriminatory politics in our own arenas. They ask that we act as witnesses and transmitters of their existence, their resistance strategies, and their worldview. Yet their worldview is ample and complex, as seen in speeches, their murals, and interactions. The whole world seems to be represented in the caracoles, even though the Zapatistas fight to stay put: here a flag from the Basque country, here a photo of a Marcos mural in Belfast, the rainbow flag, a condom wearing a Zapatista mask. I say worldview rather than ideology because the Zapatistas are pragmatists, not ideologues. As the evening celebration shows, all indigenous peoples committed to resistance against the bad government are welcome—regardless of the religious, linguistic, and regional tensions that often separate the groups. Indigenous Catholics, Evangelicals, even Muslims who are fighting each other throughout the state are dancing together here. And so were we, the nonindigenous guests, the many who had responded to the invitation.

And all night and throughout the week, the Mexican Air Force buzzed the caracoles, just in case WE had forgotten that they could.

> Avanzo un metro, se aleja un metro
> Avanzo dos metros, se aleja dos metros
> Avanzo diez metros, se aleja diez metros
> Sé que nunca lo alcanczaré
> Sé que una utopía
> Que es un sueño

Entonces . . .
¿Para qué sirven los sueños, las utopías?
Para avanzar!
(Painted on the wall in Oventic, Chiapas)

I move forward a meter and it moves away a meter
I move forward two meters, and it moves away two meters
I move forward ten meters, and it moves away ten meters
I know I will never catch up
I know it's a utopia
That it's a dream
So
What good are dreams? Utopias?
To keep us moving forward!

FOUR

Making Presence

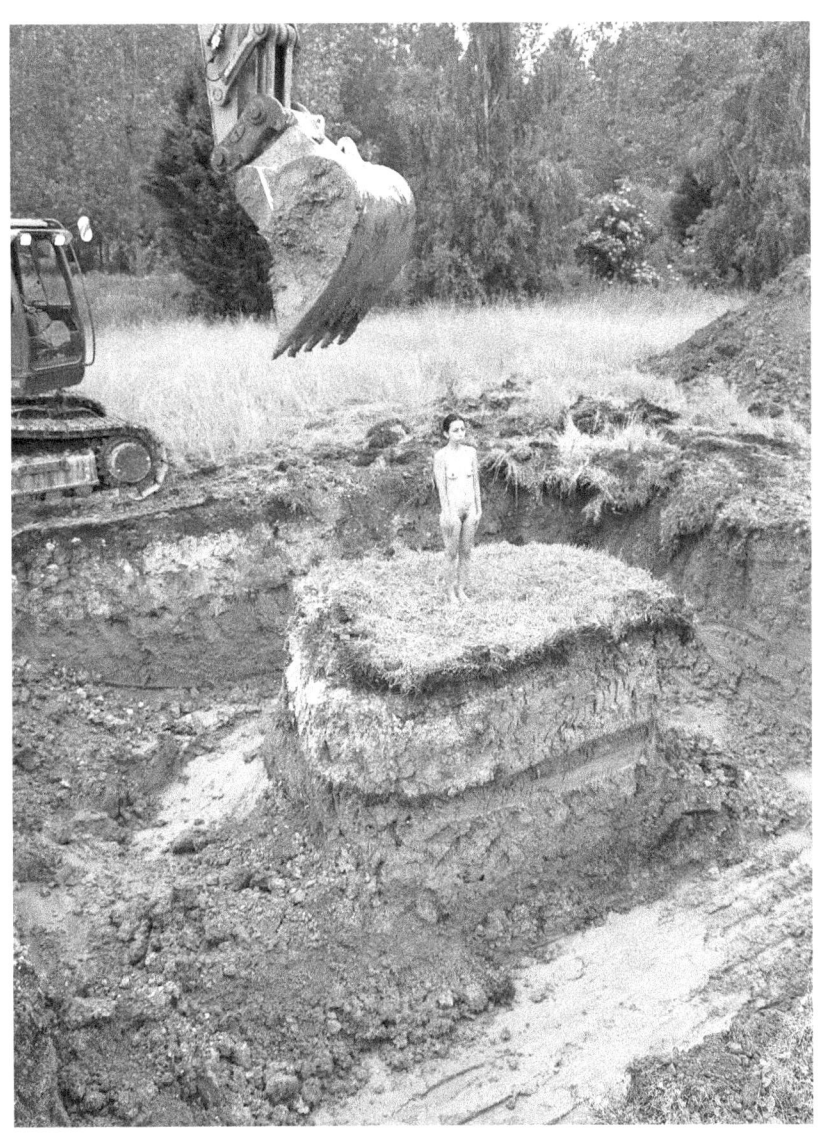

In the photograph, we see her, a diminutive woman, standing naked as a backhoe methodically crashes down, digging a hole in the earth all the way around her (fig. 4.1). In the video we hear the grinding machine before we see it. The giant claw crashes down, grabs massive mouthfuls of earth, gyrates jerkily, noisily, and throws them to the side, gyrates wildly back, closer and closer to her small body. The hole gets deeper. The machine groans, and buzzes, and smashes just behind, in front, or to the side of her.

She stands still, looking into the distance, her hair braided down her thin back, her hands resting on her thighs. There is nothing erotic about her. Resolutely nonglamorous, her body refuses to transmit a promise of pleasure. Rather, it bears signs of wounding. What's that on her right leg? She seems to have a scar right above her pubis.

The simplicity and the power of the piece are impressive. The frail human body seems both central and incidental. The tenacious materiality of the earth, so green and rich, crumbles under the claw. Gentle gusts of wind push her hair onto her face. She stands silent, rooted like a tree. She may as well be a tree or a rock, an indistinguishable form of materiality that obstructs the machine. Her face impassive, her eyes open, blinking but never flinching. She breathes deeply, as if she were trying to stay calm. But we see the muscles contracting in her neck.

She sees it, and registers it, and does not collapse or falter. The "it" is her certain death in the ensuing demolition—the backhoe that lurches closer, the pit that opens wider and deeper in front of her. Aside from the painful vulnerable materiality of her body, she has only attitude, the slightly defiant show of human dignity and resolve in the face of devastation. She may be a part of the material world under siege, but as a human she nonetheless clings to the part of her humanity that distinguishes her from trees and rocks. ¡Presente! her attitude demonstrates. The unspoken mandate: Get out of the way! Disappear! is met with stillness, a silent animative of refusal. You'll have to disappear me. ¡Presente!, here, as an act of resistance in the face of obliterating power, resonates like a mute war cry. ¡Presente! but absolutely isolated. The machine seems intractable and inhuman, as if it were simply doing its job of digging up the land she just happens to be standing on. But we can see a man at the controls. Presente, always to, with, and among others, even when that other hides its face.

4.1 (overleaf) Regina
José Galindo, *Earth*, 2013.
COURTESY OF THE ARTIST.

The gnashing mechanical noise deafens and invades. Yet her body remains absolutely still. The performance is all about proportion and scale, the smallness of the human, the vulnerability of the earth, the magnitude of the crime. In contrast to the relentless, lurching, mechanized violence, the countryside has been domesticated. Swaths of the tall grass have been cut. We see a fence and behind it, a house. The material supports of life over there seem intact. Occasionally, a car drives by in the distance. It's all so civilized. Life apparently goes on.

The only thing that moves is the enormous backhoe jerking back and forth. Even the camera moves minimally. The close-up fades into a wide-angle shot and back in again. Increasingly insulated, she soon stands abandoned on a tiny island of earth. The pit is now many meters deep, and it's clear that she can never get out. It's simply a question of time. Regina José Galindo's live performance lasts an hour and a half; the video of the performance runs about thirty-five minutes.

Where are we? Where is the spectator, the witness, the bystander, the activist who might intervene?

"How did they kill people?" the prosecutor asked.

"First, they would tell the machine operator to dig a pit. Then trucks full of people parked in front of the Pine, and one by one the people came forward. They didn't shoot them. Often they would pierce them with bayonets. They would rip their chests apart with bayonets and take them to the pit. When the pit was full, the metal shovel would drop on the bodies."[1]

Between March 1982 and August 1983, Efraín Ríos Montt's military dictatorship in Guatemala enacted a scorched-earth policy against its Mayan population. In addition to disposing of humans as if they were merely things, indistinguishable from other matter, they destroyed the material basis for their survival. Under the code name Victoria 82, the army exterminated Maya Ixil communities and destroyed their livestock, their crops, and their sacred corn seeds, their living link to their past. The Mayas are, after all, the people of corn. Their fate is bound to that of their land. They demolished men, women, children, and even fetuses—"the seed that must be killed"—the Maya's hope for the future.[2] Genocide, another form of preemptive violence, creates the "ruins yet to come."[3] Time present and time past lead to eradication of time future; genocide is the permanently present, in this scenario. The trial court found that, under Ríos Montt's rule, women were a "military objective."[4] Soldiers raped women and girls not only as the spoils of war but as part of the systematic and intentional plan to destroy the Ixil ethnic group by exercising violence on women's bodies as a way to unravel the social connectivities that maintain the Ixil population.[5]

The military also terrified people into abandoning their cultural practices. The dance-drama *Rabinal Achi*, which dates back to sixteenth-century Guatemala with roots in Mayan court drama of the fourth to tenth centuries, enacts the encounter between two almost identical noble warriors.[6] The Rabinal warrior captures the Quiché warrior preparing an attack on his territory. The piece stages the dignified and highly choreographed process (literally dance) of negotiation with which one treats one's enemy. The two characters duel verbally—each actor sums up what the other has said before adding his own words. The action reinforces the circularity of the dialogue as the two dance and threaten each other. They mirror each other in word and movement. The dancers wear masks, identical except for the strip of color of the rim at the edges—one blue, one green. Our enemy is almost identical to us, the Quiché propose. While the Quiché warrior will be shown every honor, offered all politically viable options for survival (abandon his kingdom, marry the Rabinal king's daughter and join his court), it is clear that he must die on the sacrificial stone.[7] He will never relinquish his ties to his people and his lands. He asks only to be allowed to return home once more to say goodbye. Permission being granted, the Quiché warrior goes home and returns, as promised, to Rabinal to accept his punishment. That drama could not be performed during the Ríos Montt period when the military targeted the village.[8] Death squads roamed through Rabinal smashing babies' heads against walls, raping young women, and killing civilians point blank. The military had a very different idea of what one does to opponents.[9]

The mandate issued by the military was "Indian seen, Indian dead."[10] Over 200,000 people were killed, most of them Mayans. An additional one million people were displaced between 1960 and 1996. "A UN truth commission later specifically found that the state was responsible for acts of genocide in four designated regions of Guatemala between 1981 and 1983. In the predominantly Ixil towns in Quiché, between 70 and 90 percent of the communities were wiped out during this period."[11]

Ríos Montt was the first head of state in the world to be convicted in his own country of genocide and crimes against humanity.[12] While he kept insisting during the trial that he did not know what the army was doing, documentary filmmaker Pamela Yates had earlier filmed him saying, "If I can't control the army, then what am I doing here?"[13] The prosecution used this video during the trial—art here functions unambiguously as truth telling:

the now elderly Ríos Montt, sitting in the courtroom, watched the younger Ríos Montt speaking at the height of his powers. He was sentenced to eighty years in jail. Ten days later, his conviction was overturned.

Yet Guatemalan artist Regina José Galindo chooses not to include the testimony or the trial in her video performance, *Earth*. Only a handful of spectators and three cameras witnessed the live event in Les Moulins, France, in 2013.

I asked Galindo why viewers are not made aware of the testimony.

"I never speak or give information," she answered. "I don't make it didactic; I just carry out an action."[14]

What does this action do or transmit? Does it denounce, expose, or bear witness? Galindo is presente, but present to what, to whom, with whom?

I agree of course with Galindo when she maintains, "the work has several meanings." Like all art, the piece works on multiple expressive, communicative, and political levels simultaneously. Her stark act of being ¡presente! provokes what Nicholas Bourriard might call a series of encounters ("art is a state of encounters") with other artists, publics, and political and historical moments.[15] Performance can bring atrocity to light stripped of the specifics of the when, who, and where. Violence too strips the body under attack of all particularities—she stands as quivering, fleshy materiality that nonetheless makes a claim to presence. The work, clearly grounded in Guatemalan history under Ríos Montt, transcends the particulars to present extermination as a constant. Art from the space of death shows the now and always of criminal practice, as genocide and as environmental ruin, in Guatemala and beyond. The performance balances on the very edge of the poetic and the historical, as differentiated by Aristotle: "Poetry is both more philosophical and more serious than history, since poetry speaks more of universals, history of particulars."[16] Galindo's simple but rigorous aesthetic framing of the action allows it to resonate on multiple levels—the particular and the so-called universal.

We can understand her standing by the widening pit as a reflection on the human existential condition: the well of desperation gets deeper, the inevitability of her fate, the silence and isolation more profound and unspeakable. The very earth collapses around her. Ancient Greek tragedy, one particular aesthetic form, is all about asymmetrical relations of power—Oedipus confronting his inexorable fate. Antigone goes to the cave to meet her death: "Alive, I tread the chambers of the dead. / What law of Heaven have I transgressed against?"[17] Closer to (Galindo's) home, *Rabinal Achi* presents the warriors as twins. Wearing almost identical face masks, the two figures reflect each other in word and movement.[18] Repeating each other's words functions as a mnemonic device but also, I would suggest, as an early example of active listening. Did I understand what you just said? Did I get it right?[19] Violence and war, in the traditions of the Mayan highlands, require close attention to one's other as a part of oneself. Disrespecting one's enemy destroys one's own integrity. The highly codified frameworks within which confrontations take place contain the violence, protecting the individuals exercising it from becoming monsters, and ensuring social stability and continuity.

Earth resonates because of the stark, forceful image of the human confronting certain destruction, because of the devastation of the earth, and because the violence and injustice remain constant. Here, though, I want to rein in its universalizing potential for a moment to explore the urgency of the action's intervention in a specific historical moment as a response to the politics of extermination. In 2013, Ríos Montt, as I noted, was tried and found guilty of genocide. After intense political machinations, a higher court overturned the decision and sent it back down to a lower court to languish. The charges and record remained, poised between oblivion and reactivation. Time ran out—Ríos Montt died at age ninety-one in 2018, having evaded punishment.

Galindo intervenes with *Earth*. Faced with the political foreclosure of a juridical response even before Ríos Montt died, she responds. Galindo stands resolute, a mute victim/witness who sees what's happening and can do nothing to prevent the inevitable. The very land, as with the Mayans, is being taken out from under her feet. Unlike Antigone, no words express the self-awareness of her predicament. What have I done? No interlocutor or Chorus utters or responds to the question: Why? Seemingly stripped of agency, she has done nothing to merit her demolition except exist. Now, the violence seems incidental—she, unlike Antigone, cannot even qualify as an individuated victim. In ancient Greek tragedy, victims usually die at the hands of their kin. This anonymous death strips her of kin but, with racist virulence, highlights ethnic kinship as grounds for extermination: Indian seen, Indian dead. The fierce subjectivity and political agency demonstrated by Antigone seems impossible for Galindo's unidentified, mute figure. The backhoe of Western colonization continues to uproot and evacuate the very possibility of naming and caring for these victims. Galindo's corporeality, though stubbornly material, also stands for the collective body that needs to disappear so that modernity can happen. She stands there, on the land, an impediment to progress, synonymous to many Latin American leaders with modernity.[20] In this version of progress, land too is there to be exploited. The performance, on this level, is so literal. Combatants no longer face each other honorably, as in *Rabinal Achí*. The murderers conceal their faces behind the mechanization of the job. No one is guilty. Leaders hide behind their self-granted amnesties and highly paid lawyers. The separation between the one who orders the violence and the one who carries it out eliminates all sense of personal responsibility. The enormous repercussions of Antigone's unjust death will not be visited on Guatemala or her murderers. The grandeur of these earlier works, the exquisite dance that emphasizes the moral implications and social aftershocks of inflicting death on one's other, has vanished, leaving only silent victims, mass graves, and unexamined crimes. Murderers go unpunished, justice foreclosed. Nobody, apparently, cares enough to end the calamity.

In 1997, fellow Guatemalan artist Daniel Hernández-Salazar confronted the see-speak-hear-no-evil attitude of this fellow citizens with the atrocities committed in their country. Every egregious crime had been met with silence. He created three photographs using the forensic remains of victims—their bullet-pierced shoulder blades resembled angel wings. Following the 1998 murder of Bishop Juan Gerardi, who was shot dead immediately after he presented the report on human rights violations, *Guatemala: Nunca Más* (Guatemala: Never again), Hernández-Salazar added the angel with the silent scream (fig. 4.2).[21] Speak up! The images spread throughout the city of Guatemala, plastered on walls, on buses, everywhere, even on the cover of the *Guatemala: Nunca Más*.

Angels were in the air. In 1999, dressed very much like an angel in a gauzy long dress, Galindo suspended herself from the iconic arch of the post office building in downtown Guatemala City and recited poetry. Her words were lost in the wind.[22]

While the works I put in conversation with *Earth* center on death—the unjust death, the honorable death, the unacknowledged death—*Earth* acts from the very space of death. We do not hear from Antigone after she enters

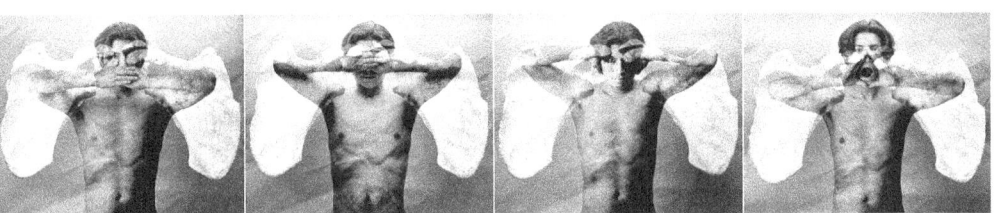

4.2 Daniel Hernández-Salazar, *Esclarecimiento/Clarification*, 1998. COURTESY OF THE ARTIST.

the cave (until we hear others tell of her death); Cawek, the defeated warrior of *Rabinal Achi*, kneels down to be sacrificed, accepting death as the appropriate response to his bellicose trespasses. Hernández-Salazar's angel screams out to whoever will listen. In *Earth*, the woman's nameless, naked, vulnerable body waits stoically to be returned to the earth, not in the respectful, caring burial that mourners usually perform to accompany natural death but by the brutal thrust of the metal claw. Her posture reminds me of Comandanta Ramona's words at the beginning of the Zapatista uprising: "We were already dead. We meant absolutely nothing."[23] Galindo's character inhabits that space of the "already dead," people pronounced socially dead long before governments dispose of the corpses. Her frail, slightly bruised body is disposable, the refuse of the political in Chantal Mouffe's understanding of the term as the "ontological dimension of antagonism."[24] She's nothing. A no one. Nadie. Ninguno. Octavio Paz coined the verb *ningunear*, recognizing that denying someone personhood is an active process of violence.[25] No angels lament her passing or look back in warning.

As the political turns murderous, politics as "the ensemble of practices and institutions whose aim is to organize human existence" also collapses.[26] There is no body of adjudication, no legitimate executive body, no space where people can come together to make a claim for appearance, just the rapidly shrinking earth on the edge of a gaping pit. Only those in power maintain their firm grounding. The face in the cab of the bulldozer might change, but the killing machine keeps moving forward. Galindo takes her stand here, in the face of the catastrophe, making visible the steady demolition as strategic and rationalized political practice.

The Death Space

There is no *post* or *pre* in this [indigenous] vision of history that is not linear or teleological but rather moves in cycles and spirals and sets out on a course without neglecting to return to the same point.—SILVIA RIVERA CUSICANQUI, "Ch'ixinakax utxiwa"

In this one art *acción*, Galindo captures the historical violence of biopower from the times of the conquest to the present. This is a sweeping claim, I know, but I hope to demonstrate it not by presenting a cohesive overview of political history in the area, but rather through repeating scenarios.[27] Much like *Earth*, the continuous nature of the violence can be comprehended as an ongoing performance. Alternatively, it can be captured through stills (as in still photography) animated to appear as an ongoing act. Using the methodology of the performance itself, then, I separate the never-ending tragedy into three isolated (but internally contiguous) scenarios that meld almost imperceptibly from conquest, colonialism, ongoing coloniality, and imperialism.

SCENARIO I

"They forced their way into native settlements, slaughtered everyone they found there, including small children, old men, pregnant women, and even women who had just given birth. They hacked them to pieces, slicing open their bellies with their swords as though they were so many sheep herded into a pen. . . . laughing and joking all the while," writes Dominican friar Bartolomé de Las Casas in 1542, a warning to the Spanish monarch Philip II of the atrocities his countrymen were committing in the Americas.[28] The Spaniards, early extractivists, sought gold and other valuable resources in the new territories; the people they found there were disposable—they could either help the conquerors find the resources or be fed (literally) to the dogs.[29] "Indians" came into being through a double strategy—the first undid preexisting entities and affiliations (Taíno, Mexica, Maya, Zapotec, Olmec, and so on) and converted them into an undifferentiated mass, Indians. The second announced a new entity that need never be fully recognized as human, one that could be exploited or exterminated at will. The separation between the conquerors and the conquered was absolute—the autochthonous people were so resolutely nonhuman "that when the European men massacred them they somehow were not aware that they had committed murder."[30] Arendt, in this citation, is writing of the massacres of Africans on what she calls the "Dark Continent." Her understanding of racism does not extend to the Americas, for they, she states in an example of glaring unfamiliarity with the context, "had not created a human world." Nonetheless, her observation that Europeans treated the conquered as inhuman remains on point.

Las Casas's text, immediately translated into all major languages in Europe, was widely read—an early exemplar of the colony as a state of exception governed by the sovereign but that lay beyond the boundaries of the state proper. The asymmetrical relations gave the conquerors absolute power over the conquered, feeding their sense of omnipotence, affirming their right to violate every legal and moral injunction. Las Casas retells the atrocity in the hope that "recognition of the truth will make the reader more

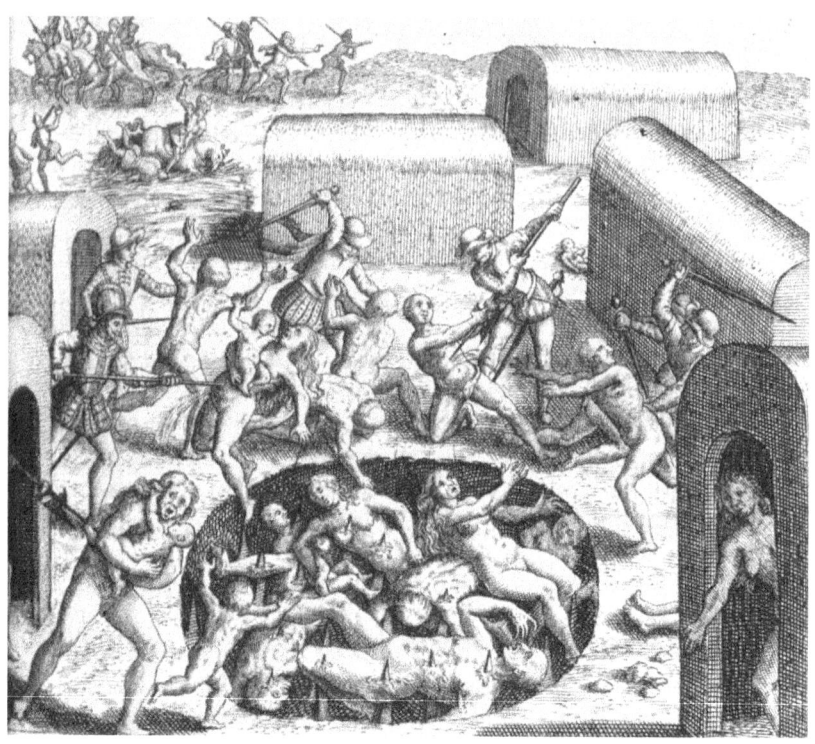

4.3 Theodore de Bry (sixteenth century), illustrations for Bartolomé de Las Casas, *A Short Account of the Destruction of the Indies.*

compassionate towards the sufferings and the predicament of these poor, innocent peoples and oblige him [the reader] to adopt an even more stern and censorious attitude towards the abominable greed, ambition and brutality of their Spanish oppressors."[31] This is an extraordinary document for many reasons. For one, Las Casas names the Europeans as monsters and murderers instead of inverting those terms. Second, it conveys his assumption that reading about (or seeing) injustice will make readers or viewers care enough to intervene.

The demolition wrought by conquest and colonization happened in all social arenas simultaneously—the military, religious, cultural, and epistemic. The newly created Indian provoked major ethical and moral debates in Europe. Back in Spain, Bartolomé de Las Casas debated humanist scholar Juan Ginés de Sepulvida in Valladolid (1550–51) regarding the indigenous populations they encountered. In 1537, "the papal bull *Sublimis Deus* . . . established the status of the Indians as rational beings."[32] The discussion focused on whether Indians have souls and the capacity to be converted to Christianity or, if found lacking, could they be worked to death? The question itself performed the violent ontological project of evacuating the subjectivity of this newly found object, Indian.

The sixteenth-century colonialist project, then, coproduced and refined the European systems of rational thought in which the isolated, individuated subject came into being as a product of his own self-recognition, best summarized in the seventeenth-century Cartesian "cogito, ergo sum." The European, the subject of knowledge, turns all else into an object of knowledge.[33] The annulment of reciprocity and relationality had devastating effects on those not covered by the defining "I." As Aníbal Quijones argues, "the 'other' is totally absent; or is present, can be present, only in an 'objectivised' mode."[34] There can be no intersubjectivity, no subject-subject recognition of human connectivity. That evacuation of the human capacity for recognizing and acknowledging others as part of a shared, complex, living environment is what makes the "terror system," to use Michael Taussig's term, so terrifying.[35] Western epistemology relied on notions of rationality and objectivity and practices of taxonomy and categorization to legitimate certain kinds of knowledge. Writing and print culture, as I argued in an earlier work, helped cement and circulate knowledge as external to oneself through the separation of knower from known.[36] The many ways of knowing and transmitting knowledge practiced by indigenous communities were repressed—epistemicide, in Santos's term.[37] Western theories of progress, development, and modernity, posited within the spectrum of primitive to European, labeled the indigenous peoples as the anathema of progress, congenitally underdeveloped. Indigenous peoples in Guatemala have long been seen as an obstacle to the progress that underwrites modernity. "Cruel modernity," Jean Franco notes, is "massacre on behalf of 'progress.'"[38]

From the sixteenth century, the foundations of what Foucault calls biopower are in place. Biopower, for him, refers to "the set of mechanisms through which the basic biological features of the human species become the object of a political strategy, of a general strategy of power."[39] As I said in chapter 1, I disagree with Foucault's dating of the phenomenon of biopower "starting from the eighteenth century" when "modern Western societies took on board the fundamental biological fact that human beings are a species."[40] Foucault does not consider the debates and practices governing the treatment of indigenous peoples and, shortly afterward, African slaves. These preview the governing of populations through the implementation of racialized categories that become central to biopower.[41] While Las Casas won what some consider the first human rights debate in Valladolid, the outcome had no practical application for the indigenous communities that came in contact with Europeans.[42] The mechanisms of control of the general populations that Foucault associates with biopower were already beginning to take shape—humans could be bought and sold, stripped of their names, kinships, religious practices, languages, to be relocated and worked to death. Human subjectivity was divided into the "people of reason" (*gente de razón*), the Hispanicized, Cartesian self-referential subject "cogito ergo sum" and the "people without reason," the indigenous and African populations relegated to the legal status of minors. We see too the initial formations of racial castas or caste systems that flourished in the seventeenth and eighteenth centuries. The denial of political subjecthood of people considered populations to be managed, thus, happens before the shift Foucault writes of as happening in the eighteenth century: "The population no longer appears as a collection of subjects of right, as a collection of subject wills who must obey their sovereign's will through the intermediary of regulations, laws, edicts and so on. It will be considered as a set of processes to be managed."[43]

The management and eradication of populations continued through the centuries-long period of colonialism and, later, with no clear interruption during what Aníbal Quijano calls ongoing "coloniality" and Pablo González Casanova calls "internal colonialism."[44] Colonial domination may have ended in Latin America in the nineteenth century with the wars of independence, but that the new nation-states built themselves on systems of differentiation and racism ensured the dominance of the descendants of the Europeanized elites.

SCENARIO II

In 1982, just at the end of the Ríos Montt dictatorship, Rigoberta Menchú, the testimonial voice of *Yo, Rigoberta Menchú*, tells how her mother was kidnapped, tortured, raped, and laid out as bait by the Guatemalan military to lure in her family members so that they too might be captured. The description is too painful to include here. After her mother died, the soldiers "were there right by her; they ate near her, and, if the animals will excuse me, I believe not even animals act like that, like those savages in the army. After that, my mother was eaten by animals; by dogs, by the *zopilotes* there are around there, and the other animals helped too. They stayed for four months, until they saw that not a bit of my mother was left, not even her bones and then they went away."[45]

Again, this scenario conveys the dominant, unchanging characteristics— the armed forces, representative of the country's highest power, reduce the indigenous woman to bait and a sexual object. By torturing her, they also torture her family, who have to stay away even as she suffers. The military use affective relations to annihilate relationality itself—seeking to destroy the mother and all her family members. How could her family even think of saving her? She was another of the "already dead." Is there a clearer example of what Mbembe calls "the *generalized instrumentalization of human existence and the material destruction of human bodies and populations*"?[46] Rigoberta Menchú's mother, like many before and after her, was eaten by dogs. Menchú's testimony became an instant classic—it was read broadly and adopted as a text in high schools and colleges. Menchú herself won the Nobel Prize. Some readers were certainly "more compassionate towards the sufferings and the predicament of these poor innocent peoples," as Las Casas hoped, but the destruction of indigenous communities continued unabated well after the Peace Accords were signed in 1995, and into the present.[47]

The current waves of violence in Guatemala started with the CIA-backed 1954 coup against Jacobo Árbenz, the progressive, democratically elected president who tried to reign in the United Fruit Company and legislate land reform. In response to the Cold War, the U.S. increased its support of the Guatemalan military, including the training of its officers (including Ríos Montt) in the infamous School of the Americas. "Since 1946, the SOA has trained over 64,000 Latin American soldiers in counterinsurgency techniques, sniper training, commando and psychological warfare, military intelligence and interrogation tactics. . . . Hundreds of thousands of Latin Americans have been tortured, raped, assassinated, 'disappeared,' massacred, and forced into refugee [status] by those trained at the School of Assassins."[48] Ronald Reagan circumvented Congress to ship armaments to Guatemala in spite of evidence of escalating massacres. He visited Central America in December 1982 and declared, "President Ríos Montt is a man of great personal integrity and commitment. . . . I know he wants to improve the quality of life for all Guatemalans and to promote social justice."[49]

Fast forward to the postdictatorial present in which violence has been privatized and includes many corporate and additional state and nonstate actors. The extermination of the hundreds of thousands of Mayans and the dispossession of their lands has left many traditional lands free for the taking. There is a long history, as Greg Grandin notes, of land expropriation and human exploitation in Guatemala.[50] The indigenous peoples, who happened to be standing on the land, have disappeared. Canadian mining companies, backed by French capital, now extract resources from that earth, bucketful by bucketful. Galindo's performance subtly reveals the networks and practices that create and sustain this ongoing violence, including the recent neoliberal policies that enable the *dictaduras* and what some have come to call the *dictablandas* (soft rather than hard power), such as those in Mexico and currently in Guatemala.

For centuries now, those in power have pushed indigenous communities off their resource-rich lands. Conquest gave way to colonialism, colonialism to coloniality, dictatorship to so-called democracy. The names only distract momentarily from the continuity of brutal practice. Nowadays, the government grants "concessions" to international mining, hydroelectric, and agricultural businesses that force people to leave their communities and even their country; it colludes with the murder of those who resist or protest. The burgeoning drug trade has complicated the volatile situation by redirecting the drugs to new routes through Central America and Mexico on their way to consumers in the U.S. The recently removed president, Otto Fernando Pérez Molina, who won the 2011 elections, was also a military officer trained in the School of the Americas. Guatemala's transition from dictatorship, as in much of Latin America, was not a transition to democracy but to a particularly savage brand of neoliberalism. The sharp rise in femicides attests to a virulent misogyny coupled with racism.[51] The Central American children arriving at the U.S. border in the mid- and late 2010s, separated from their families, placed in freezing cold rooms (*heleras* or iceboxes), and housed in cages, are only the most recent chapter of the history of that ravaged region. *Rabinal Achi* made it clear—the humiliation and degradation of one's opponent, now coterminous with indiscriminate violence, wrecks the entire social fabric into the future.

Earth took place in France, an interesting choice. Why France? Part of the answer is pragmatic—Lucy and Jorge Orta in Les Moulins offered Galindo an artist's residency in 2013. They could provide her the land and the financial support to carry forward a project of this size and expense. The timing of the residency was fortuitous—Galindo felt the urgency of responding to the recent testimony from the trial. Another reason for staging this performance in France, however, builds on Galindo's strategy of staging work that calls out the complicity of the country she performs in, another powerful animative. In her 2010 piece, *Looting*, she paid a dentist in Germany to extract eight gold fillings from her teeth:

On one side, conquest, war, scorched earth policies, pillage of the soil, the humiliated. On the other, the conqueror, he who gives the orders, the man from the Old World, he who raises his hand and keeps the gold.

In Guatemala, a dentist perforates my molars and places 8 fillings of Guatemalan gold of the highest purity.

In Berlin, a German doctor extracts the fillings from my molars. These small sculptures, 8 in total, are exhibited as objects of art.[52]

In the United States, for the Hemispheric Institute's twentieth anniversary in late October 2018, which coincided with the Trump administration's political frenzy about the caravan of migrants at the southern U.S. border, Galindo performed *Carguen con sus muertos/Carry Your Dead* through the streets of New York (fig. 4.4). She lay in a body bag while volunteers carried her through the neighborhood and those of us attending the anniversary accompanied the funeral cortege. "Is there a dead body in there?" people would ask us. "Yes, our dead. Those we are responsible for," some of us would reply.

The choice of France for *Earth* reveals two deeper connections—one that points to the history of colonial violence in Guatemala and another to its updated, neoliberal presentation. Marie-Monique Robin, in *Death Squadrons: The French School*, outlines how the French army developed counter-revolutionary and dirty war strategies in Indochina and perfected them in Algeria, including covert action, secret centralized information, surveillance, psychological warfare, terror tactics, and torture. This model was exported to the U.S. at the beginning of the Cold War, and the word "disappearance" enters our lexicon in 1954 in Guatemala, which, along with other Latin American countries, became "empire's workshop" as the U.S. perfected its own counterinsurgency prowess.[53] It was there, Grandin argues, that the U.S. developed its counter-insurgency chops and "tactics of extraterritorial administration."[54]

Regina José Galindo, standing still at the edge of the pit in France, connects these various moments and practices. Still. Still here. The performance, moreover, demands the rigorous physical practice of stillness. Stillness requires enormous muscular effort. "Stillness," as Nadia Seremetakis reminds us, "is the moment when the buried, the discarded, and the forgotten escape to the social surface of awareness."[55] That stillness conjures up all the pasts. As with *Oedipus*, "It is precisely the sudden and paradoxical emergence of a pattern connecting the distant past to the present, which gives the movement of events so much of its force."[56] The scenarios are

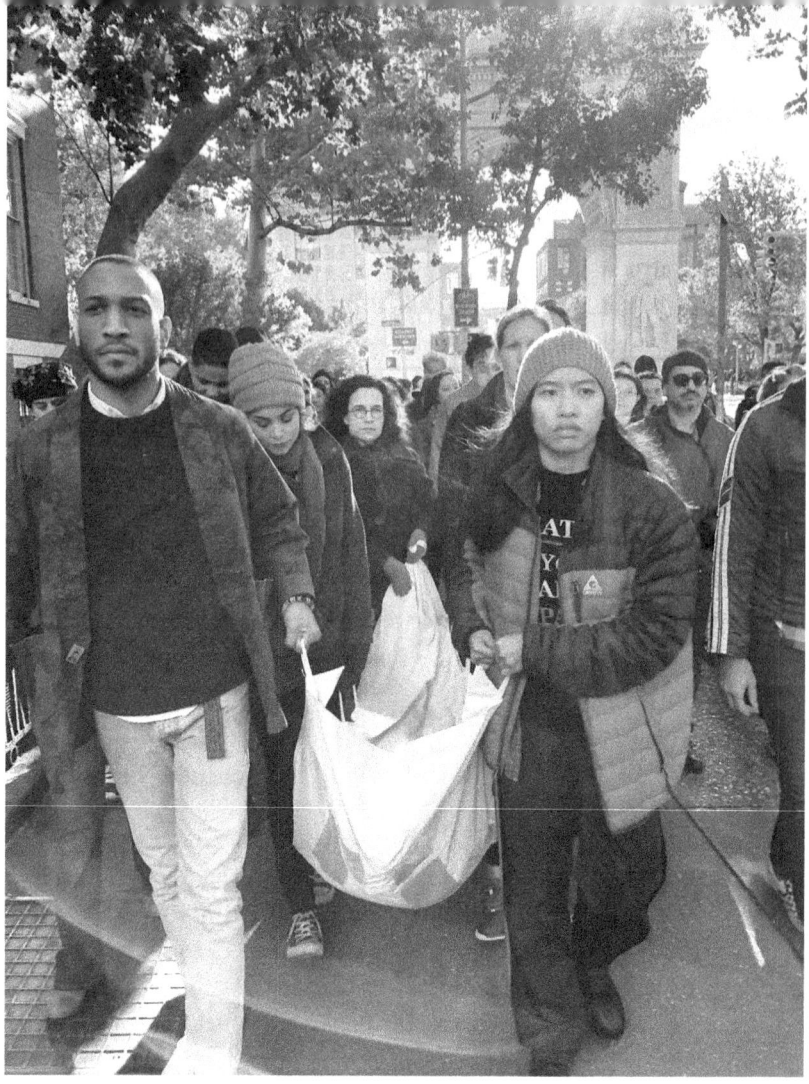

4.4 *Carguen con sus muertos*, New York City, October 26, 2018. PHOTO: DIANA TAYLOR.

almost interchangeable. A scenario, as I defined in an earlier work, serves "as an act of transfer, as a paradigm that is formulaic, portable, repeatable, and often banal because it leaves out complexity, reduces conflict to its stock elements, and encourages fantasies of participation."[57] The basic elements remain the same, albeit with variations, century after century. Conquest, colonialism, and coloniality as Quijano argues, all contributed to cementing a "new world order" predicated on the same objective, the "violent concentration of the world's resources under the control and for the benefit of a small European minority and above all, of its ruling classes."[58]

Biopower and biopolitics, I agree with Mbembe, very rapidly become necropolitics as Amerindians and African slaves experience "social death," that is, "expulsion from humanity."[59] Necropolitics, for him, refers to a "specific terror formation" that includes, among other things, territorial fragmentation, surveillance (inwardly and outwardly oriented), and "the overlapping of two separate geographies that inhabit the same landscape." Necropolitics creates "death-worlds . . . new and unique forms of social existence in which vast populations are subjected to conditions of life conferring upon them the status of the living dead."[60] I would question Mbembe's use of "new" here but rather see these death spaces as being continually refashioned to serve the needs of evolving local powers and global capital. Moreover, the "dead" we see continue to talk back, ¡presentes!

Art from the Space of Death, Necroart

How can one convey asymmetrical power relations more directly or more simply? "Don't you see?" she might be asking us. Or better, where are we, the spectators, to witness this atrocity? Performance can bring atrocity to light, stripped of the specifics of the when, who, where.

Galindo's body faces an enormous pit, the very vacuum of the political that withholds recognition of indigenous peoples. Alone, except for the shadowy figure of the backhoe driver, her gaze (as is often the case in Galindo's work) resists human contact. She does not look at him or beg for mercy. She does not look inward or betray traces of individual subjectivity. Why communicate a sense of interiority, of humanness, or hope of connectedness that for centuries has been denied? Neither does she seek reciprocity or acknowledgment from the spectator. What spectator? Buber's I/Thou has been severed; she accepts her condition as a "nothing."[61] Her impassive face accentuates rather than hides her human vulnerability, even as she cannot hope to make a moral demand on others, as Levinas envisioned.[62] The performance, like the Guatemalan context, negates the possibility of a space of appearance that "arises out of acting and speaking together."[63] There is no together, no shared space for empathetic connection or recognition. Galindo stages the demolition of the between and the beside. This is the death space.

No one, it seems, is there to see. Two hundred thousand murdered. Who was there to witness and demand an end to the genocide? No one. The spectators were missing. No one on both sides—the victims denied personhood and the nonpresence of those who might have borne witness to the crimes. Violence has destroyed the victims, the witness, the audience (perhaps those the Zapatistas would call "civil society"). This performance stages the crisis of care I have pointed out through the various scenarios. No one seems to care. Not individually. Not collectively. Not politically. No one has ever cared about these populations. Caring, in one sense, is about positionality. Who cares about the "over there" when there's so much to care about here? As Richard Nixon made clear to Donald Rumsfeld, "As long as we've been in it, people don't give one damn about Latin America."[64] In case he hadn't been clear enough, he added, "'People don't give one shit about' the place."[65] It is not a priority for the United States even though, or perhaps because, Latin America is where it "acquired its conception of itself as an empire."[66]

Caring acknowledges the interconnectedness between ourselves and others, ourselves as only a part of that larger entity. Studies on empathy "as an affective capacity or technique via which 'we' can come to know the cultural 'other'" keep the hierarchical self-other distinction firmly intact.[67] Empathy, the way I understand it, is an innate, adaptive capacity living creatures have to connect with other forms of life (not exclusively human) through neurological mechanisms. As biologist Frans de Waal puts it, "Seeing someone in pain activates pain circuits to the point that we clench our teeth, close our eyes, and even yell 'Aw'!"[68] This understanding does not carry the colonialist fantasy of understanding or knowing our cultural other but rather recognizes the interconnections between living organisms that could potentially produce cultures of care. People have the capacity to care about those they do not know, as I explore in the epilogue to this study. But even an innate, involuntary biological capacity collapses when confronted with othering. Resisting othering and recognizing interconnectivity might enable us to register or acknowledge that the pain of others is often politically induced: some benefit from the exploitation of others. We can get used to it, or we have to work for a political system in which pain or deprivation are more equally distributed.[69] A study on empathy finds that "despite its early origins and adaptive functions, empathy is not inevitable; people routinely fail to empathize with others, especially members of different social or cultural groups."[70] Not only "Who cares?" but "They deserve it." Not caring, in fact, has been promoted as hip and attractive in today's U.S. culture. Memes of "Who cares?" circulate constantly. In June 2018 when Melania Trump, first lady of the United States, visited the migrant children held in detention on the U.S.-Mexico border as part of the family separation program, she wore a jacket that read, "I really don't care, do u?"[71]

Galindo stands alone. No one serves as a witness to the violence.

How to perform the ongoing annihilation without evacuating the copresence that underwrites the performatic contract? Performance, almost by definition, relies on spectators to complete it. Galindo's look, in the video of her performance, is alienating, and for many, off-putting. It's hard to take spectatorial pleasure from this performance. This work falls outside the Aristotelian tragic aesthetic form that allows us to take pleasure in the pain of others. As opposed to works that fill us with pity and fear, Galindo's *Earth* destabilizes the viewer and denies us being. True, this is a work of art. Galindo will not die in that pit. But by depicting the death of intersubjectivity, the character denies herself and by extension us, the viewers. If as, Jean-Luc Nancy maintains, "being cannot *be* anything but being-with-one-another," then how can a scenario that annihilates her validate us? Interrelationality has failed. This performance builds on the failure to recognize some humans as human. How can spectators become a "we" without some form of shared recognition? The basis for solidarity has crumbled beneath our feet, giving way to a very profound solitude.

Nothing apparently can be done to evade the devastation.

And yet she does something. In the face of *nothing can be done*, she exerts her choice. She stands still. She enables us to see it. Not with her, perhaps, but through her. Again, the "failure" succeeds in exposing the viewer's role in the ongoing nature of the devastation.

Galindo's performance for the camera forms part of another aesthetic lineage, now in contemporary performance practice. Artists such as Francis Alÿs, Ana Mendieta, Guillermo Gómez-Peña, The Yes Men, and others intervene through video for a variety of reasons that might involve strategies of circulation, target audiences, political cover, self-protection, and philosophical and aesthetic reflection.

The video of this action has a life of its own. Though not equivalent to the act, it is not simply its documentation. The performance continues to act on many of those who have seen the video or perhaps just the photographs. The image of the vulnerable woman on the edge of the abyss lasts with us not because it documents the horror of an actual event (as in the testimony of the massacres). It lasts because, on some level, we know it's true, whether we understand the video to be about the ongoing practices of femicide, violence against indigenous communities, and/or extractivist policies. It encapsulates the image of the disposable nonsubject whom no one cares about or acknowledges. Criminal practices, such disappearances, are hard to see directly. They take place at the margins of the public gaze and are visible, if at all, through acts of performance or documentation.

At the same time, the video does make a claim to its status as an archival artifact. It reminds us that some video is true in another sense as well. The image of Ríos Montt facing his younger self on film during his trial indicates that art, documentary filmmaking in this case, can also provide evidence that holds up in court. The videos and documented testimony of the victims being thrown into the pit are also part of the archival record. Yet I would argue that this is not an archival performance. It does not reveal a specific transaction or event such as a particular massacre. Although it performs testimony, the work is not directly about testifying or witnessing. If anything, Galindo withholds reference to the detailed testimony that inspired her. Rather, the aims of the work seem broader, more far reaching, more about embodying the country's ferocity, the unilateral and seemingly endless violence directed at women, at indigenous people, at the defenseless, at the environment. Her minimalist gestures depersonalize the singular massacre to expose the ongoing traffic in weapons, drugs, resources, and people. The disappearance and disposability of populations constitutes an unending moneymaking, transnational event.

Yet *Earth* is also an artwork by a major artist. It has been shown at the Tate, the Guggenheim, and other major museums around the world. The video of the live performance circulates, separated from the physical presence of the artist and the context that gave it rise. The performance is frozen; it is now an original. Galleries and museums can buy it. The embodied performance, the physical endurance and stamina required of Galindo as she stood for an hour and a half facing the backhoe, has become something else—the universally intelligible cultural product that circulates successfully in the art market. People probably assume the video refers to some violence or other, but here too, who knows? Who cares?

Galindo does.

No matter where she performs, this political background informs her approach to her work. She recounts being at work in an office when she heard that Efraín Ríos Montt was running for office as president of Guatemala in the 2003 elections even though the constitution forbids the participation of former dictators and coup leaders in the democratic process. She says she went home, locked herself in her room, screamed, and kicked her legs. On a lunch break shortly afterward, she put on a simple long black dress, took a basin full of human blood, and walked slowly, dipping her feet every few minutes in the blood, all the way from the Constitutional Court to the National Palace in Guatemala City. When she stopped at the National Palace, the sight of the soldiers stationed outside so incited her that she walked up to them with the same determined, implacable expression on her face we see in *Earth* and placed the bowl of blood at their feet. She then washed her feet, changed her clothes, and went back to work. The Regina José Galindo lunch hour. This piece is called *Who Can Erase the Traces?* (2003).

When Guatemalan author Francisco Goldman asked Galindo in an interview what their poor country had done to deserve so much tragedy, she responded, "You ask me what Guatemala has done to deserve all this? Maybe the more appropriate questions would be: What have we *not* done? Why have we been so fearful and tolerated so much fear? Why have we not woken up and reacted? When are we going to stop being so submissive?"[72]

For Galindo, the difference between artists and activists is that activists protest specific issues, and they evaluate the efficacy of the act by whether or not it can change the outcome of the cause. As an artist, she claims the right to reflect on these issues in a more personal, idiosyncratic manner. She will not claim her work has testimonial weight. She has no illusions that she can change the political situation, or make people care about atrocities that seem very far away. But she does everything in her power to make the situation known in the most powerful way possible.[73] I think she would agree with Ricardo Dominguez that "activists break the law, while artists change the conversation theatrically, by disturbing the law."[74]

But Galindo also wants to avoid the romanticism of those who struggle for social justice. And unlike activists, she does not believe that it's crucial (or perhaps even possible) for her to change the system of power. In 2008, she was invited to participate in *Horror vacui*, a group show of young Guatemalan artists around the theme of denunciation. How had they intervened in a society marked by criminal violence? Galindo's contribution was to pay an intelligence expert who had worked for the security forces during the dirty war to investigate the artists participating in the show, just as he had during the dictatorship. He prepared a dossier about each artist containing personal data (address, names of family members, daily routine, bank transactions, everything). The intelligence expert came to the show and exhibited his findings: all those artists who considered themselves denunciators had not, in fact, decried anything that was not already well known. He concluded that they posed no threat to the army or the government and were, rather, more like children at play. She presented this as the performance *Infiltrado/ Infiltrated*.

So what is the political force and efficacy of Galindo's performance? Perhaps none. She certainly would not call herself a denunciator. Does her standing naked by the open pit communicate anything that was not well known before? Maybe, says Galindo, it is sufficient for the performance to impel the spectators to reflect on the issue. For her, this modest goal is sufficient. But she needs to do something. On International Women's Day, March 8, 2017, she staged *Presencia*, a performance during which she recited the names of victims of femicide: "Patricia, Saira, María de Jesús, Cindy, Sandra, Carmen, Ruth, Mindi, Florence, Kenia, Velvet, Flor de María, Karen. All of them with life projects, family, work, dreams. All of them were silenced, snatched up in the most violent ways on earth, against their will. They were all murdered in Guatemala. Wounded, humiliated, tortured, and murdered for the sole reason of being women."[75] Galindo puts on their clothes; saying their names, she wants to acknowledge their lives and their deaths: "Their bodies are no longer here, but they remain in memory, in their dresses, in their objects."[76]

Some say that there is nothing people can do to change the world, or even the immediate situation. There are many reasons for not acting: they are not from this country, or from this community, and so on. How does someone dare involve herself in the business of other people? Is she exploiting them? Appropriating their pain, their stories? Is that ethical? The asymmetries of power leave others feeling impotent. Who is able to effectively confront military might? Or deeply ingrained economic inequalities? But for people like Galindo who feel the need to intervene, these excuses don't hold up. The question is not *if* something can be done but *what* can be done and how to do it in a way that is powerful, responsible, and ethical.

I asked Galindo about her future plans. She confessed she didn't know.[77] She can't make plans. She has a notebook filled with project ideas, and she is working on a new performance now. But life is too uncertain in Guatemala to plan ahead. She was offered a prestigious two-year residency in Berlin and was excited about going, but she was denied a visa. So how can she plan? "Guatemala doesn't have a future," she said, "and I don't know if I have one either."

And still, she keeps working, exposing herself to the cruelty and corruption and injustice she encounters everywhere. ¡Presente!

Whenever people lament that there's "nothing we can do" about some awful situation or other, I suggest they go tell that to Regina José Galindo.

FIVE

Traumatic Memes

Buscamos la vida en caminos de muerte. [We look for life on the roads of death.]

Con los padres de las victimas, sostengo: no hay nada peor que estar enfermo de incertidumbre. Y vivos los queremos. [With the families of the victims, I affirm that nothing's worse than to be sick with uncertainty. We want them back alive.]

—ENRIQUE GONZALEZ ROJO ARTHUR

I

When I first met the family members and classmates of the 43 disappeared students of Ayotzinapa, Mexico, I almost felt I recognized them. The enlarged photographs of the missing young men crowded the room. I recognized the photographs, but also the strategy of mothers using the oversize images to claim justice for their disappeared. In April 2015, the families and advocates of the students arrived in New York as part of their caravan throughout the United States seeking international support for human rights. A six-hour extremely brutal attack on September 26, 2014, by federal and local police in cohort with members of drug cartels left three students dead, forty-three disappeared, and fifty or more tortured who survived by escaping and running for their lives.[1] The Mexican government proffered various ludicrous explanations for the events in lieu of an investigation. As a member of an International Jury of the People's Permanent Tribunal (PPT), I heard family members tell of the anguish of disappearance and blame the Mexican government for obstructing justice.[2] The testimonies resounded amid the photographs of serious faces. At the end of the session, everyone shouted in unison: "Vivos se los llevaron, vivos los queremos"

(They took them alive, we want them back alive). We said their names out loud, followed by "¡Presente!" Presente, here, was complex—the reiterative act of showing up, a form of witnessing, a denunciation, an invocation, a tenacious animative against officially mandated absence and forgetting, and a sign of solidarity and contestation powerful enough to conjure up the disappeared as vitally present. We all were there to acknowledge and support the families of the disappeared and to lend mass and weight to their claims. Instead of a few calling for justice, there were many. The missing filled the room, made present through the pronunciation of their names, the photographs of their faces, and the stories others told of them. The family and friends continued to present their demand—they wanted their loved ones back alive. At the end of the event, I asked one of the mothers of a disappeared student if she knew of the Madres from Argentina. She had never heard of them. Here, I look at how presente works to illuminate absence, how its againstness keeps the disappeared visible, clamoring from the space of death, even in and through the vacuum created by forced disappearance.[3]

While the devastation caused by forced disappearance as an ongoing political practice in Latin America since the mid-twentieth century is widespread, what struck me were the commonalities in how certain groups made the loss visible both personally and politically. The photos, the grieving mothers, the chants making political claims ("They took them alive, we want them back alive") were very familiar to someone who has followed mothers' movements since the Madres de Plaza de Mayo, wearing their children's diapers as head scarves, started protesting in the late 1970s in Argentina. The

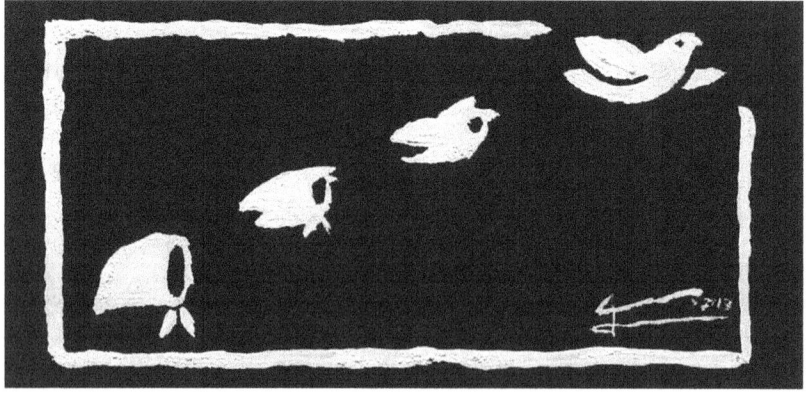

5.1 Francesc de Diego Fuertes, *Madres Palomas*, 2003. COURTESY OF THE ARTIST.

fact that I recognized this cluster—mother-photo-chant—suggested that it replicated and circulated as a traumatic meme, an animative that refuted official mandates that families get over it and move on. The mothers' representational strategies had spread, had become memetic.

Here, I use presente as an optic to explore some of the factors that made the 43 a cause célèbre nationally and internationally. In a country where hundreds of thousands of people have been killed or disappeared since 2006, why did the 43 become so emblematic? I will look at some of the reasons that have been advanced in the media and in academic studies and propose an additional explanation: the family, fellow students, and human rights advocates who insisted that their missing were indeed ¡presentes! and demanded them "back alive" from the government animated powerful, traumatic memes to further their cause. The grieving mothers, the chants (or *consignas*) demanding justice, and the use of photo IDs tapped into recognizable traumatic memes that made the tragedy immediately register with a public now only too familiar with disappearance.

Traumatic memes capturing the affective and political dimension of forced disappearance circulate throughout the world to make violence and loss visible. The evolutionary biologist Richard Dawkins coined "meme" in his 1976 book *The Selfish Gene* to rhyme (imperfectly) with "genes," accentuating what he saw as the biological mechanism vital in the reproduction of cultural codes, and with the Greek *mimeme*, which he says "comes from a suitable Greek root."[4] As *mimeme* does not exist as a Greek root, I assume that he's referring to *mimesis*, from the root *mimeomai*, "I imitate" (infinitive *mimeisthai*).[5] Memes, which he calls cultural "replicators," are behaviors, gestures, ideas, tunes, practices, and so on that catch on and spread from person to person in a version of the survival of the (cultural) fittest.[6] "Just as genes propagate themselves in a gene pool by leaping from body to body via sperms or eggs, so memes propagate themselves in the meme pool by leaping from brain to brain via a process which, in the broad sense, can be called imitation."[7] Good ideas, the belief in God, and the notion that the world is flat are cultural units that catch on and then seemingly replicate themselves. "Happy Birthday," for example, is sung throughout the world, including in many places where people do not speak English. Nonetheless, everyone immediately knows what it signals. Memes are cultural items of social thought or practice (ideas, jokes, styles, and other forms) transmitted through repetition. Like viruses, like social practices, they are successful only if they catch on, if people continuously transmit them. "For a meme to survive and spread in a competitive environment it must have attributes which give it advantages over other memes."[8] Gradually, the notion and use of memes themselves became rampant, memetic. But instead of the version of virus-like genetic "mutation" Dawkins had identified in cultural memes, he noted that memes were now "altered deliberately by human creativity" through digital transmission as what An Xiao Mina calls "internet memes . . . a piece of online media that is shared and remixed over time within a community."[9] Online memes have become so prevalent that some forget the biological paradigm first put forward by Dawkins. Interestingly, for reasons I reflect on later, most of the memes I discuss here are not transmitted online. What interests me here is how populations use and alter memes to make a political intervention, epigenes as different from Dawkins's genes, in an another imperfect analogy, and how successful memes spread from bodies, through public space, the internet, back through bodies and so on in a rampant whirl of circulation.

Whether they start as a mutation (as in the replication of genetic code) or as a deliberate alteration (say of a photograph), memes are never for the first time.[10] They become themselves through the force of repetition, by catching on.[11] The fact that they have been creatively altered matters. So too does the force of the uptake. It makes no difference whether or not the cultural unit was designed to spread—it becomes memetic at the moment of propagation, "never for the first time" but for "the second to the nth time."[12]

Memes repeat through a mechanism of sameness and change. The structure remains, immediately recognizable, while inviting others to adapt it for their needs. While memes have links to mimesis, the nature of the repetition differs. In very broad strokes we could differentiate between memetic repetition-as-replication and mimetic repetition-as-imitation. Singers of "Happy Birthday," for example, are not imitating others. On key or off, they're engaging with a cultural form they have incorporated from who knows where. While mimesis is an extremely complex philosophic and aesthetic term that ranges from "representation" to "imitation" to "a family of concepts," for the moment we can limit ourselves to the over-simplified meaning of the classical Greek *mimeisthai* as "to imitate."[13] For Aristotle, a dramatic work imitates action. In this sense, mimesis often involves corporeal repetition of actions. We learn to walk and talk by following others. You sing; I will try to sing as you do. Learning, for Aristotle, becomes pleasurable through mimetic repetition. Memes, unlike mimesis, emphasize replication and copying, often bypassing the body-to-body contact—as in ideas jumping from brain to brain or proliferating digitally. It would seem we do not have to be physically present with and to another for the transmission to occur. Memes have multiple and different ways of entering our system.

Where does agency lie? Mimesis seems more and less deliberate than memesis. "Aristotelian definition of human 'action' has a strongly intentional cast" and "must make reference to the reasons, desires, and choices of the agent."[14] Yet much of what we learn (such as smiling or walking as a baby) can hardly be thought of as fully intentional. Nor can we limit mimesis to human activity, though corporeality and intentionality remain central. Memesis often seems to function virally, beyond control, especially if people find something noteworthy or useful. Nonetheless, as I will describe, political memes often require strategic thinking.

People commonly use words such as "contagion" and "virus" to describe mimetic and memetic transmission. The viral component, after all, was central to Dawkins's theory. Does that mean that people have no choice but to transmit materials from their memespheres?[15] It depends. Jingles may enter our heads and be difficult to shake, however hard we try. We tend to be hosts, not agents, in Dawkins's paradigm.[16] But singing "Happy Birthday" or using a political meme entails choice. Memes are an invitation to join in. As Mina argues, they "spread across borders and territories to involve much larger groups of people participating in solidarity than might previously have been possible."[17] Nonetheless, it's hard to assess where ideas and cultural forms originate. Mimetic and memetic repetition serve different though at times related and overlapping functions. The political force of memes lies in their ability to catch on, repeat, circulate ideas, interrupt a governmental discourse (as an animative, for example), and reproduce uncontrollably, finding both agents and hosts to continue to disseminate them.

The traumatic meme, like all memes, depends on the simplicity of structure for its power and efficacy. The Woman + Photo + Chant/Demand is actually a cluster of memes, a "memeplex," a term developed by Dawkins to describe "mutually supportive [elements that] . . . clearly help to secure the longevity of the memes of which they are composed."[18] The memeplex I study here—the grieving mother, the photo, and the chant—includes memes recognizable in their own right. The Virgin Mary or Pietà is only the best-known Western example of the grieving mother. The centrality of mothers, as opposed to fathers or other family members, in these movements varies from place to place. Because this particular memeplex becomes recognizable after the Mothers of the Plaza de Mayo in Buenos Aires settled on it through trial and error, three central reasons account for the predominance of mothers. First, the Argentinean mothers had to leave their husbands at home in order to go to the plaza—the military would have killed them otherwise, calling the protest an act of armed resistance by subversives. Second, in many of the patriarchal, Catholic countries where we first see this memeplex, such as Argentina, Chile, Guatemala, or El Salvador, mothers enjoyed a privileged symbolic status denied other women. The military did not want to be seen gunning down unarmed mothers. Third, once the memeplex was circulating globally, transmitting a recognizable story of disappearance and criminality, others protesting the disappearance of their kin could use it to telegraph their loss and their demands for justice. The use of "mothers" is often a strategic choice and does not entirely reflect the composition of the group.

In 1977, the Mothers of the Plaza de Mayo moved around the square, wearing their head scarves and holding or wearing the photo IDs of their disappeared children, demanding that their children be returned alive. The act of performing the photographs functioned as an animative. The official photo ID gives a subject an identity vis-à-vis the state. The state recognizes the individual, bringing her or him into presence as a citizen. Now the state refused to recognize its citizens, conjuring up the missing as subversives who had gone underground of their own volition. Underground, yes, or into the bottom of the River Plate, and certainly not of their own volition. The mothers' photos would not go away, reminding the government of its responsibility to its citizens. You took them, the women seemed to say, but where? We want them back. Other women, such as the Saturday Mothers in Turkey, sit surrounded by the photographs of their men disappeared by the Turkish military in the 1980s and '90s. The Iranian Mothers of Khavaran formed in 1988. Among the photographs in the exhibit *Yuyanapac* (I remember) that document the violence of Peru's internal conflict (1980–2000), one shows a woman holding a small photo ID of her missing loved one in her hands.[19] Look, these photographs challenge onlookers. These are the faces of the many victims of forced disappearance. They have names, faces, families, and friends who love them. Where are they? Each variation contributes something of its local context while remaining immediately identifiable. Always, however, these traumatic memes speak to the specific violence of forced disappearance and insist that the missing remain ¡presentes!, an emotional and political presence. In the case of Ayotzinapa, many clamoring for justice were men. The fathers joined the mothers, and the classmates were necessarily male, given the gendered separation in the *escuelas normales*. Those using traumatic memes in Ayotzinapa had no idea where they came from. Memes circulate freely, available for use. No one owns them. Memes cite and build on previous practices without acknowledging where they started or who performed them. Only the most transmitted ones succeed.

The cluster or memeplex of traumatic memes—the grieving mothers, photos, and the demands—accumulates affective and symbolic power in each new iteration. Memes, clearly, are not in themselves traumatic. They are not necessarily animatives, refusing the powerful performative, as I examine in chapter 2. They are agnostic—as capable of transmitting images and slogans linked to racist virulence (Melania Trump's "I really don't care, do u?" in chapter 4) as they are in making claims for human rights. Nonetheless, given their reiterative nature, they serve as a potent mechanism of reproduction of the affective traumatic charge. Trauma too, I have argued, is never for the first time. It is also known by the nature of its repeats.[20] If, as Cathy Caruth argues, traumatic "repetitions are particularly striking because they seem not to be initiated by the individual's own acts but rather appear as the possession of some people by a sort of fate," then the contagious meme seems the perfect form of transmission.[21] This is not to say that the meme is or repeats the trauma. Rather, it is a form of transmission that conveys the grief, identifies the loss, and makes the claim, all without providing the viewer with specific details of the disappearances. That's its power.

Encountering the grieving women, the photo, the demand for justice moves me, as a viewer, in profound and deeply contradictory ways. I feel pity, outrage, tenderness, frustration, a sense of impotence coupled with a sense of responsibility and political urgency. The meme summons me. I, too, want to be ¡presente! I struggle to imagine the protesters' loss yet resist the pain of engaging emotionally too deeply.[22] The traumatic memes "carry an impossible history within them."[23] The more we engage, however, the more some of us try to understand, acknowledge, witness, and denounce (rather than absorb or identify with) the particular situation.

Traumatic memes, thus, are doubly charged, repetition as form and repetition as content, accentuating the againness of the loss, the pain of the victims and survivors, and the impunity of the perpetrators. Forced disappearance, these memes communicate, exceeds violence against individuals; it's an ongoing state practice that also undermines entire families and communities left in permanent states of uncertainty and anguish. Are they alive or dead? What happened to them? These traumatic memes underline the durational and globalized nature of protest as a response to continuous and globalized criminal practices. Here, then, I look for the signs of the loss, criminality, and resistance by tracing the traumatic meme back from Ayotzinapa to their first known appearance. Traumatic memes pull images and memories of disappeared people back into the public sphere. They too are ¡presentes!

II

In Mexico, between 2007 and 2018 some 250,000 people have been murdered and 37,400 to 120,000 or so disappeared.[24] The wild disparities in the number of disappearances depend on whether authorities include the migrants from Central America who disappear in Mexico. Those are the official figures. Actual figures are believed to be much higher. The victims, if noted at all, become nameless ciphers in the official rosters. Most of the bodies lie in mass graves or have been dissolved in acid by *pozoleros* (a macabre play on *pozole*, the pre-Columbian stew popular in Mexico). Very few of these crimes have been investigated, and fewer than 1 percent of the perpetrators have been charged and brought to trial. Many of the criminals, human rights groups surmise, belong to the government, the military, the paramilitary, the police force, and drug cartels.[25] International corporations, supported by the Mexican government, contribute to the violence by hiring paramilitary security forces to target those who oppose their land grabs and extraction of natural resources. It's impossible at times to tell who is responsible for the violence—the state, the corporations, or the narcos. Often the three work in tandem, creating a narco corporate state. Impunity reigns on all levels. Investigations, if attempted at all, inevitably get bogged down, evidence goes missing, and documents lost. Fighting crime in Mexico belongs to the realm of lost causes. The deaths and disappearances seem to be accepted as the new reality since President Felipe Calderón took office 2006 and declared his U.S.-backed war on drugs.

Yet in the midst of this new macabre norm, the September 26 attack shocked Mexico and the world. The 43 prompted a national and international outcry that almost toppled the Mexican government. The number "43" became a meme, a rallying call for millions of people throughout the country (fig. 5.2).

The tag line, "They wanted to disappear us, and we appeared throughout the world," captures the global force of memetic circulation. People took to the streets demanding a governmental investigation, and proclaiming "Fue el Estado" (It was the state) (fig. 5.3), and "Nos Faltan 43" (We're missing 43). Signs saying "−43" appeared everywhere (fig. 5.4). While these memes circulated online, they dominated the public sphere. It was hard to walk anywhere without seeing them chiseled into the sidewalk, painted on the walls,

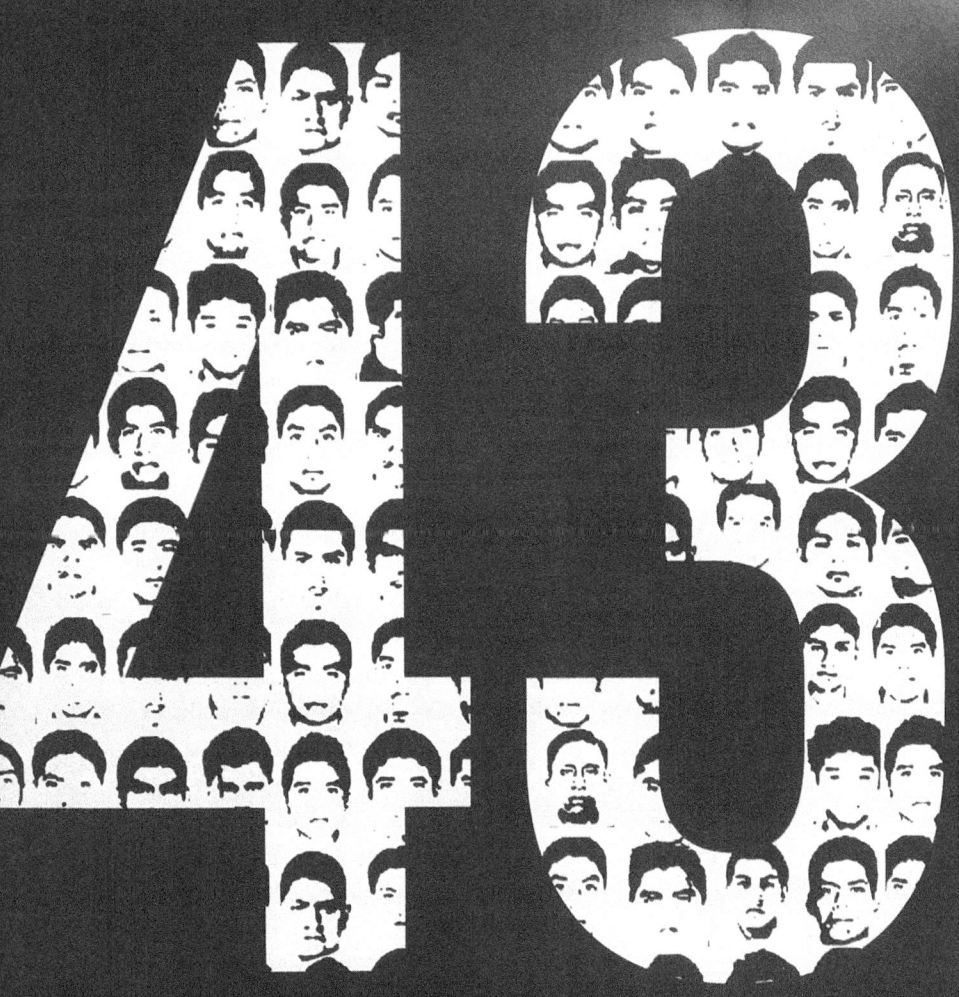

Figure 5.2. "43. Quisieron desaparecernos y aparecimos en todo el mundo." Poster. Date unknown.

and stuck to lampposts and car bumpers. Moving through cities and towns in Mexico on foot or by car, it was fascinating to look down, up, to the sides, and notice where the memes had been placed. What neighborhoods. What kinds of cars. People with and without internet encountered the meme many times a day. Why, I wondered, this outrage over 43 disappeared students when more than 200,000 others have been killed and/or disappeared without repercussion?

Journalists and scholars have offered a number of important reasons. The victims were students, which certainly contributes to the outpouring of repudiation. The Mexican government has long targeted students and teachers, regarding them as unruly and critical. The massacre of some three hundred or so students in Tlatelolco Square, a working-class neighborhood of Mexico City, at the height of the student movement in 1968 was only the most egregious example, and it has carried symbolic weight ever since (see chapter 2). Every October 2, people throughout Mexico honor the students who died in Tlatelolco. "El 2 de octubre no se olvida" (The second of October is not forgotten). The fact that students from Ayotzinapa were tortured, killed, and disappeared on their way to Tlatelolco highlights the continuities of State backed extrajudicial violence against students.

The students, moreover, were poor, indigenous, and mestizo, and thus socially and politically expendable. They came from the La Escuela Normal Rural Raúl Isidro Burgos in the state of Guerrero, which added to their vulnerability. Guerrero has always been the most insurrectionary state in Mexico, and Ayotzinapa is known for its politically activist stance. The *normales* have been in the government's crosshairs for years. It complains that the schools are sapping the economy (although it pays less than two dollars a day per student), that the students do not contribute to the national good (although they become the underpaid teachers for poor, indigenous, rural school children), and, more troubling, that the students are critical of the capitalist-militarized state.[26] In 2011, security forces assassinated two students from Ayotzinapa and tortured twenty-four others.[27] When one hundred students took several buses and set out to Mexico City to commemorate the Tlatelolco massacre, the military and security forces were alerted.

That night in 2014, the narco state responded in full force: a mix of military, police, and federal forces joined with drug cartels to attack the buses. No one understood why at the time. Even in Mexico, the brutality seemed completely out of proportion. The students commandeered buses every year and brought them back without incident. More than a year later, it turned out that the students had inadvertently taken two buses loaded with two

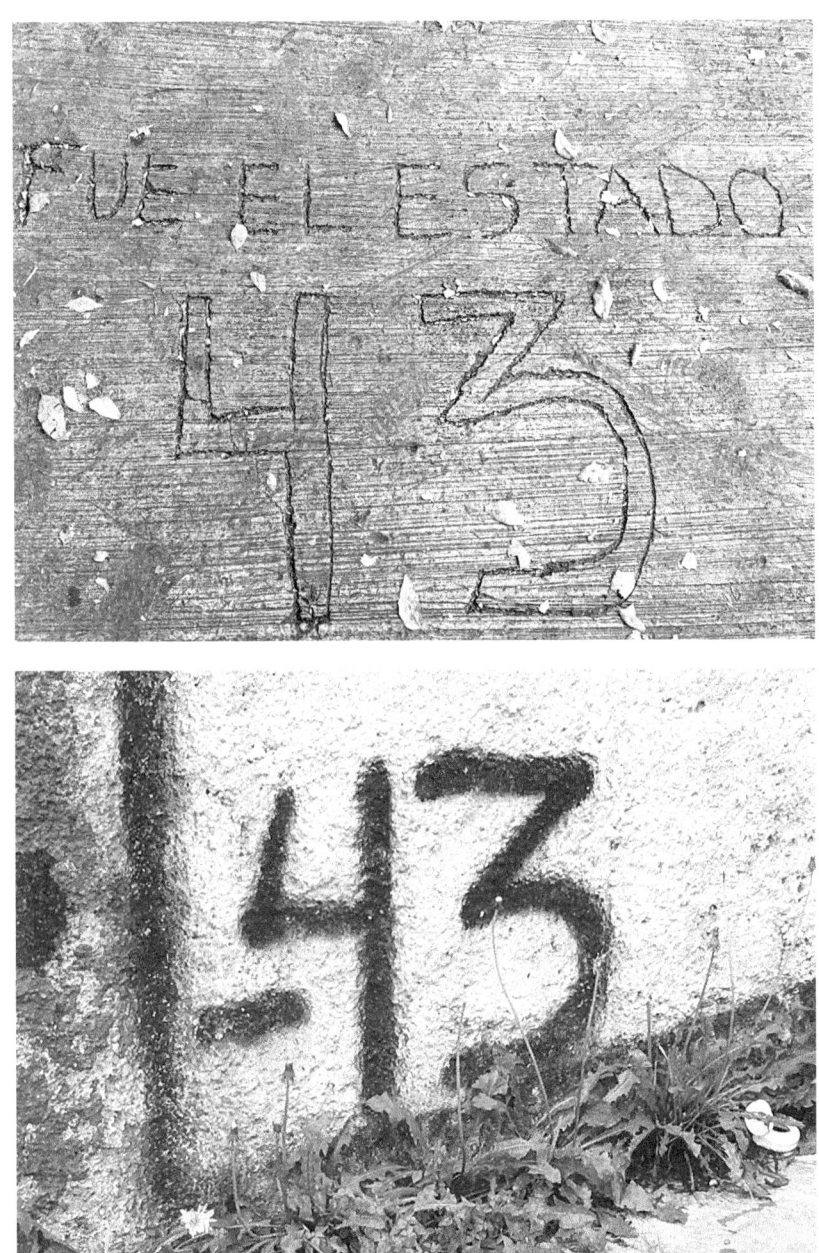

5.3–5.4 "Fue el Estado" and "–43." Date unknown. PHOTOS: DIANA TAYLOR.

million dollars' worth of heroin about to make their weekly journey to Chicago. The drug route needed to be protected.[28] That explained why the mayor, the governor, and the higher-ups in President Enrique Peña Nieto's government knew what was going on in real time.[29] The collusion of government and extrajudicial forces was clearly on display.

Another feature that provoked widespread shock was the viciousness of the assault. Julio Cesar Mondragón, one of the three students killed outright, was found dead and faceless on the street on September 27. Apparently the military had gouged out his eyes, flayed him, and taken photographs, which they posted to Twitter hours before the body was found.[30] The barbaric de-facing of the young student disclosed the dissolution of a social order in which "the responsibility of the 'one for the other,'" as Emmanuel Levinas puts it, can no longer delineate "the limits of the State."[31] Presente as nothing, the absolute form of *ninguneo*, turning a somebody into a nobody, but far worse; turning a somebody into a surplus of terror and barbarity through the desecration of the very idea of the human. Necropolitics, extending the destruction even into the very realms of death. The photographs, meant to intimidate the population, went viral on social media and sparked unbridled outrage. Why? Why the hatred? The dehumanization? What was happening? Where were the other students? Almost immediately the missing became known as the "43." In the context of countless victims, counting functions as an animative; 43, an exact number, enacted resistance. The meme as animative took on symbolic political force in a country that buries brutality in part by burying numbers.

In the years following the tragedy, the enigmas and the public furor have only increased. After flows of misinformation, the government decided to declare the students dead in November 2014 and have done with it. The students had been killed and burned in a garbage dump in Cocula (thirteen miles from Iguala) by a few no-gooders, said Jesús Murillo Karam, Mexico's attorney general. The murderers had confessed, he added. Period. When the press pushed him to explain incongruities—the evidence that the so-called culprits had confessed under torture and that it was physically impossible to burn forty-three bodies in a dumpster overnight—he walked away saying, "Ya me cansé" (I've had enough).[32] Memetically, "Ya Me Cansé" became a rallying cry. Mexicans, too, had had enough, enough of the violence, the corruption, the impunity, the arrogance, and the incompetence. The Argentine forensic anthropologists who started their work in 1986 analyzing the DNA of the disappeared in Argentina were brought in by the Mexican authorities in a show of good faith. However, relations became strained when the team found that, with one exception, the remains in the dump did not match the DNA of the missing students. The matching DNA from the one student, Alexander Mora, bore no links to the putative scene of the crime. The evidence had clearly been tampered with, increasing the families' suffering and the national ire.

Seeking international support, the families and advocates of the 43 began their caravan throughout the U.S. in 2015 to let people know about the cover-up in Mexico. These van or bus trips by family members and advocates have become a crucial part of the rights strategy for migrants in Central America and Mexico who felt that by being presentes, they could bring international attention to their struggles for justice. As families of the 43 prepared for the caravan, former president Vicente Fox publicly told them to "get over it": "It is good that they love their sons so much. It's good that they miss them, and cry so much for them, but now they need to accept reality."[33] But what reality? The false one that the government kept force-feeding the population with doctored proof? They met the mandate to accept and forget with the animative to fight and remember.

In 2015, the Inter-American Commission of Human Rights appointed an interdisciplinary group of independent experts (Grupo Interdisciplinario de Expertos Independientes, or GIEI) to examine the situation.[34] The GIEI arrived and worked closely with the families, government officials, bureaucrats, and all involved with the 43. Their resulting report pointed to the multifaceted deception promulgated by the government.[35] The 43, the GIEI suspected, had been taken to a military base where all or some were incinerated. They asked to search the nearby military base of the Twenty-Seventh Infantry Battalion without success. Their request to continue investigating was officially denied by Mexico, and the group was informed it needed to leave the country. Peña Nieto's government no doubt hesitated to blame itself and its own military forces for its systematic use of extrajuridical violence. Anabel Hernández, a respected journalist for the weekly news magazine *Proceso*, asserted that the army "ordered, orchestrated, and organized" events related to the disappearance of the 43.[36]

Murder might be a straightforward act of brutality, but forced disappearance is a political project. It entails the purposeful mangling of bodies and evidence beyond recognition. Thus it always involves the state. As Mexican theorist Roberto González Villarreal makes clear, "disappearance is not an excess, not an error; it is a specific repressive technology."[37] Disappearance, he continues, "is not an event but a process, an assemblage of actions, omissions, confusions, in which many agents participate."[38] So those shouting "Fue el Estado" were right even if the president did not order the killings, tortures, and disappearances. It was the state, from the president on down, that created the disappeared by allowing all evidence to go missing and by threatening those who searched for facts. Those involved in the functioning of disappearance include social actors from the military and security forces, the executive branch, the judiciary, the technicians who handle evidence, the bureaucrats responsible for filing documents, the compliant members of the media, and on and on. The politics of death, carrying the violence to the desecration of the dead, and permanent states of exception during which people can be tortured, assassinated, vandalized, and disappeared, dominate contemporary Latin American democracies just as they did during the U.S.-backed military dictatorships of the 1970s and '80s.[39] And just as in that period, the Argentine forensic team is back. The Madres de Plaza de Mayo's cries of "¡Presente!" and "¡Vivos se los llevaron, vivos los queremos!" can be heard again today as the mothers, fathers, and family members of the 43 give voice to their trauma, protests, and demands.

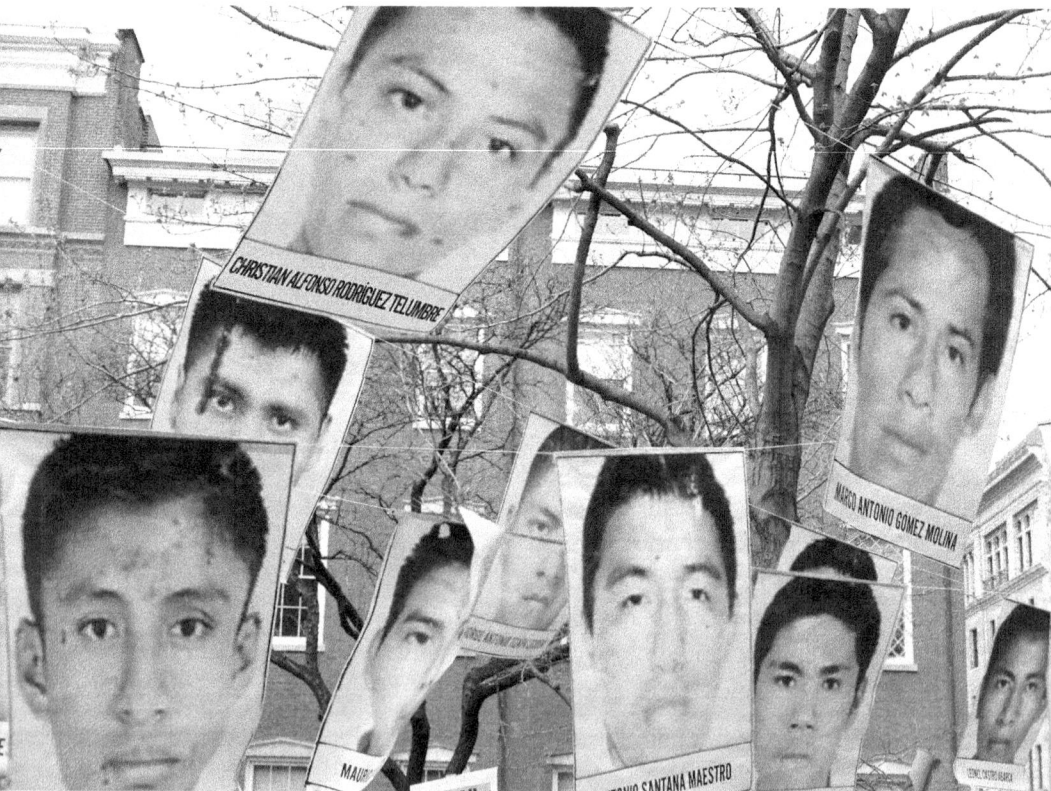

5.5 Photographs of the 43 in Washington Square Park, New York City, April 2015.
PHOTO: DIANA TAYLOR.

When the caravan came to New York in that April 2015, the group held a rally in Washington Square Park the day after meeting the PPT. They strung hundreds of enlarged photographs of the 43 from the trees, filling the park with the presence of those absent (fig. 5.5.).

The space was alive with photographs, cries of "back alive," and calls for justice, producing an affective density and intensity—a memesphere. The parents animated the photos of their missing sons with stories about their dreams and accomplishments. The students were alive, present, resisting even from the space of death. The hundreds of people who attended the rally repeated the forty-three names, one after another, punctuated by the shout, "¡presente!" Those who happened to be walking through the park and joined us shared the palpable sense of sadness and indignation as we followed the families from the park, up the avenues, to the Mexican Consulate to demand answers. Bystanders and even police officers asked what we were protesting. When we told them about the 43, some looked shocked and saddened. Others joined us, carrying signs saying 43. The meme was contagious.

III

How did that meme make its way to New York in 2015? Where did it start, and how did it travel around the world? Given the unrestrained ways memes circulate, tracing them does not always prove a productive endeavor. More than once I reflected on the irony of my physically going from place to place, speaking with people and scouring the walls and sidewalks for traces, seeking photographs in archives, museums, and newspapers, trying to track down an idea, gesture, or symbol that can jump from brain to brain. Rearguard theory, no doubt, staying close to the ground. But every once in a while, I would catch sight of the meme and, from there, learn about the context. Memes can make visible the continuity and circulation of practices that other forms of print and embodied transmission sometimes leave out. The political practice of disappearance, predicated on the notion of cover-up, makes it difficult to identify the crime. Are the people really gone? When can we authoritatively classify them as missing and, beyond that, as disappeared, victims of an intentional political act?

The traumatic meme, circulating since the late 1970s, demands an answer—and provides one. Returning contestation to the public sphere, it displays evidence of governments' criminal attacks on their people, their youth most particularly. While the memes may not carry much specific information, they provide hints that can point to the relationship between the memesphere and historical and political reality. Following this trace, in fact, reveals an enormous amount about political practices. The memes alert us to disappearances that otherwise go unnoticed by all but the loved ones of the disappeared. Registering the appearance of the meme is like catching sight of a large shadow. Is there an airplane overhead? What, we wonder as we look up, disturbs the light?

To the best of my knowledge, the first grieving mothers carrying photos and demanding "back alive" were the Madres in Argentina in 1977, a group of unarmed, middle-aged women wearing white scarves and holding or wearing photographs of their disappeared children; they walked counterclockwise around the Plaza de Mayo demanding information about their whereabouts. These women, nonpolitical actors, came upon the cluster of memes by trial and error. They needed to be noticed as mothers insisting that the government recognize the missing as citizens, thus the photo IDs. The demand, "back alive," reflected their early hope of getting their loved ones out of jail. When that hope faded, "back alive" signaled that they would not accept that their loved ones were dead until the government acknowledged the murders and punished the perpetrators. Only then would they accept closure.

While disappearance as state political strategy did not originate in Argentina, the junta was keen to perfect it.[40] They launched a full-blown campaign to discredit the Madres (the "madwomen of the plaza") and muddle the facts. In answer to the question "Where are they?," official sources came up with all sorts of answers: surely they'd left the country, run off with someone. Vanished. Get over it, they might as well have said.

The Madres' staging countered the junta's vacuous disclaimers with its simplicity, constancy, and determination. The performance they developed came out of the conditions of impossibility imposed by the laws and prohibitions of the dirty war that forbade all sorts of actions: congregating in public, sitting in public for any length of time, protests of all kinds. Walking two by two, carrying and wearing the photo IDs of their children, the Madres evaded the military's prohibitions. As civil society had collapsed, and with it all possible "space of appearance" in which people come "together in the manner of speech and action," the Madres subverted the space of prohibition into a potent site of reappearance and resistance.[41] Gradually, the mothers' role shifted into a performance of a collective, political motherhood, mothers now of all the disappeared. The Madres continue their protest into the present.

However, we cannot call this apparently initial instantiation of a traumatic cluster memetic, as memes are, as I said, "never for the first time," always a repetition.

Informally tracking what I much later came to think of as traumatic memes, I went to Chile in 2003 to meet with the group of Chilean mothers of the disappeared. They have a small organization compared with the Argentinean Madres but have been organized longer, as the Pinochet dictatorship started in 1973 and disappeared a far greater percentage of Chile's population. Pinochet chose not to kill most of his opponents but to disappear, torture, break, and release them, as I show in chapter 7. Releasing the traumatized, ghostly population of survivors, Pinochet thought, would be a message to further terrorize the general public. The Chilean mothers disagreed that the Argentinean Madres were the first to perform the photographs of their children by publicly carrying and wearing them in the streets to make demands for justice.[42] They too had used photo IDs of their children, but displayed together as a group, as the disappeared. While my aim is to explore how and what these traumatic memes make visible, rather than adjudicate claims about where they started, my research shows that the idea of wearing the photographs, taking them out on the street, animating them in order to make a demand was initiated by the Madres de Plaza de Mayo. But, as important to my argument, the protest by the Chilean mothers reveals a different (though deeply interrelated) history of authoritarian necropolitics. Because the great majority of the Chilean victims returned, broken but alive, the 38,254 people tortured and temporally disappeared did not have people protesting in the streets for them, nor were they acknowledged or compensated by the government until the Valech Report came out in 2004. The "disappeared" officially refers to the 1,248 people who remain disappeared. The dissimilarities in the memetic practices make visible these sociopolitical differences between these two movements.

From the southern cone, the traumatic cluster became memetic and jumped to many parts of the world: the Saturday Mothers in Turkey, 1995, the Mourning Mothers and Mothers of Khavaran in Iran that started in 1981, the Committee of Mothers of Disappeared Migrants in Honduras, the Comadres in El Salvador in the late 1970s, and the Tiananmen Mothers in 1989 in China, among many more.[43] Not all enactments are identical—some mothers dress in black, for example, or remain stationary and silent. Each uptake reflects contextual particularities even as it gains in affective impact by virtue of previous iterations. Each, in isolation and in tandem, points to the proliferation of disappearance as explicit state strategy.

Clearly, there are many possible routes through various parts of the world that one could take to explore the replication of the traumatic memes and the specific historical conditions that made them useful, even necessary. My route tracks the meme through Central America during the 1970s and '80s, when mothers' movements demanded information about their disappeared in situations that shared many historical similarities.[44]

Walking through the Museo de la Palabra y la Imagen in San Salvador, I saw the photograph (fig. 5.6). Who were these women? I asked Carlos Henriquez Consalvi, director of the museum and former revolutionary leader (alias Santiago) who led "Radio Venceremos," which organized and encouraged the resistance to the military during the civil war in El Salvador during the 1980s.[45] He pointed me in the direction of the Comrades.

The Comadres, I found out, came into existence informally in El Salvador after the 1975 military massacre of students from the National University

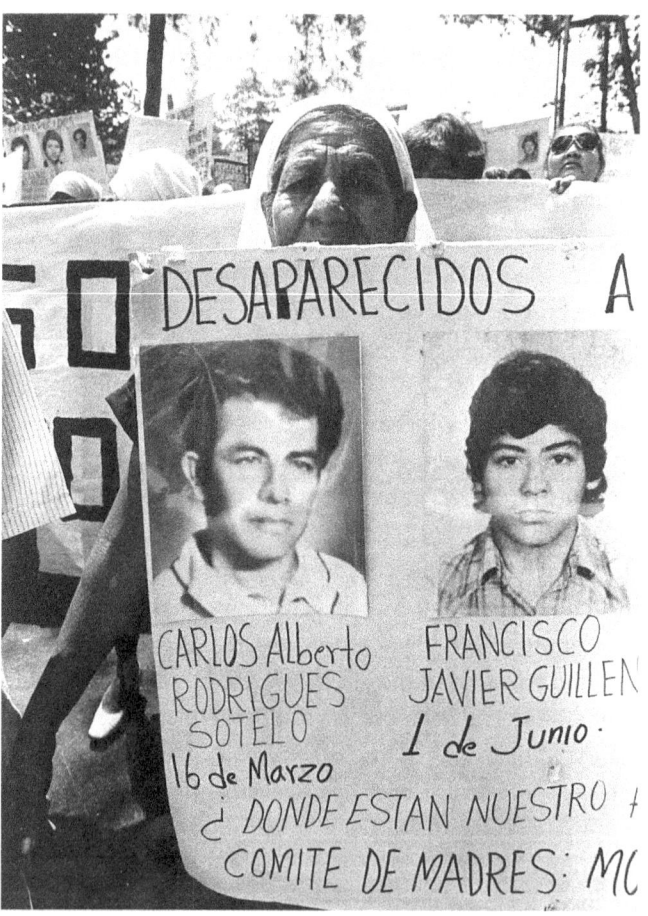

5.6 Marcha de madres de presos politicos y desaparecidos (March of Mothers of Political Prisoners and the Disappeared). Date unknown. San Salvador. COURTESY COLECCIÓN MUSEO DE LA PALABRA Y LA IMAGEN.

who, like the students in Tlatelolco, were protesting for better conditions.[46] Women began looking for their missing children, much as the Argentinean Madres did, and started wearing black initially to identify themselves to each other and the world. Their movement predates the Madres by two years, but they formalized their organization and changed their strategies toward the end of the 1970s and early 1980s, the period when the traumatic meme jumped from the southern cone to Central America and Mexico. Mothers who had lost children during the U.S.-backed wars in Central America started using the white head scarves, waving the photographs of their disappeared, and shouting their demands (fig. 5.7).[47]

Who carried the memes? Did they know of the Argentinean Madres? One older Madre in El Salvador told me that the Argentinean Madres visited the country in the 1990s at the invitation of Catholic priest Jon de Cortina, who founded Pro-búsqueda (Pro-search) in 1994 to find the children disappeared during their civil war, many of them given up in illegal adoption.

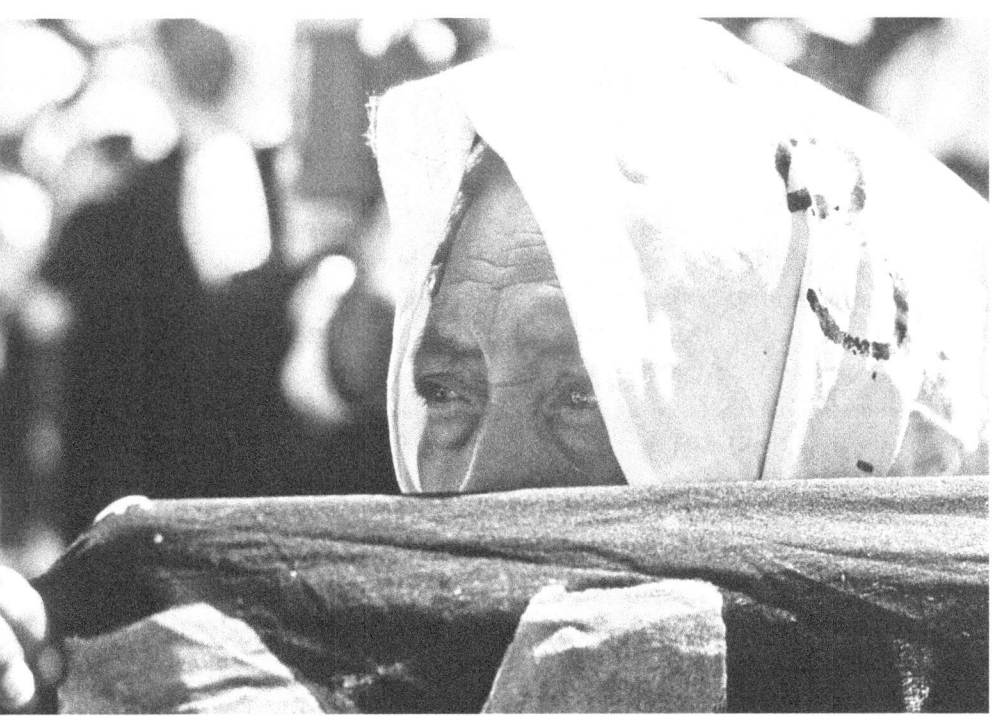

5.7 Madre de desaparecido en marcha en San Salvador (Mother of a Disappeared Person in the March in San Salvador), 1987. PHOTO: GIO PALAZZO. COURTESY COLECCIÓN MUSEO DE LA PALABRA Y LA IMAGEN.

But the photographs of the El Salvadorian women with the white scarves told of earlier transmissions. How had that happened? I spoke with people who suggested that I speak to other people—fittingly rearguard and slow, I thought, walking and talking with others. A search through archives in El Salvador did not turn up any local press photographs of the Argentine Madres. I spoke with others who suggested the descriptions might have circulated by word of mouth or by radio, something harder to track. For there they were with the photos, the women in white scarves, shouting for the return of their disappeared.

In the late 1970s, the traumatic memes leaped to Mexico. This was important because it showed that disappearances cannot be limited to the U.S.-backed dictatorships and wars that have tormented Latin America. These practices persist under so-called democratic governments such as Mexico's.

One of the most important social movements that made evident the routine practice of torture, disappearance, and extrajudicial killings in Mexico during the late 1970s—and that took up the traumatic memes—was that of the Doñas of Comité ¡Eureka! The Doñas lost their children to state terrorism in Mexico in the 1970s and '80s. They, too, held photographs of their missing children while calling for their safe return. Comité ¡Eureka! was started by Rosario Ibarra de Piedra in 1977 after years of looking for her son Jesús, a student who was disappeared in 1974 for his activity in the Liga Comunista 23 de Septiembre. The Greek word "eureka" means *ya encontré* or "I have found it," him, or her. It denotes not just finding the desired thing, but also a process, a heuristic, a way of life and exploration. This is what the search for the disappeared became for the Doñas.

Here too the search entailed walking and talking. Paula Monaco Felipe, a journalist friend in Mexico who accompanied the families of the 43 and published a book on Ayotzinapa, introduced me to Sara Hernández, the wife of Rafael Ramírez Duarte, disappeared in 1977. Hernández has kept a record of ¡Eureka!'s news clippings, posters, and other materials in her apartment. While she did not represent her husband in the demonstrations—that role was reserved for his mother, Della Duarte viuda de Ramírez, in part because ¡Eureka!, like the Argentinian Madres, saw the affective advantage of defining themselves as a mother's movement—she followed ¡Eureka! closely and kept their files.

Sara's binders of materials offer evidence of the transfer of the traumatic meme as exiles from the Argentine and Chilean dictatorships were granted asylum in Mexico in the late 1970s. Comité ¡Eureka! learned of the Madres' strategies through them. The Doñas deliberately and strategically placed their disappeared within the sad trajectory of disappearances in Latin American dictatorships. They blasted the government for its hypocrisy in granting asylum to exiles of state terror while exercising terror tactics on its own population: "¡No Sólo en Argentina y en Chile Hay Desaparecidos Políticos! ¡En Mexico Hay Cientos También!" (The disappeared are not only in Argentina and Chile! In Mexico we have hundreds too!) [48]

While the Doñas started animating the photographs of their disappeared, their practice reveals an intriguing variation on the traumatic memes. They wore the photos not in the plain plastic sheaths used by other Madres but rather framed them as relics enshrined in pearls and velvet around their necks. This handmade and religious dimension underlines the religious homogeneity among the Doñas. Madres in Argentina included many Jewish mothers in their organizations, as the military specifically targeted Jews. The use of the photograph identifies the political demand—mother searching for missing child—yet its style captures some of the specific characteristics of the group.

Today, the traumatic memes appear in Guatemala, Peru, Bolivia— everywhere that state terrorism disappears its opponents. Currently, the Madres organizations of Central America use the photos and chants to make their demands in their search for their children who have gone missing. They have joined the mass migration of young people toward the U.S., pushed by a variety of hemispheric factors involving corrupt governments in the grip of multinational mining and agro corporations and by the violence of the drug trade.

One Salvadorian mothers' group, COFAMIDE (Comité de Familiares de Migrantes Fallecidos y Desaparecidos de El Salvador [Committee for Families of Migrants, the Dead and Disappeared of El Salvador]) consciously uses the traumatic memes they have seen in videos of the Argentinean Madres.[49] Their use of the photographs and slogans, however, has an added dimension. The migrants who leave often change their names and nationalities to avoid deportation once they cross into Mexico—so the photo ID is key not just in presenting the evidence of loss (as it is now with the Argentinean Madres) but in identifying their loved ones. And because their children left as migrants, they have changed the slogan "Vivos se los llevaron" to "Vivos se fueron, vivos los queremos" (they left alive, we want them back alive).

The crimes against migrants also qualify as disappearances, as the Madres cogently explain. They, too, enter the Kafkaesque world of systemic dissimulation and cover-up. Official forces deny requests for information and refuse to carry out investigations. If coffins are returned to families, as sometimes happens, they come with instructions not to open them. Families do open the coffins, of course, to make sure their loved one is inside. In coffins coming from Mexico, they tell me, they have found body parts, or bodies of the wrong gender. One rights advocate told me they have seen coffins filled with dead animals or stones.[50] In short, the various governments along the route, including the U.S., actively participate in obfuscating the situation and destroying the evidence.

Mothers' movements throughout the northern triangle have organized caravans to find their missing, who, they hope, are somewhere in Mexico. Marta Sánchez started the Movimiento de Migrantes Mesoamericanos to help women who were already embarked on the search.

The crime of disappearance, she told me when I joined the Central American mothers recently, is not just organized, it's officially authorized.[51] The government is fully involved in it. While the participants were not familiar with the traumatic memes, Sánchez was, and she suggested that they organize as mothers, sensing the symbolic power of situating the demand for justice within a recognizable framework. Unlike the Madres in Argentina, these women do not employ the language of motherhood to physically protect themselves. But mothers throughout patriarchal Latin America still enjoy a special status not available to other women. The Central American Madres, then, started wearing the photographs of their children and chanting the well-known slogans (fig. 5.8). When their caravan arrived in San Cristóbal de las Casas in the southernmost state of Mexico on November 16, 2016, where a commission of international observers I participated in received them, they were greeted by hundreds of supporters.[52]

As they walked through the throng, carrying and wearing the photo IDs and chanting "Vivos los queremos," people joined in the chants. Some of their children have in fact been found alive—some in jails, in brothels, or held captive—ashamed or unable to contact their families. Most of the more than 100,000 disappeared, however, will never be found. Their remains lie unidentified in one of many mass graves. The Madres continue their search. "Buscamos la vida en caminos de muerte" (We look for life on the roads of death), they say. For the past twelve years, they have embarked on exhausting caravans through Mexico, stopping, asking, showing the photographs, and staging public protests. Walking for them too is a heuristic methodology, a way of finding the truth about their loved ones. The Central American Madres have become a powerful force for human rights in the area and beyond. Sánchez told me that their movement has sparked similar ones among migrant families in Africa—a second generation of memetic transfer that

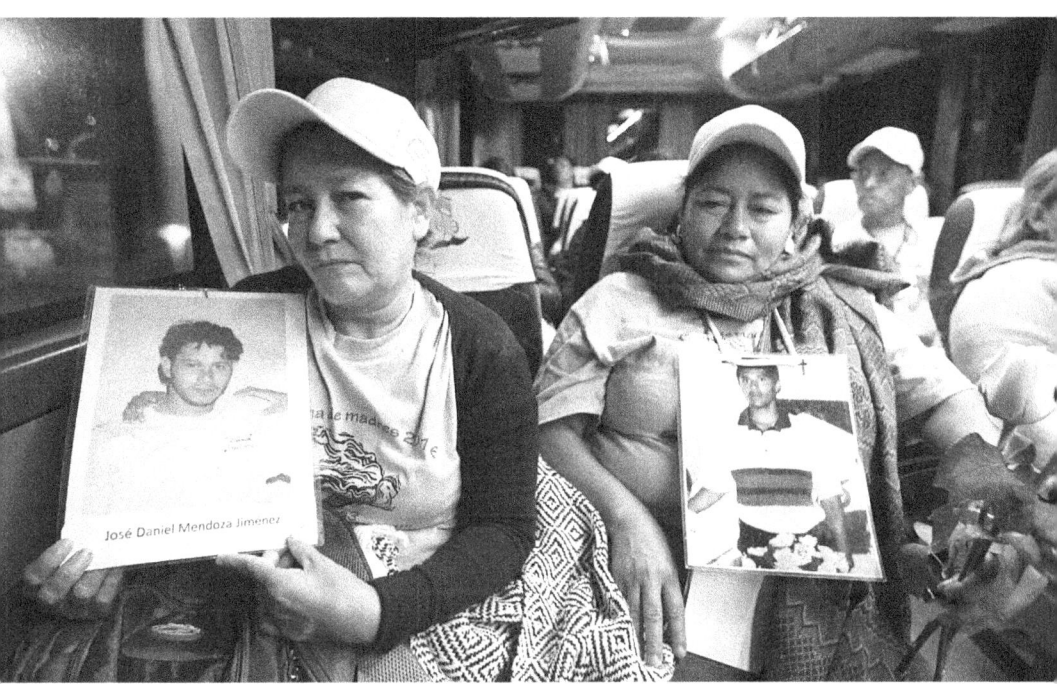

5.8 Central American Madres on the caravan, 2016. PHOTO: RAY MARMOLEJO LE
GAREC.

points to different heinous social and political conditions. Sánchez carried
out an international summit of mothers' movements for 2018, a worldwide
enactment of protest characterized by these traumatic memes.[53]

So when the families of the Ayotzinapa students wanted to make their
search and demands internationally visible, it is not surprising that they, too,
turned to the traumatic memes, even if they had never heard of the Madres
or the Doñas. As early as October 4, 2014, they adopted the language ("Vivos
se los llevaron") and visual strategies (the enlarged ID photograph) made
famous by earlier mothers.[54] Although the parents did not know of these
memetic strategies, their children's schoolmates from Ayotzinapa were po-
liticized and likely aware of them. As human rights advocates joined them,
they drew from their repertoire of consignas (slogans) and images associated with Comité ¡Eureka!, the Central American Madres, and Argentina's
Madres. The memes made visible not just the trajectory of necropolitics but
also a strong trajectory of necroresistance.

When the caravans traveled through the United States, with family members performing the photographs and "back alive," many onlookers knew

it was about loss and disappearance, though many did not know how they knew. The replication and transformation of the memes underlined both the disappearances and the resistance. It seems impossible now to imagine the one without the other.

IV

What can the mothers' demands for bringing them "back alive," the ¡presentes!, and −43 with the display of photos and images do against the processes of disappearance as a political strategy? Traumatic memes, having gone global, light up the map. They instantly mark the continuities of criminal practices and performed resistance across space and time. We who become witnesses can observe, investigate, hear testimony, and make our own political demands.

Traumatic memes open the space of appearance up to question. What kind of people can claim visibility and recognition in that interaction? What happens to those viewed as "what" rather than "who," those without access to the "revelatory quality of speech" that Hannah Arendt sees as fundamental for "human togetherness" and appearance?[55] If the "space of appearance" is forged by the presence of people interacting and speaking to each other, then silencing and forced absence creates the space of disappearance, the nullification of life itself, the collapse of political and discursive space.

The disappeared lie scattered in the desert or at the bottom of the ocean or in mass graves. As those responsible obfuscate, we might follow geographer-artist Trevor Paglen's lead in linking political to spatial practice to consider the river bottom and the mass graves as the necessary extension of the state.[56] Everything that government programs try to hide turns up somewhere. The act produces material effect. Conversely, the mass grave or the protest points to the act. The shadow signals the existence of the plane.

Those responsible for state terrorism continue to cover their tracks. Nobody knows for sure where the disappeared are. "¿A dónde van los que se van?" (Where do they go, those who go?) asks Argentinian singer-composer Liliana Felipe in her song by that name, dedicated to her disappeared sister. The erasure of space for the disappeared, she says, threatens the space of political response and grief. When people disappear, she told me, "You don't have a place to put your grief."[57]

Traumatic memes also powerfully transmit the continuities among the disappeared themselves—young protesters, unruly students, migrants, or the poor. The particularities might change—victims used to be called subversives in an ideology-infused regime; now they're *desechables* (throwaways), disposable in today's global capitalism that renders many lives precarious. During the dictatorships, the military kept records of their victims. Nobody counts today's dead and disappeared. Truth commissions throughout the Americas examined the crimes against humanity committed by the armed forces. They all declared, "Never again!" But who, besides the symbolic PPT, will bring up these so-called democratic governments on charges? Nonetheless, the photographs of the young faces, the −43s, and the women's chants provide evidence of ongoing criminal, state-supported violence.

What's particularly powerful about memes in the transmission of memory and political contestation is that they can free themselves from space (memorials and monuments—and the authorization and finances that represents), from bodies (the physical limits of the mothers, for example), and replicate throughout public space—online and off. People with and without internet encountered the memes many times a day. The mothers' bodies had given the first impetus to the traumatic memeplexes and memes, such as

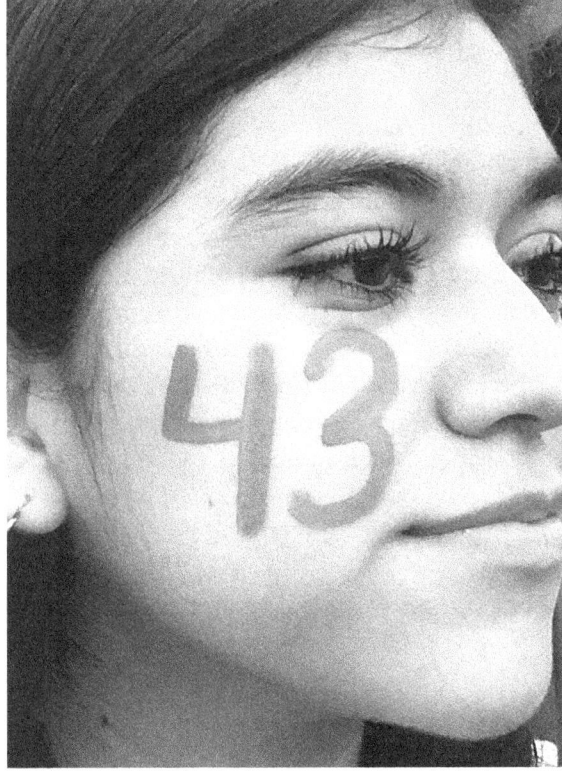

5.9 Embodied memes.
PHOTO: DIANA TAYLOR.

"43," which circulated widely and then were picked up again by other bodies, those with no personal ties to the victims. Now the 43 belonged to everyone who struggles for human rights and social justice in Mexico.

The mothers' movements are affective, contagious, as well as communicative. Their performance of grief and outrage delivers a strong emotional message. How do we make sense of their loss? Traumatic memes reappear, always asking the same question, always receiving the same official answer: silence. "It's hard to give an answer," says Sister Valdette Willeman, from the Center for Returned Migrants in San Pedro Sula, Honduras, where she works with deported migrants and with the families of those who continue to search for their loved ones. With disappearance, she says, "There is no answer."[58]

The social movements by mothers of the disappeared now span forty years. The Madres de Plaza de Mayo remind us that protest is a durational performance. Their resistance affirms the force of bonds that unite—love, care, loyalty, perseverance. Although they were originally dismissed as the crazy women of the plaza, their persistence contributed directly to the first Kirschner government bringing the perpetrators to trial. Protest, the Madres show, can work. The symbolic, and at times actual, power of the "powerless" inspires others to keep demonstrating, even though the odds against them seem overwhelming.

The Madres' performance, like the enactments of grief and resistance, is far from over. It offers no closure. Like the Madres, who show up decade after decade to make their demands, the memes repeat. They come back again and again to the now and always of criminal practice. Part of the reiteration comes from the fact that the crimes have not been acknowledged or adjudicated either by the state or by civil society. Part of the memetic repeat stems from the traumatic nature of the injury. For the Madres and Doñas and Comadres throughout the Americas (and beyond), the claim and the pain become transmittable, bearable, and politically efficacious through the ever-present, increasingly ubiquitous, traumatic memes.

SIX

We Have Always Been Queer

To María Elena Martínez,
the primogenita *of this work on Juana la Larga,*
who did not live to see the outcome

The Sting

In June 2014, during the Hemispheric Institute's Encuentro (eight-day con-ference/performance event) in Montreal, a very queer dispute erupted in the assembly of some eight hundred participants. A "queer" dispute because almost everyone on all sides of the clash self-identified as queer and trans and because it questioned the meaning, scope, temporality, and politics of the terms as well. The dispute also questioned the ability of communities of self-identified WE's to walk and talk together across divides. Who are we? What do we do, study, practice, care about? The Hemispheric Institute came into being to open spaces of exchange, of mutual appearance and recogni-tion, for artists, scholars, and activists in the Americas who share struggles for social justice. We-making too, the founding aspiration behind Hemi and this book, seemed a failed performance.

Jesusa Rodríguez and her Argentine wife/artistic partner, Liliana Felipe, two of Mexico's most radical performance artists and activists, had presented a play, *Juana la Larga* (Long Juana), developed from archival documents they encountered through their conversations with queer Mexican historian María Elena Martínez. Juana Aguilar, an eighteenth-century intersex per-son from Central America, was accused by the Inquisition of committing "abominable sins" (sodomy) with men and women.[1] This was their first per-formance piece, they said, that directly addressed the issues of sexuality.[2]

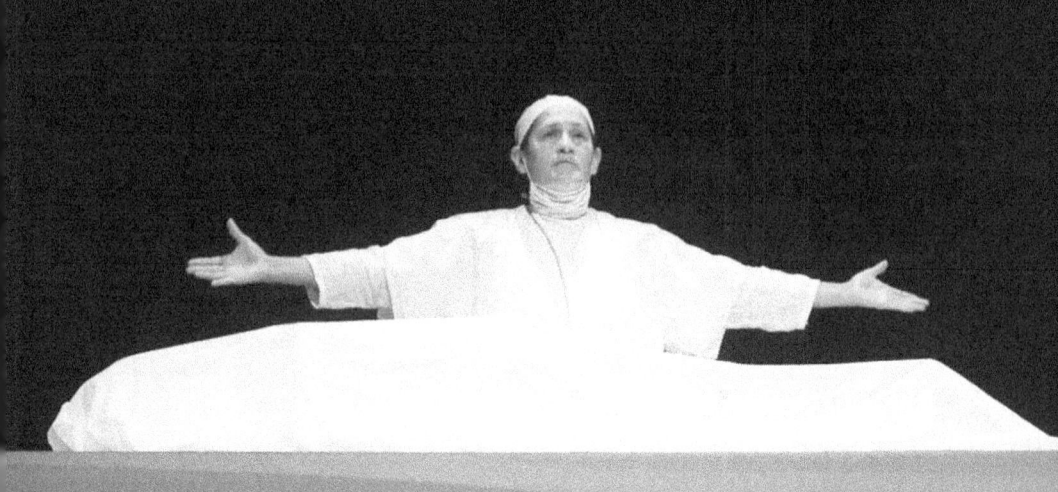

The body, after all, is all we have.

6.1 Jesusa Rodríguez in *Juana la Larga*, Hemispheric Institute Encuentro, Montreal, 2014.
PHOTO: JULIO PANTOJA.

The reaction to some elements in the performance threatened to derail the entire Encuentro. The Encuentro, as trans theorist Jack Halberstam noted, "turned, overnight, from a wildly imaginative series of performances, talks, and theatre productions into a somber event."[3]

First, the way-back story.

According to the archival documents Martínez showed Rodríguez and Felipe, the Royal Protomedicato—the official authority in medical matters—asked Narciso Esparragosa y Gallardo, a well-respected surgeon, to examine Juana Aguilar's sexual organs and determine whether "she" could have committed the crimes of sodomy attributed to "her." The report written by Esparragosa performs a complicated conjuring into present/e of Aguilar. It notes that "she" dressed as a female and used the female pronoun in referring to "her," as will I for lack of a more appropriate pronoun, given the historical context, though always in quotations. Esparragosa explored Aguilar's body repeatedly and minutely, concluding that Aguilar was not a "hermaphrodite" as the foolish midwives and old-fashioned doctors who had examined "her" previously had affirmed. Hermaphrodites, supposedly "una idéntica persona con dos sexos" (one self-same person with two sexes), don't exist.[4] They're mythical, he went on to say, "chimeric," made up as "monsters of nature." Esparragosa, proud of being an eminent, learned, and enlightened figure of the new age at the dawn of the nineteenth century, sets out to unmask the phantom through his use of observation and reasoning.[5] He explains his method: he will first meticulously describe the "natural" appearance of female genitalia to later demonstrate all the ways in which Aguilar deviates from the norm.[6] He pays special attention to the clitoris, and notes that especially large ones have been observed previously, especially among women from Egypt and other "oriental" countries. Clitoridectomies make those women "apt for marriage."[7] While he grants that the clitoris enhances sexual pleasure in women, he condemns the "reprehensible abuse that some women have committed of satiating their lasciviousness, defrauding that which nature has given to men."[8] The carefully examined anatomical observations turn immediately into a racist, misogynist, and violent discourse and unexamined worldview.

During the physical exam of Aguilar, Esparragosa identifies features (two glands the size of cocoa beans and menstruation) associated with one or the other gender. He concludes that Aguilar, "far from uniting two sexes," has neither: not a hermaphrodite, not a man, not a woman, but "sexually neutral . . . like certain bees." "Rare phenomena!" he asserts repeatedly. Not the monster of nature, like the hermaphrodite, Aguilar becomes monstrous in medical terms. "She" is so deviant, so singular and rare as to escape all possible classification. A "trick of nature," perhaps, like the chimera and mythological creatures he so handily dismissed.[9] How, then, to label or classify Juana la Larga, who is apparently all lack? Admitting that he cannot, he continues to assign Aguilar the female pronoun, inadvertently distinguishing a volitional, social, and sexual identity from an anatomical one. "She" enters the literature as a "truly unhappy person," a submissive mute creature with "misplaced and confused organs."[10] Esparragosa enters the literature as a loquacious expert, legitimating, as Martha Few writes, "medicine's authority, and his own as a medical practitioner, to judge cases of sexual ambiguity."[11]

Juana may have been declared "sexually neutral, like certain bees," but the sting kept stinging. Medical, legal, social, sexual, and even psychological identity were all in play in this investigation, mutually constructed through and against a silent, captive person. Aguilar's fate literally comes down to the clitoris. After rubbing Aguilar's clitoris repeatedly without being able to produce an erection, Esparragosa determines that "she" is physically incapable of having committed the crime of sodomy attributed to her. At worst, she might have engaged in "obscene confriction that usually happens between two women" but that cannot amount to much as it lacks "seminal pollution."[12] Juana la Larga's case, therefore, "falls outside everything that the laws have sanctioned in this matter."[13] Given her anatomy, he argued, she should not be found guilty of the acts brought to the Inquisition. Here we have an early version of what today the law knows as the "impossibility defense . . . a criminal defense occasionally used when a defendant is accused of a criminal attempt that failed only because the crime was factually or legally impossible to commit."[14] To prove his findings, Esparragosa cited leading European authorities on the topic and commissioned a local artist to draw Aguilar's genitals from two different perspectives and made copies, available upon request. He submitted his report and, for good measure, published it in the *Gazeta*, Guatemala's official daily.

The documentation shows that Juana Aguilar endured at least ten years of public shaming. "She" was turned into the object of legal charges, medical probes, debates, and other physical violations such as having "her" genitals drawn and story circulated through the news.[15] In fact, "she" is nothing more than "her" genitals, denied a voice and perspective in all the proceedings. "She," as a person, is unmade.

Rodríguez and Felipe were drawn to the case for several reasons. As María Elena Martínez recounts, Rodríguez loved "the theatricality of the name . . . at once concrete and derogatory."[16] They empathized with the sting of discrimination, injury, and violence Aguilar experienced at the hands of the church, the law, the press, and the medical authorities. Both women relished poking fun at the Catholic Church and the Inquisition and took advantage of any opportunity to ridicule those men who condemn or disparage same-sex pleasure.[17] Octavio Paz suffered a similar fate in their play about Sor Juana Inés de la Cruz.[18] Gradually, Rodríguez became interested in Esparragosa, in part because her father was a thoracic surgeon up to date with Western practices. She was struck, Martínez notes, by "Esparragosa's reading of Aguilar's body through European lenses and a Western medicine that labelled her as strange and monstrous to exert its authority over her . . . as well as his misogyny, homophobia, and paternalism."[19] As important, Rodríguez and Felipe urgently wanted to call attention to the escalation of violence against cis and trans women—"women of all sexes," as they put it. Sixty-four thousand women and girls are killed in the world every year, one every three hours in Mexico alone.[20]

The performance takes place on a stage with a mortuary table. An inert body lies covered by a shroud. In the dark, a nun hand puppet screams out from between the dark curtains that cover the back of the stage: "Get out of here immediately, children of concupiscence! Get your sinning fannies out of those chairs and save your souls from ruin! The third bell hasn't sounded yet. You still have time. Leave before it's too late!!" The third bell rings. Oops. Too late.[21]

Rodríguez, dressed as a physician, stands over the body, later to be revealed as Juana. She uses the anatomical dummy to reflect comically on a series of issues ranging from violence against women to homophobia to colonialism through a string of cabaret-style numbers punctuated with songs played and performed by Felipe, a major musician in her own right. From the opening line, "the highest secrets of life are written in the body," they raise expectations only to shatter them. In a grandiloquent voice Rodríguez proclaims, "Practically all societies, past and present, have asked themselves: what is man's place in the cosmos?" Majestic piano notes. Regular voice: "Well, today we won't talk about that." Laughter. Pause. "Today, we'll talk about the place of woman." Every line sets up a punch line.

The performance was humorous, as almost all of Rodríguez and Felipe's work is. Less a play than a cabaret piece, it is a collage of skits and songs. Though usually hilarious, the impersonations at times push, even violate, the boundaries of acceptable taste. Gendered and sexual violence, for starters, is not usually considered a laughing matter. They make fun of Spaniards, Argentines, Barbie from the U.S., the Canadian immigration service, and everyone else, including lesbians and themselves. They use accents and facial expressions as they rant and rave against all manifestations of colonial and authoritarian power: "Coño!" (a very common expletive meaning cunt) Felipe repeatedly exclaims as a macho Argentinean character.

The use of caricature, songs, vaudevillian gags, oversimplifications, and double entendres to tell a very complex history of conquest, slavery, misogyny, homophobia, and violence against women draws the audience into a rhythm of push and pull. In one duet, Rodríguez and Felipe perform a synchronized dance of the clitoris, "the only organ in the human body designed only for pleasure." In another, they wrestle with the colonizing and disciplinary puppet nun with the Castilian accent who derides them for not being funny: "So old fashioned! Man, what an ugly way to grow old. You should know when to retire." They play constantly as they veer in and out of acts and words that point to different kinds of violence. In their "master class in anatomy," they make jokes about definitions, chromosomes, orgasms, and other supposed markers of gender and sexual identity. They call in experts to elucidate the conundrums: Dr. Helen O'Connell, Australian urologist and "mother of the clitoris," and Dr. Katsuhiko Hayashi of Japan. Rodríguez did a particularly offensive rendition of yellow face to depict the Japanese doctor. "Why do that?" I asked Rodríguez later. She told me she developed the facial expression, or facial mask as I call it,[22] to impersonate former president Gustavo Díaz Ordaz, the man responsible for the massacre of the students back in 1968. He had a famous overbite, the butt of many jokes in Mexico, and it seemed a shame not to use it, she thought. She considered it funny, not racist. Part of the blind spot stems from Mexico's ideology of *mestizaje* that claims to supersede race itself—how can there be racism if we're all mestizos?[23] Humor, in fact, has long been used to reproduce and naturalize "racialized systems of domination,"[24] something that those of us from Mexico usually come to learn and unlearn the hard way. Rodríguez and Felipe considered it simply part of their laughing at everything and everyone to make their point, and the sting is sharp—violence against women continues unabated across all arenas: political, domestic, medical, archival, and so on.

Then, twenty-two minutes into the performance, Narciso Esparragosa y Gallardo comes onstage, a bespectacled Rodríguez in a wig and muttonchop whiskers dressed in an embroidered red velvet overcoat, lace ruffled shirt, breeches, white silk stockings, and low-heeled shoes with buckles (fig. 6.2). S/he begins to deliver an abbreviated version of the report. Her/his Castilian accent and tone is slightly nasal; s/he extends grand words slowly, caressing every syllable in a deliciously pedantic drawl. His first name, Narciso, fits him perfectly. S/he struts about the stage in a self-admiring mode, massaging the words in her/his mouth. "Seminal pollution" sounds like a delicate perfume or fine wine. Rodríguez clearly enjoys the skit and makes fun of herself as she forgets her lines and has to peek at the subtitles projected on the examination table downstage center to catch up. She even asks the person running the translation slides to back up a little. Humor breaks all bounds. On the table behind Esparragosa, the anatomical dummy of Juana is now upright, silent, obedient. Plastic casts of the male and female organs stand on the table beside it. The doctor points to and glances at the female organs, at times notably mystified, while he pronounces his findings: Juana is not male or female and therefore has no sex at all ("se es nada"). Juana la Larga is therefore "nothing."

The performance winds down with a cabaret riff on ongoing colonization and imposition of Western worldviews, starring more puppets (fig. 6.3). Covering the dissection table and the anatomical body with a map of America, North and South, Rodríguez declares that First Nations peoples were put on the dissecting table by accident. "What do you mean, by 'accident'?" Felipe asks sharply. "I mean, by Occident," Rodríguez corrects herself. The

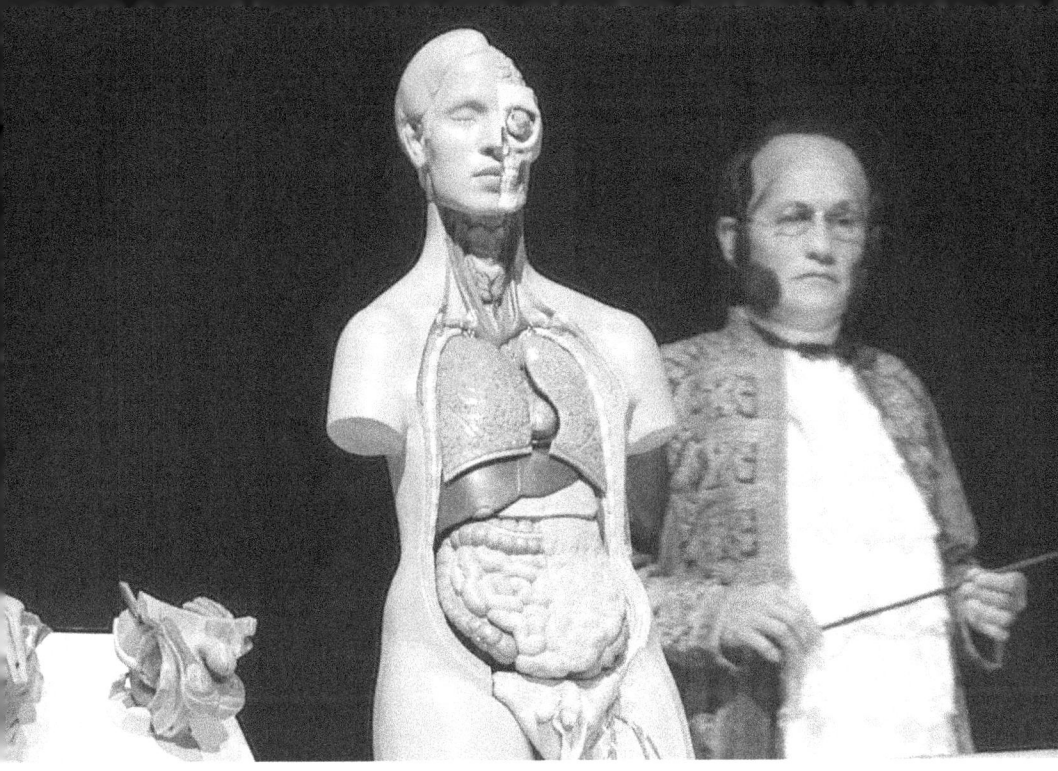

6.2 Jesusa Rodríguez as Narciso Esparragosa y Gallardo in *Juana la Larga*, Hemispheric Institute Encuentro, Montreal, 2014. PHOTO: JULIO PANTOJA.

Conquistador puppet complains that Mexicans are so ungrateful—Spain "brought them civilization and the one true god, Coño!, and they're still complaining." The Barbie claims the whole continent for the U.S., the only "Americans," and people better get used to it. The Conquistador and Barbie compete for how many "fucking Indians" they've been able to destroy—the former fourteen million dead in eighteen years, the latter countless millions through pesticides, GMOs, exploitation, and environmental devastation. Canadian mining is not exempt from critique. A small army of tiny Zapatista female finger puppets and figures take over the American continent and perform different version of hemispheric futurity. Women, daughters of daughters of daughters, stand on the four corners of the earth, defending life and the environment. "Women of all sexes."

The performance ends to enthusiastic applause and a standing ovation.

To return to Juana's story, Rodríguez and Felipe took liberties with Esparragosa's findings that categorized Juana as gender "neutral" (as opposed to "nothing"). The results regarding the Inquisition would have been the same.[25] We could go into detail here, as María Elena Martínez does in her essay, and as Felipe alludes to in one of her skits, about the violence of Western

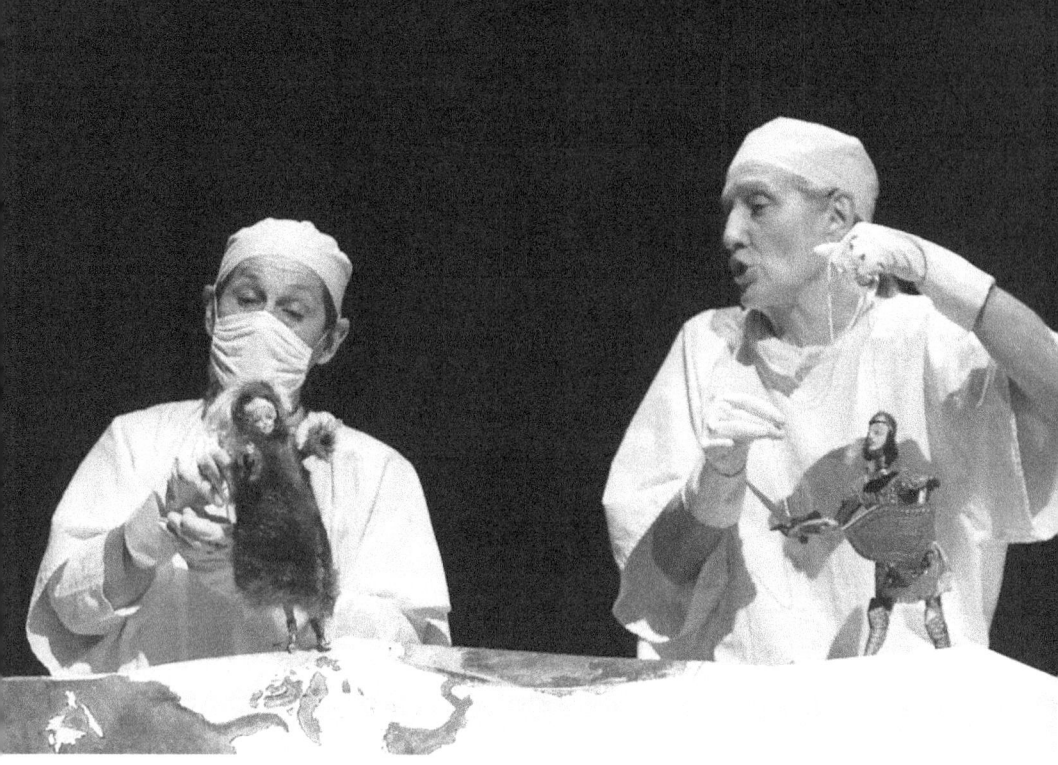

6.3 Jesusa Rodríguez and Liliana Felipe in *Juana la Larga*, Hemispheric Institute Encuentro, Montreal, 2014. PHOTO: JULIO PANTOJA.

classification systems and taxonomies, the brutal and inhumanizing ways that medicine has labeled and treated nonnormative subjects, not to mention the merciless scrutinizing powers of the Inquisition.

Rodríguez's "nothing" also stems from another genealogy—Mexico's *ninguneo*. Octavio Paz, Mexico's Nobel laureate, defines ninguneo as the "operation that consists of making Somebody a Nobody. Nothingness becomes individualized, it becomes body and eyes, it becomes Nobody." As easy as it might seem to align Aguilar's sexual "deficit" with a Freudian notion of the phallus or a Lacanian theory of lack, ningunear is not a psychoanalytic paradigm but rather a radically misogynist and racist act of ontological obliteration. Paz recounts, "I remember one afternoon I heard a noise in the room next door and I called out 'Who is there?' The voice of the domestic servant who had newly arrived from her village responded: It's nobody, Sir, just me."[26] The genealogy of producing "absence" also dates far back—at least back to the conquest. Domingo Sarmiento, an Argentine school teacher, intellectual, writer, and political activist who became president of Argentina (1868–74) tellingly described Argentina in *Facundo*, his masterpiece, as empty, desolate, completely without human habitation, nobody there but some Indians, "salvajes" (savages).[27]

While the designation "neutral" might have saved Aguilar's life, the reason for the shift to "nothing" in the performance, I believe, is far more existential and political, suggesting that women and nonnormative subjects have been treated as nonhumans in Mexico, the rest of Latin America, and beyond for a very long time. Esparragosa continues his lecture while Juana, as silent dummy, remains positioned on the table, the object of conversation. It's as if "she" were not there, reduced to an innate oddity. A puppet. A placeholder for the human. The age-old power relations seem very clear. The coming into being of women not as presence but as phantasmagoric, lingering absence has a long history. Paz sums it up: Mexican national culture considers women to be "dark, secret, and passive beings."[28] "Woman" is not included in this version of Mexicanness. In fact, because of her, "we" Mexicans are all "hijos de la chingada," sons of La Malinche, *La chingada* (the fucked one). "She" (like Juana) exists beyond the limits of the norm, outside of history, nation, citizenship, even humanity. Women can never be human beings in their own right, Paz continues, because they "are only the reflection of male will and desire."[29] This, for Paz, explains the violence against her: "Sadism begins as vengeance against feminine hermeticism and a desperate attempt to obtain a response from an unresponsive body."[30] While not affirming that this should be so, at times subtly critiquing it, he merely asserts that it is. Paz neutralizes and normalizes female nothingness, a "reality" advanced not as the product of a misogynist historical accounting of a socio-political undoing and ontological un-becoming with cruel consequences for "women of all sexes," but as a mere fact of life.

Rodríguez and Felipe make Juana the subject of their performance on sexual identity to reflect how Esparragosa, Paz, and others turn a somebody into a nobody, into a nothing, an impossibility, and then condemn them for bringing the violence on themselves. Esparragosa's examination produces the coming into absence of Juana as a silent, ambiguous, and feminized nothing through his act of unnaming and placing beyond the norm. Juana Aguilar, as a nobody, is one more in the long line of people who do not fit into the identity-granting values and categories and, thus, are forcefully and/or discursively disappeared. This disappearance is not volitional on Juana's part, not an alternative way of living otherwise from normative regulations. There is nothing liberating in this instance of sexual ambiguity. She, like many others, the performance suggests, is condemned to a brutal end.

Through the performance, however, the artists make clear that Juana Aguilar has once again become an object of display—a pretext to tell another story about gender violence. "She" as a historical person has vanished, in part no doubt because the documentation regarding Aguilar's fate has vanished from the archive.

The performance, for all its comic elements, enacted the history of conquest, misogyny, and continued dehumanization. Through the use of puppets, dummies, stereotypes, and other forms of objectification, the two artists call out the continued and escalating violence and nullification of women. Femicide, a term coined in Mexico to describe the gendered nature of the brutality, steadily escalates. A United Nations representative reported, "Violence against women isn't an epidemic, it's a pandemic in Mexico."[31]

But the performance tries to do several things at once. It resurrects the painful story of the historical figure Juana Aguilar in part to critique the colonizing practice of categorizing and disciplining sex and gender—a practice imposed through the Spanish conquest and colonization of the Americas. It tackles the coming into presence of Juana as an ambiguous and dangerous feminized figure through humor, destabilizing the assumption that gender, sexuality, and identity align in any clear way. How to determine who is a "woman," they ask, playing doctor—through their chromosomes, hormones, genitalia, orgasms, and so on? They refuse to categorize or reduce options for "women."

On the other hand, the performance wants to call attention to the alarming aggression being directed at "women" (broadly) in Mexico and the world. Earlier in the performance, Rodríguez removes the genitals from the anatomical dummy and replaces them with a revolver. This, for her, is an allusion not to the biological or anatomical components of sex but rather to the cultural problem of the production of a very dangerous masculinity. The monstrosity on display lies in the social construction of the brutal, misogynist "macho." This is not about a chimeric or ambiguous sexual identity but an intolerable fact: human beings becoming and socialized as "men" throughout Mexico are viciously killing "women," boasting, and getting away with it. Here, then, there's a tacit assumption that we know what they/we mean by "men" and "women." Throughout the performance the tension oscillates between the desire to destabilize gender and sexual categories, pointing out the violence of medical and archival categorization that historically cemented current notions of difference and, at the same time, make an urgent point: that "women," brought into presence through a process of systematic and violent differentiation, are being targeted and killed for being "women." The performance attempts to resolve this tension between "women" and unsettling gender in the last line with a celebration of "women of all sexes."

The Hornet's Nest

The next morning, via Facebook, the eight hundred or so participants of the Encuentro learned that a trans member of the audience felt humiliated and laughed at by both the artists and the audience members during the performance. He said it had brought him to the point of tears and that he had resisted the temptation to walk out. A number of queer friends agreed and reposted the text widely. Those who had not seen the post heard about it at breakfast. The buzz circulated in Spanish, French, Portuguese, and English via the morning chatter and the did-you-hears. The sting announced the hornet's nest. Annie Sansonetti pointed out:

> A hornet's nest is an apt metaphor. . . . It's what hornets guard when threatened. Rodríguez and Felipe's performance and the discussions thereafter might allow us to feel the sting of the bee—the sting of being queer, of feeling trans, of queer and trans desire (wanting and longing).
>
> Think of the sting of being nothing, of being laughed at, of laboring in the name of building a communal nest. The sting: a pinch. The sting is what happens when we begin to walk together—when we are too close for comfort. The sting is fleeting, one-at-a-time, worse before it is better, and an affecting aftermath of desire.[32]

The next hours were full of discussions, accusations, and demands for clarification. In a brief impromptu town hall meeting that the organizing committee of the Encuentro and I decided to call that same day in the midst of a packed performance schedule, Rodríguez explained that her intention had never been to make fun of trans people—on the contrary. Her artistic and performance work has always pushed for gender rights, sexual rights, and other forms of human rights. Humor must be directed at the perpetrators of violence, never the victims. She did mean to offend machos, she added, who define themselves by annihilating femininity in all its manifestations. A tall, strong, trans woman wearing a red dress, pearls, and high heels came up to the three of us on the slightly raised platform and thrust her hand within inches of my face. "It's not their fault," she shouted at me. "It's your fault." Fault? Do we go to the language of "fault," as "lack" and "defectiveness," by "default"? I let the gesture pass, even as I felt physically attacked.

For all the talk in the audience of the need to create safe spaces, I did not feel safe. Again, Rodríguez reiterated that the violence against women, including trans women, in Mexico is so virulent that she and Felipe had wanted to bring it to the foreground. She apologized if they had inadvertently hurt people in the audience.

A contingent of the Encuentro's participants wanted more time to talk about the issues that had been raised. Stephen Lawson, the queer Canadian performance artist (of 2boys.tv) and curator of the Encuentro, asked us all to postpone the discussion until the next day so that artists who had come from throughout the Americas to share their work might be able to continue with the programming. The majority of those in the room agreed, and performance artist Lois Weaver of Split Britches organized a Long Table for the following afternoon at the Library of Performing Rights that she created for the Encuentro.

The Long Table

Long Tables, developed by Weaver in 2003, offer a performance as an alternative form of discussion to traditional roundtables and town hall meetings. Based on the notion of a dinner table conversation, she developed an etiquette that allows anyone to speak as long as they are seated at the table that normally accommodates twelve people at a time. If all the seats are taken, the person who wants to speak taps someone at the table on the shoulder and requests the chair. The Long Table ends after an hour and a half. While allowing for full participation, the seating arrangement encourages us to look at people as we speak to them. The face-to-face offers a very different form of engagement than a disembodied Facebook communication. Language, affect, self-presentation—everything, in short—becomes part of the transmission. Being present, face to face, offers a more relational modality for discussion than throwing out a comment from the back of the conference room or through Facebook. Etiquette, also a disciplinary regime, replaces the traditional hierarchy of invited speakers, while imposing its own structures of comportment. Lois Weaver read the rules of etiquette:

> There is no beginning
> It is a performance of a breakfast, lunch, or dinner
> Those seated at the table are the performers
>
> The Menu is up to you
> Talk is the only course

There is no hostess
This is a democracy

To participate, take a seat at the table

If the table is full, you can request a seat
Once you leave the table you can come back

There can be silence
You can break the silence with a question
You can write your questions on the table
There can be laughter

There is no conclusion[33]

The table was set with sheets of paper as a table cloth and markers instead of cutlery. A hundred or more people stood waiting for people to claim a seat at the table. Rodríguez sat at the table, as did I. Felipe chose not to. The trans man who posted on Facebook sat next to Rodríguez but did not speak. The trans woman who confronted me did not attend the Long Table and said she would not talk to any of us. Others at the table, nontrans queer activists and theorists, made some points: the trans community bears the burden of always having to explain itself—we should not contribute to that burden; the trans movement is a central one that needs to be heard and understood; there were language issues and points of untranslatability. What (and who) was the audience laughing at? Was the audience laughing at what the artists said, or at the translation that kicked in a minute or so before or after? Some pointed out the dangers of censorship; others reiterated that Rodríguez should have explicitly referenced the trans population as she played with genitals; others felt uneasy with artists being called on to apologize for their work. A queer theorist from Puerto Rico who is a professor at a U.S. university pointed out the dangers of mistranslation and misrecognition around terms and concepts combined with the challenges of engaging historical documents. The play, after all, he stressed, dealt with the eighteenth-century Spanish Inquisition! "I understood it was a parody and that Jesusa was opening a space for conversation," he said. But he added, "It sounds to me like the white people from the North are once again telling the women of color from the South how to do their work." A Jamaican artist/scholar agreed that the discussion reflected a North/South divide: "the huge gap between what Jesusa was trying to get at" and the attitude that "those backward Third World people need to be taught things." Queer performance artist Peggy Shaw reminded everyone that women have never been safe, and women have always had to explain themselves, and they're used to seeing themselves ridiculed onstage and off. She expressed her position succinctly: "If you have a problem with a show, go make your own fucking show." For the first time, a self-identified trans person spoke, saying, "The only person I can speak for is myself" and telling Rodríguez, "I want to be in solidarity with you."

And so it went.[34]

Rodríguez repeatedly asked for someone to explain the specific thing/image that had offended them.

When the Long Table ended, the trans man who had posted the comment on Facebook leaned over to Rodríguez and asked her quietly if he could speak with her.

The discussion did not finish there. Unease and suspicion hovered over the entire Encuentro.

Jack Halberstam, who was present at the exchange, referred to the incident in his piece, "You Are Triggering Me! The Neo-liberal Rhetoric of Harm, Danger and Trauma": "A play that foregrounded the mutilation of the female body in the 17th century was cast as trans-phobic and became the occasion for multiple public meetings to discuss the damage it wreaked upon trans people present at the performance." He goes on to note that "controversies within queer communities around language, slang, satirical or ironic representation and perceptions of harm or offensive [sic] have created much controversy with very little humor recently, leading to demands for bans, censorship and name changes."[35] Here, the queer community is charged with lacking humor. Later, in Trans*, he sums up the problem differently: "Rather than receiving the play as an interesting piece of period theater, audience members became irate and angered by the depiction, especially since some parts of the hermaphrodite's character were played for comic effect."[36] Here, the comedy is faulty for trying to be funny, and the one audience member who expressed feeling harmed comes to stand for the entire audience that gave the performance a standing ovation. Clearly, this was not just "an interesting piece of period theater." It had ignited political concerns and sensitivities across a broad range of issues. While Hemi Encuentros intend to animate participants to discuss and listen to issues that play out differently across the Americas, here the opposite had happened as participants tended toward retreat and retrenchment to firmly held convictions.

Rodríguez's answer to Halberstam's blog post sidestepped the harm issue and noted instead the cultural differences around humor. She also pointed to different understandings, or perhaps assumptions, around queerness:

I've dedicated my time to studying ancient Mexican culture, our heritage. Its worldview is based on a dual conception. This dual principle is male and female at the same time . . . (Ometecuhtli and Omecíhuatl). This dual principle encompasses everything in our culture. From the very origins, opposite forces are conceived as complementary and not simply as opposites (which is the case in Christianity). This duality, simultaneously male and female, shapes everything and includes everything. So the hermaphrodite dual concept is integrated into all that exists, it is a basic concept that imprints Mexican culture with a special seal, including, of course, sexuality. This doesn't mean that we don't follow the controversies taking place in the West, or that we're unaware of the predicaments of so-called "modernity," but no matter what, we see them through this lens because it's in our roots and our origins, and is therefore reflected in our language.[37]

In other words, riffing off of José Esteban Muñoz, in Mexico we have always been queer. According to Muñoz (who himself was a gay U.S. Latino), "we have never been queer, yet queerness exists for us as an ideality that can be distilled from the past and used to imagine a future." Queerness, for Muñoz, is about futurity, "about the rejection of the here and now and an insistence on potentiality or concrete possibility for another world."[38] For Rodríguez, among many others, queerness and trans have always been with us, have always been us, although the same inquisitional forces that tried to execute Juana la Larga have attacked and literally demonized it (as *cosas del diablo*) for over five hundred years. It's not only a fundamental part of Mesoamerican life, but the trans *muxe* or *muxhe* are a socially accepted gender category in some parts of Mexico today. A muxe, in Zapotec communities, "is an assigned male at birth individual who dresses and behaves in ways otherwise associated with the female gender; they may be seen as a third gender."[39] The broad, encompassing notion of queerness and trans, for Rodríguez and Felipe, I believe, is a given. The political stakes of the piece for them, rather, are communicating the brutality of the misogyny and ninguneo—reducing the someone to a no one.

Becoming presente, or absent, as queer and/or *cuir* or trans across these cultures, then, is a process that includes differing notions of temporality, of ontology, of the cosmic order. Different ideological systems interpellate us differently. As Rodríguez and Felipe suggest in the performance, many concepts were brought in with the conquest and colonialism—linear temporality being one of them. The bells at the beginning of the performance that precipitate the puppet nun's trigger warnings about lust and perdition reflect the imposition of Western notions of time through church bells that began to call out the hours for all to hear. By edict, the indigenous population had to live within hearing distance of the church bells. Time plays a role in *The Final Judgment*, one of the earliest known plays to be staged in the conquered Americas, screaming out much as the puppet nun does: "I am time . . . calling out to them, reminding them of things day and night. I don't shut my mouth for a moment."[40] Church bells changed the soundscape of Mesoamerica into the postconquest present. Like Juana la Larga, this play too is about subjugating women and disciplining desire understood as lasciviousness.

But for indigenous populations in Mexico and other parts of the Americas, as with many communities of Afro-descendants as I mention in chapter 1, time does not function as past, present, future. Where native languages and cultural beliefs and practices survive as living forces, the future is not fully distinguishable from the past. We move forward into the past; our present simply enacts the second of alignment between the past that is never over and the future that is always here. Para-times, para-spaces coexist, nested in and alongside each other. Guillermo Bonafil Batalla analyzes the "living presence of Mesoamerican civilization" and calls this "Mexico Profundo" and the Western imposition of civilization "the imaginary Mexico."[41] When at the end of the performance Rodríguez and Felipe circle back to the conquest (using a wooden puppet of a conquistador and speaking with an outlandish Castilian accent) and place it next to the tiny doll figures of the Zapatistas, it's not to underline the linear passage of five hundred years since the conquest, but the continuation of conquest by many means—the now, again, and always. The move also underlines the ongoing presence, force, and resistance of indigenous people and worldviews. Close to 15 percent of Mexico's population is indigenous, although a far greater percentage actively engages in indigenous cultural and belief systems. One of the underlying principles of this system is that identities exist in a state of constant complementarity and change. The Aztec "nahual" is only one way of naming the ongoing transformation and shape-shifting power that makes up the cosmos and everything in it.[42] Labeling tries to fix them in time and language. Rodríguez writes elsewhere of her desire to transcend categorization in her work and "leave behind its gender prejudices—what's important is that spectators confront their own capacity for transformation, male, female, bird, witch, shoe, or whatever."[43]

The understanding that terms such as gender and sexuality and queer and trans are not understood the same way throughout the Americas, and—more importantly—cannot be reduced to one more North-South tension—was again underlined at the Encuentro by the keynote delivered by a Cree queer writer from northern Canada, Tomson Highway:

> Aboriginal languages divide the universe into that which is animate and that which is inanimate, that which has a soul and that which has not. In this conception, gender has no place whatever. Whether male or female biologically, we are all he/shes emotionally, psychologically, and spiritually, as is God. And the resulting superstructure is thus not the straight line of monotheism but the circle of pantheism, a system wherein god is biology is nature is the land. A yonic—that is, womb-like—superstructure as opposed to phallic is what we speak of here, a design where there is room for many genders.[44]

In this very queer cosmology, he laments the loss of spaces and geographies that allow for his language and culture to survive.

The Long Table, then, became one more site for the difficult practice of self-naming and self-localization—in addition to other negotiations that we perhaps failed to recognize, let alone name and locate. As Anjali Arondekar notes, one becomes "non-trans through seizing political affect . . . non-US through seizing political affect."[45] The process of self-constitution, she continues, entails designating whomever one deems "improper as anachronistic." Instead of focusing on the shared experience of violence, risk, and harm, the conversation became about where people came from, whom they spoke for, on what authority, and how they labeled themselves. Tomson Highway's keynote had explicitly made the connection between location, naming, and risk—he knew that within the capitalist, expansionist economy, he was deemed an anachronism, an improper outlier, a Cree, queer subject from a First Nations land that most refer to as northern Canada, who understood himself as part of a yonic system of constitution within a phallic world and thus doomed to disappear. The death sentence had been passed—it was simply a question of time. He had resolved to die laughing. Humor, for him as for Rodríguez and Felipe, was a political affect that served to highlight the very concrete danger: within this economy of subjectification, certain populations are disposable. Harm and risk, for them, are collective, shared. They're all nothing, absent, nobodies.

Highway's keynote, in fact, anticipates several of the issues raised by the Long Table. On the one hand, the vision of complementarity and repair. On the other, the impossibility of communication, the perceived anachronism of other ways of being and doing, the singularity of the neoliberal subject, and the nontransferability of humor. The participants at the Long Table did not all understand each other across languages and cultures. Instead of aspiring to the expansiveness offered by queer and trans, Rodríguez's "duality that . . . shapes everything and includes everything," everyone individually felt the sting. The language of hurt and injury "create[d] the borders between selves and others," as Sara Ahmed puts it.[46] The anachronism explicitly addressed at the table was not just a political form of exclusion, as in Highway's understanding of himself as a doomed subject within a system he could not control, forcefully thrown back (as opposed to a throwback) to other times and spaces marked for disappearance because they were incompatible with neoliberalist, masculinist expansion. The discussion also had disciplinary overtones in trying, as Martínez warned against, "to make [Aguilar] a part of 'gay and lesbian'" and now trans history. "Succumbing to a classificatory impulse," she adds, is "not unlike that which is present on Esparragosa's investigation."[47] This might have been a warning for those who insist on labels, but it's a warning too about the very power of labeling, a sovereign power of determining or delimiting rights and legitimacy. Ultimately, the two understandings of anachronism are related; the differences lie in perspective and positionality. (Who classifies? Who gets classified to nothingness?)

Translating humor, of course, posed yet other problems. Some at the Encuentro felt that Highway was making fun of them. "I love white people, don't you?" he asked, looking at us, laughing himself silly as he stopped to "readjust his girdle," as he put it. Many, however, followed the laughter to where he was asking us to go—a place of mutual nervousness and suspicion. His performance asked us to sit with it, find our way through it, and understand that others were experiencing similar unease. The fact that we don't know and understand each other, and thus have no way of assessing our stakes or investments in the arguments, severely complicates even the most well-meaning cross-cultural discussions. We might be uneasy, but we were there. Presentes, though perhaps too tentative for exclamation marks.

Die Laughing

So, is humor—à la Rodríguez, Felipe, and Highway—an apt modality to address grievous and seemingly insurmountable wrongs? Comedy always has its costs. Too often, as in the example of the yellowface "humor," comedy strengthens stereotypes, making them palpable, normative. Not funny, many insist, rejecting claims to humor. Part of the hurt expressed by the person who posted to Facebook was precisely the laughter, the sting of feeling laughed at and shamed. Some people at *Juana la Larga* also found the yellowface racist, as did some audience members at Tomson Highway's lecture. Can humor address such violent histories? What to do with the genre, gender, racial, and sexual troubles emanating from the continued use of camp and humor as queer, indigenous, and trans methods? Comedy is risky, not just because there's always the threat of failure hovering around jokes but because it puts the comedian and the audience at risk of insult, injury, misunderstandings, and hostility. Australian stand-up comedian Hannah Gadsby insists in *Nanette* that she is giving up comedy because the self-deprecating nature of the form further humiliates those like her who "exist in the margins."[48] Furthermore, comedy undercuts the importance of the very difficult story she has to tell. Like Juana, and like Rodríguez and Felipe, Gadsby's story is about the soul-crushing undoing she faced coming into presence as a lesbian in Australia and about the rapes and batterings she received from men. "I learned how to disappear," she says.[49] Nadie. Ninguno. Nobody. She too wants "to try and change toxic and predatory male culture," she continues. "Laughter is not medicine. . . . It's just the honey that sweetens the medicine." Laughter creates and relieves tension, she adds, much as Lauren Berlant and Sianne Ngai note it creates and dispels anxiety.[50] The tension and anxiety are always there, but comedy activates them and then helps relieve the pressure. Laughter might be a way to cover or "manage disruptive difference," but it does not resolve the issues.[51] The racism, colonialism, misogyny, homo- and transphobia, arrogance, and violence that Rodríguez, Felipe, and Highway all bring to the fore only become more evident. Do we dare look these in the face and address them? Berlant and Ngai make a crucial observation: comedy and laughter draw "insecure boundaries" and help us "test or figure out what it means to say 'us.' Always crossing lines, [comedy] helps us figure out what lines we desire or can bear."[52]

Do we stay with it and try to negotiate those boundaries, or walk out?

Hemi Encuentros, the performances of encounter, seek specifically to test these boundaries, these zones of instability and untranslatability, and explore the issues (however painful) that connect and divide artists, scholars, and activists throughout the Americas. These curated events enact the ideals articulated throughout this study: the promise of the conversations among many others beyond the disciplinary fence, the Zapatista struggle for a world in which many worlds are possible, a more relational sense of subjectivity developed by walking and talking with others, a collective awareness of harm and repair, the hope that if others knew and listened they might understand and care. Encuentros stage who "we" are. They challenge us to reexamine not just what we see but how we see. They bring people together to explore our common and disparate concerns and strategies. Can we ever be a WE or find ways in which our various and overlapping WE's can speak and listen to each other? Or do we walk away? The way we do this is the way we do everything. The Long Table is one of the performance modalities that helps address the tensions frontally, face to face. Sometimes these interactions work. That is, people feel they have been able to acknowledge the sting and move through murky areas—emotionally, politically, economically, culturally, epistemically, and so on—in order to hear and perhaps understand other perspectives.

This Long Table, for example, opened a space for a brilliant rebuttal to the yellowface. The Asian American work group at the Encuentro performed a skit of people dressed in yellow costumes from a previous art show. The fabric had "it's a small world" on it and was designed to critique racial stereotypes, as one member of the group put it. They did, in fact, make their own fucking show.[53] They seemed willing to concede that in Mexico and other countries these jokes might not be considered racist. By performing the stereotypes, however, they let no one off the hook for not knowing how they experienced that depiction as racism. If there's a commitment to unlearning some of the unexamined assumptions we take from colonialism, this action asked us to follow through.

Other times, these interactions feel like failure. Participants sitting at the Long Table seemed entrenched, not open to listening and exchange. As one member of the Asian American group put it: "The most shocking part was that no one really saw us. After we talked about it and realized: We didn't interrupt anything."[54] People at the Long Table talked past each other or not at all. My sense was that the disconnect was less about understanding the important trans movements, the ways that trans lives and theories diverge from queer or the ways that we inadvertently hurt each other, and more about the ways that identity struggles can blind us to related forms of violence. We were all talking about violence—the violence trans communities face every day, the violence of racial stereotyping, the violence against women, the violence of dispossession of indigenous peoples, lands, and worldviews. Moreover, these forms of destruction are connected—sharing deep roots in patriarchal and imperialist structures that thrive in neoliberalism.

Part of the problem of turning the violence into a personal grievance put it beyond discussion: "I felt Highway was laughing at us," or "your representation was hurtful to me," or "I didn't feel safe when she thrust her hand in front of my face." Conversation ends: I cannot argue with your feelings or you with mine. Pain and hurt become individual, almost a neoliberal form of possession, "my pain." We might try to respect them and say "sorry you feel that way" and try to learn from them, but it's impossible to have a critical discussion. "What about the pain of others?" Ahmed asks.[55]

> Time to stop.
> Pause.
> Listen.
> It's possible to share and heal.
> Acknowledge: It's hard to unlearn.
> Sometimes it takes a while.

In hindsight, and in conversation with others, I came to rethink what I experienced as the gesture of aggression against me at the town hall meeting. Repeating the scene again and again, I moved from the personal to the communal sense of injury. The gesture still stung me, individually, but it was part of a more generalized hurt. I thought it might be understood as a form of matricide (killing the first-world feminists that came before us) as some suggested, but it might (also) be an instance of what Susan Stryker calls "transgender rage . . . a queer fury, an emotional response to conditions in which it becomes imperative to take up, for the sake of one's own continued survival as a subject, a set of practices that precipitates one's exclusion from a naturalized order of existence that seeks to maintain itself as the only possible basis for being a subject."[56] Rage, perhaps, against ninguneo. Maybe we aren't supposed to feel safe in times like these. When the bee stings, there's an urgency to its motion. The bee is in danger too. Perhaps this is something like transgender urgency set in motion: a call to action, to be present, a reminder that transgender matters, if we have always been queer. It all matters.

Talking about violence and hurt, ongoing, repetitive, and relational, allows us to develop strategies of coresistance, solidarity, intergenerational alliances, or at least an understanding that communities have a different sense of what/when/how something constitutes an issue, an injury, a desire, a sting. Women have always been explaining themselves; feminists have always been explaining themselves; people of color have always been explaining themselves; queer and transgender groups have always been explaining themselves; indigenous peoples have always been explaining themselves. And, related, they are all at risk. Halberstam's proposal that trans* people find "alternative ways of being in relation to others" such as "privileging friendship networks" and "altering relations to seeing and being seen" has long served other communities.[57] Surely, as the one trans person who spoke at the table noted, there are grounds for solidarity. As Peggy Shaw reminded us during the Long Table, if we are going to cast everything as a war, we need to remember who our enemy is.

What does "at risk" mean here? Communities and groups of peoples referred to in this discussion—women, queer and trans people from the global south and north, communities of color, and indigenous groups are at risk of physical violence, desubjectification, discrimination, and economic marginalization at the hands of the very same forces. These are not sequential forms of oppression—as in the old ones resolve, giving place to new. The violence and hurt are lived as past and very present. Rather than separate, I turn to anachronism as a viable politics to call attention to the seemingly constant state of againness of dispossession. Repetition here works not only as a working-through but as a transectional politics. In 2014, the Long Table performed the failure of the "dramatics of discourse," Foucault's scene of enunciation.[58] Injury seemed to be the main item on the menu, and people could not hear each other. We all felt the singular sting that happens when we begin to walk together—when we are too close for comfort. At risk, however was the very possibility of envisioning modes of coresistance, perhaps even coemergence, that might help us and each other practice other forms of knowing, being, and coming into presence. But change happens over time, and the effects and affects of those conversations keep doing their work. I could hear now what I couldn't hear then. My hope is that these interactions—the walking and talking together—have only just begun. ¡Presente! yes, for better and for worse.

SEVEN

Tortuous Routes
Four Walks through Villa Grimaldi

Prologue

This chapter invites the reader to accompany me on several walks through Villa Grimaldi and to think through the many issues this site (and others like it) raise in terms of memory, history, place, performance, trauma, witnessing, and political contestation. Villa Grimaldi is one of the most infamous of the 1,170 spaces used for torture, detention, and killings under the regime of Augusto Pinochet listed in the 2005 "National Commission on Political Imprisonment and Torture Report" or "Valech Report."[1] While it may be clear what the site is (former torture center) and what it's about (the atrocities committed by the Pinochet dictatorship), it's less clear who these spaces are for and what they actually do. Is it for the survivors, painful proof of the violence done to them? A reminder and warning for the local population? Or for those who know little about this terrible history? The sites ask something of us, the visitors. The visits, landscaping, audiotapes, video testimony, artwork, and resource centers attempt to transmit a sense of what happened there, to them, and at the same time engage us as coparticipants in the drama.

Here I trace four (of many) visits I made to Villa Grimaldi between 2006 and 2016. Why, I wonder, do I go, and why go back, again and again? I'm not from Chile. I had nothing to do with Pinochet's dictatorship. If anything, as a young adult living in Mexico City, I remember the Chileans who came to Mexico as exiles. We felt very proud of our make-believe democracy. And yet I go back.

How, and for whom, does a memorial site bring the past into presence?

Figure 7.1, a photo taken by Lorie Novak, shows the metal shards that the military tied to the bodies of their victims to weigh them down before dumping them in the sea in the Death Flights. The magnifying glass

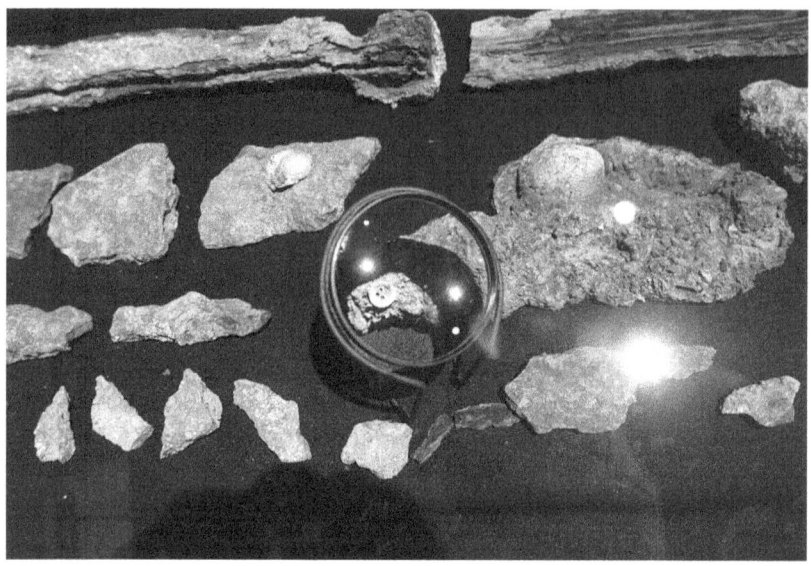

7.1 Button from a victim of Pinochet's Death Flights, Villa Grimaldi, Chile, 2012. PHOTO: LORIE NOVAK.

focuses on a button ripped off the clothing on one of the bodies. I had not noticed it the first time I saw the shards. Nor the second. The button is small, and the magnifying glass unobtrusively positioned among the metal. For too long I didn't know what I was looking at. The *punctum*, as Roland Barthes puts it.[2] The detail that affects and "pricks" me. Plastic outlasts the human. But the button is also the *studium* that provides information. The material link to the disappeared person wearing the clothing. Evidence of atrocity. The photo, like my many visits, reminds me that I need to shift focus and attention in order to see, understand, and feel the drama of which I gradually, and begrudgingly, became a part. I understand repetition as form, through these walks, repetition as content, repetition as an affective response, repetition as a heuristic, repetition as a performance pedagogy.

Trauma as Durational Performance

2006: Pedro Matta, a tall, strong man, walked up to us when we arrived at the unassuming side entrance to Villa Grimaldi, a former torture and detention camp on the outskirts of Santiago de Chile. Matta is a survivor who twice a month or so gives a guided visit to people who want to know about what happened there. Chilean colleagues thought I'd be interested in visiting the site with him. He greets us and hands me the English version of a booklet he has written: "A Walk through a 20th Century Torture Center: Villa Grimaldi, Santiago de Chile, a Visitor's Guide." I tell him that I am from Mexico and speak Spanish. "Ah," he says, his eyes narrowing as he scans me, "Taylor, I just assumed . . ."

The space is expansive. It looks like a ruin or a construction site. There's some old rubble and signs of new building—a transitional space, part past, part future. A sign at the entrance, Parque por la Paz Villa Grimaldi, informs visitors that 4,500 people were tortured here and 226 people were disappeared and killed between 1973 and 1979. I take a photograph of the sign that explains that this place is simultaneously a torture camp, a memory site, and a peace park. Like many memory sites, it reminds us that this tragic history belongs to all of us and asks us to behave respectfully so that it might remain and continue to instruct. Lesson One, clearly, is that this place is our responsibility in more ways than one.

I look around; the place seems empty.

"This way, please." Matta, a formal man, walks us over to the small model of the torture camp to help us visualize the architectural arrangement of a place now gone: Cuartel Terranova. "Terranova" (new land) designated unexplored territories on ancient maps. Who knew the Chilean military was given to ancient scholarship? The mock-up is laid out, like a coffin, under a plastic, slightly opaque sunshade that in itself distorts vision (fig. 7.3).

As in many historically important sites, the model offers a bird's-eye view of the entire area. The difference here is that what we see in the model is no longer there. Even though we are present, we will not experience it in person. So, one might ask, what is the purpose of the visit? What can we understand by being physically in a torture center once the indicators have disappeared? Does the space offer up evidence unavailable elsewhere or cues that trigger reactions in visitors? Little beside the sign at the entrance reveals the context. My photographs might illustrate what this place is now, not what it was. So, why? It's enough for now that we are here in person with Matta, who takes us through the *recorrido* (walk-through). Walking and talking, presumably, will bring the past into focus. Matta speaks in Spanish; it makes a difference. He seems to relax a little, though his voice is very strained and he clears his throat often.

Park for Peace map

Headquarters Terranova map

1. Memorial Plaque
2. Remains of a wall
3. Entrance gate
4. Site to unload prisoners
5. First torture chamber
6. Men's cells

7. Isolation cells
8. Women's cells
9. Second torture chamber
10. Male collaboration cell
11. Prison ward's shack
12. Third torture chamber

13. Bathrooms
14. Storage for confiscated goods
15. Site for hanging
16. Isolation and punishment cell
17. House for female collaborators
18. Tower (isolation, punishment and torture)

19. Photographic lab
20. Silkscreen room
21. Swimming pool
22. Parking lot (torture with vehicles)
23. Water fountain (symbol of life and hope)

N

JOSE ARRIETA

The compound, originally a beautiful nineteenth-century villa used for upper-class parties and then weekend get-togethers for artists and intellectuals, was taken over by DINA, Augusto Pinochet's special forces, to interrogate the people detained by the military during the massive roundups. As thousands of people were captured, many civilian spaces were transformed into make-shift detention centers. The military appropriated sites identified or run by progressive intellectuals and left-wing movements—the Londres 38 torture center had been the office of the Socialist Party; the Center of Humanistic Studies at the University of Chile became the Communications Center for the military, and so on.[3] Villa Grimaldi, with its solitary confinement tower and cages for prisoners, was one of the most feared. One of the attractions of the villa for the military, Matta explains, was its proximity to a remote military airport controlled by Pinochet, head of the Air Force. It proved a convenient place to upload prisoners to the notorious night flights, during which their bodies were dumped into the sea, alive, weighted down with metal. In the late 1980s, one of the generals sold the place to a construction company belonging to the Pinochet family to tear down and replace with a housing project. Survivors and human rights activists could not stop the demolition, but after much heated contestation they did secure the space as a memory site and peace park in 1995.[4] Matta, among other survivors and human rights activists, has spent a great deal of time, money, and energy to make sure that the space remains a permanent reminder of what the Pinochet government did to its people. Three para-times and spaces, all nestled in and alongside each other, with three overlapping and interconnected histories, create this complicated space that even now has multiple functions simultaneously: evidentiary, commemorative, reconciliatory, and pedagogical.

The miniature detention camp positions us as spectators. We stand above the model, constructed like a toy theatre, looking down on its organizational structure (fig. 7.4). It was built, Matta told us, by students of architecture using his and other survivors' notes and plans. The main entrance to our top left allowed passage for vehicles that delivered the hooded captives up to the main building. Matta's language and our imaginations populate the inert space. He points to the tiny copy of the large main building that served as the center of operations for DINA—here the military planned whom they would target and how, and they evaluated the results of the torture sessions. Those

7.2 (facing) Map, in Pedro Matta, "A Walk through a 20th Century Torture Center: Villa Grimaldi, Santiago de Chile: A Visitor's Guide." Villa Grimaldi, Chile, 2006.

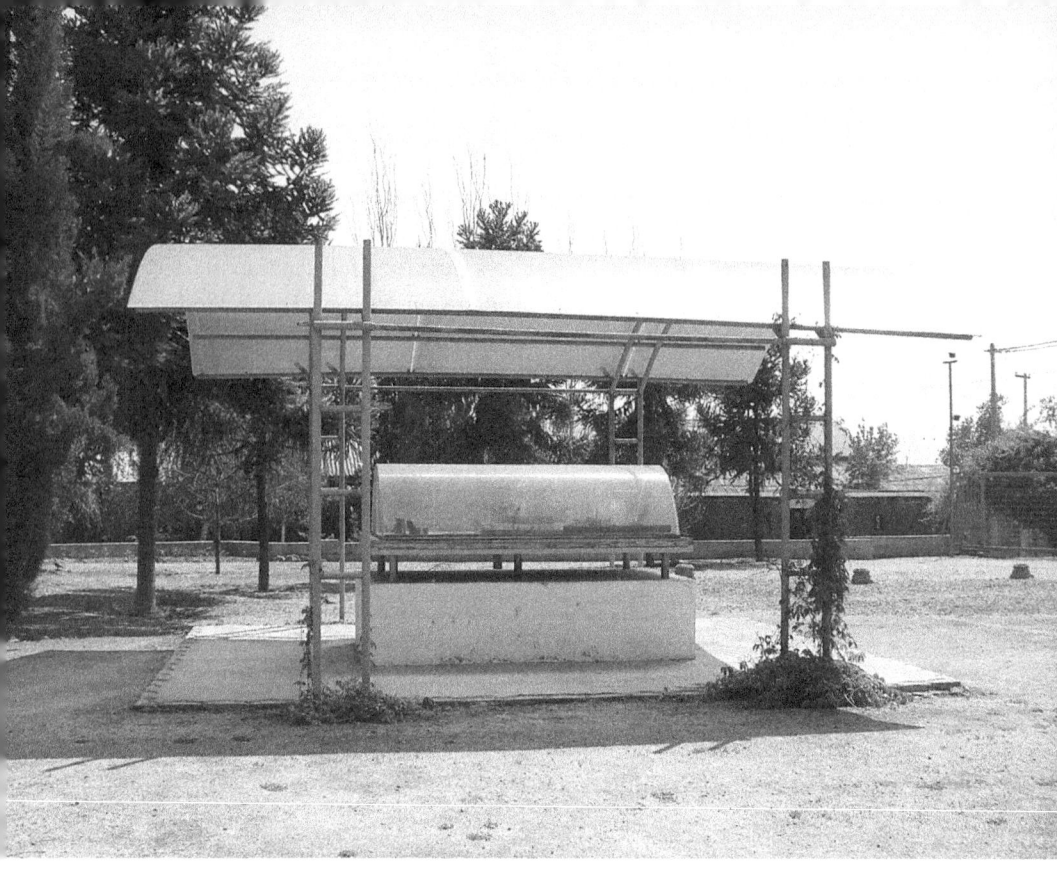

7.3 Model of Terranova, 2006. PHOTO: DIANA TAYLOR.

in charge of Villa Grimaldi had offices here, and there was a mess hall for officers. The space housed the archives, and a short-wave radio station kept the military personnel in contact with their counterparts throughout South America. Plan Condor, the transnational network of repressive military regimes operating in Latin America, in cooperation with the CIA, shared intelligence and helped persecute progressive leaders and militants on the run.[5] The model showed the small buildings that ran along the perimeter where prisoners were divided up, separated, and blindfolded—men there, women there.

Miniature drawings made by survivors line the periphery—hooded prisoners pushed by guards with rifles for their thirty seconds at the latrines; a hall of small locked cells guarded by an armed man; a close-up drawing of the inside of one of the cells in which a half dozen shackled and hooded men are squeezed in tightly; an empty torture chamber with a bare metal bunk bed equipped with leather straps, a chair with straps for arms and feet, a table with instruments (fig. 7.5). The objects reference behaviors. We know

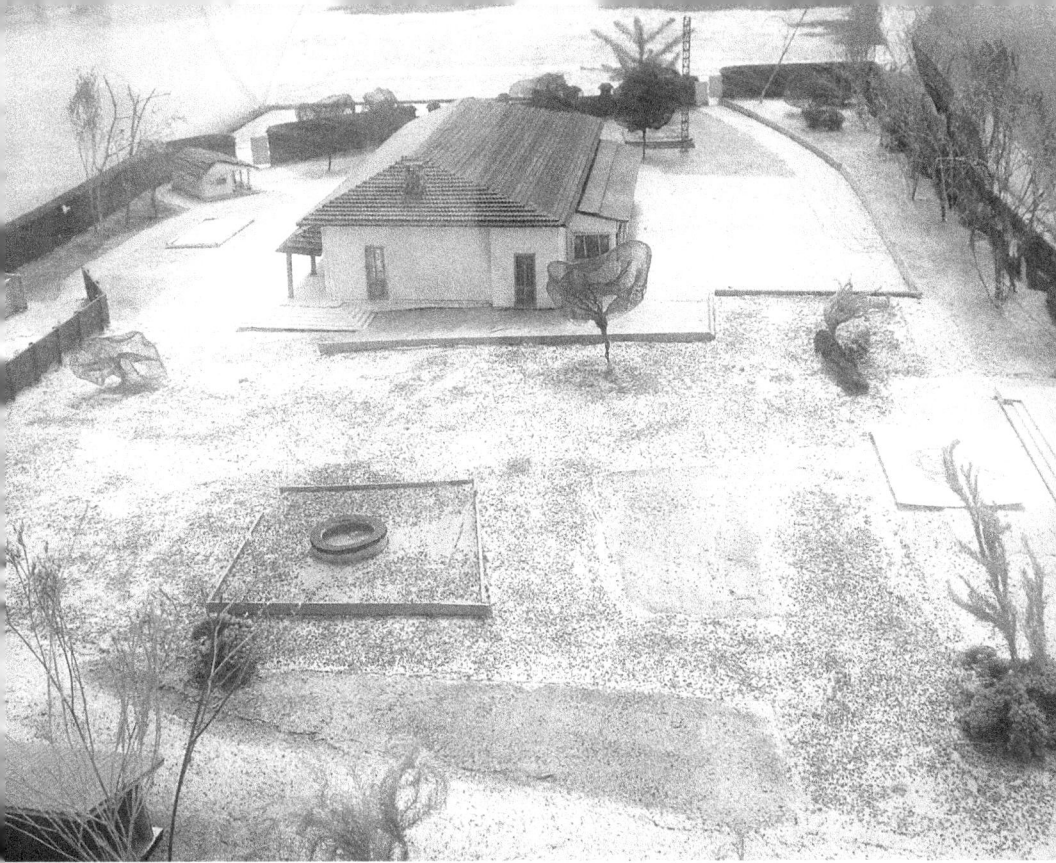

7.4 Model of Terranova, 2006. PHOTO: DIANA TAYLOR.

exactly what happened there/here. Matta points to other structures. It is clear that the displacement offered by the model gives him a sense of control—he no longer needs to fully relive the image to describe it—he can externalize and point to it over there. The violence, in part, can be transferred to the archive, materialized in the small evidentiary mock-up. He is explicit about the criminal politics, and very clear in his condemnation of the CIA's role in the Chilean crisis. He blue eyes pierce me, and then he remembers I am not *that* audience—an audience, but not that audience.

Looking down at the model in relationship to the larger space, I see we are standing on the site of the main building, usurping the military's place. Looking offers me the strange fantasy of seeing or grasping the whole, the fiction that I can understand systemic criminal violence even as we position ourselves simultaneously in and above the fray. We are permitted to identify without identifying. We are not implicated except to the degree that we can understand the information transmitted to us by the mock-up and by Matta, our guide. This happened there, back then, to them, by them. . . .

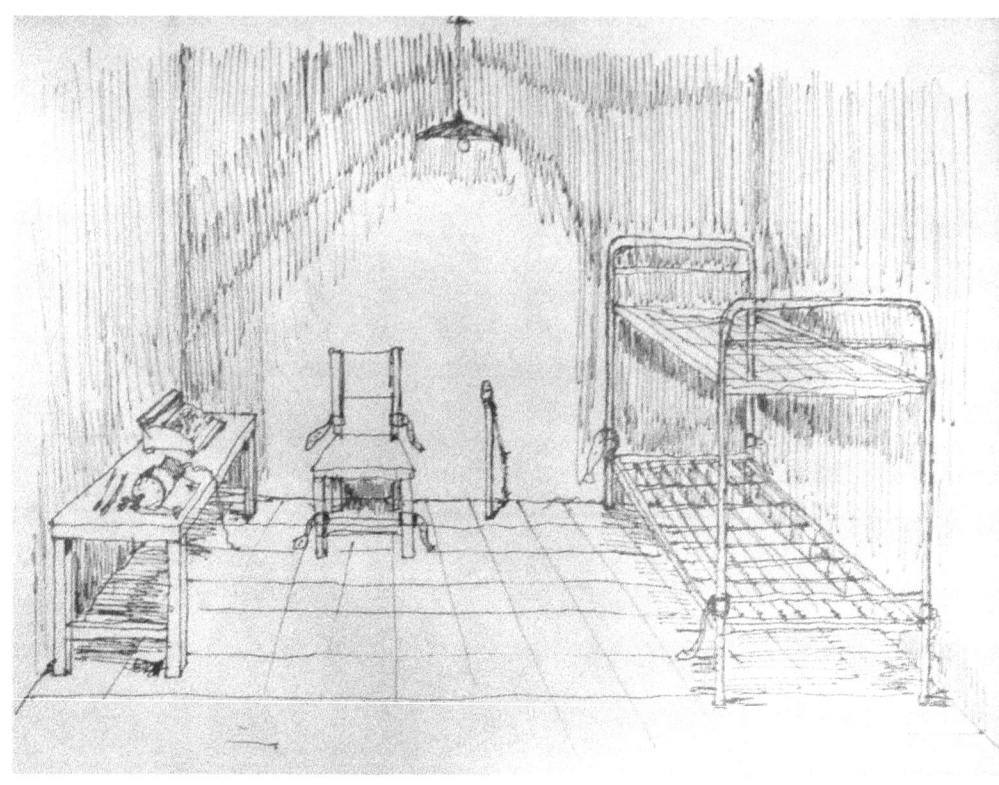

7.5 Miniature drawing made by a survivor, Villa Grimaldi, 2006. PHOTO: DIANA
TAYLOR.

Recounting performs the spatial and temporal displacement. The encounter, at this point, is about representation and explication of the facts. I take
photographs, wondering how the tenuous evidentiary power of the photo
might extend the fragile evidentiary claim of the model camp. I know what
happened at Villa Grimaldi, of course, but wonder if being there helps me
know it differently. Can I, with my camera, do anything to further make
visible the criminal violence? The other violence, the economic policies
that justified and enabled the breaking of bodies, remains safely outside
the frame.

We look up and around at the place itself. There's not much to see of the
former camp. The remains of a few original structures and replicas of isolation cells and a tower dot the compound, emptied though not empty—empty
of something palpable in its absence. No history. No one responsible. Much
later, activists planted rows of birch trees (*abedules*) to symbolize the fragile

and solitary condition of the ex-prisoners, along with their resistance.[6] With the camp demolished, Matta informs and points out, but he does not seem to connect personally or emotionally to what he describes. Some objects have been reconstructed and placed to support the narration—this happened here. A model wooden cell, one meter by two meters, demonstrates how four or five prisoners were forced to stand upright in a tiny space for extended periods of time. The armed forces called them Casas Chile as an ironic put-down of Salvador Allende's initiative to provide the poor with housing, small and cramped though it was. Matta told us that he learned to sleep standing up in one of those cells. I imagine some visitors must actually try to squeeze themselves in the tiny, upright isolation cell. They might even allow someone to close the door. Do performance pedagogies such as immersion and simulation allow people to feel or experience the camp more fully than walking through it? Possibly. Rites involving sensory deprivation prepare members of communities to undertake difficult or sacred transitions by inducing different mental states. The basic idea—that people learn, experience, and come to terms with past/future behaviors by physically doing them, trying them on, acting them through and acting them out—is the underlying theory of ritual, older than Aristotle's theory of mimesis and as new as theories of mirror neurons that explore how empathy and understandings of human relationality and intersubjectivity are vital for human survival.[7] But these reconstructed cells disconcert me. I am embarrassed to even think of entering in Matta's presence—he was subjected to this cruelty, not me. How can I pretend to experience what he did? Rather the opposite; the less I see intensifies what I imagine happened here. My mind's eye—my very own staging area—fills the gaps between Matta's formal matter-of-fact rendition and the terrifying things he relates.

Matta walks us toward the original entryway—the massive iron gate now permanently sealed as if to shut out the possibility of further violence. From this vantage point, it is clear that another layer has been added to the space. A wash of decorative tiles, chips of the original ceramic found at the site, form a huge arrow-like shape on the ground pointing away from the gate toward the new peace fountain ("symbol of life and hope," according to Matta's booklet) and a large performance pavilion. The architecture participates in the rehabilitation of the site. The cross-shaped layout moves us from criminal past to redemptive future. Matta ignores that for the moment—he is not in the peace park. This is not the time for reconciliation. His traumatic story, like his past, weighs down all possibility of future. He continues his recorrido through the torture camp.[8]

Matta speaks impersonally, in the third person, about the role of torture in Chile—one half million people tortured and five thousand killed out of a population of eight million. I do the math . . . one in sixteen. There were more tortures and fewer murders in Chile than in neighboring Argentina, where the armed forces permanently disappeared thirty thousand of their own people. Pinochet chose to break rather than eliminate his enemies—the population of ghosts, or individuals destroyed by torture, thrown back into society as vacant, ghastly presences would be a warning for others. This coming into absence is the unmaking of the world. Life in Chile devolved into one of silence, suspicion, and fear of public space. Matta speaks about the development of torture as a tool of the state from its early experimental phase to the highly precise and tested practice it became. Matta's tone is controlled and reserved. He is giving archival information, not personal testimony, as he outlines the daily workings of the camp, the transformation of language as words were outlawed. *Crimenes*, *desaparecidos*, and *dictadura* (crimes, disappeared, and dictatorship) were replaced by *excesos*, *presuntos*, and *gobierno militar* (excesses, presumed, military government).

As we walk, he describes what happened where, and I notice that he keeps his eyes on the ground, a habit born of peering down under the blindfold he was forced to wear. I see now that he's back in that terrifying, unreconstructed space. The shift is gradual—he begins to reenact ever so subtly as he retells, entering into a dark space in which we stand but cannot see. He moves deeper into the death camp. Pointing at an empty spot: "Usually unconscious, the victim was taken off the parrilla (metal bed frame), and if male, dragged here."[9] Maybe the lens of my camera will grasp what I cannot grasp. Looking down, I see the colored shards of ceramic tiles and stones that now mark the places where buildings once stood and the paths where victims were pushed to the torture chambers. As we follow, we too know our way by keeping our eyes on the ground: *sala de tortura* (torture chamber), *celdas para mujeres detenidas* (cell for detained women).

I follow his movements but also his voice, which draws me in. Gradually, his pronouns change—"they tortured them" becomes "they tortured us." He brings us in closer. His performance animates the space and keeps it alive. His body connects me to what Pinochet wanted to disappear, not just the place but the trauma. Matta's presence performs the claim, embodies it, *le da cuerpo*. He has survived to tell. ¡Presente! Being in place with him communicates a very different sense of the crimes than looking down on the model. Walking through Villa Grimaldi with Matta brings the past up close, past as actually not past. Now. Here. And in many parts of the world, as we speak.

I can't think past that, rooted as I am to place suddenly restored as practice. I too am part of this scenario now; I don't need to lock myself up in the cell to be doing. I have accompanied him here. My eyes look straight down, mimetically rather than reflectively, through his downturned eyes. I do not see really; I imagine. I *presenciar*; I presence (as active verb). Embodied cognition, neuroscientists call this, but we in theatre have always understood it as mimesis and empathy—we learn and absorb by mirroring other people. I participate not in the events but in his transmission of the affect emanating from the events. My presencing offers me no sense of control, no fiction of understanding. He walks through the Patio de Abedules; he sits on the semicircle that remains from the camp; he tells. When he gets to one of the original trees, used to torture prisoners in various ingenious ways, he acts out some of the hanging positions he and others endured. He suffered a permanent lesion in his shoulder, he told us, and his heart was affected. In front of where the torture rooms stood, he relates that the tortured body begins to release water from all its pores. Although completely dehydrated, the person cannot drink water because the remaining electricity in the body would electrocute him or her. It takes a few hours to de-electrify. And electricity, he continued, makes the body contract, so the torturers would tie the victim down with a leather strap. Prisoners were left with lasting damage to their spinal columns, and often their sphincters. When he gets to the memorial wall marked with the names of the dead (built twenty years after the violent events), he breaks down and cries. He cries for those who died but also for those who survived. "Torture," he says, "destroys the human being. And I am no exception. I was destroyed through torture." This is the climax of the tour. The past and the present come together in this admission. Torture works into the future, yet it forecloses the very possibility of future. Torture creates the "ruins yet to come."[10] The torture site is transitional, but torture itself is transformative—it turns societies into terrifying places and people into zombies.[11]

When Matta leaves the memorial wall, his tone shifts again. He has moved out of the death space. Now he is more personal and informal in his interaction with us. We walk and talk about how other survivors have dealt with trauma, about similarities and differences with other torture centers and concentration camps. He says he needs to come back. The walkthrough reconnects him with his friends who were disappeared. Whenever he visits with a group who is interested in the subject, he feels he is doing what he wishes one of his friends had done for him had he been the one disappeared. He transmits. He keeps them ¡presentes! Alive. He's a living

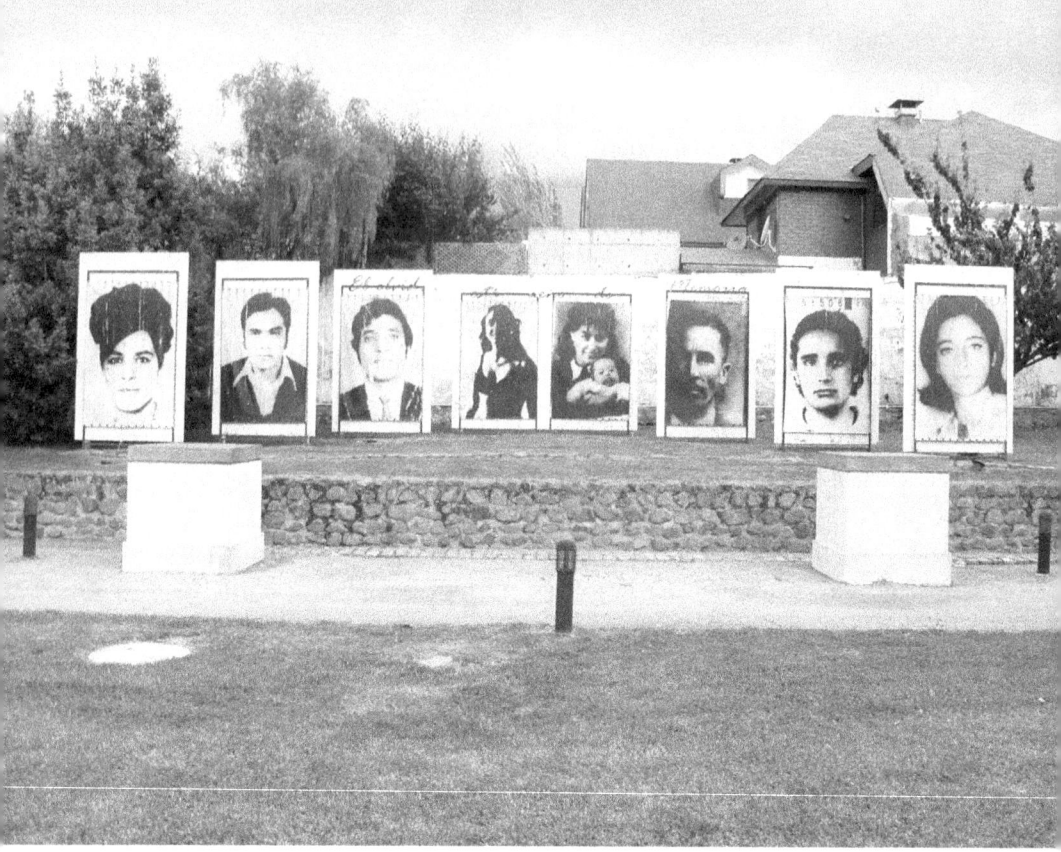

7.6 "El pasado está lleno de olvido." PHOTO: DIANA TAYLOR.

monument, demanding justice, refusing erasure. His activism originates in the death space—now necropolitics from the dead that fight back. Afterward he goes home physically and emotionally drained, he says, and drinks a liter of fruit juice and goes to sleep—he doesn't get up until the following morning. His body still hurts from the torture, and he has developed debilitating aftereffects. We continue to walk, past the replica of the water tower where the high-value prisoners were isolated, past the *sala de la memoria* (memory room)—one of the few remaining original buildings, which served as the photo and silkscreen rooms. At the pool, also original, he relates one of the most chilling accounts told to him by a collaborator. At the memory tree, he touches the names of the dead that hang from the branches, like leaves. Different commemorative art and memorials for the dead have been installed by some of the political parties and organizations most virulently hit by the armed forces—the Chilean Communist Party and the MIR, the Revolutionary Left Movement, among others, line the periphery like small grave plots. Near the exit, a large sign with names of the dead reminds us, "El pasado está lleno de olvido" (The past is full of forgetting) (fig. 7.6).

And of course, the ever hopeful Never Again (*Nunca Más*). He barely notices the fountain—the Christian overlay of redemption was the government's idea, clearly.

After we leave the site, we invite Matta to lunch at a nearby restaurant that he recommends. He tells us about his arrest in 1975 for being a student activist, his time as a political prisoner in Villa Grimaldi, his exile to the U.S. in 1976, and his work as a private detective in San Francisco until he returned to Chile in 1991. He used his investigative skills to gather as much information as possible about what happened in Villa Grimaldi, to identify the prisoners, and to name the torturers stationed there. One day, he says, he was having lunch in this same restaurant after one of the visits to Villa Grimaldi when an ex-torturer walked in and sat at a nearby table with his family. They were having such a good time. The two men looked at each other, and Matta got up and walked out.

Later a colleague tells me that Matta does the visit the same way every time—stands in the same spot, recounts the same events, cries at the memorial wall. Some commentators find this odd, as if the routine makes the emotion suspect. Are the tears for real? Every time? Is there something fake about the performance? Is Matta a professional trauma survivor? But the re-enactment, I believe, is central both to trauma and to performance. Trauma, like performance, is known by the nature of its repeats, "never for the first time." We speak of trauma only when the event cannot be processed and produces the characteristic aftershocks. Trauma, like performance, is always experienced in the present. Here. Now.

Trauma, studies show, lays down new memory tracks. Neuroscientists suggest that these paths are physiological as well as material, fixed in the brain as a specifically patterned circuit of neurons. Being in a situation or place can automatically provoke certain behaviors unless other memory tracks are laid down to replace them.[12] A cue or trigger can suddenly send the mind to para-spaces and times, experienced as viscerally and immediately present. Various kinds of treatments, such as immersion therapy and virtual reality, aim to gradually and carefully expose people to the place or thing that traumatized them until they can separate out the cue from the uncontrolled emotional onslaught. For people trapped in the stairwells of the falling World Trade Center, for example, stairs may take on a terrifying dimension that makes it difficult, if not impossible, for them to use stairs or even take elevators. The therapy helps them internalize that the stairs are not in and of themselves dangerous or life threatening. Moreover, they may be able to access the memories of the day when they choose to, without being overwhelmed and disoriented by intrusive thoughts and feelings. The old cues no longer automatically transport the person back to the traumatic injury.

For a survivor of torture, going back to the torture camp is a deliberate reentry into a painful memory path. Memory, we know, is linked to place— one clear reason why that place needs not only to exist but to be marked for the violence to be acknowledged. For any guide, routine serves a mnemonic function—people can remember certain events by associating them with place.[13] Through the recorrido, the act of walking, the body remembers. Matta, I believe, has been able to separate out some of the traumatic experiences from his daily life, choosing to encounter them and even allowing himself to feel them in safe settings such as these guided visits. These tours then give him a way to keep his past alive yet under control. A change in Matta's routine might well change the affect. But routine also protects against unexpected affect—survivors can often recall some aspects of their torment and not others—there are some places (literally and physiologically) where no one dares to go.

For Matta, both victim and witness, trauma is a durational performance. His experience does not last the two hours of the walk-through nor his many months of imprisonment—it has lasted years, since he was disappeared by the armed forces. His reiterated acts of leading people down the paths exemplify trauma and the trauma-driven actions to channel and alleviate it. As with the Mothers of Plaza de Mayo, the ritualized tour offers him both personal consolation and revenge. Memory is a tool and a political project— an honoring of those who are gone, and a reminder to those who will listen that the victimizers have gotten away with murder. His tour, like the Mothers' march, bears witness to what gets spectacularized—a society in which judicial systems cannot bring perpetrators to justice—and what gets invisibilized: rapacious economic systems that disappear certain populations. Yet the walk-through, like the march, also makes visible the memory paths that maintain another topography of place and practice, not of terror but of resistance—the will not only to live but also to keep memory alive.

Matta has been instrumental in building the evidence, investigating and collecting documentation on what happened at Villa Grimaldi and other torture centers, such as the names of those detained there and those who worked there. He worked to preserve Villa Grimaldi as a memorial site. He helped construct the model; he wrote and published the booklet, "A Walk through a 20th Century Torture Center." He has actively participated in creating the external material markers that designate this a dark site. He has led countless groups through the site and even prepared for a visit without him present. The book maps out every move; the brutal images in the margins make visible every practice: "Here the torture began. . . ." The book, given the nature of print media, tells same story the same way every time. It outlines the path and numbers the stops: here people were tortured with electricity. . . . The numbers in the book—like a tour guide—align with the map. Actually, it's a double map—one layer shows the torture camp, while a semitransparent layer of onion paper outlines the peace park, with the pavilion, the fountain, and the numbered places of interest: "storage of confiscated goods" and "sites for hanging." A red dotted line outlines the recorrido exactly as Matta conducts it. This trace, then, is the trauma made visible in the archive, envisioned by Matta to outlast him and transmit meaning to those who come after to visit the space.

Being in the site with Matta, however, is a powerful affective experience—one of a kind for me even if it's a repeat performance for him. What does Matta's performance want of me as audience or as witness? What does it mean about witnessing and the quality of being in place? He needs others (in this case me) to acknowledge what happened there, to accompany him and carry on the struggle for the preservation of historical place and memory, that is, to become witnesses. "To witness," a transitive verb, defines both the act and the person carrying it out; the verb precedes the noun—it is through the act of witnessing that we become a witness. Identity relies on the action. We are both the subject and the product of our acts. Matta is the witness for those who are no longer alive to tell; he is the witness to himself as he tells of his own ordeal; he is a witness in the juridical sense—having brought charges against the Pinochet dictatorship. He is also the object of my witnessing—he needs me to acknowledge what he and others went through in Villa Grimaldi. The transitivity of "witness" ties us together—that's one reason he's keen to gauge the nature of his audience. Trauma-driven activism (like trauma itself) cannot simply be told or known; it needs to be enacted, repeated, and externalized through embodied practice.

Torture, of course, produces the opposite of witnessing—it silences, breaks personal and social bonds, and guts all sense of community and responsibility. No walking and talking with others allowed. Torture isolates and paralyzes both victims and bystanders, who are tempted to look away, turn a blind eye. Percepticide, I've called this elsewhere.[14] Better not see. It's too dangerous to see, to notice what's going on around us. This is why regimes continue to practice torture even though they know that they receive no actionable information. It's inaction they seek. My job, as I understand it, is to take action (maybe with a small *a*, as opposed to inaction), to acknowledge the violence generated by our governments, to follow Matta in his reenactment, to make connections to the other events I know to be true, to write and teach about the place, or donate money, or bring other people.

Still, I can understand what Matta is doing here better than I can understand what I am doing here. I wonder about aura and worry about voyeurism and (dark) tourism. Is Matta my close-up—bringing unspeakable violence up as close as possible? If so, to what end? This too is multilayered in the ways that the personal, interpersonal, social, and political come together. Walking through Villa Grimaldi with Matta, the oversize issues of human rights violations and crimes against humanity—too large and general on one level—take on an immediate and embodied form. It enables us, to paraphrase Fredric Jameson, "to insert ourselves, as individual subjects, into an ever more massive and impersonal or transpersonal reality outside ourselves."[15] In our everyday lives, we have no way of dealing with violent acts that shatter the limits of our understanding. We all live in proximity to criminal violence—and though some of us have felt it more personally than others, this violence is never just personal. This is the strength and weakness of this kind of memorialization—it's so personalized and concentrated that it tends to focus just on the designated victims and space. But if we focus only on the personal trauma, we risk evacuating the politics. Standing there, together, bringing the buildings and routines back to life, we bear witness not just to the personal and collective loss but to a system of power relations, hierarchies, and values that not only allowed but required the destruction of others.

Matta, the booklet tells us, "feels a strong desire to transform history into memory." He makes the past alive for others through the performance of his *recorrido*. Yet trauma keeps the past alive in Matta as well—the future is not an option for him as long as Terranova continues to call him to that place. The future in fact might be a very different project. In the best of all possible worlds, the future would mean turning this memory into history, the testimonial walk-through into archival and juridical evidence, Matta's personal admonition into legally binding indictments against perpetrators, and visitors into motivated witnesses, human rights activists, and voters. Someone else, maybe someone who has never been tortured, would lead the tour, with or without Matta's guide. But that future is predicated on a past in which justice has been done and/or trauma transcended or resolved. That future is nowhere in sight even though the arrow points us toward the fountain symbolizing life and hope. The tour does not offer us the end of traumatic memory or the end of performance. Looking downward, we follow Matta as he negotiates this transitional space between remembrance and future project.

Contested Presents

2012: I heard that the renovations on Villa Grimaldi had been completed under President Michelle Bachelet's government, herself a victim of detention and torture in Villa Grimaldi; her father a general killed by Pinochet. The space had been renovated and outfitted with an educational and resource center. An audio tour was available in several languages. It felt important to go back—this time without a survivor, to try to understand how presence and voice affected my understanding of the space. As before, no taxi driver knew anything about the place and finally, one simply dropped me off at the address on José Arrieta. The outside looked very different, more institutional though understated. Inside, the homemade sign at the gate, reminding me to behave, was gone. A steel plinth mapped out the timeline. Villa Grimaldi, I sensed, had been incorporated into the international memory site industry. Thus yet another layer had been added to the site. My photographs from my earlier visit suddenly took on new evidentiary significance. A lot had changed. I picked up the headphones and transmitter from a young woman at the new resource center and chose the tour in Spanish. The room contained books and charts giving information—listing the detention centers in Santiago and identifying some of the officers who worked there. As before, there was no one there, and I asked the person in the resource center if I might be allowed to look in the new buildings. She said there was no one to show me but, sensing my disappointment, she handed me the keys and asked me to lock up and bring them back to her after I was finished.

Even without the sign asking me to behave, or a survivor sharing his ordeal, the keys on the heart-shaped key ring made me feel very responsible. I put on the headphones and started my walk. The quiet, rhythmic voice of the unidentified female audio guide informs the listener that the "Peace Parque Villa Grimaldi stands on the site of a former secret center for kidnapping, torture, and extermination." Without knowing who was speaking, I assumed that the young, fresh voice had been untouched by the violence she was describing. This was a new generation. The instructions were clear from the outset—move to the different points in the audio tour, marked on the xeroxed map.

Now the site is much more ordered. The paths are clearly marked and illuminated—some of the beauty of the nineteenth-century villa restored with the wading pools and multiple fountains. The site has been integrated, visually and politically, into the surrounding neighborhood. The neighboring houses are clearly visible. Their view of the park must be quite pleasant. What do they actually see? The torture site has been domesticated—the visceral pain I felt with Matta has given way to repose. This clearly transmits the sense of a different political moment. With the opening of the new Museum of Memory and Human Rights that same year, it appears that the contestation has given way to a time of acceptance and memorialization.

The recorrido followed the same route taken by Matta—the handmade model camp was gone, replaced by a new glossy and machine-made replica (fig. 7.7). Everything was brittle and white, as in a deep freeze. The model made visible the original structures on the site and those added to it over time when it became an official site. I recognized the structures, but not the feeling. It had been drained of color, sapped of its human history. It was a different kind of emptying than I had felt the first time I visited—the brutality of the demolition had been replaced by the negation of life itself.

Moving to the locked iron gate on my own, I stop to peer out the aperture. Now the designated stops are marked by plaques with the audio numbers and new tile markers, enacting the mandate both to fix in place and to update. But there are some new buildings, locked. I find the key and let myself in. The cases running the length of the cube-shaped building balanced on its side exhibit pieces of metal that the military had attached to the bodies they threw in the ocean so that they wouldn't float. For a long time I look at the exhibit and finally pay attention to a small magnifying glass positioned in an odd way. What is that? Finally I see it. The button accentuated by the magnifying glass offers proof, if any is still needed, of what happened to the bodies. In plain sight. How had it taken me so long to see it?

I keep walking. The crisp soft voice of the audio draws on a great number of testimonies and gives far more detail than Matta did. There are more dates, figures, facts. The separation of data into short bits makes sense, of course—supposing that the listener will have time to move from place to place. I wander as I listen and feel free now, without a survivor present, to walk into Casas Chile, and peer out the peephole. I take a photograph and wonder what I'm doing. Does the photo prove that I am here? Or that it was there? But where? This replica did not form part of the torture center

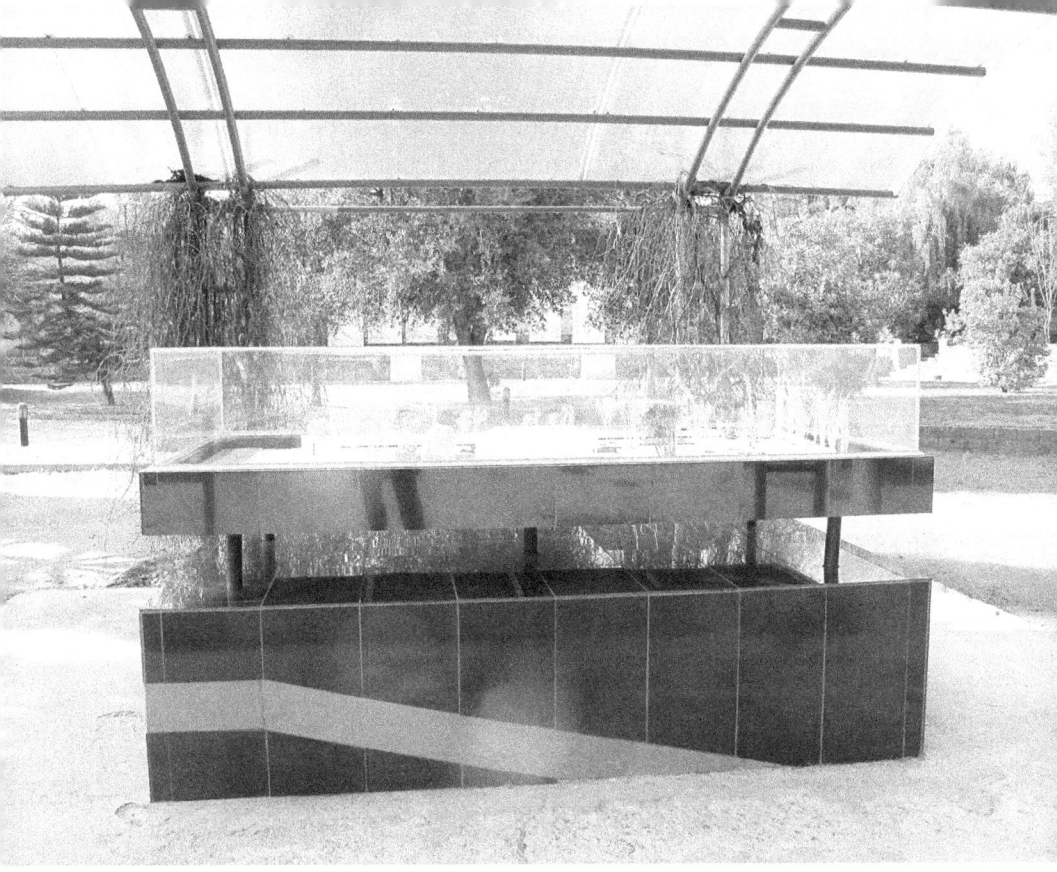

7.7 Model of Terranova, 2012. PHOTO: DIANA TAYLOR.

that I am ostensibly visiting, knowing full well that the detention center, and the objects, and the people are long gone. The audio conveys a break with the past—no para- about it. I continue on the designated path and listen. The segments are disturbing, not just in their content but in their fragmentation. They start and end abruptly—often after a particularly interesting or disturbing image.

Segment 5: Patio de Abedules—the men were allowed to sit on the bench in the open air for a few minutes a day under strict supervision. Because they could not see, they depended on their sense of smell and developed a secret code of sounds to communicate. The audio goes dead. Wait, say more!

Segment 6: Cells and torture rooms . . . the women's cells had a window painted over through which they could see the men being taken to the torture rooms. They could identify the men and their torturers. Next door to them was a room called the *parrilla* (or grill) where prisoners were stripped, bound to a metal bed, and tortured with electricity. End of section. No, let me down easy!

Next segment . . . the same controlled tone speaks of unimaginable brutality and describes a woman captive with a voice like Edith Piaf's who sang to drown out the screams of the torture. No, wait! Next segment . . .

Even when the guide cites specific testimony, there is no change in tone. As I walk, the voice points out the rose garden, planted in honor of female victims. Survivors had spoken of smelling roses at the compound. The women were raped there. So it seemed fitting to name each plant after a woman who died there. Again, the need to individualize terror.

I fumble with the buttons on the digital recorder and feel silly with the headphones even though the site is empty. I get impatient as the voice tells me in a matter-of-fact way the political acts that led to the creation of this torture center. The details—the names of the generals, organizations, and so on—overwhelm me. I feel face to face with History, and I miss the human scale. The temporal and affective gaps expand. I feel tempted to pull the headphones off, but resist temptation. When the audio segment comes to an end, I pause, search the map for the next stop, and move toward it.

I take in the facts but the voice does not speak to me, and I find the disconnect between the tone and tale distracting. It's as if we could separate out the different moments, routines, and spaces. The pauses between segments too seem very different from Matta's recounting. His silences were full of memory. His face, body, mood transmitted his thinking processes and affective swings. I cannot identify the silences of the audio—they were simply blank nothing, not even tape. If forgetting and silence are full of memory, full of life, the audio has a hard time capturing that life. I felt dutiful, but not engaged, as I followed the voice around Villa Grimaldi. Walking and listening were part of a pedagogical exercise in Never Again.

I keep walking off on my own, peering around. Suddenly, I come across all the original handmade materials in a heap, under tarps, in a shed behind a building. The names of the dead have bled on the sign, reminding us that "forgetting is full of memory." Memory, now updated with the new model and signs, is also full of forgetting. Someone's memory-making labor has been superseded (figs. 7.8–7.9).

All at once I feel very alone as I continue the walk-through and, as before, wonder what I am doing there. If Matta needed me *presenciar* and *acompañar*, I realize now how much I needed him to experience Villa Grimaldi as a practiced place.

The voice without the body radically changes my experience of being in place. Alone, I do not respond, and (perhaps related) I feel less responsible. There is no "I" or "me" envisioned in this audio tour—no human being

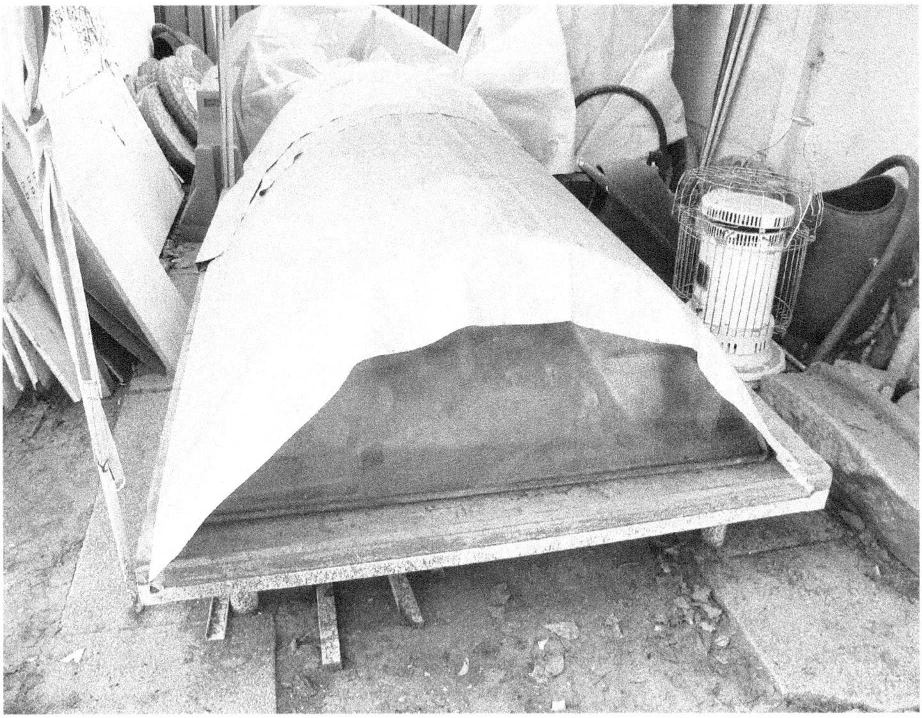

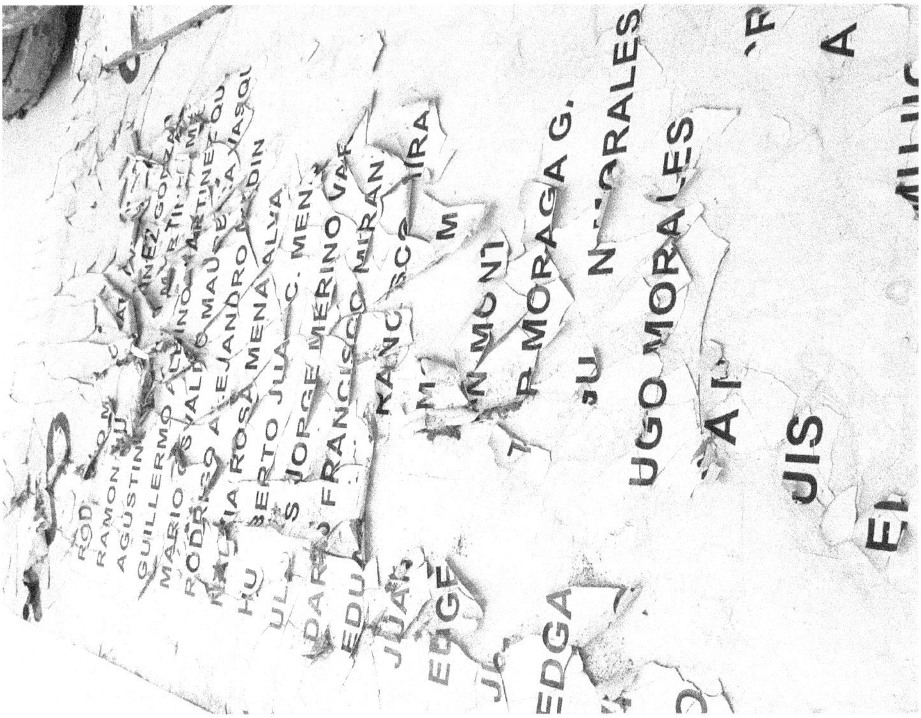

7.8–7.9 Faded memories, 2012. PHOTOS: DIANA TAYLOR.

who challenges me or holds me in part responsible for what happened. The communicative pact is now between two unknowns whose reasons for participating in this project remain unexplored. Instead of bringing the past up close and making evident the networks that link us not just affectively but politically, the audio shuts (and locks) the gateway to that past. From a safe now, I enter into the land of long ago and far away. As I listen, I know this is the place things happened to "them," but I find it hard to connect or imagine.

What does this tour ask of me, the visitor? The voice thanks me for my visit. It explains that Villa Grimaldi is a material and symbolic trace of state terrorism under Augusto Pinochet. The explanation clearly lays out the criminal practice linked to neoliberal economic politics. It says that the visit is a look to the past. Still, "we hope" (says the unidentified voice) that it prompts reflection on the present and an impetus to halt human rights abuses throughout the world. If "I" am interested in knowing more, then please visit the web page, and so on. She also gives me a phone number.

I take the headphones and the keys back to the office and ask about the narration of the audio. The person at the desk said she thought they had chosen a well-known young actress from a telenovela (soap opera) with no direct ties to the violent past because they wanted the younger generations to identify. This, then, is no longer about Matta, and trauma, and justice deferred. It is about asking the next generation to understand their history. The multilingual audio tour also reaches out to international visitors. Here is the very future envisioned by Matta with his booklet, but he is nowhere part of this new post-survivor moment. Memory has been actualized, and now the battle lines have been drawn differently. With Bachelet out of office after the constitutional ban on sequential reelection, right-wing businessman Sebastián Piñera became president in 2010. Villa Grimaldi and the Museum of Memory had lost almost half of their operating budget. I spent some time talking with the woman in the visitor's office. Her father had been a prisoner at Villa Grimaldi. He never spoke of his experience, though he has come back to the camp/park/memory site a couple of times. The repose offered by the domestication of Villa Grimaldi and the lulling voice is not as untroubled as it seems. These are still contested spaces, contested presents, and contested pasts.

This Is Not the Place

In 2013 I once again returned to Villa Grimaldi, this time accompanied by a group of colleagues from the U.S., Turkey, and Chile who were part of the

Women Mobilizing Change project and wanted to experience the tour with Pedro Matta.[16] Teresa Anativia, a close friend and survivor of Villa Grimaldi, accompanied us. She and Pedro know each other, and the tour this time was less scripted as the two of them spontaneously recollected incidents that took place in various parts of the site. Teresa could speak far more directly to the things that women had experienced there. She had already told me some of the terrible things that DINA had done to her and her companions in that place, and she had told me too about the first time she and other survivors had returned after the space had been reclaimed.[17] They all met—about 150 survivors, she recalls, outside the site and entered together. Once inside, the priest José Aldunate locked the *portón* shut forever. Never again would someone come through that terrifying entryway. The survivors hugged and wept in silence. She recalls that everyone shut their eyes as they embraced their fellow survivors. They had never seen each other before. They had never heard each other's voices. "The silence at a reunion of the blind who had been together and had never seen each other," as she put it. They started to look around the space, covered with brambles and barbed wire, and recognized nothing. "We looked for those places and we couldn't find them. I know I will never find them," she concluded. Afterward, sitting there, I asked her if returning to Villa Grimaldi had upset her.

"No," she said. "This is not the place."

Then she added, "But my bones hurt."

The redesigned space, landscaped gardens, roses, beautiful trees, the water pools and pavilion had nothing to do with the place in which she had been tortured, violated, and denied her humanity.

That "place" remains in her; she carries it with her everywhere. As Charlotte Delbo, the Holocaust survivor, writes in *Days and Memory*: "I don't live with Auschwitz, I live next to it."[18]

What then, does the renovated Villa Grimaldi do?

At one point, during the early years of the survivors' struggle to secure the space as a memory site, the place was probably intended, in part, as a place to externalize and put one's grief. They had lost an enormous amount in that place. A tortured woman lost the twins she was carrying. Teresa and Pedro both admitted to losing not only friends, but part of their own humanity—their ability to trust others. Their bodies changed, and they carry the pains and fractures induced by torture into their older age. The loss and grief that accompany disappearance and torture belong to that realm of invalidated grief. The Madres in Chile, like those of the Plaza de Mayo in Argentina, never knew if their children were alive or dead. The government did not acknowledge their loss. How can one grieve under these circumstances?[19]

While those killed in Villa Grimaldi are named in the rosters of victims on the current Villa Grimaldi website and carved into the Memory Wall, survivors have no place. The 1991 Rettig Report, issued after the Truth and Reconciliation Commission, listed only the cases of those disappeared and murdered by the Pinochet regime. The Valech Report, issued by the National Commission on Political Imprisonment and Torture (2004–5), acknowledged those who had been tortured and detained, as well as children of the disappeared. The Chilean state used that list to make reparations to survivors, but the names and circumstances have been locked away for fifty years, as if to make sure no one is brought to justice. Torture and disappearance, we know, continue to affect the victims and their families for generations.

Places like Parque de la Paz Villa Grimaldi remind us of what happened within those walls, the unmaking of so many worlds for those who passed through Terranova. I cannot capture that place with my camera. Matta conjures the past site for others to see, and Teresa Anativia does not recognize it anymore, though she feels it in her bones. These memory sites transcend the violence and pain in search of peace and reconciliation. The park performs a restorative, world-making gesture. Its existence refuses the long-standing

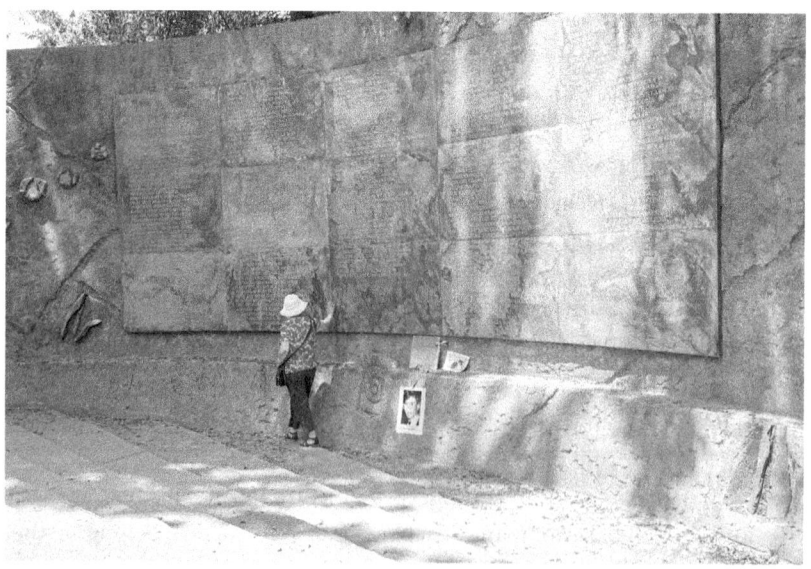

7.10 Teresa Anativia at the Memory Wall, Villa Grimaldi, 2013. PHOTO: LORIE NOVAK.

official mandate to forget. Being in the park with them, I feel the power of place and its crucial evidentiary importance. I sense the pain they associate with it, and I accompany them for a little while on their very long journey toward justice, acceptance, and renewal.

Transmitting Trauma

Our Mobilizing Memory working group for the Hemispheric Institute Encuentro in Chile in 2016 decided to go to Villa Grimaldi, and I asked Pedro Matta to walk us through. Matta was incredibly helpful to me. He met with me several times and showed me his journals and the log books with the names of the military assigned to the different detention centers that he had investigated and compiled over the years. He asked to be paid for the walk through Villa Grimaldi. He is a survivor, but he's also a teacher and researcher of Chile's terrible past. I agreed.

Back in the working group, some participants objected to paying Matta. Why would a survivor charge to tell his story? Was that ethical? Is he a professional survivor? I stressed his importance as a researcher and teacher. Some participants decided not to go to Villa Grimaldi. After a back and forth with the rest as to how much we would pay him, some thirty-five of us met Matta at the gates. Teresa Anativia joined us.

The question, again, was what language he would speak. The group decided that he should speak in Spanish, and I volunteered to translate for the rest.

Again, we started at the new, shiny model with the explanation of how Cuartel Terranova had worked, and then we began the walk around the villa.

At first, the translation was easy—Matta transmitted facts, and so did I. Here this happened—back then, to them. All distanced, all third person. We walked to the locked entry gate, and then the first torture chambers. Gradually, as before, Matta's pronouns slipped. "They tortured them" became "they tortured us." The words gnawed into me.

"They tortured us," I had to say. "They strapped me down here, put electrodes to my genitals, to my temples, in all my orifices. My body arched with the shock. I was sweating so much I was at risk of electrocuting myself." As I said these words, my body began unconsciously to take on Matta's gestures and movements. His pauses became my pauses. My body became the medium. It happened gradually, imperceptibly, the further we got into the past that was not past, the torture that had never stopped or gone away. I lost the distance so vital to witnessing. Witnessing accompanies but does not take the place of the injured person. This was not walking and talking.

As my voice echoed his, I lost the sense of my own boundedness and emotional integrity.

Against my wishes, I began to embody the pain. I felt the words violating my body. My resentment and anger grew as I said the words. I felt forced to say them. Unlike Matta, I had no control over the words I used. Unlike those listening to him, I could not walk away. Suddenly, I had been deprived of agency. How did this happen? My anger increased. I felt like crying. Why don't these people learn Spanish, damn it? Let me stay outside, listening, taking photographs. He kept telling his story in a low, undramatic way. He used no adjectives, I realized now that the words were in my mouth. My senses locked down, focusing only on what he was relating. Translating became inhabiting, identifying with him and what he was recounting. I didn't want to be there. But maybe I was also channeling his feelings of not wanting to be there either.

Anger became my distancing device. At the end of the trajectory, I thanked Matta and handed him the money, promising myself I would never come back again. He might be a professional survivor, but I am not a professional witness.

And yet, of course, I am.

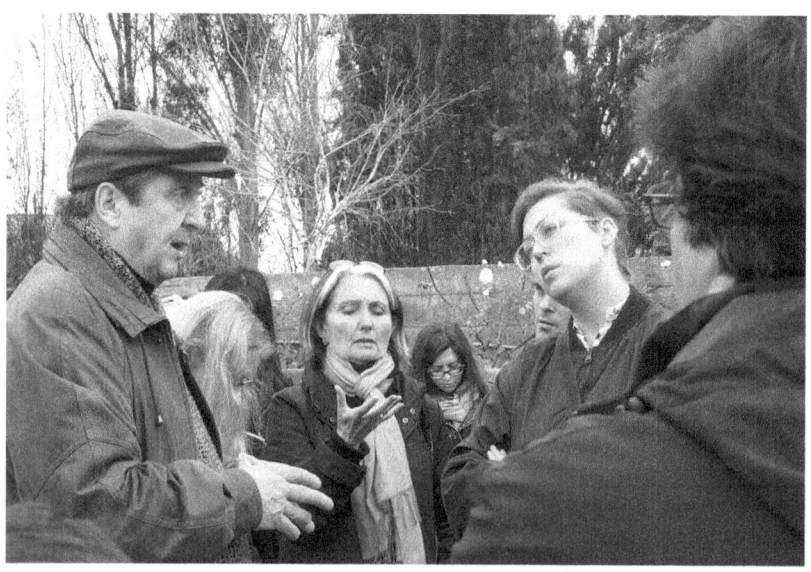

7.11 Diana Taylor translating for Pedro Matta, Villa Grimaldi, 2016. PHOTO: LORIE NOVAK.

Trauma in the Archive

It is not an exaggeration to state that future knowledge of this site will be available only through archival materials—the audio tour, the replicas, the memorial wall, the art pieces staged in the experiential practice that characterizes current memorialization practices. Villa Grimaldi now also offers virtual tours on its website.[20] We enter the space that has been set up in such a way that the archival objects might spark an affective reaction in the visitors. But it's hard for me to imagine that these objects will move someone who has not been involved in the practice, who has never been to the site, or who has no connection to what happened there. The punctum, or the prick, might emanate from outside us but it needs to spark something in the viewer/listener. Trauma lives in the body, not in the archive

The Parque de la Paz continues to be a highly practiced place. The violently contested history of spatial practices returns and disturbs the present. Memory is being constantly updated.[21] Personal testimonies become part of the historical narrative. On the evidentiary level, Villa Grimaldi demonstrates both the centrality and complexity of place in individual and collective memory. What happens to that space is tantamount to what happens to Chileans' understanding of the dictatorship: will people repress, remember, transcend, or forget? The warring mandates about the space rehearse the more salient public options: tear it down to bury the violence; build a commemorative park so that people will know what happened; let's get beyond violence by hosting cultural events in the pavilion; forget about this desolate place, forget about this sorry past; let's use this place to educate future generations.[22] Nowhere is there talk of justice or retribution.

The questions posed by these dark sites extend far beyond the fences built around them. The small model near the entrance is to Villa Grimaldi what Villa Grimaldi is to Chile, and what Chile is to the rest of the Americas: a miniature rendition of a much larger project. Over a thousand civic and public places like villas and gyms and department stores and schools were used for criminal violence under Pinochet. How do we know that the whole city did not function as a clandestine torture center? The scale of the violations is stunning. The ubiquity of the practice spills over and contaminates social life. We might control a site and put a fence around it, but the city, the country, the southern cone, the hemisphere has been networked for violence—and beyond, too, of course, and not just because the U.S. opted to outsource torture. I actually do always know what happened here/there and accept that this, like many other sites, is my responsibility. I do participate in a political project that depends on making certain populations disappear. I am constantly warned to keep vigil, to "say something" if I "see something." Though I shirked responsibility when I first met Matta—the Mexican government had nothing to do with the Chilean coup—there is another layer. After years of my own self-blinding, I realized that the Mexican government under then-president Luis Echeverria disappeared thousands of young people, about the same age as I was then. Now that I live and work in the U.S., I know my tax dollars pay for Guantanamo, for torture in prisons and migrant detention centers and who knows what else. The walks remind me I just need to look closer, look again at *what* I see and *how* I see. The *how* determines the *what*. Something has been restored through the walks, with all their differences, that brings several of these worlds into direct contact. As the multitiered space itself invites, I recognize the layers and layers of political and corporeal practices that have created these places, the politics of historical transmission, the personal histories we bring to them, and the emotions that get triggered as we walk through them in our own ways. I experience the tour as performance, and as trauma, and I know it's never for the first, or last, time.

EIGHT

Dead Capital

It seems as if culture consists in deeply martyring matter and pushing it through a relentless gut. It's a consolation to think that not even excrement can be forced to leave the planet.—JOAQUÍN O. GIANNUZZI, *Lixo ao amanhecer* (Trash at Dawn)

I

Bom Retiro 958 metros, a performance by Teatro da Vertigem, leads us on a walk through São Paulo's phantasmagoric world of things. Things, in this performance, revolve around fabric. Things such as dresses and fine cloth sold in shopping malls; things such as homeless people's blankets and torn wedding gowns; things such as remnants of cloth and used clothing tossed in garbage cans; things in their devolving states of glory, comfort, disuse, and decomposition. Teatro da Vertigem, directed by Antonio Araújo, gradually leads us through a deeply disorienting experience. Walking, we spectators feel pushed and pulled by forces we can hardly define. This world, in which everything and everyone have lost their ch'ulel and ich'el ta muk—their life force and dignity—brings us face to face with questions of materiality and circulation as people and things become unraveled, fall out of presence. This chapter bookends the camino largo of the Zapatistas as we continue to move implacably toward the unmaking of the world. I hold on by the proverbial thread that leads through this most visceral examination of materiality, the thingness of cloth, its history, its politics, the people that make it, and the people that it unmakes.

Sixty to eighty people can attend a performance. After gathering at the Oswald de Andrade cultural center in the immigrant, working-class neighborhood of Bom Retiro, we pick up a map with instructions to the meeting place: turn left after leaving the building; cross Lubavitch Street; go down four blocks and turn left to our destination, 259 Prof Cesare Lombroso Street. The buildings and street names tell a part of the history. De Andrade argued in his "Manifesto Antropófago" (Cannibalist Manifesto) that cultures remain strong by eating and digesting others: "Only Cannibalism unites us. Socially. Economically. Philosophically."[1] Lubavitch Street reflects the early Jewish immigration to this neighborhood. Lombroso argued that criminality was passed down through generations and could be recognized through physiognomy.[2] The locations reveal terrifying theories of transmission, cemented into the very geography of place and practice. Shop signs in Korean tell of the new waves of immigrants that mostly replaced the (now) well-off Jews who moved to better residential areas. Bolivians, working for Koreans, are the new lowest of the low.

The evening back streets are empty and the shops shuttered close. We wind our way in groups of twos and threes along the uneven sidewalks. But this is not the Aristotelian peripatetic walking and talking with others. As I walk, I am careful to keep my eyes on the shadowy, uneven ground. I notice various pieces of fabric bursting out of garbage bags tilted against the streetlights along the way, things left over from other things, dresses, pants, jackets. Walking further, I detect something strange about the streetlights. A few steps later, a street sign shows a person at a sewing machine (fig. 8.1). What is going on? Did Araújo alter the cityscape?

I'm concerned about an elderly woman who walks beside me, an artist from Mexico I had met previously. I worry for her on the treacherous sidewalks and hold onto her arm. What if she falls and breaks something? Is Vertigem liable? I stop to look at something written on the wall. Is it part of the performance? Everything takes on a new intentionality. All the random bits and pieces of everyday life seem aligned or assembled in a slightly altered order, inviting us to decipher them. When I turn back to walk, the old woman has gone—I see her ahead of me, single-mindedly moving toward the performance site.

Finally, everyone converges at our destination, apparently just a dim and desolate street. A woman with a vacant stare sits in a chair listening to a radio in front of a closed door. We hear the crackle of static. Suddenly, workers delivering boxes of merchandise come crashing down the street, *bestias de carga* or beasts of burden, the script calls them.[3] Soon shoppers carrying large bags join them, hammering the door to get in. They all line up and pause in front of the large metallic door that covers what we discover is a shopping mall. Then they push it open (fig. 8.2). That pause—a tableaux

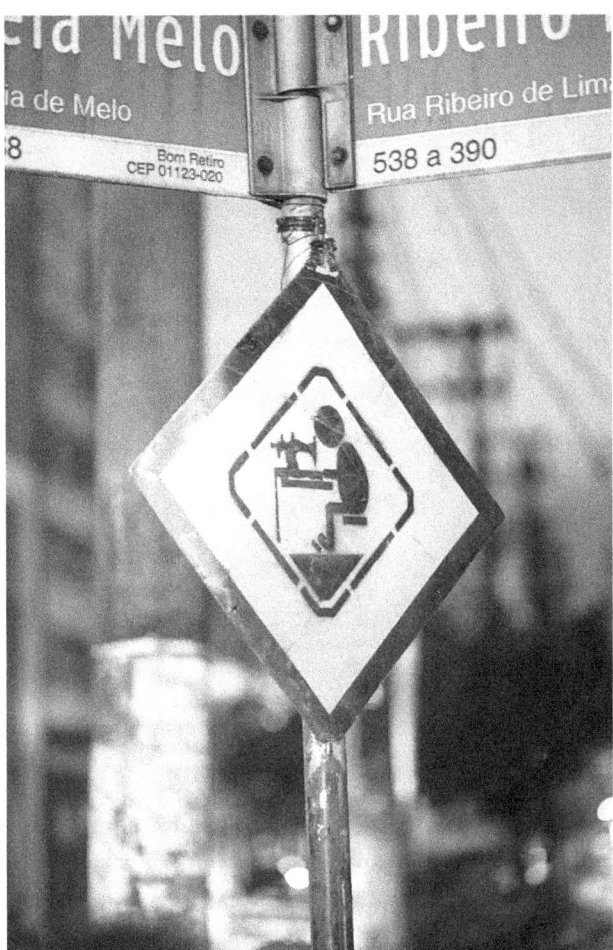

8.1 The street sign shows a person at a sewing machine. Teatro da Vertigem, *Bom Retiro 958 metros*, Hemispheric Institute Encuentro, São Paulo, 2013. PHOTO: FRANCIS POLLITT.

vivant—captures the anticipation of the before and after; that all-powerful moment of exchange of goods in capitalism.

Suddenly, gloriously, the light from the mall spills over us like daybreak. Sonorous rumblings herald us inside. Everything is alive! The lights and music pulsate like heartbeats. An invisible hand guides us deeper and deeper into the dark maze of the shopping mall. We have been initiated into the temple of things.

Over the next two hours, spectators physically experience the vertiginous pull and push of things. I say things instead of objects because "object"

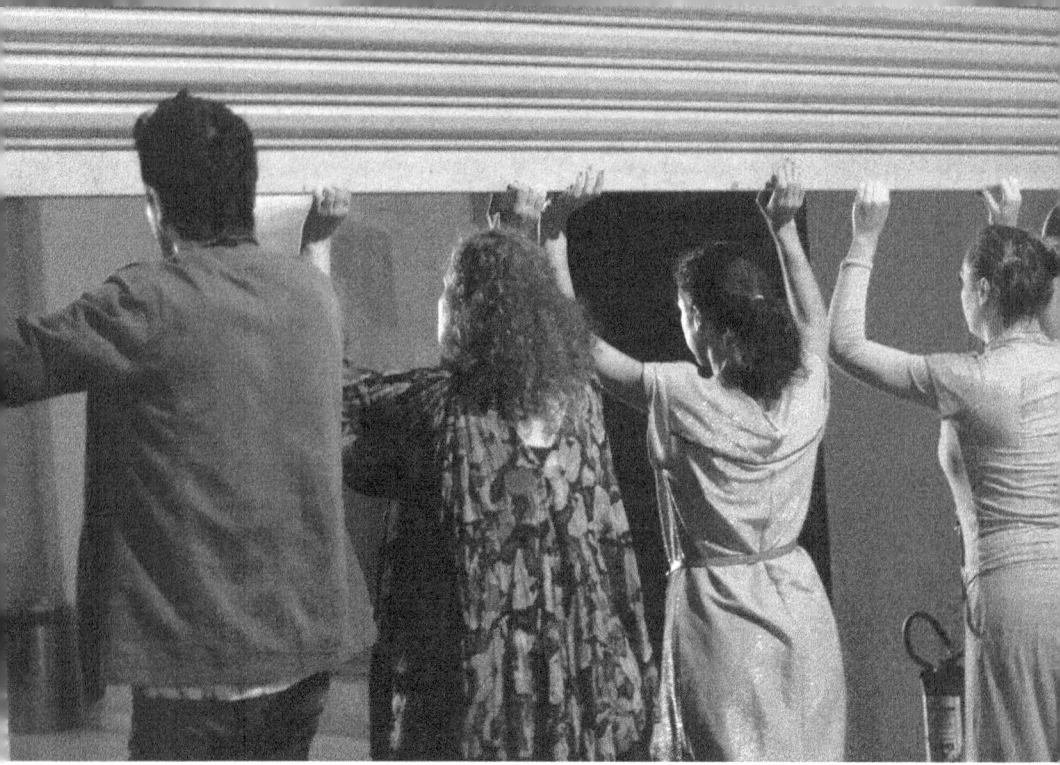

8.2 The shoppers lift the metallic door. Teatro da Vertigem, *Bom Retiro 958 metros*, Hemispheric Institute Encuentro, São Paulo, 2013. PHOTO: JULIO PANTOJA.

suggests a degree of phenomenological stability. A chair is a chair. You can label a chair and put it in the archive or in your living room. Objects, according to W. J. T. Mitchell, "are the way things appear to a subject."[4] They are nameable, categorizable. Things, on the contrary, are more ambiguous; they conjure up process, transformation, and substitutability. They elude the subject's taxonomic system and might even upend the subject-object binary. The chair/thing is tree, wood, planks, splinters, junk, a weapon or instrument, firewood, but it can also be the memory of my grandmother and almost anything else we can imagine. As Bill Brown notes, the word "thing" indexes "a certain limit or liminality, to hover over the threshold between the nameable and the unnameable, the figurable and unfigurable, the identifiable and the unidentifiable."[5] I can use "thing" to speak of another thing. One thing leads to another. So too here, spectators participate in a journey that follows the logic of mutable things. As we enter one area, it magically lights up. The space seems full of wonder, and I look around like an aging Miranda in this strange new world. It glitters. The things in it glitter. Who is pulling the strings? But as audience members begin to move past this shadowy environment, it transforms into something else. I notice that it's shabby. The tawdry things in the wanna-be-upscale shopping mall take on a sudden luminance, then fade. Again, I am confused about what is part of the performance and what is not. Does this mall function during the day as a real mall, or is it a set for the performance? Are those things in the display windows real merchandise? I catch the reflection of my face in the shop window—one more thing among things. We push each other to get a better look. Then the performance shoves us forward. Does performance stand in for the real or add another level of practice, and another lens for perception?

These bright and shiny things seem to have "thing-power," as Jane Bennett puts it, "the curious ability of inanimate things to animate, to act, to produce effects dramatic and subtle."[6] They lure us toward them. Yet the closer we look, the more they seem dead matter, their power emanating from elsewhere. As a spectator embedded in a saturated visual arena, I try to think the thing, the movement/flow, and the visual sphere of which I am a part. As things cannot be understood phenomenologically—there is no such thing as a thing—they need to be understood in context and practice. And the intractable movement that pushes us through the performance produces anxiety and desire; we pursue enchanted goods even as we catch a glimpse of the hidden, excruciating conditions of labor. Being a spectator in this Debordian society of the spectacle in which the "spectacle is the other side of money" and everything has become an image drives me deeper into the quandary in which the more I see, the less I know.[7] The mall seems to serve as a distorting mirror that traps us in an endless operation of terrifying self-reflection. Thing, movement, and visuality, in this funhouse version of contemporary society, produce perceptual instability.

The only way I could start thinking about the sensations and complexities of unraveling and desubjectification that the performance opens was by moving through and experiencing it. Here I will retrace my steps to observe how *Bom Retiro* performs its own analysis of the frenetic tempo of consumer desire and desperation. The act, Artaud reminds us, promotes the reflection.[8] Walking through the performance grounded me in one material reality even as it specularized and dematerialized another. Following the strategy of the performance, I pause along the trajectory, hold an idea up to the light, and then let it go into the general swirl of ideas and images. In short: I propose to adopt performance both as an object of analysis and as a methodological lens—a peripatetic exercise, a theoretical walk.[9]

Having been sucked into this familiar space (a mall) in the strangest of ways, we follow a lone woman. She stops at an illuminated shop window to stare at a red dress. It obsesses her. "The stores are always closed!" says the Consumidora. "You have to get here earlier, a lot earlier; you should sleep here," the disciplinary Red Dress replies.[10] Things here have a life of their own; they exert control. The short scene shows the mutual construction of things, economic policy, desire, subjectivity, and theatricality. Brecht's Marxist, anti-illusionist approach (*Verfremdungseffekt*) that makes the familiar unfamiliar to enable critical insight (so effective on the walk over) has been turned inside out. Capitalism, he knew, constantly seeks to enchant the ordinary and pacify the viewer.[11] Nor does the immersive nature of the performance allow us to pretend that we're participants in an Artaudian theatre of cruelty. True, here we witness the "revenge of things," but the agitation should not be confused with the exaltation he sought in the liberation of life forces.[12] We don't need to read Balibar to know that "every concept of politics," including of course economic politics, "implies a concept of the subject."[13] The Consumidora is nothing more than her function, driven by the singular and constricted desire to acquire. We look at her looking at the dress, also part of this constricted desiring-machine.[14] The lights in the shop pulse, like living hearts.

The lights dim where we're standing and suddenly illuminate something down the hall. Audience members hurry along to get a look at the action. I begin to feel the stress of constant vigilance. As a participant/spectator I watch, but I also watch out. The relentless one-way thrust of the seemingly chaotic performance makes me feel as if I'm being pushed to a rhythm that contracts and releases. The combination of being on guard and pushed forward puts me in a quasi-paranoid state of tunnel vision—I scan the environment to assess the risks and prioritize what to focus on. Where is that old woman? Is she all right? Ghostly mannequins line the passageway. One holds a Grande Promoção sign—15 percent off—seems alive (fig. 8.3). Wait. She is alive!

Her blank eyes betray a hint of terror. This is the netherworld of dead capital. Rebecca Schneider observes that for Marx, "dead capital is capital that is not in immediate use, such as the machinery of a factory in off-hours or a theatre on Monday night. Capital that is not immediately engaged with living labor, or otherwise revested by circulation through the live, is dead capital."[15] Playing on Marx, this performance shows that capitalism has now killed even the living bodies of labor. Its deadening machines, unlike Deleuze and Guattari's interconnected desiring-machines that transcend human-nature divides, blur boundaries between life and death.[16] Our theories of capitalism, like the mannequins, begin to clutter the darkened corridors.

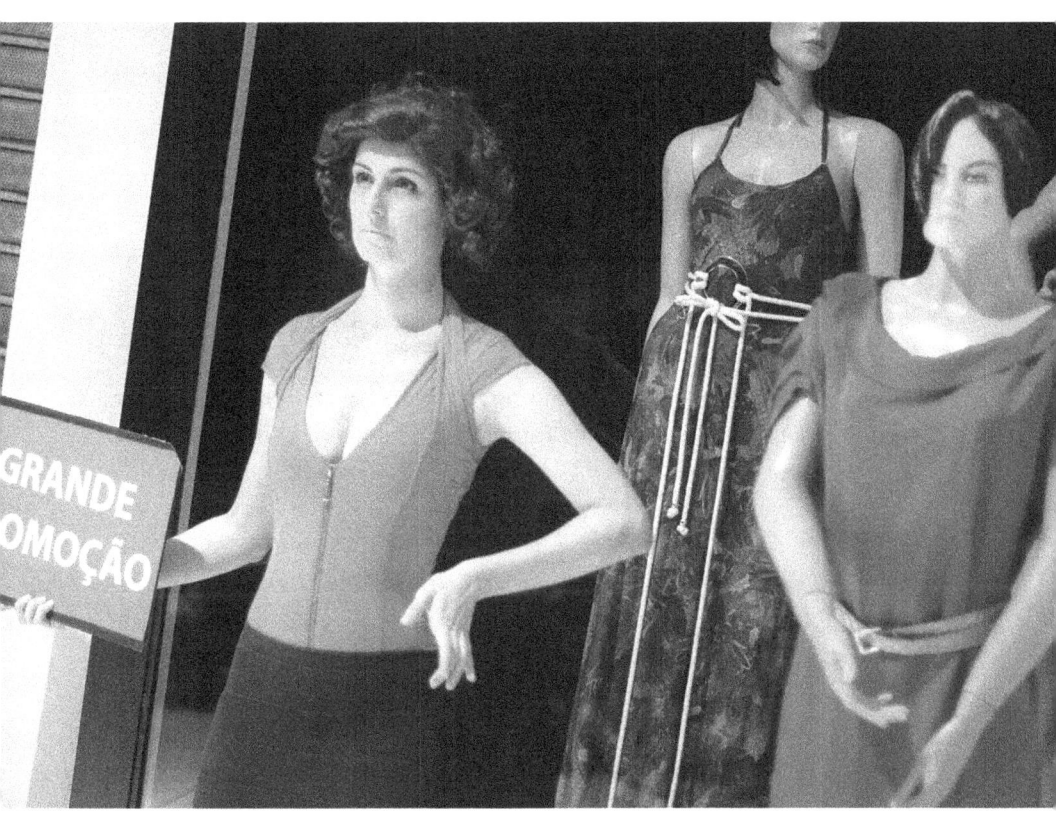

8.3 Grande promoção. Teatro da Vertigem, *Bom Retiro 958 metros*, Hemispheric Institute Encuentro, São Paulo, 2013. PHOTO: JULIO PANTOJA.

As one window up ahead lights up, the one behind goes dark. "Watch your step," warns a voice. The experience is not frightening, really. It's astonishing, humorous in a macabre way, and bewildering by moments, but it has a sharp edge. It conjures up the environment of terror I've lived in since 9/11, the mandate to stay alert coupled with the confusion of not knowing what is real, or dangerous, or threatening, and what isn't. If you see something, say something—the ubiquitous mass transit warning of the New York area. Is terror a relatively new phenomenon, a U.S. import like some of the things in the store? Or have I so thoroughly internalized it that I carry it with me now wherever I go? It's hard to gauge what matters and what doesn't, to know what to look at or what I've missed.

After some time I notice that the "phantom guides," as the script calls them, clad head to toe in fabric, move both the lighting and sound systems along with us (fig. 8.4). They manage our environment, silently and invisibly transforming it. The invisibilization of labor in capitalism, performed by these shrouded figures. It's not clear that they are always the same humans, but they (like the mannequins) look the same and function interchangeably. Transformation here does not mean coming into presence as subject, or being in motion as a process of individuation. Rather, the phantom guides come into being as anonymous, faceless beings through the systemic process of ninguneo or denial of subjectivity.[17] Like the mannequins (like migrants, like the disenfranchised), they have been broken down to body parts—arms and backs to pick the grapes or push the baby carriages. They are interchangeable and disposable. Racism, violence against women, queers, and the poor, and generalized doping further dehumanize. The performance underscores this by using some thirty or so actors to play the hundreds of figures and shadow that populate this universe. Everyone, quite literally, is always morphing into something/someone else.

Instead of a brave new world, we've entered "a whole new world." Faxineira Filósofa (Philosophic cleaning lady), the Afro-Brazilian woman, sings about the new as she recycles the Disney song. As a philosopher, an Afro-descendant, and a woman in the service industry, she knows her place. Like generations of her ancestors, she continues to clean. The performance invites us to follow the physical and metaphorical threads. Capitalism grew and thrived on and through the body that could be thingified and sold. Slavery, the savage violence of exchange, constitutes the inaugural act of capitalism, which grew out of the trade in humans.[18] The slave trade gave rise to a broad and complex network of global relations. Terror, clearly, has always been the underside of capitalism. Humans have long been treated as things. The trade in textiles, cotton specifically, sustained the circular system in which "the product of Indian weavers paid for slaves in Africa to work on plantations in the Americas to produce agricultural commodities for European consumers."[19] A defective female mannequin, imported from Korea, finds it hard to believe she is not as gorgeous as those on display. Trash, the characters in the performance call her, she's nothing but trash.

Most shop windows on our journey are dark and shut tight. But once in a while we see something inside the shops; Bolivian women work through the night sewing the red dresses that other women will wear (fig. 8.5).

The thingification of humans, especially women, Vertigem makes clear, continues long after slavery has officially been eradicated. A female actor plays Radio Infinita, the radio that never sleeps for workers who never sleep. The radio is a person/thing; her eyes are transistors; antennae pop up from her head. She is live but not exactly alive, offering 50 percent off sales, talking

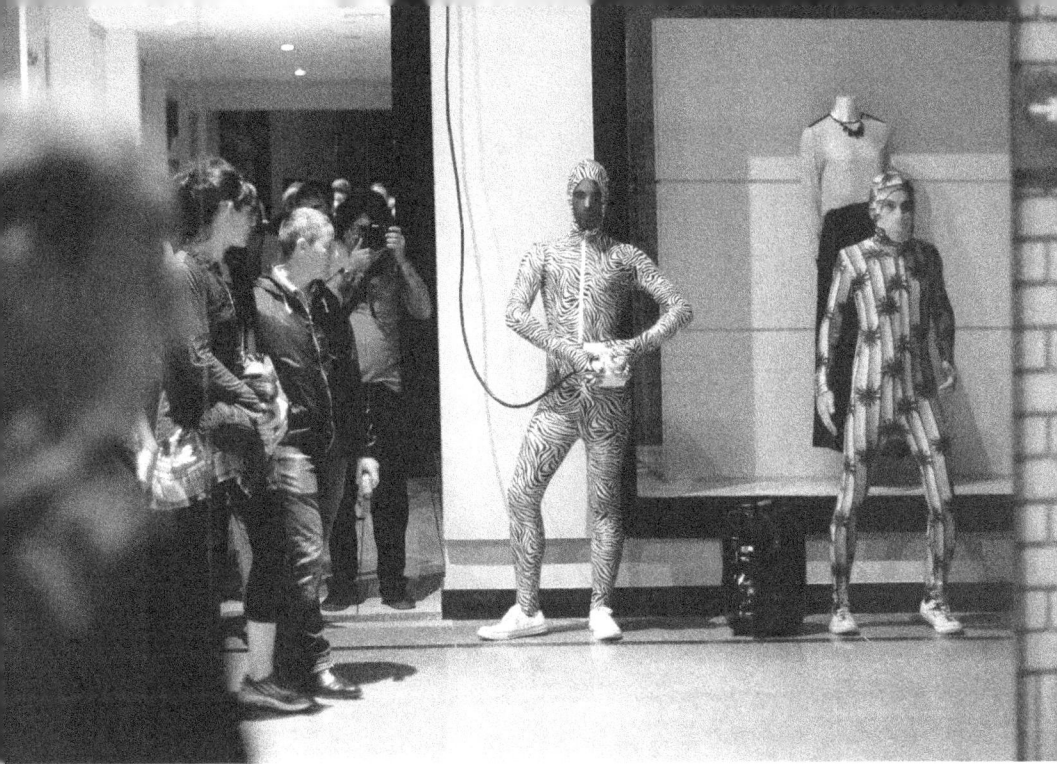

8.4 Phantom guides manage our environment. Teatro da Vertigem, *Bom Retiro 958 metros*, Hemispheric Institute Encuentro, São Paulo, 2013. PHOTO: JULIO PANTOJA.

to this "world of dreams" sponsored by clonazepam, the sleeping pills. Radio Infinita transmits terror alerts—we hear that the recent attacks are being investigated and those responsible punished.

In the corridors, a deliveryman fondles a female mannequin.

At times, the audience follows behind a happy group of shoppers, running toward a fire sale. An Errante, a disruptive figure who punctuates the performance, sets an enormous floor-to-ceiling banner on fire. At one point, he pulls out Radio Infinita's tongue. Is he a terrorist? A revolutionary? Always a wild card, he goes running off. What I see is stunningly beautiful and utterly depressing: both sides of the capitalist coin on view at the same time. I'm a trapped in a system, or a machine, or an organism that I cannot assess but that pushes me along. The experience has no outside, no place from which to name and analyze the rush of things that engulf and move us. The movement seems irreversible.

We move through haunted spaces of circulation and exchange, an empty mall full of wants and longings. Desire transports us to a space of imagined future-being/having. To have, seemingly an equivalent of to be, robs our identity. Want steals our present. What gets preserved for the consumer in

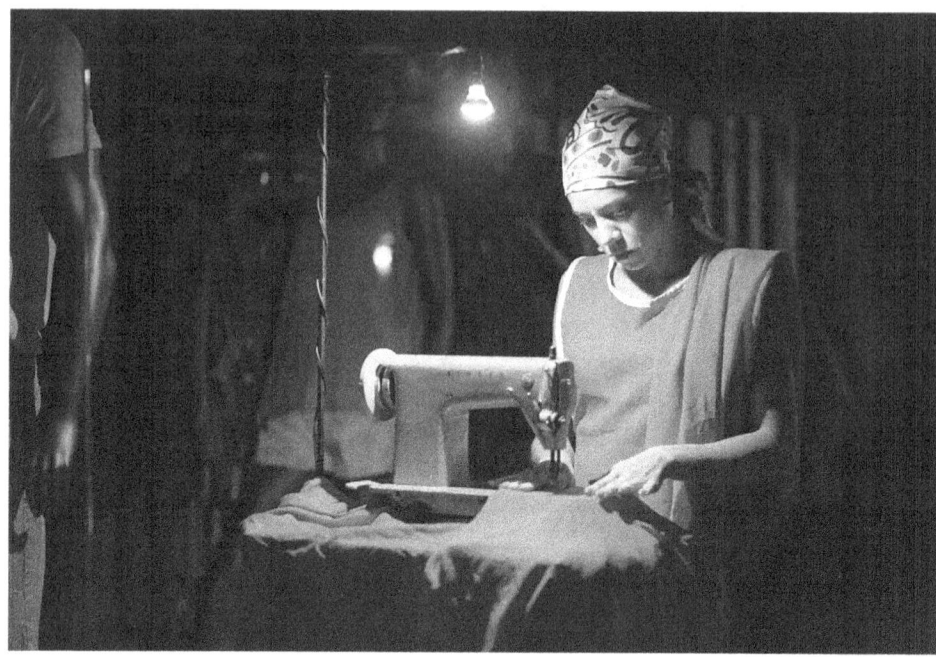

8.5 Bolivian women working through the night. Teatro da Vertigem, *Bom Retiro 958 metros*, Hemispheric Institute Encuentro, São Paulo, 2013. PHOTO: FRANCIS POLLITT.

this world is not the object but the desire, the insatiable desire to possess. The more the characters run toward the goods, the closer they get, the farther the goods slip from their touch. What moves us spectators is the desire to see. We've become voyeurs; the pleasure of watching relies on the separation and distance from the object of the look. As we run after it, it recedes. What if we were to catch up to it? A before/after ad shows a fat man as "before," and a smiling slim man "after." The Errante surreptitiously replaces the image of the slim man with one of a cadaver. That's what happens when/if we catch up. A character in the play tells us that we're in the realm of the "Dibuktronik," the devil of things without owners.[20] Things manage and make us one of them, one more thing among things. We too are dead capital. Anti-presente. The living model has been marked down again. She's now 30 percent off.

Many cultures believe that things have a life of their own. The Mayans, both ancient and contemporary, as noted in earlier chapters, have a word, ch'ulel, for the animation in all things, human and nonhuman.[21] Ch'ulel refers to the life in everything. Humans, animals, mountains, rivers, trees, corn, and other forms of material existence in this indigenous world view share a life force. Ich'el ta muk acknowledges their value, grandeur, and dignity. These are not things or objects but agents or even subjects. Human life depends on these other forms of existence. In chapter 1, I put the concept of ch'ulel in conversation with N. Katherine Hayles's writing on cognitive biology. She argues that "all life forms, including those lacking central nervous systems such as plants and microorganisms" share cognition.[22] Views such as these have of course been debated and challenged. If all things have a life force, does that mean, as Terry Eagleton puts it, "that you reduce human bodies to the status of coffee tables?"[23] While clearly none of these vital materialists are arguing that simplistic position, it seemed clear to me (at least before I entered the mall) that humans belong to the material world, yet not in the same way as things—the fabric, the trash, and the broken mannequins. Debates around new materialisms focus on the degree of agency accorded to the nonhuman. Vital materialists (such as Deleuze, Manuel De Landa, Bennett, and myself) affirm the liveliness of materiality, of its capacity to precipitate action or change, the blurriness even at times between the animate and the inanimate. Some scholars trivialize vital materialism, sustaining the usual objection that it "is out to decenter the all-sovereign subject into the mesh of material forces that constitute it."[24] The all-sovereign subject or imperial I, this performance seems to suggest, has been consumed, digested, and spit out by a self-defining, self-referential, deadening system that has displaced it. Vertigem, however, seems to be making an urgent economic, rather than philosophical, argument. Capitalism has desecrated matter and destroyed the material supports for human life. It has killed the ch'ulel in things and in people. We are in the land of the production of death. Everything around us might be animated, but not alive. If everything is dead, what moves things? The invisible hand of capitalism, arguably an inanimate but extremely powerful force. The phantom guides, like seemingly all else here, are governed by the consumer logic of things as substitutable, discardable, and replaceable. Things (mannequins) seem no more dead than the shadow figures are alive.

Our journey through the maze is interrupted by bangs and screams—the drug-addicted homeless population outside the mall beats on the metal grate, demanding to be let in (fig. 8.6). Again, Araújo stages a breathtaking tableaux vivant at the locked entrance to the mall. The addicts, with blankets thrown over their shoulders to keep them warm, pose as mirror images of the consumers and delivery people at the beginning of the performance. They too belong to the crazed world of supply and demand. Theirs is the universe of rocks, *pedra*, crack. "I am also a person," pleads the Cracômano, trying to

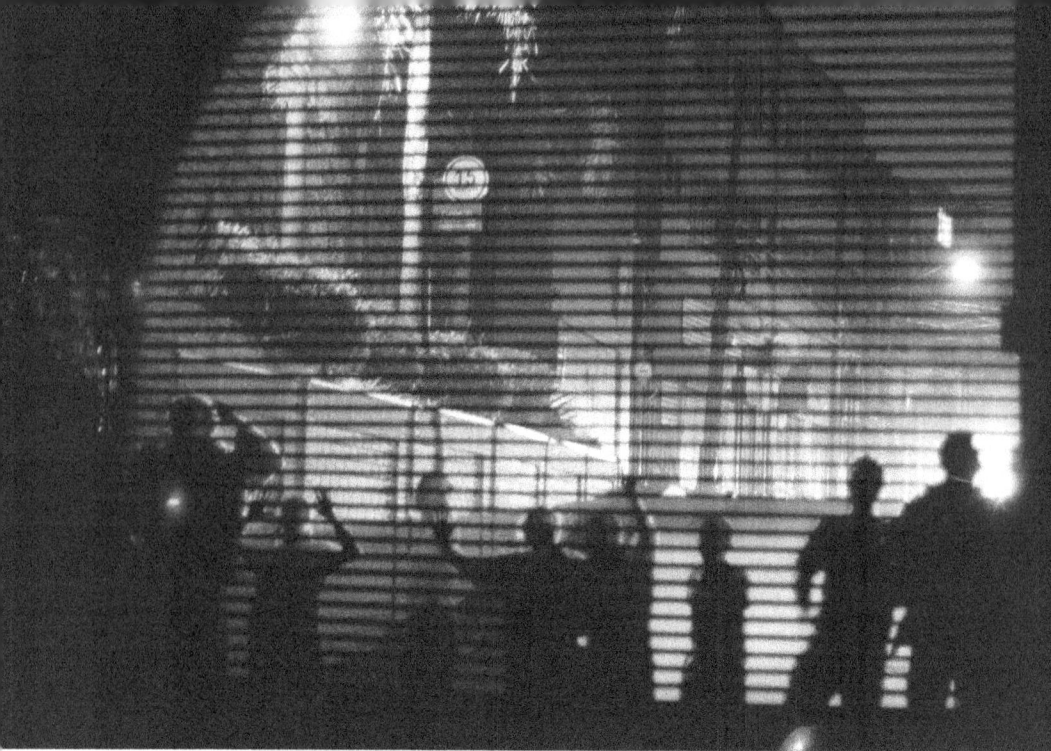

8.6 The drug-addicted homeless population outside the mall beats on the metal grate. Teatro da Vertigem, *Bom Retiro 958 metros*, Hemispheric Institute Encuentro, São Paulo, 2013. PHOTO: JULIO PANTOJA.

sell stuff to the shoppers and audience. His small pedra is his, all he needs. In *cracolandia* or crack land, as Brazilians call it, things also have a life of their own—the rock talks back to the addict. Throughout the performance, it gets larger and takes up more and more space. The addict might hold the rock in the beginning, but by the end he belongs to the rock. These mirror images, the mall and cracolandia, illustrate the degree to which people live in interconnected economies, the violence outside associated with drugs and poverty and the privatized violence of capitalism inside the gates, though those connections are often obscured.

But again, a rush of activity makes it impossible to hold onto a reflection. All of a sudden, a crowd of consumers overtakes us. They rip off their old clothes and throw them to the floor. They rush out of the mall, euphoric with their new acquisitions, trampling all the clothes on the ground. The audience too walks over the discarded fabrics on the way out. Fabric has a complicated history even aside from the slave trade, I think as I step on it carefully. The blankets over the shoulders of the crack addicts, like the blankets on the shoulders of Holocaust survivors, remind us there's a politics to cloth, an economy, a social performance of value and care. Disappeared people in Peru and elsewhere have been identified through small remnants of clothing. Regina José Galindo, in *Presencia 2017*, wore the dresses of murdered and disappeared women in Guatemala to tell their stories. Cloth has a history, no matter what Eagleton says. As I follow them out of the mall, walking on these textiles, I feel I am being asked to witness another kind of violence and disappearance.

We follow the shoppers, the homeless, and other members of the audience out of the mall and into a dark passageway between buildings. Despite our many differences, for a moment we're all the same—we are the people who move through spaces that don't belong to us, transitional spaces that don't belong to anyone. The move to the dark outside is far less noticeable than the initial entry into the mall. Even though the shadow figures accompany us, there is no music, no glorious light, just the sound of a train passing very close by. Did Araújo plan that?

I keep looking for patterns, for internationalities. The performance consists of interwoven threads, acts, scenarios, themes, characters, colors, sounds, and images that repeat in different patterns. The high points, undersides, flashes, poses are all there redistributed. Radio Infinita continues speaking. Terror continues to threaten our dreams. Looking up at the dark windows of the silent buildings, we see the silhouettes of women sewing at their machines (fig. 8.7).

A bride in a crumpled wedding dress appears stranded on a high narrow ledge of a wall. She's lost, she tells us; she was looking for a store and doesn't know how she got trapped on that ledge or how to get off. The Consumidora wanders the streets, homeless now too, looking for the closed shop with the red dress. Audience members walk past smashed mannequins and other refuse that lie abandoned on the sidewalks. Phantom guides push female seamstresses down the streets in carts and glass boxes (fig. 8.8). Thingmobiles. Women as objects on display en route to disintegrating into things.

The deliveryman, now naked in a cart, masturbates against his female mannequin.

As we approach a crowded city avenue, two women notice that they're wearing the same red outfit. Enraged, they claw and rip at each other until they're both naked. The women stop and look at each other again, jump into each other's arms, and devour each other in what seems to be a kiss. The libidinal desiring machine however has been undone by the capitalist desiring machine—they are joined not by desire but by the consumer thread that unravels from their mouths as they back away from one another. A bus passes

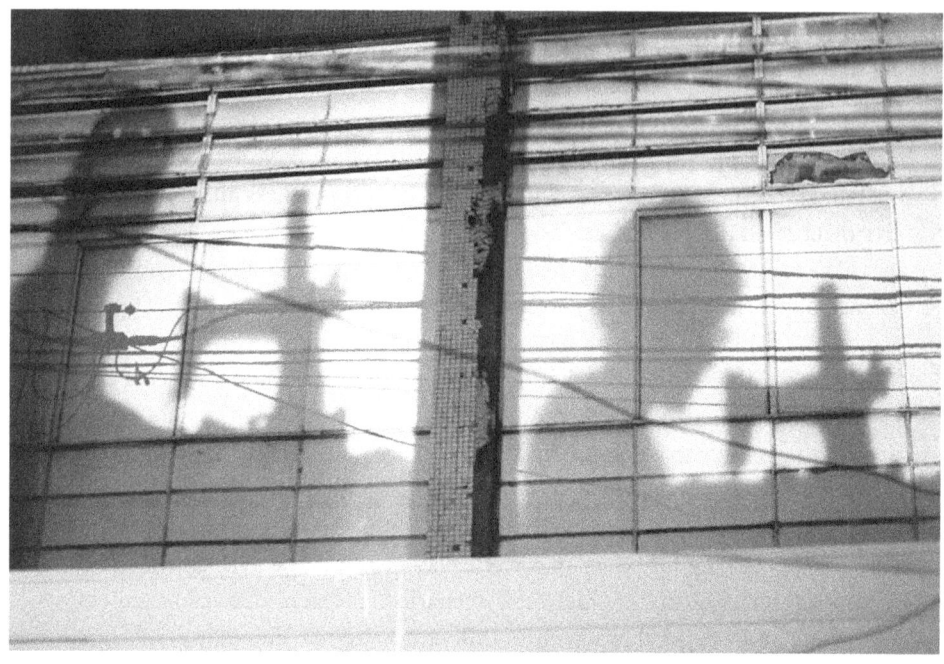

8.7 Silhouettes of women sewing at their machines. Teatro da Vertigem, *Bom Retiro 958 metros*, Hemispheric Institute Encuentro, São Paulo, 2013. PHOTO: JULIO PANTOJA.

by with curious passengers peering out the windows. Did Araújo stage that? It's a real bus. Those are real people, I assure myself, aware of how foolish I sound even to myself.

Only now am I beginning to grasp the enormous scale of the performance. The city too is a protagonist, a throbbing organism. Everything happens at the same time; we hear airplanes, trains, buses, and everything becomes part of something else—not least the performance we're a part of. We're in traffic—not just street traffic but also the traffic in drugs, in women, in undocumented labor, pirate radio, the traffic in dreams and desires. Everything, like the cloth, is in process of decomposing, recomposing, and being discarded. Outside, the city resembles the shopping center far more than we might have anticipated. It's a larger version of the same. It shocks me to physically experience something that I know intellectually: the deadening machine knows no limits. We keep walking down the city streets, crossing avenues and catching sight of things that may or may not have been designed for the performance. After a while, it doesn't matter, I think. It's a coproduction of transformation and transmutation—Antonio

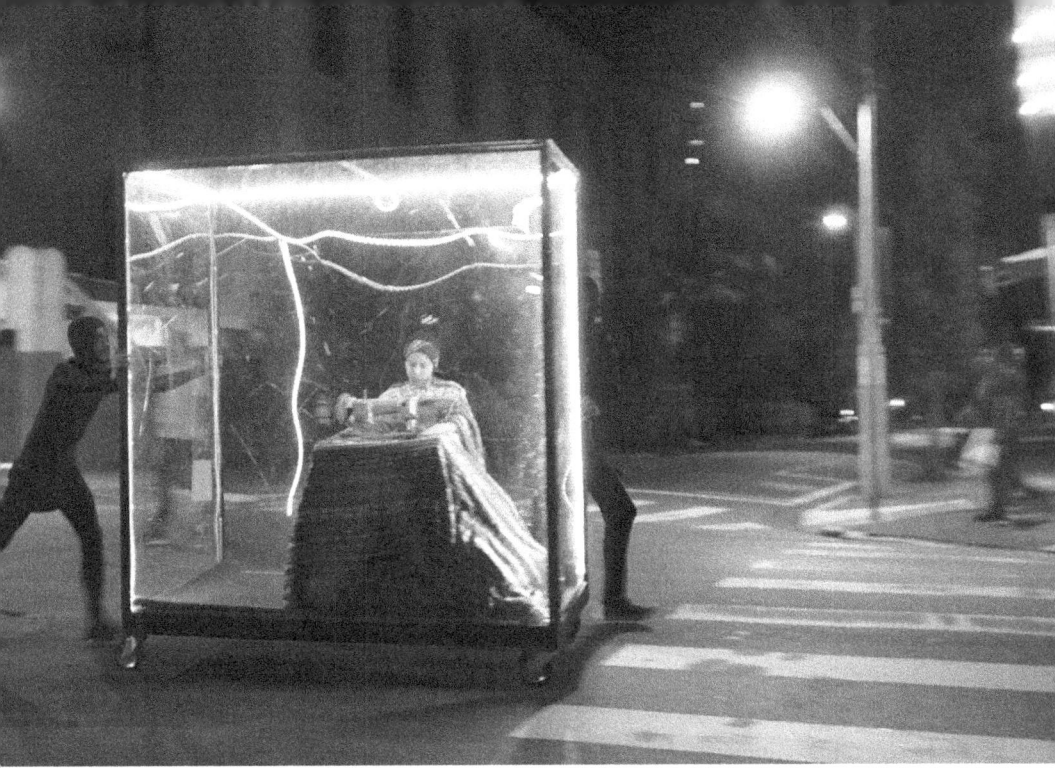

8.8 Phantom guides push female seamstresses down the streets in carts and glass boxes. Teatro da Vertigem, *Bom Retiro 958 metros*, Hemispheric Institute Encuentro, São Paulo, 2013. PHOTO: LORIE NOVAK.

Araújo, Vertigem, and the city of São Paulo. The cannibalism of capitalism unites us.

Audience members make an effort to be attentive to each other—stepping back so that others can get a better look, trying to make sure people don't get trampled. But although we're all part of the event, we're also atomized. Impossible to walk and talk together. The performance pulls us this way and that. I feel as if I were leaving my body behind, part of the frenzy, pushed by desire—my desire to see and experience and make sense of this environment that looks so foreign and familiar at the same time.

While Vertigem creates astonishing images, I would argue that this is not a performance that privileges the image. Rather, it reflects (on) an image-making society that collapses human interrelationality. In the society of the spectacle, "the social relation among people [is] mediated by images."[25] The visually stunning tableaux capture the thing for a second, display it as in a light box so we can see it, then release it again into the crash of circulation. We will never see it in the same way again. While we rush to get a glimpse of something, our inner Debord chides us for being enthralled by images.

We crane our necks, trying to see what's just outside the frame of vision, "as if the image launched desire beyond what it permits us to see."[26] But this not the animation of erotic desire but a greedy desire of the promise of more to come in capitalism. There is no privileged or hegemonic spectator in this performance who can evaluate and see everything. This image-making machine is way beyond our control. No frame or stage could contain it—it has too many moving parts.

As we walk on, some locals lean out of their windows, looking at their street made strange, knowing that for a moment they too form part of the performance. They look at us, amusing objects of their gaze. I look up at them looking at me. The fleeting encounter brings us into presence as an image for each other—the glimpse of the couple in the lit window for me; for them, I'm framed as a body in a crowd looking up. Looking, the encounter recaps, is relational, mutually defining. Yet the objectifying power of the look produces us as separate, unknowable to each other except as image. The living model, now 90 percent off, stands in the middle of the street, gradually becoming trash (fig. 8.9).

We continue walking, one foot in front of the other, following the crowd without a sense of inner purpose or direction. We stop facing the building's multistoried glass façade. Each window is a mini stage. People move inside; things happen. I now feel like a consumer at a peep show when just a few blocks back I felt like an amusing object for the locals looking out their windows. Object, viewing subject, voyeur, consumer, critic, amazed audience member, cautious pedestrian, all describe certain watching and looking experiences I've had throughout the evening. Seeing has been confusing—simultaneously pleasurable and disorienting, humanizing and dehumanizing.

Looking, seeing, watching—all the usual acts associated with spectatorship—are especially fraught in this performance. Theatre, from the Greek *théâtron*, a "place for viewing," asks us to look. But here looking sustains the nightmarish society of the spectacle reduced to vision and visuality in which the "reigning economic system" traps us in "a vicious circle of isolation."[27] The performance simultaneously critiques and relies on ocularcentrism. It produces us as spectators and disorients us, muddling our insights. One of the challenges is that the terms of the phenomenon—spectatorship—are also the terms of its theorization. The words "sight," "spectatorship," and "theory," as commentators have noted, all come from the Greek *théâ*.[28] The theoretical lens I employ is deeply bound up with my object of analysis. If insights about sight always border on the tautological, *Bom Retiro* accentuates the predicament. We not only have trouble navigating our way through these deeply

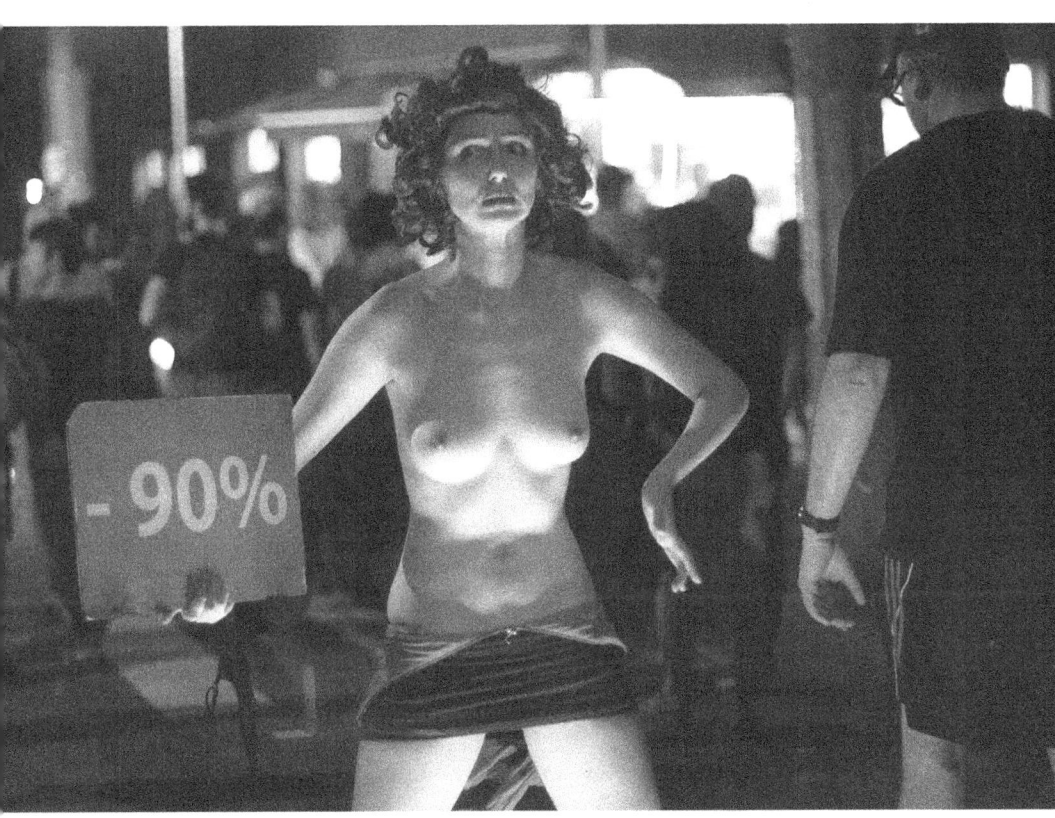

8.9 The living model gradually becomes trash. Teatro da Vertigem, *Bom Retiro 958 metros*, Hemispheric Institute Encuentro, São Paulo, 2013. PHOTO: JULIO PANTOJA.

entangled epistemic systems, but we are also the product of them, as spectators, as thinkers. We don't have other tools to think with, or know how else
to articulate thought. The vicious cycle kills the connectedness, relationality,
and the capacity to dialogue with and to care about others that might lead
us out of this dead end. But, like all else in this performance, the experience
of looking takes place within the crush of movement, not at a distance or
outside it. As spectators we are isolated, but not alone. We constantly react
to the pulls and pushes.

The door opens and the woman with the vacant stare from the beginning
of the performance ushers us into a large foyer of a building in disrepair.
The phantom guides lead us downstairs to a very large, completely disin-
tegrated theatre.[29] We enter a world of red. The faded red plush velvet of
the seats reminds us this was once a place with aspirations of its own. In its
prime, this theatre was part of the Jewish cultural center, a stronghold of the

resistance to the dictatorship. Now, back in a so-called democracy, people have forgotten all about it.[30] The Consumidora continues her search for her red dress. Suddenly the room is full of shadow figures in red dresses, their faces covered in red cloth. They ceremoniously embrace her, put the dress on her, cover her face, and welcome her into their deadened world. The addict comes back, now melded with his rock. "It's now one of my organs, one of my limbs," he yells. "Only surgery can separate us." We've witnessed the culmination, the consummation of people melded with things. This is the exact opposite of ch'ulel.

Again, chaos breaks out. Agentes Sanitários (sanitation agents) come into the theatre with their long brushes and disinfectants. They fill the space with sounds of clashes, thumping, yelling: "ATTENTION, DO NOT PANIC! EVACU-ATE THE AREA!" The sound of sirens and alarms punctuates the words coming from the loudspeakers. Unceremoniously now, workers in tall rubber boots and plastic bins hose down the floors around our feet, expelling us from the theatre. The enchantment's over, folks. We, now just dead things, waste, join the crush of circulation to be disgorged. We've been pushed through the gut of the beast, processed, and ejected. One now with "martyred matter" or excrement from the opening poem, we've been shat out. The sanitation crew cleans up behind us.

Pushed out onto the street, we see a large dumpster immediately in front of us. It's filled with the broken figures we've come to know throughout—the living model, now 100 percent off, lies in the trash (fig. 8.10). So does the defective model, and the Faxineira Filósofa. It's painful to see the women lying broken, undone by the endless violence of thingification. If they were just things . . . I think. The defective mannequin continues to chat away happily about things, *coisas*, though her limbs are askew. The trash pile is the site of human degradation and decomposition, in the process of transformation to another form of materiality. As in the photograph of corpses piled high in containers at Buchenwald, this image shows the victims while leaving the killers and the killing machine out of the frame.

As we walk past the container, members of the large cast begin to gather on the street, ready to take their bow. The spectators come together as a traditional audience. The actors thank Petrobras, Brazil's massive, and now infamous, petroleum company, for the financial support they needed to produce this play. By law, Petrobras is and has the last word. Capitalism, we are reminded again, constitutes the force behind everything we see and experience, including this performance.[31] But appearing behind the actors, the woman from the beginning of the play looks at us enigmatically. Is this really

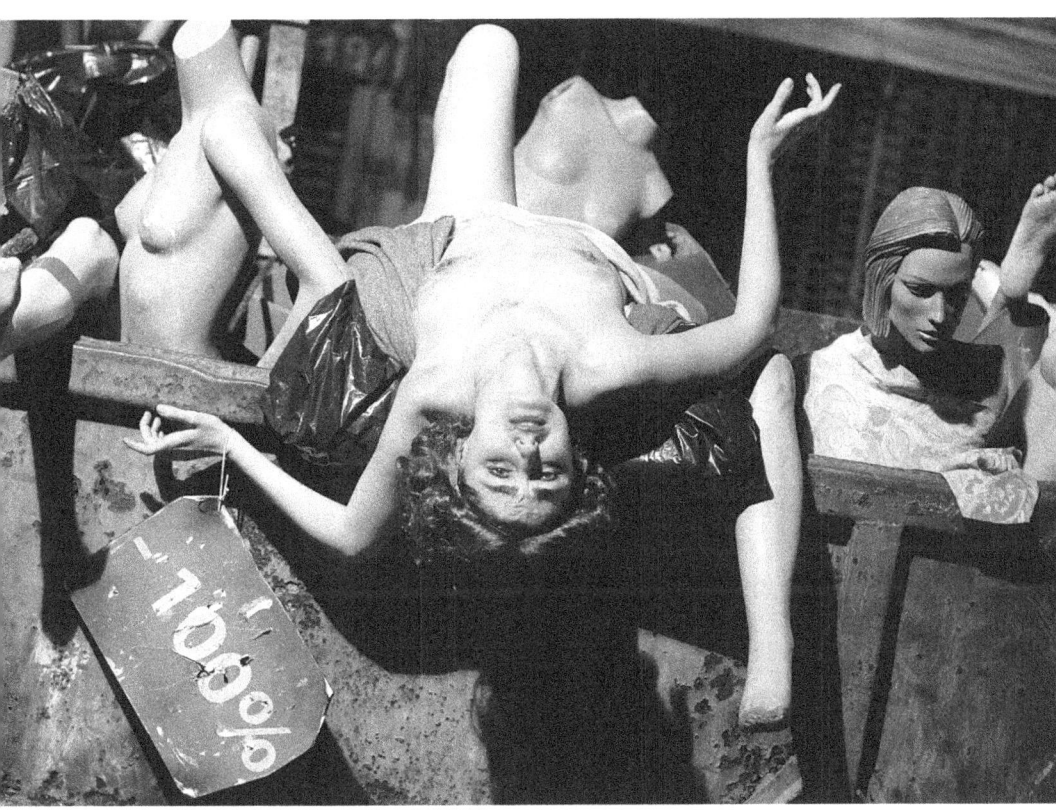

8.10 Trash. Teatro da Vertigem, *Bom Retiro 958 metros*, Hemispheric Institute Encuentro, São Paulo, 2013. PHOTO: JULIO PANTOJA.

the end? Or the beginning of a new scenario? As spectators, we hesitate. Errante posts a banner announcing one more fire sale. Is this a new game? Capitalism never ends. Most spectators congregate for a few minutes, uncertain what to expect, then disperse separately into the night.

II

I had to go back. I needed to understand what was real, what fake, about everything I had seen the night before. As important, I wondered, were those even the right questions to ask of what I had experienced? I'm not the anxious spectator now; I take my time. I walk the route, sit down, make notes, walk around some more, and talk to some people on the street. In the daylight, I see many of the same elements from the performance. Yes, the mall functions and the stores are now open for business, most of them selling knockoffs of designer fashions in vogue who knows when or where. Homeless people line the sidewalks. Some of them pull carts full of their personal belongs along with them. Crackolandia is a few blocks away, but addicts have found their way to this spot. The forgotten theatre from the end of the performance, I realize, sits right around the corner from the Oswald de Andrade center where we had started. We had come around full circle, 958 meters. Our walk-through is not the camino largo (or unending walk toward autonomy and self-definition by the Zapatistas), but a seemingly futile, irreversible loop. We had physically moved through the vicious, self-reproducing cycle of capitalism. The agitated movement made it impossible to recognize the pattern the night before, though clearly there was no destination, no ending, just circulation, transmission, absorption, regurgitation. The excruciating push through the landscape of deformed and deforming mirrors seemed one-way, but it twisted and turned back on itself. We were back where we started.

Looking around the unremarkable area, I recognize that everything we saw in the performance is right here. I hurry past similar places every day but don't really perceive them. I never pause to connect the dots or tie the threads as Araújo did. If the way I do this is the way I do everything, I need to ask myself why I don't stop, look, and look again. One possible response: why focus on the detritus of capitalism, when we know it intellectually already? Another: there are certain things we cannot afford to register if we're to continue to lead contented lives. In *Disappearing Acts*, I wrote that percepticide or self-blinding seemingly defended people from fully noting the criminal violence taking place around them during the Argentinean dictatorship. The *what* was indisputable. The military disappeared people, at times in broad daylight before people's eyes. Self-blinding for the population became one way to deal with it, a *how*. Now, for me, the widespread poverty, the homelessness, and the violence against migrants are among the *what* that troubles me and makes me look away. The encounter with people living on the street activates my self-deception, "understood epistemologically . . . in terms of what a perceiver is able to recognize or discern when she perceives."[32] *How* do I react? I'm busy, what can I do, and so on. I pretend I don't see. Although I despise the people who label the poor or the homeless or migrants a danger or a nuisance, I too often act as they do.

Capitalism, as Vertigem made clear, distracts us, keeps us (pre)occupied, calling our attention to sales and special offers even as it robs us of our capacity to relate to and to care about others. The immersive nature of *Bom Retiro* targets not just the *what* of capitalism's ruins, but the *how* of ruination. How does capitalism encourage us to turn a blind eye? As a developer in Silicon Valley who worked on Pokémon Go, an augmented reality game that used real people without their knowledge, revealed, "We are learning how to write the music, and then we let the music make them dance."[33] Shoshana Zuboff explores how "surveillance capitalism . . . depends upon one-way-mirror operations engineered for our ignorance and wrapped in a fog of misdirection."[34] The "epistemic inequality" this produces stems from the vital fact— we know, they don't. Surveillance capitalism keeps consumers reacting to remote control prompts and affective triggers to produce "psychic numbing and messages of inevitability to conjure the helplessness, resignation and confusion that paralyze their prey."[35] Walking through the performance exposes the spectators/participants to constant uncertainties and fears even as it fuels destructive hungers and desires. By living the promise of pleasure together with the deadening results, the performance links what capitalism tries so hard to keep separate—the thrill and the devastation caused by the frenzy for acquisition. But at the end of the play, those of us who think that we profit from the system get thrown out just like everybody else.

Araújo chose this area, I imagine, for the concentrated way it encapsulates a brutal history of modernity. He looked at everything; every element was allowed to communicate its hope and degradation. Everybody and everything had wanted to be a better version of who and what they are. The conflicts and deprivation, he demonstrated, are generated by the structural environment in which we find ourselves. This is the world that historical materialists warned us about—"the conflicts between forces and relations of production"—that lead to alienation.[36] São Paulo, yes, but other places work too—he directed another version of this piece in Santiago de Chile.[37] He could probably do it in New York or Mexico City or any of our major cities, addressing their own particular cultural and historical formations. This is our contemporary landscape. The brilliance and lucidity of his production allow us to recognize and own it as our new, manipulated, and fake real, produced and governed by the remote and invisible hand of capitalism. This walk undoes us. Every step takes us farther from utopia, farther from any aspirations of care and relationality—human and nonhuman, animate and inanimate. No animatives here. No brave acts of refusal. Dystopia. Antiutopia. Cacotopia actually seems a fitting word, given the performance's scatological and very dark humor.

The performance, however, does not lead us into a dead end. The movement, we now know, snakes back on itself. What started as a Cannibalist Manifesto written as a critique of colonialism ("Without us Europe would not have had even its sorry declaration of the rights of man," Andrade wrote) now turns into a critique of self-consuming capitalism. Acknowledging the shift in the seemingly inevitable opens the possibility of more change. What Santos writes of colonialism applies to capitalism: "It is as difficult to imagine the end of colonialism as it is to imagine that colonialism has no end."[38] Vertigem marks the continuities of oppressive practices, even though the historical conditions have changed. Nonetheless, as the poem conveys at the beginning, everything exists in a constant state of transformation.

By provoking a disorienting, lived engagement with the seemingly permanent, immutable economic system we tend to examine from a rational, disembodied perspective, Vertigem alters our perspective. The walk-through forces us to shift our habitual state of awareness to reexamine both the *what* and the *how* we see. What are these shoddy items in the window? Who are these broken figures? Are they alive? Dead? Why does my face reflect back to me when I look at them?

Seeing, then, is confusing, but not because the things Vertigem offers up—the mannequins, phantoms, characters, cityscapes, ruins, and so on—are always morphing into something else. It's the spectators' incapacity to grasp, identify, and hold on to a sense of a reality that creates the instability. Our own ontological and epistemic stability seems up for grabs. They're playing the music and we're dancing. . . . But our perceptual instability is the point. We begin to see ourselves as things, products, among all those other dead things. But the seemingly endless refraction of the mirror also turns back on itself, reflecting the grotesqueness of the mirror as operational system and its inadequacy as metaphor. What we can also glean, in other words, is not the deformation of the subjects but of the reflecting, distorting mechanism of capitalism. Again, it's important to reflect on not just *what* (the mirror) but *how* we see. The image of the mirror distorts. The mirror as metaphor runs through Western and non-Western cultures equating knowledge, self-knowledge, and much else with vision, but it fails to deal with the other senses that contribute to our experience and understanding of the world.[39] We do not actually live the world at a distance or, in the surveillance capitalism paradigm, online; we are part of it and eat, hear, smell, and touch it every day. It all sticks to us. The performance highlights the danger of giving ourselves up to the scopic frenzy produced by capitalist society, but asks us to look better, get closer, touch, listen, and look at our environment so that we can decipher the many layers of interconnectivity. The walk to the performance space offers its own pedagogy, encouraging us to use our bodies and all our senses to explore our interconnectedness and embeddedness in the world.

The isolation that spectators sense during the performance, moreover, obfuscates the reality that we are in fact together. We are walking together through these tawdry malls and frenzied streets. Yet, as a collective force, we have agency. We are not just dead capital. Brecht, Artaud, Butler, Balibar, Deleuze and Guattari, and the other theorists who last night were pushed against the walls with the mannequins come back together and in full force, insisting that we claim our capacity to act as spectators and as scholars. Action, reversal, inversion, and subversion, the Errante reminds us, can alter the landscape. The enigmatic woman stands outside the performance, reminding us that there is an outside, and that it's not over.

NINE

The Decision Dilemma

This book has explored various ways in which subjectivity is brought into presence or absence to be performed and reperformed in the public arena to question ongoing colonialist, authoritarian, and neoliberal rule. The struggle to become a person, with, to, and among others, has been a recurring theme throughout. This commitment to interrelationality, to walking and talking with others, has taken some strange turns in my meanderings through the Americas. Here, I explore one of the strangest, a direct encounter with Monsanto. As a corporation, Monsanto enjoys the status of a legal person. If Monsanto is a person, why not impersonate him? Jesusa Rodríguez, Jacques Servin of The Yes Men, and I embarked on a performance of environmental activism.[1] Our impersonation of Monsanto precipitated some interesting legal conundrums. Impersonation, as a practice of masquerading, troubles the boundaries between person, performance, and the law while, at the same time, masking and contesting continuing colonialist practices of exploitation and nullification. Impersonation, from an "assimilated form of Latin *in-* 'into, in' (from PIE root *en 'in') + persona 'person'" challenges us to reflect on what constitutes a "person."[2] Who counts as a person, a Somebody as opposed to a Nobody? How can individuals refuse, contest, and be *presentes* in relation to the corporation as a person with legal standing and rights?

Impersonation, pretending to be someone else, originally meant "represent in bodily form" in the 1620s.[3] It comes with rules and repercussions. While it may be fine to pretend to be a police officer onstage, it's against the law to do so in real life. Impersonation encompasses both theatrical and fraudulent behaviors—everything from actors to con men to criminal acts. Performance and theatre, by definition, enact identities, critical positions, situations, and emotions that do not coincide with the actor's. Not me, but

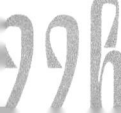

not necessarily *not* not me. "There is a gap at the heart of the mimetic continuity," as Jacques Rancière put it.[4] Audiences recognize and participate in the gap, the as-ifness, or the deception. As Coleridge put it, people willingly participate in the "suspension of disbelief" when the story is infused with "human interest and a semblance of truth."[5] The law, however, has trouble with semblance and is often based on agreements, defined as "a meeting of minds with the understanding and acceptance of reciprocal legal rights and duties as to particular actions or obligations, which the parties intend to exchange; a mutual assent to do or refrain from doing something; a contract."[6] However, terms such as "meeting of minds" and "intent" and "assent" might well be fictions suggesting that people ("parties" in legalese) clearly understand what they are agreeing to.[7] What do impersonations intend to do? What do people assent to when participating in them? Some of the most effective political performances in the twentieth and twenty-first centuries (to focus on more contemporary examples) risk legal censure to mine the delightfully slippery terrain of impersonation.

Orson Welles's 1938 radio broadcast, "War of the Worlds," for example, terrified his audience. He pretended to be a newscaster giving live bulletins about an invasion from Mars. He found it shocking, he said afterward, that listeners would believe in Martians.[8] Should there be a law, a critic asked him, against such enactments? And what would that legislation be? Sophie Calle, a French artist, dressed up in a wig and stalked a stranger, photographing even the most banal aspects of his existence (*Suite Venitienne*, 1980). In 1981, she pretended to be a maid to enter hotel rooms and photograph strangers' belongings. At least one of her subjects sued her for invasion of privacy.[9] Reverend Billy of the Church of Stop Shopping has been arrested repeatedly throughout the U.S. for reciting the First Amendment and exorcising cash registers. Reverend Billy, aka Bill Talen, is an actor pretending to be an evangelical preacher to take on corporate interests.

What's at stake in these performances that makes some want to impose legal controls and punishments on them? Is their intent to deceive or harm their subjects or their audiences? Or do these artists intend to make visible deep-seated assumptions (about national paranoia, privacy, and savage capitalism) that go unexamined? Do we agree on what the artist intended to achieve? Who is the authority? Does "freedom of speech" outweigh accusations against "false," even malicious, speech?[10] Who gets to decide? The judge? The art world? A legal definition of "agreement" as "specify[ing] the minimum acceptable standard of performance" only further complicates the issue.[11] It's a genuine challenge to define performance.[12]

The usual definitions of impersonation cite the intention to deceive, to profit, or to harm behind the act that makes it a criminal offense. The issue is actually not that straightforward. Theatre aims to deceive and reaps financial benefits at the box office from doing so. People going to the theatre, however, know they will be deceived; they participate in and enjoy the deception. Yet certain performances might well start before the audience realizes it. A Chicano director, Daniel Martinez, staged his play in an old theatre in a run-down part of downtown Los Angeles. The well-off theatregoing audience had to stand in line in front of the people who lived on the streets. The homeless folks looked at the audience with great curiosity. The theatregoers did not know that the performance was (about) them until they walked inside the theatre and saw projections of audience members coming in from the street and from the lobby.[13] The Brazilian theatre director Augusto Boal developed "invisible theatre."[14] Two actors, pretending to be ordinary citizens, stood at a bus stop and started an argument about the ongoing war. Was war justifiable? Soon a group of people started to congregate and join in the argument.

So when is impersonation unlawful? According to a legal dictionary, impersonation is by definition a crime: "The crime of false impersonation is defined by federal statutes and by state statutes that differ from jurisdiction to jurisdiction."[15] "False" impersonation? Is there "true" impersonation? The tautological definition again reflects the lack of agreement on what impersonation means. Impersonation is always false, if by "false" we mean the pretend nature of taking on a persona or role that does not coincide with the actor's own. Yet the definition confuses impersonation with fraud, as if every act of impersonation were fraudulent. Under federal law (18 US Code 912), someone who pretends to act as a U.S. officer or employee "as such, or in such pretended character demands or obtains any money, paper, document, or thing of value, shall be fined under this title or imprisoned not more than three years, or both."[16] Under the New York penal code 190.25, criminal impersonation applies to those impersonating police officers or physicians, while subsections 1 and 2 classify as a misdemeanor an act whereby a person "pretends to be a representative of some person or organization and does an act in such pretended capacity with intent to obtain a benefit or to injure or defraud another."[17] What about a political performance that parodies a corporation and its website?

So back to the Monsanto incident, which allows me to examine the ambiguity inherent in person, persona, impersonation, and what it means to be ¡presente! by impersonating and trying to unmask a corporation.

Etymologically linked to *corporare*, Latin for "embody," the word "corporation" came to refer to a "legally authorized entity" in the 1620s.[18] Corporations, thus, came into presence as having "bodies." They have been considered persons for a long time, expanding the temporal frame of what we normally understand as durational performance.[19] "In every common-sense, everyday way, a corporation is not a person. Corporations don't date, don't have families, don't go catch a movie on Friday night. They also don't go to jail when they do something criminal. But in the eyes of the law, corporations enjoy many of the same rights—including free speech and religious expression—and protections afforded to individuals."[20] In an 1892 case, it was established that "since a corporation has no soul, it cannot have actual wicked intent . . . and in 1909, the Supreme Court found it 'true that there are some crimes which, in their nature, cannot be committed by corporations.'"[21] We're back to the "impossibility defense" that I mentioned in relation to Juana la Larga of chapter 6: "A defendant is accused of a criminal attempt that failed only because the crime was factually or legally impossible to commit."[22] Corporations, it seems, have all of the rights and none of the liabilities of persons. However, pretending to be that body or person, as we discovered, can have adverse effects. Here, then, I examine the ways in which impersonation led to conundrums about which kinds of impersonation are naturalized, which are found to trouble the limits of the law, and which kinds of political subjectivities they bring into presence.

Over the years, the Hemispheric Institute has offered a number of courses called Art and Resistance in Chiapas, Mexico, as mentioned earlier in this work. Hemi, housed at New York University, offers graduate-level courses through the department of performance studies, where I teach, and accepts students from NYU and from universities throughout the Americas. In 2013, as usual, the goal was to create an immersive, multilingual environment in which collaborative learning could take place through doing as well as through traditional text- and discussion-based seminars. In addition to researching the topic of resistance as a series of acts—from armed resistance to civil disobedience, revolt, refusal, protest, foot-dragging, and so on—we always offer a workshop that ends in a public performance directed by Jesusa Rodríguez.

This was the third time Rodríguez and I had taught the course, although we always changed the topic. That year we focused on the health, social, and economic problems caused by genetically modified (GM) corn. Monsanto had asked permission from SAGARPA, the Mexican Secretariat of Agriculture, to plant GM corn commercially in Mexico. They had planted it experimentally since 2009. Although Mexico's National Biosecurity Commission had issued a moratorium on planting GM corn in 1998, President Felipe Calderón lifted it in 2009 after a personal meeting with Monsanto.[23] Activists throughout Mexico were mobilized to intervene against further invasion of GM corn. Genetically modified organisms (GMOs), they agree, impoverish local farmers and can pose health dangers. They threaten the diversity of the crop, the environment, and the cultures that developed in connection to agricultural practices. Monsanto, like other corporations, funds scholars to contest the evidence against them. Its goal is not to prove that GMOs are safe or beneficial to society, but to create enough doubt in people's minds so that safety and economic issues become a matter of opinion rather than fact.[24] Mesoamericans have been developing corn for the past ten thousand years. They think of themselves, by extension, as the people of corn. Hundreds of countries have condemned planting GM crops and understand them as especially threatening to countries of origin, those places where the crops were first grown and developed.[25]

In July 2013, as usual, the thirty-five participants from throughout the Americas (and beyond) staged a wonderful street performance of the People of Corn combating big bad Monsanto. As is typical of both theatrical and legal fictions, the mammoth agricultural complex was reduced to one representable character, Monsanto. For us, Monsanto wore a tuxedo, a top hat, and a pig's face. On his arm, a glorious drag performer dressed in a variation of the national flag pranced around as the adoring Motherland, eager to pick up the pennies that fell from Monsanto's wallet (fig. 9.1).

The performer could not wear the actual flag, as that is against the law in Mexico. The People of Corn, covered in body paint, sang and danced to the God of Corn. The performance moved toward the Plaza de la Paz in front of the cathedral, gathering more spectators as it moved along. The performance ended there with a public volleyball game between Monsanto's evildoers and the People of Corn. Everyone was invited to participate on either side, though almost everyone took the side of the People of Corn. A young Mayan girl threw the ball that defeated the Monsanto team, to great applause and shouts of joy (fig. 9.2). The group carried the beaming girl on their shoulders in triumph (fig. 9.3).

In 2013, as in previous years, we invited artists, scholars, and activists to participate in the course. Lorie Novak, a photographer and professor of photography and imaging at NYU, joined us for the second time. Jacques Servin of The Yes Men, who was a visiting professor in performance studies, also

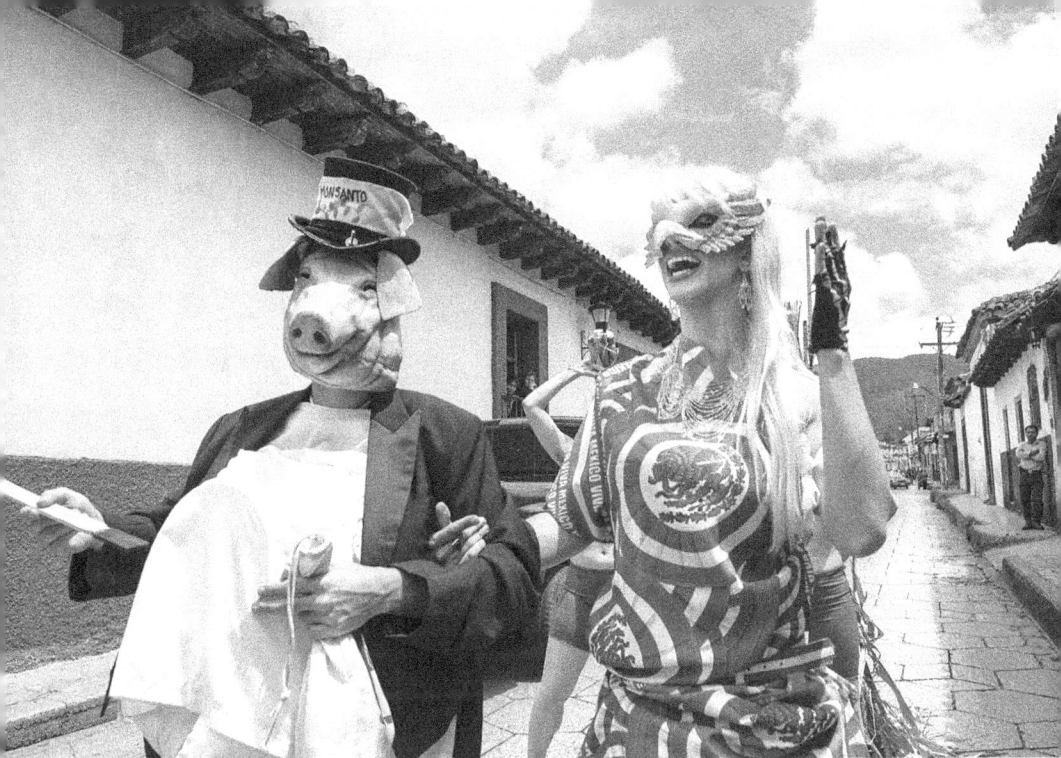

9.1 Monsanto and the Mexican Motherland. San Cristóbal de las Casas, Chiapas, 2013.
PHOTO: LORIE NOVAK.

participated. Andy Bichlbaum (Jacques Servin) and Mike Bonanno (Igor Vamos) are The Yes Men, artivists who parody powerful corporate leaders and spokesmen through what they call "identity correction," that is, "impersonating big-time criminals in order to publicly humiliate them, and otherwise giving journalists excuses to cover important issues."[26] So while The Yes Men use the media, they do not target the media. Rather, as they say, they give journalists the excuse to talk about serious and ongoing issues that do not necessarily qualify as newsworthy.

Servin (as Bichlbaum) writes in *Beautiful Trouble*:

When trying to understand how a machine works, it helps to expose its guts. The same can be said of powerful people or corporations who enrich themselves at the expense of everyone else. By catching powerful entities off-guard—say, by speaking on their behalf about wonderful things they should do (but in reality won't)—you can momentarily expose them to public scrutiny. In this way, everyone gets to see how they work and can figure out how better to oppose them. . . . This is identity correction. . . .

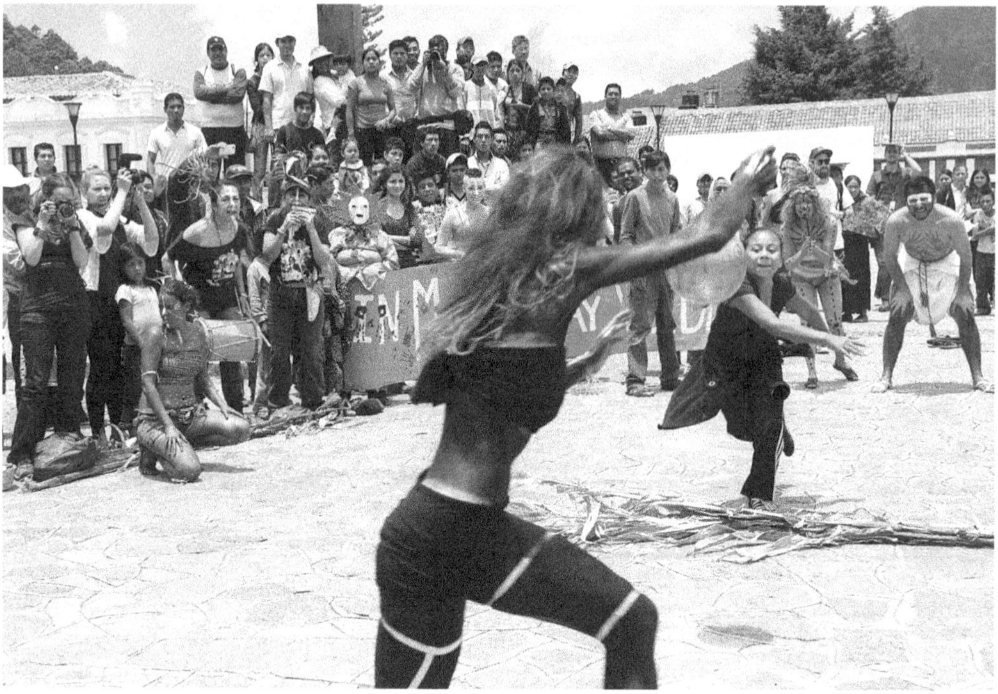

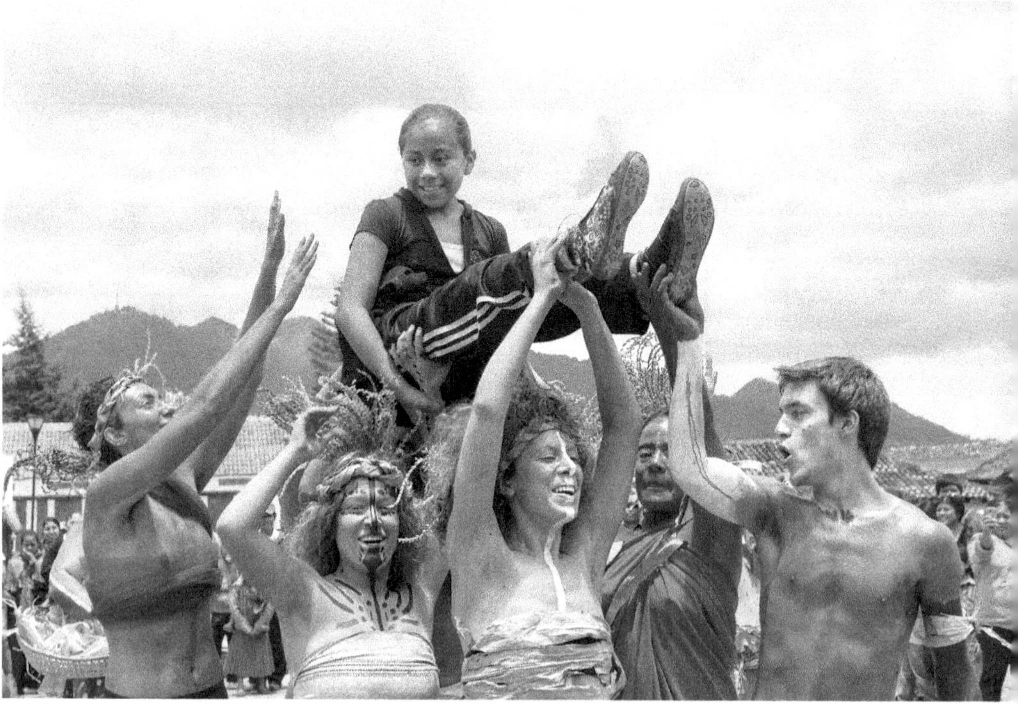

9.2–9.3 Defeating Monsanto. San Cristóbal de las Casas, Chiapas, 2013. PHOTO: LORIE NOVAK.

Instead of speaking truth to power, as the Quakers suggest, you assume the mask of power to speak a little lie that tells a greater truth.[27]

Telling a lie to tell the truth closely aligns with what Carrie Lambert-Beatty calls parafiction. Along with the other paraworlds mentioned in this study, parafiction marks the coexistence and besideness of "fiction or fictiveness." Parafiction "remains a bit outside . . . has one foot in the field of the real." She continues, "Parafiction real and/or imaginary personages and stories intersect with the world as it is being lived."[28] While pretending to be big bad Monsanto might belong to the fictive, big bad Monsanto continued to do terrible things in the real world. For Lambert-Beatty, parafiction focuses less on the "disappearance of the real than toward the pragmatics of trust. . . . For a moment at least, for various durations, and for various purposes, these fictions are experienced as fact."[29] While The Yes Men actions certainly have a foot in the real, one of the legal questions they raise is about the degree to which they are "experienced as fact." In all cases, however, they do shake fictions of trust.

Since 1999, The Yes Men have been getting into all sorts of mischief with their parafictions, impersonating a spokesperson from Dow Chemical on the BBC *Newshour*, another from Halliburton, yet another claiming to be from the U.S. Chamber of Commerce in a live forum, and so on. During these impersonations, the two often build false hope that companies will finally do the right thing (compensate the victims of the Bhopal disaster in Dow's case) or that the U.S. Chamber of Commerce would support environmental legislation.[30] When the organizations rushed to declare that in fact the announcements were a hoax, that they had no intention of doing the right thing, they fell into what is known as a "decision dilemma"—the "damned if you do and damned if you don't" gold standard for activists. The target looks ridiculous no matter what it does.[31]

Typically, The Yes Men start their action with a fake website that looks real. Servin and Vamos create nearly identical sites and simply change the URL slightly. Their fake Dow Chemical site drew some criticism from Dow, but nothing else. When the BBC was looking for a Dow Chemical representative to speak on the twentieth anniversary of the Bhopal disaster, they found Jude Finisterra (Servin as the saint of lost causes positioned at the end of the world) happy to comply. On the air, Servin played Finisterra with a straight face, the very picture of concern and thoughtfulness befitting a well-meaning executive (fig. 9.4).

At moments, as often with Servin's various personas, he looked slightly baffled.[32] The complexity of it all often throws his characters slightly off

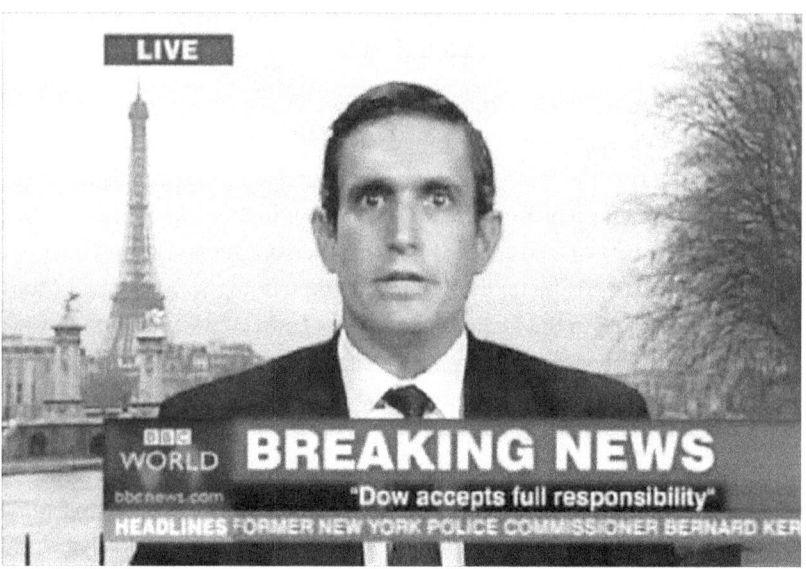

9.4 Jacques Servin as Jude Finisterra assures BBC viewers that Dow Chemical will do the right thing by all the victims of the Bhopal disaster.

kilter, comically giving them a somewhat lost feel. The film *The Yes Men Fix the World* (2009) shows a very nervous Servin almost running out of the BBC studios, like David getting away from Goliath. Chalk up one for the little guy. Dow stock prices in Europe dropped precipitously. Trust had been shaken, although it seemed that the sinking stocks meant investors could not trust Dow to value money over lives. Dow was too savvy to sue The Yes Men, but they did send "spies," as Servin calls them, to keep track of their doings.[33]

The U.S. Chamber of Commerce, on the other hand, demonstrated less caution. It was so incensed at The Yes Men's fake site that it issued a takedown notice in 2009 demanding they take down the "infringing material."[34] The Electronic Frontier Foundation, defending The Yes Men, argued that the "Parodic Site is obviously designed for purposes of criticism and comment and protected by the fair use doctrine."[35] The argument was that parody, with only one foot in the real, clearly belonged to a different (not real) register based on humor and criticism rather than fact.

As with the Dow case, The Yes Men decided to impersonate a Chamber of Commerce spokesperson to push the hoax further. In 2010, Servin as Andy as the spokesperson gave a press conference pretending to be a representative of the U.S. Chamber of Commerce, announcing the chamber had reversed its plans to derail responsible congressional legislation on climate change.[36] The chamber, which presents itself as if it were a government agency, sued The Yes Men for "fraudulent acts . . . [that] deceived the press and the public and caused injury to the Chamber." In a way, the chamber suggests that the hoax violates public trust in its pretend status as an official, seemingly politically neutral state agency. "These acts," the complaint continued, "are nothing less than commercial identity theft masquerading as social activism."[37] The chamber insisted that these "conducts" are "destructive of public discourse" because they "disguise the true motives of the persons who took that property." The defendants, Servin and Vamos, the lawsuit states, are "engaged in a business [they] call 'identity correction.'" The complaint repeated that the acts were fraud, not "hoaxes," used to promote The Yes Men's films and increase the sale of T-shirts. The Yes Men maintained it was all mimesis, as in ideas that "cluster around the motif of artistic 'deception.'"[38] The chamber's complaint quotes Servin as telling the *New York Times*, "We're comedians, basically. It's all theatre." The tension illuminated different understandings of both "lies" and the "real," with each side claiming they were committed to defending or exposing the truth. As the lawsuit dragged on and on, the chamber finally gave up its suit. The Yes Men then sued them for dropping the suit. The legal framework ironically enabled The Yes Men to develop even more theatre. "Sometimes it takes a lie to expose the truth," The Yes Men say. All the brouhaha provoked by the hoaxes proved invaluable in keeping the companies' wrongdoings in the public eye.

Impersonating corporations leads to a funhouse world of mirroring, masking, and masquerading as a person that troubles perception, making it look as if power always resides elsewhere, impossible to locate. Corporations are hard to pin down. Who is, or rather was, Monsanto now that Bayer has bought them out?[39] The corporation? Or the people who run it? Or the people who carry out company policies? Or the stock holders? In the Citizens United case, for example, the Supreme Court "held that if individuals have free speech, then so must collected groups of individuals. Corporations are groups of individuals and, therefore, they have free speech rights."[40] Who exactly are these individuals who have rights but never have to accept responsibility for what the company does? Corporations also mask their transnational networks by buying real estate and branding it with their name. Here but not here. Presente, but not really. Bureaucrats wear suits and ties to embody and represent the financial interests of the mega rich who hide behind corporate labels and identities. Ventriloquists reiterate faux facts, little lies, and big lies that emanate from who knows where. Meanwhile actors are called fakes.

In 2013, when Servin was with us in Chiapas, activists were anxiously waiting for the news of whether SAGARPA would grant Monsanto's bid to plant GM corn commercially. Rodríguez communicated with activists from throughout the country, coordinating events and efforts to intercede. For years she had led nationwide protests through her Resistencia Creativa project that uses art, humor, performance, and other creative practices to inform Mexicans about the dangers posed by GMOs.[41] As we sat in the Zapatista restaurant on Real de Guadalupe, an upscale walking street in San Cristóbal de las Casas, the idea came to us—we would create a Yes Men action against Monsanto. Some local activists and some participants in the class wanted to join in. In a few days we had prepared our digital action. In true Yes Men fashion, we launched a fake website claiming to be Monsanto's. Our press release, on the fake Monsanto website, announced that the request for expanded GMO cultivation had been granted by SAGARPA and thanked all those people in government for their invaluable help in moving Monsanto's interests along to fruition. We, of course, thanked them by name and carbon copied them in our communiqué (fig. 9.5).

> MEXICO CITY (Aug 14, 2013): The planting of genetically modified (GM) cornfields on a large commercial scale has been approved by the Mexican Secretariat of Agriculture (SAGARPA). The permit allows the planting of 250,000 hectares of three varieties of GM corn (MON-89034-3, MON-00603-6 and MON-88017-3) in the states of Chihuahua, Coahuila and Durango. This is the first time GM corn will have been planted on a large commercial scale in Mexico.[42]

Our release went on to add that Monsanto, aware that critics would decry the threat to the diversity of corn in Mexico that would now be contaminated or displaced by the GM crops, would enact certain measures. "One such initiative is the National Seed Vault (Bóveda Nacional de Semillas, BNS), whose charter is to safeguard the 246 native Mexican corn strains from ever being fully lost." "Fully lost," we felt, was a nice touch. Researchers and celebrity chefs could come and examine the native seeds in the vault.

Another initiative, we claimed, was the creation of the Codex Mexico (Codice México), a digital archive preserving the vast wealth of Mexican culture for centuries to come. The five-hundred-year-old *amatl* (bark) manuscripts that contain much of what we know about preconquest and early

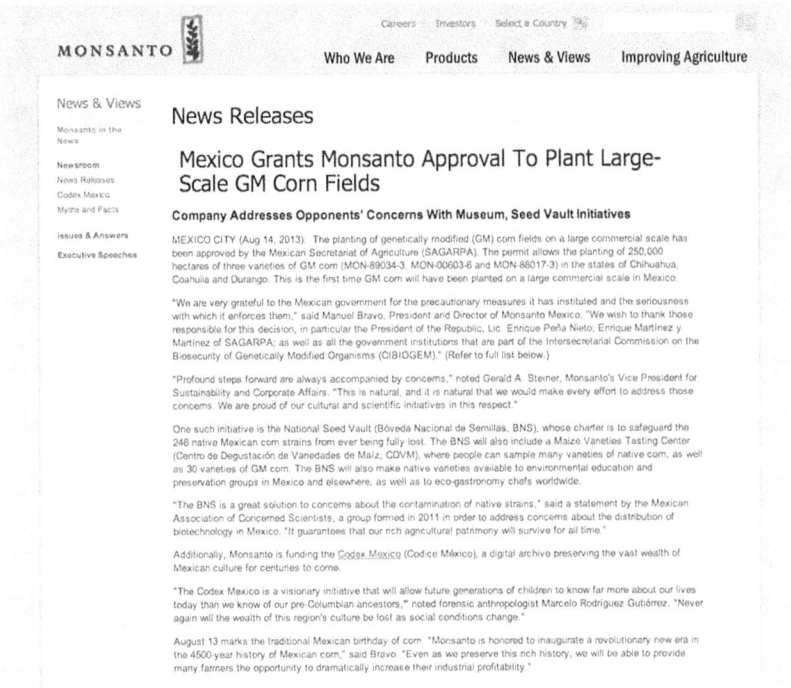

News & Views

Monsanto in the News

Newsroom
News Releases
Codex Mexico
Myths and Facts

Issues & Answers

Executive Speeches

News Releases

Mexico Grants Monsanto Approval To Plant Large-Scale GM Corn Fields

Company Addresses Opponents' Concerns With Museum, Seed Vault Initiatives

MEXICO CITY (Aug 14, 2013) The planting of genetically modified (GM) corn fields on a large commercial scale has been approved by the Mexican Secretariat of Agriculture (SAGARPA). The permit allows the planting of 250,000 hectares of three varieties of GM corn (MON-89034-3, MON-00603-6 and MON-88017-3) in the states of Chihuahua, Coahuila and Durango. This is the first time GM corn will have been planted on a large commercial scale in Mexico.

"We are very grateful to the Mexican government for the precautionary measures it has instituted and the seriousness with which it enforces them," said Manuel Bravo, President and Director of Monsanto Mexico. "We wish to thank those responsible for this decision, in particular the President of the Republic, Lic. Enrique Peña Nieto; Enrique Martínez y Martínez of SAGARPA; as well as all the government institutions that are part of the Intersecretarial Commission on the Biosecurity of Genetically Modified Organisms (CIBIOGEM)." (Refer to full list below.)

"Profound steps forward are always accompanied by concerns," noted Gerald A. Steiner, Monsanto's Vice President for Sustainability and Corporate Affairs. "This is natural, and it is natural that we would make every effort to address those concerns. We are proud of our cultural and scientific initiatives in this respect."

One such initiative is the National Seed Vault (Bóveda Nacional de Semillas, BNS), whose charter is to safeguard the 246 native Mexican corn strains from ever being fully lost. The BNS will also include a Maize Varieties Tasting Center (Centro de Degustación de Variedades de Maíz, CDVM), where people can sample many varieties of native corn, as well as 30 varieties of GM corn. The BNS will also make native varieties available to environmental education and preservation groups in Mexico and elsewhere, as well as to eco-gastronomy chefs worldwide.

"The BNS is a great solution to concerns about the contamination of native strains," said a statement by the Mexican Association of Concerned Scientists, a group formed in 2011 in order to address concerns about the distribution of biotechnology in Mexico. "It guarantees that our rich agricultural patrimony will survive for all time."

Additionally, Monsanto is funding the Codex Mexico (Codice México), a digital archive preserving the vast wealth of Mexican culture for centuries to come.

"The Codex Mexico is a visionary initiative that will allow future generations of children to know far more about our lives today than we know of our pre-Columbian ancestors," noted forensic anthropologist Marcelo Rodríguez Gutiérrez. "Never again will the wealth of this region's culture be lost as social conditions change."

August 13 marks the traditional Mexican birthday of corn. "Monsanto is honored to inaugurate a revolutionary new era in the 4500-year history of Mexican corn," said Bravo. "Even as we preserve this rich history, we will be able to provide many farmers the opportunity to dramatically increase their industrial profitability."

9.5 Communiqué from "Monsanto."

colonial Mexico are called "codexes." Our "'Codex México is a visionary initiative that will allow future generations of children to know far more about our lives today than we know of our pre-Columbian ancestors,' noted forensic anthropologist Marcelo Rodríguez Gutiérrez. 'Never again will the wealth of this region's culture be lost as social conditions change.'" This new conquest, we suggested, would be kinder and less devastating than the last. To illustrate the contribution of the codex, Lorie Novak included corny photographs and empty captions: "Mexican Corn."

Monsanto, faced with the decision dilemma of responding to or ignoring the prank, did not take long to respond. Just as we were sitting down for a celebratory margarita (fig. 9.6), Monsanto had us on the phone demanding that we take our hoax site down. They insisted we issue a retraction immediately. We agreed, of course. Another press release, by us but again seemingly from Monsanto, "denounced the release as a hoax, crediting a group of students and activists called *Sin Maíz No Hay Vida* (Without Corn There Is No Life)."[43] There we fully explained what Monsanto was up to. The reveal, The Yes Men's revelation of the hoax, always happens within twenty-four hours

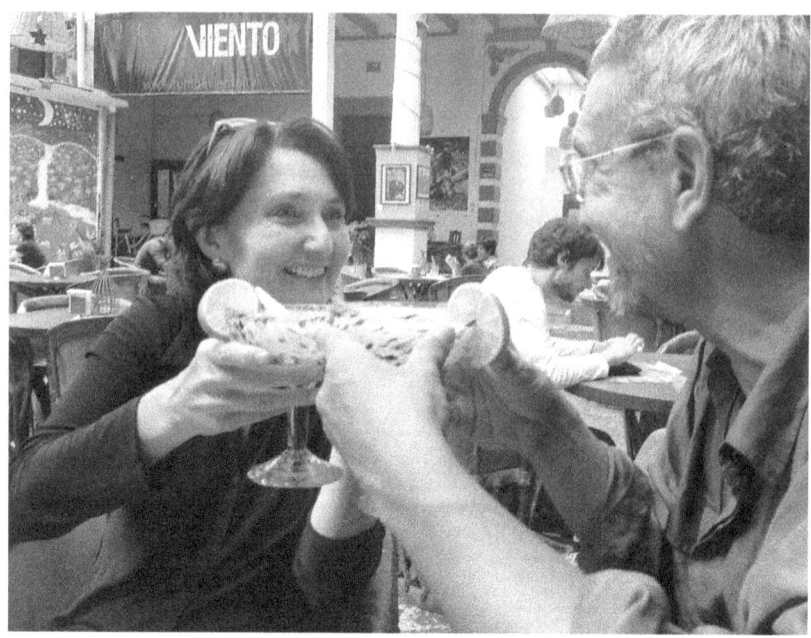

9.6 Diana Taylor and Jacques Servin having a celebratory margarita. San Cristóbal de las Casas, Chiapas, 2013. PHOTO: LORIE NOVAK.

of the act, if it hasn't already been uncovered. The lie may be useful in illuminating a larger egregious act, but it is not allowed to stand.[44] Unlike fraud, our intentions were neither to profit nor deceive but, rather, to provoke a conversation. A few news outlets knew that both our press release and our denouncement were a prank—no one familiar with Monsanto's strategies could believe that the corporation would issue such declarations—but they took advantage of the excuse to throw light on the corruption shrouding Monsanto and SAGARPA. Given the widespread activism around the GMO issue, we were leaked a confidential email that Monsanto had just sent to SAGARPA, apologizing for the confusion that our "reprehensible action" had caused and promising to get things under control.[45] Monsanto reiterated the need for confidentiality. Monsanto, imposters too, had to perform their role as responsible and efficacious collaborators for the authorities. We also published that email.[46]

On September 13, 2013, Monsanto contacted the president of NYU to complain about the street and digital actions. They wanted to know about the course, see the syllabus, and understand the relationship of the actions to NYU. They demanded an apology from NYU.

This created a new drama, one that dominated our fall semester in 2013 at NYU. This drama was complex. In Victor Turner's language of social drama, it could be characterized as consisting of a breach or rupture caused by a transgressive act (launching the fake website?), a crisis (which spanned the fall semester), the reparative acts (involving Monsanto lawyers, NYU, and myself), and the resolution (hopefully to come).[47] The series of acts that constituted the drama shifted between overt and covert, play and "dark play" in Richard Schechner's words.[48] Play, like the law perhaps, is usually regulated by rules and agreements, but it was not quite clear during that time what we all thought we were agreeing to. Had we even agreed to agree? More in the realm of dark play, we did not all know who were playing. The law structured its performance of authority and consensus, agreeing that we were in violation. Servin and I started coming into presence as a problem, a problem for Monsanto and, by extension, a problem for NYU. We defended different rules based on freedom of speech that included the right to parody and critique.

In several ways, Monsanto started to appear as a person and persona invested with personality before my eyes. Persona, in classical Greek theatre, is literally the mask through which the actor speaks the words. No one ever saw the face of the being that uttered the words, only the mask or persona transmitting them. Monsanto's spokespeople were literally mouthpieces, ventriloquists conveying language. I never knew who, if anybody, was behind the mask. The mask of Monsanto removed the "object from our grasp," to paraphrase Brecht.[49] But contrary to Brecht's "alienation effect" that builds on dialectical materialism "to unearth society's laws of motion . . . [and] treats social situations as processes, and traces out all their inconsistencies," this form of alienation made the powers more inaccessible and potent, unlocatable yet ubiquitous.[50] Monsanto's spokespeople impersonated and embodied a corporation (*corporare*) that itself impersonated being a person.

On a different level, Monsanto seemed to be a person with feelings. It (he? she?) claimed to have been hurt and embarrassed, and needed an apology. Corporations legally count as persons after all; they have rights and, apparently, they have emotions. "Monsanto" had complained to NYU. But again, who is Monsanto and to whom did he/she/it complain? In what guise? Where were the people behind these masks? That legal fiction functions as its own form of impersonation. The fiction of the corporation as a person was, it seemed, an acceptable and permissible impersonation, while impersonating a corporate impersonation was not.

Lawyers for NYU repeatedly questioned Servin and me. We stressed that the digital action had nothing to do with NYU. It was not on the syllabus or part of the course. We forwarded the materials, syllabus included, requested by Monsanto. We reiterated that NYU had no reason to issue an apology.

We had a few questions of our own for Monsanto. We asked the lawyers to ask what Monsanto objected to—the street action or the digital action. Is impersonation on the street different from impersonation online? It could not be that simple. We had impersonated Monsanto before, in a street action comparing the insatiable agribusiness to the insatiable mouth of Tlaltecuhtli, the Aztec god/dess of the earth who devours her creations. It would seem that embodied actions in some distant town in southern Mexico did not resonate much. Yet again Servin had been sued for impersonating a Chamber of Commerce representative in the flesh. The difference, Servin and I concluded, was not about the online or offline nature of the impersonation but about the reach of the prank.

We also wanted to know how our action had harmed Monsanto. After all, it was just play. A performance, such as the street action, can be considered a form of representation. Monsanto in a pig's mask was a representation. A performative, on the other hand, can be considered a speech act, a form of incitement.[51] We, like The Yes Men before, claimed ours was intended as an art project—a performance rather than a performative. We were not trying to do something, make something happen, we said. This was not an animative—a refusal to play the game. On the contrary, we were playing. And arguably, if readers had actually believed the fake website, it might be said that we were trying to make Monsanto look good, as if it cared about bio- and cultural diversity.[52] Privately, of course, Servin and I actually hoped Monsanto could show we had injured them—that would have been proof of the efficacy of activist performance. But no proof of injury or efficacy was forthcoming.

Before long, an NYU lawyer and a top administrator came to visit me in my office. Phrases such as code of ethics, academic freedom, and conflict of interest came up. Apparently, our action had placed us on the wrong side of each. The lawyer and senior administrator from NYU told me with straight faces that I might be guilty of conflict of interest. Really? How so? I asked. Apparently the Hemispheric Institute site linked to The Yes Men's, where they sold T-shirts. But then I asked the senior administrator, "Weren't you once one of Monsanto's lead counsels? Some might call that a conflict of interest." The lawyer hastened to add that conflict of interest was not necessarily a bad thing, it just needed to be managed. The administrator straightened herself up uncomfortably in her chair and scratched "conflict of interest" off her list of our infractions.

Violation of an ethical code? An important university person had recently sent an email on official letterhead asking employees for donations to a right-wing politician, payable through his office. Was that a violation of NYU's ethical code, I asked them? Just asking. That violation was also scratched off the list of my infractions.

The administrator reminded me that I was not covered by academic freedom.

Monsanto, I said to my visitors, had seemingly infinite resources and strategies to counter any critiques or evidence of wrongdoing against them. All we (professors) had to shield us was academic freedom.[53] Were they really going to go after me on the grounds of academic freedom? They must have agreed it wasn't worth their while to continue the conversation, but they did admonish me not to do it again.

As I put in an email to members of the administration who continued to question whether my actions were covered by academic freedom: "For me, as a performance studies scholar, the hoax and writing and acting are all ways to express ourselves in the face of enormous corporate interests that do very real harm." Polluting the environment, destroying local economies, meddling in educational institutions, and harming humans all theoretically count as violations, but which violations matter and which do not? The law, apparently, legitimates certain performances, turning away from the harms they permit, and negatively sanctions others (plays, pranks) on the basis of a harm they are said to cause.

Nonetheless, the logic around academic freedom seemed paradoxical: if my use of a hoax were part of a course, it would be covered by academic freedom. If it were not covered because it took place outside the limits of my institutional commitments, then why would NYU have to weigh in? Again, there's no clear agreement on what academic freedom might mean and what it covers, especially now in the Trump era. Greg Lukianoff defined it in *Fire's Guide to Free Speech on Campus* "as a general recognition that the academy must be free to research, teach, and debate ideas without censorship or outside interference." Following that definition, those who study and teach there must be able to pursue knowledge without corporations impeding and subverting academic work.[54] Monsanto and other corporations and military entities fund research at all of our universities. There is a rotating-door hiring process between these industries and universities, as the role of ex-Monsanto lawyer, now current highly placed administrative officer, makes clear. These businesses influence what areas of inquiry are important, prioritized, and funded. And yet I am not allowed to critique them? Is that academic freedom?

If we must make a choice, as the law apparently requires, then we will need to agree on underlying values. Which performance is more important to society: a group of concerned artists and academics impersonating a hurtful corporation, or a corporation intent on impersonating hurt feelings?

After many back-and-forths, it seemed that the street action, which was officially related to the course, did not really bother Monsanto. While the actor wore a pig's mask to impersonate Monsanto, no one actually believed it was Monsanto—it was a performance; the joke was clear, and it took place far away, in a small Mexican city. The digital action, on the other hand, reached a far broader audience (including the people who were considering granting permission to Monsanto). It might be argued that people for a short period of time actually thought the fake announcement came from Monsanto, which got them activated—thus it was a performative, language that acts, that makes something happen. In any case, that level of exposure was no laughing matter, and Monsanto was taking it very seriously indeed, operating behind closed doors as usual to intimidate their critics.

As the fall semester wore on, it seemed that Monsanto no longer insisted on a formal public apology from NYU. A confidential apology, available only to "persons who need to know," as an email put it, would be sufficient. As before, I argued strongly against this, stating that Monsanto would use the (confidential) apology to justify itself and discredit critique before Mexican lawmakers.

Civil liberties lawyers argue that the ambiguity around the legal understandings of impersonation could clamp down on free speech. Matt Zimmerman, the lawyer with the Electronic Frontier Foundation that defended The Yes Men from the Chamber of Commerce, notes, "the concern is it gives a lot of discretion to law enforcement to go after First Amendment activity. . . . The resulting consequence of that is that people will feel chilled and intimidated and hence decide to not engage in perfectly legitimate forms of social protest because they're worried that not only might they be sued, but they could actually go to jail."[55] Political speech is, after all, what the First Amendment protects, according to Christopher Dunn of the New York Civil Liberties Union: "Political, religious and other speech often is intended to be annoying. But that is precisely the type of speech the First Amendment was designed to protect."[56]

In October 2013, a Mexico City judge, Marroquin Zaleta, issued a temporary halt that prohibited SAGARPA from granting Monsanto permission to plant GM corn in Mexico, either on an experimental, pilot, or commercial basis.[57] A December 2013 ruling upheld that position.[58] Subsequent court rulings have prohibited the planting of GM corn in Central America. Agro-BIO and other firms have lobbied to overturn Judge Marroquin Zaleta's 2013 ruling and demand he be taken off the case.[59] The struggles continue into the present, but the prohibition against planting GM corn stands, at least in theory. In practice Monsanto aka Bayer continues to plant its genetically modified crops.

Did our digital action prove efficacious? Did we really derail or at least postpone Monsanto's plans? Although we would love to think so, this hoax was one of thousands of interventions that artists and activists constantly carry out to keep GMOs out of Mexico and other countries. We did not know most of them, but we were reassured to be among people who use their talents to keep (further) bad things from happening. These networks of core-sistance can make a difference. Unfortunately, local activists are usually the ones taking the heat from corporations for intervening in their plans.[60]

But the action did place many in a decision dilemma. Would NYU tell Monsanto to go away and reiterate that NYU had nothing to do with the digital action (my suggestion)? What would happen to Jesusa Rodríguez, to Jacques Servin, and to me? Would the Hemispheric Institute have to distance itself even further from direct actions such as this one?

As of this writing, the Hemi-NYU-Monsanto conundrum seems to have been resolved or, better, dropped. Instead of reaching a resolution, the issue went away. Monsanto, of course, was too smart to go after The Yes Men. Monsanto just wanted a letter from NYU declaring our action unethical. They were even willing to accept a confidential letter, read by only a few key people. I could not find out if NYU ever issued the letter of apology. Although Bayer absorbed Monsanto, deemed too toxic a brand, and Monsanto Roundup now masquerades as Bayer Roundup, "Bayer Chairman Werner Baumann said in a statement, 'We will listen to our critics and work together where we find common ground.'"[61]

Happily, in any case, we were history.

But I too had been caught up in an identity correction. Coming into presence as an activist as well as a scholar has shifted my sense of temporality, responsibility, my worlds of interlocutors, and my understanding of the stakes. I remember one of the conversations we had at the first Hemi Encuentro in Rio de Janeiro in 2000. Apparently many participants found it strange that we would convene artists, activists, and scholars to think and collaborate together. Finally after working together for a few days, some of the artists spoke up: "We know why the artists and activists are here, but what are you [the scholars] doing here?" I responded that artists and activists often work with their bodies—everything from voice, to body art, to movement, to putting one's body on the line. But who, I asked, complicated our understanding of the body as raced, gendered, sexed, and so on? "Okay, you can stay." We agreed to work together. But it's still difficult to refuse disciplinary lines and loyalties, the age-old divisions between the knowing and the doing. I have to do something, but accept that I can only do what I can do. If there's a price to pay, so be it. After the administrator and the NYU lawyer warned me "not to do it again," I said that I would write the incident up in an essay. "If they [Monsanto] come after me for that, I'll write more." But again, it's not that simple. I too have been forced to confront my mask of power and recognize how risk is unevenly distributed not just throughout society but in my own practice. Jesusa Rodríguez risks her life (which has been threatened more than once). Now a senator in Mexico, Rodríguez is taking the fight against GMOs to the Senate floor. Jacques Servin has a collection of injunctions, cease and desist letters, and other warnings. He answers the performative with an animative; he turns his back and keeps laughing and finding ways to correct corrupt political and corporate identities. Visiting and adjunct faculty face more risks of losing jobs than do tenured, full, and distinguished professors. Servin was not reappointed to NYU. Organizations such as Hemi also run the risk of losing support and funding. In short, the prank had repercussions for all of us, in different ways.

Armed with scholarship and creativity, I continue to do what I can from where I am. What can I do when it seems that there's nothing to be done, and doing nothing is not an option? Lots of things, apparently.

Have I changed tactics in regard to knowledge, action, truth, and power? YES MA'AM!![62]

¡Presente!

Epilogue

What to do when it seems that nothing can be done and doing nothing is not an option?

This study has looked at ways in which certain artists, activists, and scholars throughout the Americas have responded to this question. Some, like the Zapatistas, opted for armed resistance followed by the creation of an autonomous, communal government. Others, such as the civil servants in chapter 2, turned their backs on the official demand for compliance. Others staged protests, pranks, performances, and memes, and traveled in caravans to intervene in situations they found intolerable. There are so many ways to be ¡Presente! In closing, I will reflect on one act, one gesture, so small and yet so life affirming that it crystalizes an ethics of care, of being ¡presente! with and to others. I've come to think of this gesture as one of the most moving I've encountered in my many years of engaging in this kind of intellectual and political meandering.

In February 1995, Leonilla Vasquez asked her daughters Norma and Bernarda Romero Vázquez (both in their late teens or early twenties) to go buy bread and milk. To do so, the two young women had to cross the train tracks that ran next to their very modest house in Patrona, Veracruz, Mexico. On their way home carrying the plastic bags with bread and milk, they stopped for the oncoming train. Men, women, and children clung to the top of the train. As they stood watching wagon after wagon push past them, a couple of young men shouted, "Madre, we're hungry! We haven't eaten in four days!" The young women hesitated, then handed up their bags of food. When they got home empty-handed they thought their mother would be angry. The family had very little money. Instead, Leonilla thought and said, "You did the right thing." That night, Leonilla told us, she could not sleep.[1] Why, she

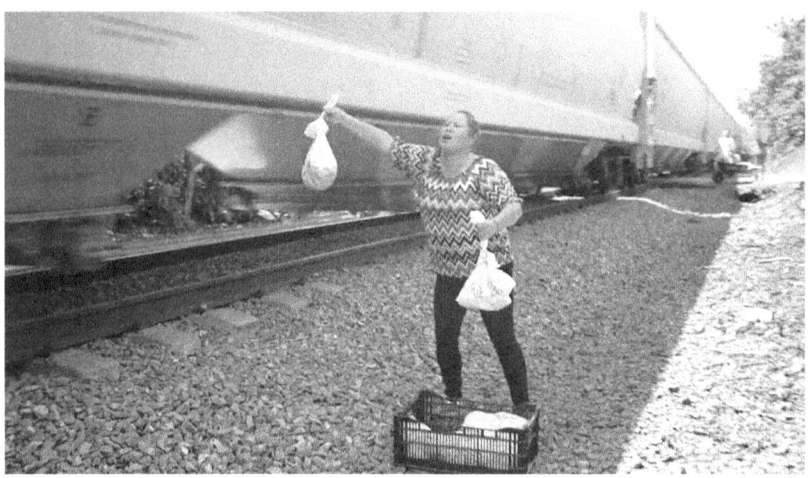

E.1 Norma, of Las Patronas, hands food to migrants traveling on top of La Bestia, the train that heads north to the U.S. border. Ecologies of Migrant Care, August 2017.

wondered, had she never thought about the hundreds of people on top of the train that goes right past her house? Who were they? Where did they come from, and where they were going? She'd only thought of them as *moscas* (flies) glued to the train. She resolved that she could not eat if they did not eat. Her daughters thought she was delusional. How can you feed them all? We don't know who they are—what if they're criminals fleeing from justice?[2]

Leonilla didn't let their objections deter her. She didn't know who they were, she said, and therefore would not judge them. But she knew they were hungry, and she would feed them. She'd do it alone. She started with a kilo of rice, a kilo of beans, and tortillas. Her husband and daughters saw her determination and agreed to help. A spontaneous act of kindness turned into a life-changing mission. Now, more than twenty years later, Las Patronas— Leonilla, her daughters, and her granddaughters—continue to prepare bags of food for three hundred to five hundred (and often more) Central American migrants riding La Bestia, which passes by their house three times a day. They ask for nothing in return.

There are many things we could say about this: the brutal nature of the migrant crisis, the terrors of La Bestia (subject of Óscar Martínez's book by that name), the gendered and radical nature of the generosity, the role of faith, the lack of humanitarian response by state or church officials, the impossibility of the task the women undertake, three times a day, seven days a week, year in and year out, providing food for people they do not know and will never see again. They call themselves "women of faith," but they're not nuns or doing church-related or supported work. Unlike the Mothers of Plaza de Mayo, ¡Eureka!, or other women's groups that have spent decades fighting for social justice, these women do not have a personal or political stake to motivate their acts. Their actions do not come from a place of struggle. No one in their family has migrated, and they have no theory on immigration policy. They know they will never solve the problem—but they tirelessly exert themselves anyway. How to explain it?

I close with a reflection (not an explication or theorization) on the empathetic gesture that turns ¡Presente! into a life project. The women hold up their hands with food and water. Not for themselves, not just for their ethnic or political kin, but for strangers. That's all. That's everything. If this empathetic gesture animates a life-affirming form of ¡Presente!, how, I wondered, might I/we be able to emulate, imitate, replicate, transform it into sustained political practice?

This gesture performs not only between bodies (the two young women holding out the bags of food to the migrants) but across various expressive arenas. From medieval Latin *gestūra*, gesture is a mode of action. It refers to a movement by the body intended to express a thought or feeling, an emotion, an idea, an opinion, and a political posture. The embodied, communicative, affective, and political dimensions of the word open up an expressive field of possibility, which ranges from the empty impulse (a token or meaningless gesture), to the small move (my gesture in offering up this book, or the Ecologies of Migrant Care project), to the accomplished act (Las Patronas giving out food). Gestures can be both fleeting expressions and iterable, quotable enactments that cite previous acts and positions— everything from Brecht's *gestus* to the hands holding the bag up toward the train. Gestures often accompany speech, but they are not reducible to verbal language. They capture the many facets and forms of expression that make up a communicative act. Gesturing ¡Presente!, Las Patronas make manifest their commitment to care for those who pass their home in need. Day in, day out, they hold up their bags of food and water. They expanded their care to migrants traveling by foot when the cartel gangs and Mexican federal agents made it too dangerous for them to ride the train.[3] With help from international organizations, Las Patronas built dormitories, washrooms, a wide-open dining room, and a laundry room to house those who stopped on their journey. They've connected to human rights organizations that help migrants with medical and legal issues. Where does the money to expand their offerings come from? One benefactor, they found out later, was a Central American woman who had reached Canada after traveling north, past their house, on the train. She had been a recipient of their kindness and wanted to extend the gesture.

Empathy too covers a broad range of meanings spanning spontaneous, neurological, visceral response in human and nonhuman animals to the predicament of others.[4] Often studies equate empathy with identification, mirroring, and even appropriation (their pain becomes our pain). People worry about "rampant empathy" that we cannot control.[5] Empathy, some say, is manipulated for political reasons. Empathy, studies prove, is innate but easy to override—young children can be taught to not care about or even to hate others. Thinking about empathy in other animals might help untangle some of these charges against empathy. My dog, for example, sits close beside me when I'm upset—she's not appropriating, identifying, or manipulating me. Yet these arguments have been instrumental in teaching us to not care, to rationalize and justify not caring. Las Patronas give examples of how people constantly try to dissuade them from helping the migrants—who are they? And what are they to you? It's not your problem. "I don't care. Do U?" as Melania Trump signaled to the world.

The example of Las Patronas, however, offers a more hopeful, relational way to think about empathy as part of this spontaneous act of doing something when it seems as if nothing can be done. Leonilla says they have to do what they can ("Lo que puedamos," as Leonilla put it). It's not about identification or compassion—they are not us. She is not mirroring them or feeling their pain—she enjoys stability, family, food and shelter, extremely modest though it be. She's not asking for anything in return. For her, the sharing of food creates and humanizes the relationship—the migrants go from being flies to being people. The women never talk about the poor migrants or the unjust system. They do not judge: "Nadie sabe como viene la gente" (We never know who people are). The migrants are hungry and they have food. It's that simple.

Las Patronas' gesture, I believe, potentializes or mobilizes an ontological and epistemic understanding of ¡Presente! as copresence, of subjectivity as participatory and relational, founded on mutual recognition and responsibility. Empathetic gestures are not contagious—others in the town, including the Catholic Church, have not followed the women's generous example, though some people at times come out to help distribute the food. But they are learnable—for Leonilla it was a choice. She reflected on her daughters' spontaneous act of sharing (the visceral response) and turned that into a lifelong practice—a responsibility.

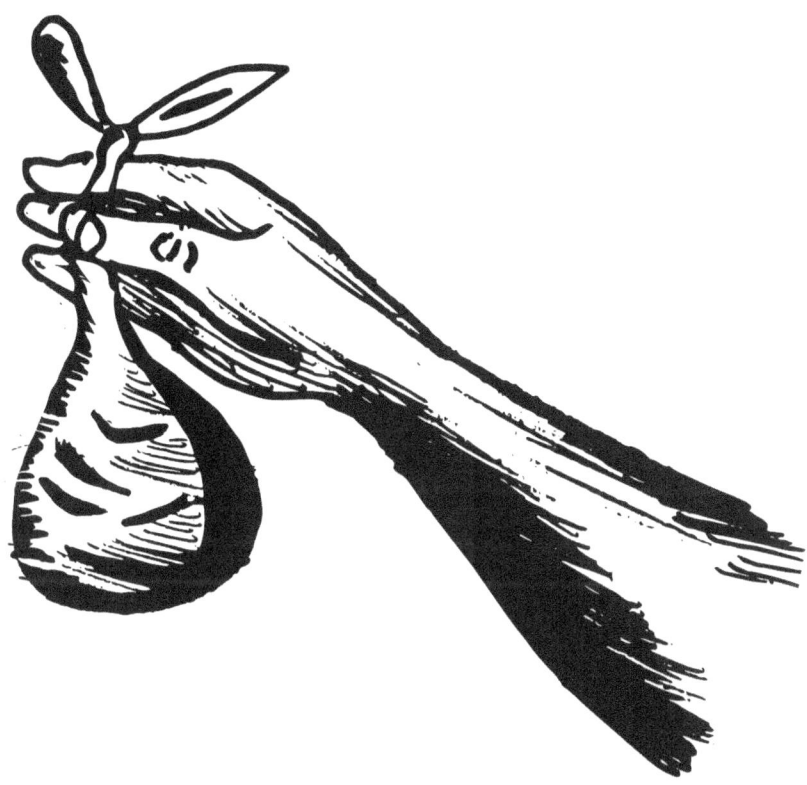

E.2 Alexei Taylor, *The Gesture*, 2019.

A gesture, Ricardo Dominguez writes, "makes manifest a set of social relations that extend beyond the performance. . . . At the core of a gesture is the potential of a body or of bodies to create new types of agency and social interventions," ways of doing, of being ¡Presente!, of standing up, showing up, responding, and accepting responsibility, when it seems there is nothing to be done.

Xuno's Dream

Just before I left Chiapas to visit Las Patronas in Veracruz in August 2017, Xuno López told me he'd had a dream in which he and I were walking together when a huge wall or building started to collapse near us. His first instinct was to run to save his life, but he realized I couldn't run. He saw that my right leg was hurt. He reached out his hand to help me and was able to get me to his family's house, where they healed me.

Xuno's dream came a month before the September 19, 2017, earthquake struck Mexico. My family and I were literally surrounded by the debris of falling buildings, the gas leaking from broken pipelines, and people running terrified into the streets. It came two years before I broke my right foot following Hemi's 2019 Encuentro in Mexico City, the last I would organize before stepping down as director in August 2020. It came in the midst of the crushing human rights calamity created by Donald Trump's xenophobic calls for a border wall. It came three years before the zoonotic infection of COVID-19 paralyzed the world, a reminder that massive animal slaughter and the destruction of natural habitats has taken them, and us, to the point of extinction. The quarantined populations and grounded airplanes made graphic that frantic capitalism and globalization is bringing the world crashing down around us. If there is a healing place and a regenerative practice, we need to find them now. Those who have accompanied me on this journey have inspired me to keep walking and talking.

¡Presente! Holding out one's hand to others, is the beginning of everything.

Notes

Prologue

1. "¡Ahí está el detalle! Que no es ni lo uno, ni lo otro, sino todo lo contrario." Augustina Caferri, "23 frases divertidas del comediante mexicano Cantinflas," About Español, July 2, 2019, https://www.aboutespanol.com/23-frases-divertidas -del-comediante-mexicano-cantinflas-696281.

One ¡Presente!

1. The PPT met in New York City on September 4–7, 2014. See the interview, "Garifuna Woman—Permanent People's Tribunal," Hemispheric Institute, 2015, https://vimeo.com/134332716.

2. The Hemispheric Institute began in 1998 as a consortium between New York University, Universidad Autónoma de Nuevo León, and the Universidade Federal do Estado do Rio de Janeiro to share and promote understanding of performance (broadly understood) in the Americas. Marcial Godoy-Anativia, managing director of the Hemispheric Institute, Pablo Domínguez, a PhD candidate at Princeton University, and I formed the core of the research team, and we convened and met with hundreds of researchers, rights advocates, artists, and religious figures from throughout the Americas working on the issue of migration from 2014 to the present. Thanks to Toby Volkman and the Luce Foundation for helping to support this research. For information about the Hemispheric Institute, see https:// hemisphericinstitute.org/en/.

3. See Óscar Martínez, *The Beast: Riding the Rails and Dodging Narcos on the Migrant Trail*, trans. Daniela Maria Ugaz and John Washington (London: Verso, 2013), for a full account of La Bestia.

4. An International Human Rights Observation Mission on the Guatemala-Mexico Border (MODH is its Spanish acronym) was held from November 10 to 16 to document and highlight the situation of systematic violations of human rights in the border region between Guatemala and Mexico. "Mexico/Guatemala: International Human Rights Observation Mission on Guatemala-Mexico

Border," *Sipaz Blog*, accessed January 1, 2020, https://sipazen.wordpress.com/2016/12/01/mexicoguatemala-international-human-rights-observation-mission-on-guatemala-mexico-border/.

5. Tomás González, interview, November 13, 2016, Ecologies of Migrant Care, https://migration.hemi.press/fray-tomas/.

6. "About Us: Praise for EMC," Ecologies of Migrant Care, accessed February 3, 2020, https://migration.hemi.press/about-us/.

7. In summer 2017, Hemi convened artists and activists from Mexico and Central America, including Jacques Servin of The Yes Men and Jesusa Rodríguez, in Chiapas, Mexico, to create satirical digital projects meant to disrupt what we all saw as the xenophobic discourses and practices regarding Central American migrants taking place in Mexico and the United States. Two of the interventions were *Somos el Muro* (We are the wall), https://somoselmuro.com.mx/, depicting a fake right-wing group of Mexicans proclaiming themselves "the wall" needed to keep Central Americans out. "Every time you do nothing to help, you are also part of the wall," one character in the video assures a bystander. *Somos el Muro* enjoyed a tepid reception and then went viral about a year after we created it, causing a massive response and much controversy in Central America, Mexico, and the U.S. See the discussion in "On the Internet, Nobody Knows You're a Joke," *On the Media*, November 30, 2018, https://www.wnycstudios.org/story/internet-nobody-knows-youre-joke; Zachary Small, "Mexican Anti-migrant Video Goes Viral, before Artists Reveal It as Satire," *Hyperallergic*, December 17, 2018, https://hyperallergic.com/475940/millions-believe-an-anti-migrant-video-from-mexico-was-real-until-artists-exposed-it-as-satire/; and for Mexico, "Muy enojados en Honduras por video con contenido xenofobo," *La Prensa*, October 30, 2018, https://www.la-prensa.com.mx/mexico/361792-muy-enojados-en-honduras-por-video-con-contenido-xenofobo. Migratón Fundación (https://migraton.com.mx/), a parody of the popular money-raising telethons, especially those purporting to help migrants, makes clear that migration is a big business in Mexico (as elsewhere). Everyone makes money, except for the migrants. Migratón's Tours, Kids, and Champions use humor to reflect on especially egregious practices. For my work as a professor, see Diana Taylor et al., *Art, Migration, and Human Rights: A Collaborative Dossier by Artists, Scholars, and Activists on the Issue of Migration in Southern Mexico* (New York: HemiPress, 2015). At Hemi, we have organized, transcribed, and subtitled the interviews and visual materials from these interactions to extend the information and reach of the migrant crisis to other domains—to policy makers, advocates, educators, journalists, artists, and activists. We continue to create a series of encounters and conferences (pedagogical, artistic, hemispheric) and to develop a research and advocacy repository of all these materials (including those from this PPT) that are available freely online to all who work to make this political and humanitarian crisis visible. See Ecologies of Migrant Care, https://migration.hemi.press/.

8. Gayatri Spivak, "Scattered Speculations on the Subaltern and the Popular," in *An Aesthetic Education in the Era of Globalization* (Cambridge, MA: Harvard University Press, 2012), 440.

9. Rigoberta Menchú said that critique was in fact a "sign of privilege." Quoted in Doris Sommer, *Cultural Agency in the Americas* (Durham, NC: Duke University Press), 2006, 4. Sommer adds: "Poor people need a next step."

10. Marlène Ramírez-Cancio, associate director of arts and media at Hemi, coins words such as "Ailóbit" (I love it!) to capture the constant creative flow of cultural codes and expressions.

11. I describe this part of my life and training a little more fully in the preface, "Who, When, What, Why," to my book *The Archive and the Repertoire: Performing Cultural Memory in the Americas* (Durham, NC: Duke University Press, 2003).

12. Silvia Rivera Cusicanqui, for example, calls out postcolonial studies in the U.K. and U.S.: "Without altering anything of the relations of force in the 'palaces' of empire, the cultural studies departments of North American universities have adopted the ideas of subaltern studies and launched debates in Latin America, thus creating a jargon, a conceptual apparatus, and forms of reference and counterreference that have isolated academic treatises from any obligation to or dialogue with insurgent social forces." Silvia Rivera Cusicanqui, "Ch'ixinakax utxiwa: A Reflection on the Practices and Discourses of Decolonization," *South Atlantic Quarterly* 111 (winter 2012): 98.

13. For a fuller discussion of Malinche, see Taylor, *The Archive and the Repertoire*, ch. 3.

14. Dwight Conquergood, "Of Caravans and Carnivals," in *Cultural Struggles: Performance, Ethnography, Praxis*, ed. E. Patrick Johnson (Ann Arbor: University of Michigan Press, 2013), 13.

15. Richard Schechner, *Between Theater and Anthropology* (Philadelphia: University of Pennsylvania Press, 1985), 36.

16. Michel de Certeau, *The Practice of Everyday Life*, trans. Steven F. Rendall (Berkeley: University of California Press, 1984), xi.

17. Jean-Luc Nancy, in *Being Singular Plural*, trans. Robert Richardson and Anne O'Byrne (Stanford, CA: Stanford University Press, 2000), writes, everything "passes between us. . . . All of being is in touch with all of being, but the law of touching is separation" (5). Nancy adds: "Being cannot be anything but being-with-another" (3). Nancy distinguishes being from presence; being is "opened by presence to presence: all things, all beings, all entities, everything past and future, alive, dead, inanimate, stones, plants, nails, gods—and 'humans'" (3). Ironically, Nancy links presence in humans to language: "'humans,' that is, those who expose sharing and circulation as such by saying 'we,' by saying we to themselves in all possible senses of that expression, and by saying we for the totality of all being." Presence, in humans, according to Nancy, allows for the articulation of a "we," albeit an oddly totalizing and self-referential one, a "we to themselves."

18. Hannah Arendt calls the "space of appearance" "the organization of the people as it arises out of acting and speaking together . . . [whose] true space lies between people living together for this purpose." Hannah Arendt, *The Human Condition* (New York: Doubleday Anchor, 1959), 178.

19. Arendt, *The Human Condition*, 179.

20. Ejército Zapatista de Liberación Nacional, "Comunicado de Prensa del Subcomandante Marcos," *Chiapas*, May 28, 1994, http://www.bibliotecas.tv/chiapas/may94/28may94.html.

Marcos es gay en San Francisco, negro en Sudáfrica, asiático en Europa, chicano en San Isidro, anarquista en España, palestino en Israel, indígena en las calles de San Cristóbal, chavo banda en Neza, rockero en CU, judío en Alemania, ombudsman en la Sedena, feminista en los partidos políticos, comunista en la post guerra fría, preso en Cintalapa, pacifista en Bosnia, mapuche en los Andes, maestro en la CNTE, artista sin galería ni portafolios, ama de casa un sábado por la noche en cualquier colonia de cualquier ciudad de cualquier México, guerrillero en el México de fin del siglo XX, huelguista en la CTM, reportero de nota de relleno en interiores, machista en el movimiento feminista, mujer sola en el metro a las 10 P.M., jubilado en el plantón en el Zócalo, campesino sin tierra, editor marginal, obrero desempleado, médico sin plaza, estudiante inconforme, disidente en el neoliberalismo, escritor sin libros ni lectores, y, es seguro, zapatista en el sureste mexicano.

21. Guillermo Gómez-Peña, "I AM: A Poetic Conversation," accessed January 6, 2020, http://scalar.usc.edu/anvc/dancing-with-the-zapatistas/i-am. In the early 1990s, I wrote a poem, "Spanglish Lesson," as part of my trilogy *The Rediscovery of America by the Warrior for Gringostroika*, which five years later would inspire Subcomandante Marcos to write his famous poem "Marcos Is Gay." Fifteen years later, I have taken Marcos's text, rewritten it, and made it my own again in "Rewriting Marcos," in *Dancing with the Zapatistas*, ed. Diana Taylor with Lorie Novak (Durham, NC: Duke University Press and HemiPress, 2015), http://scalar.usc.edu/anvc.

22. See Diana Taylor, "The Death of a Political 'I': Subcomandante Is Dead, Long Live the Subcomandante!," in Taylor and Novak, *Dancing with the Zapatistas*.

23. The epigraph for this section is from González, interview, November 13, 2016, Ecologies of Migrant Care, https://migration.hemi.press/fray-tomas/.

24. Enrique Dussel, *The Invention of the Americas*, trans. Michael D. Barber (New York: Continuum, 1995), 25.

25. Dussel, *The Invention of the Americas*, 17–26. Denise Ferreira da Silva, *Toward a Global Idea of Race* (Minneapolis: University of Minnesota Press, 2007), xxxix. See too Denise Ferreira da Silva's "analytics of raciality" (xviii) that map "the productivity of the racial and how it is tied to the emergence of an ontological context—globality—that fuses particular bodily traits, social configurations, and global regions, in which human difference is reproduced as irreducible and unsublatable" (xix).

26. Ramón Grosfoguel links the violence leading to Descartes's *ego cogito* as building from the *ego conquiro* (I conquer, therefore I am) to the *ego extermino* (I exterminate, therefore I am). Ramón Grosfoguel, "The Structure of Knowledge in Westernized Universities," *Human Architecture: Journal of the Sociology of Self-Knowledge* 11, no. 1 (fall 2013): 73–90, https://www.okcir.com/Articles%20XI%201/Grosfoguel.pdf.

27. Gines de Sepúlveda called the indigenous inhabitants of the Americas "natural slaves," basing himself on Aristotle's *Politics* (Book 1). See José A. Fernández-Santamaria, "Juan Ginés de Sepúlveda on the Nature of the American Indians," *The Americas* 31, no. 4 (1975): 434–51, doi:10.2307/980012.

28. Online Etymology Dictionary, http://www.etymonline.com/index.php?term=present.

29. Dussel, in *The Invention of the Americas*, 30–31, notes that Columbus died in 1506 convinced he had discovered Asia. "America" was named after Amerigo Vespucci, the first to realize that the new land was not only unknown but unimagined by Europeans. Francisco López de Gómara, *Historia General de las Indias*, vol. 1 (Barcelona: Orbis, 1985), 50. Esteban Mira Caballos, in "Indios Americanos en el reino de Castilla, 1492–1550," *Temas Americanistas* 14 (1998): 2, states the following: "Fernández de Oviedo writes that Columbus brought 9 or 10 indians, of whom one died at sea and two or three 'dolientes' (mourners, sufferers) stayed in the Villa at Palos, so the six remaining went to the Court of the Catholic kings" (inconsistencies in capitalizing "indians" in the original). Gonzalo Fernández de Oviedo, *Historia general y natural de las Indias* (Madrid: Atlas, 1992), 1. Girolamo Benzoni affirms that two Indians died in the crossing. Girolamo Benzoni, *Historia del Nuevo Mundo* (Madrid: Alianza, 1989), 88.

30. Frantz Fanon, *Black Skin, White Masks*, trans. Charles Lam Markmann (New York: Grove, 1967), 10. The idea of turning a somebody into a nobody defines the process of *ningunear* introduced by Octavio Paz, "Máscaras Mexicanas," in *El laberinto de la soledad* (1950; reprint, Mexico City: Fondo de Cultura Económico, 2018).

31. The practice of putting indigenous peoples on display continued for centuries. Minik Wallace, a translator, and his father and other Inuits who helped Commander Robert Edwin Peary on his explorations of the North Pole, were given to the American Museum of Natural History to be studied at the end of the nineteenth century: "After his father died, museum staff tricked Minik into thinking they had given his father a proper burial—instead they put his skeleton on display to the public." Edward Brooke-Hitching, *The Phantom Atlas: The Greatest Myths, Lies, and Blunders on Maps* (London: Simon and Schuster, 2016), 74.

32. See Greg Grandin, *Empire's Workshop: Latin America, the United States, and the Rise of the New Imperialism Project* (New York: Owl, 2006).

33. Ariella Azoulay, in "Unlearning Human Rights" (Modern Language Association panel, Rights under Repression, January 6, 2018), ties the notion of "rights" to the rights to explore and destroy existing worlds and asks who are "we" to extend rights to other people?

34. See Anthony Paglen, *European Encounters with the New World* (New Haven, CT: Yale University Press, 1993).

35. Achille Mbembe, "Necropolitics," trans. Libby Meintjes, *Popular Culture* 15, no. 1 (winter 2003): 17.

36. Aníbal Quijano, "¡Qué tal Raza!," *América Latina en movimiento*, September 19, 2000, https://www.alainet.org/es/active/929.

37. Hannah Arendt, *Origins of Totalitarianism* (New York: Harcourt, 1976), 185.

38. Arendt, *Origins of Totalitarianism*.

39. Alexander G. Weheliye, *Habeas Viscus: Racializing Assemblages, Biopolitics, and Black Feminist Theories of the Human* (Durham, NC: Duke University Press, 2014), 12.

40. Bartolomé de Las Casas, *An Account, Much Abbreviated, of the Destruction of the Indies with Related Texts*, ed. Franklin W. Knight, trans. Andrew Hurley

(Indianapolis: Hackett, 2003); David E. Stannard, in *American Holocaust: The Conquest of the New World* (New York: Oxford University Press, 1992), estimates that 95 percent of the native population of the Americas was extinguished in the fifty years following contact. Aníbal Quijano ("Coloniality and Modernity/Rationality," *Cultural Studies* 21, no. 2 [2007]: 170) estimates that "65 million inhabitants were exterminated in a period of less than 50 years." Ben Vinson III ("Fading from Memory: Historiographical Reflections on the Afro-Mexican Presence," *Review of Black Political Economy* 33, no. 1 [September 2005]: 60) notes what while the 110,000 African slaves taken to Mexico made up half the slave population taken to all the Americas, the African presence in Mexico was not felt as strongly as might be supposed because of miscegenation: "Blacks had made themselves prominently felt through miscegenation. Indeed, some have cited the period from 1600–1700 as pivotal for transforming the black population from being primarily African-based, to being largely creole and mulato." Herman L. Bennett, in *Africans in Colonial Mexico* (Bloomington: Indiana University Press, 2003), notes that "New Spain's seventeenth-century demographic distinctiveness—home to the second largest slave and the largest free black populations—may come as a revelation to those unaccustomed to thinking of Mexico as a prominent site of the African presence" (1).

41. Grosfoguel argues that while the conquest of Al-Andalus and the expulsion of Jews and Muslims from Spain on the grounds of "purity of blood" was based on "religious discrimination that was not yet fully racist because it did not question in a profound way the humanity of its victims . . . the conquest of the Americas . . . created a new racial imaginary and racial hierarchy." Grosfoguel, "The Structure of Knowledge in Westernized Universities," 79–80.

42. Europeans made up less than 1 percent of the population. The indigenous peoples (90 percent of the population) and Africans (10 percent) intermixed, cooperated, and even planned and carried out revolts.

43. See Robert H. Jackson, *Race, Caste, and Status: Indians in Colonial Spanish America* (Albuquerque: University of New Mexico Press, 1999), 3. See also R. Douglas Cope, *The Limits of Racial Domination: Plebeian Society in Colonial Mexico City, 1660–1720* (Madison: University of Wisconsin Press, 1994).

44. Established when Spanish and Portuguese conquers invaded the Americas, the caste system traveled to India in the sixteenth century. Allison Elliott, "Caste Systems in India," Postcolonial Studies, Emory University, 1997, https://scholarblogs.emory.edu/postcolonialstudies/2014/06/20/caste-system-in-india/.

45. Vinson, "Fading from Memory," 64.

46. Indians were bought ("about 650,000 Indians in coastal Nicaragua, Costa Rica, and Honduras were enslaved in the sixteenth century") and moved to various parts of the Americas. Alan Gallay writes, "Instead of viewing victimization of Africans and Indians as two entirely separate processes, they should be compared and contrasted. This will shed more light on the consequences of colonialism in the Americas, and how racism became one of the dominant ideologies of the modern world." Alan Gallay, "Indian Slavery in the Americas," *US Slave*, November 28, 2012, https://usslave.blogspot.com/2012/11/indian-slavery-in-americas-by-alan.html.

47. Ginés de Sepúlveda, "Democrates Alter, or, On the Just Causes for War against the Indians" (1544), Columbia University Sources of Medieval History, accessed January 1, 2020, http://www.columbia.edu/acis/ets/CCREAD/sepulved.htm.

48. "By this I mean a number of phenomena that seem to me to be quite significant, namely, the set of mechanisms through which the basic biological features of the human species became the object of a political strategy, of a general strategy of power, or, in other words, how, starting from the 18th century, modern Western societies took on board the fundamental biological fact that human beings are a species. This is what I have called biopower." Michel Foucault, *Security, Territory, Population: Lectures at the Collège de France 1977–1978*, ed. Michel Senellart, trans. Graham Burchell (New York: Picador, 2007), 7.

49. Aníbal Quijano and Immanuel Wallerstein, "Americanity as a Concept, or the Americas in the Modern World-System," *International Social Science Journal* 134 (1992): 549. See also Dussel, *The Invention of the Americas*.

50. Sven Beckert, *Empire of Cotton: A Global History* (New York: Vintage, 2014), 30–31.

51. "Indians" was used to denote major ethnic groups and nations such as the Aztecs and Mayas in Mesoamerica, the Aymara and Quechua people conquered by the Incas in the Andean regions of Bolivia and Peru, the Mapuche in southern Chile, Argentina, and Patagonia, and the Guaraní along the Atlantic borders of Argentina, Paraguay, Uruguay, and Brazil. Hundreds of other groups also became Indians.

52. Linda Tuhiwai Smith, *Decolonizing Methodologies: Research and Indigenous Peoples*, 2nd ed. (London: Zed, 2012), 20.

53. Thanks to Peter Kulchyski for this observation.

54. Barbara Deloria, Kristen Foehner, and Sam Scinta, eds., *Spirit and Reason: A Vine Deloria, Jr., Reader* (Golden, CO: Fulcrum, 1999), 356.

55. Leanne Betasamosake Simpson, *Dancing on Our Turtle's Back* (Winnipeg: Arbeiter Ring, 2011), 13.

56. Simpson's word, *Dancing on Our Turtle's Back*.

57. Simpson, *Dancing on Our Turtle's Back*, 96.

58. Vinson writes: "Trying to reconcile the country's extensive Indigenous presence with the prevailing, 19th- and 20th-century models of 'progress' was a large enough hurdle to surmount without having to add the burden of a black population as well." Vinson, "Fading from Memory," 67.

59. Rafa Fernandez de Castro, "Mexico 'Discovers' 1.4 million Black Mexicans—They Just Had to Ask," Fusion TV, December 15, 2015, http://fusion.net/story/245192/mexico-discovers-1-4-million-black-mexicans-they-just-had-to-ask/.

60. "Afro-Mexicans," Wikipedia, last edited January 4, 2020, https://en.wikipedia.org/wiki/Afro-Mexicans.

61. Aimé Césaire, *A Tempest*, trans. Richard Miller (New York:, Theatre Communications Group, 2002), Characters.

62. Christopher Columbus, "Columbus' Letter of His First Voyage," in *Four Voyages of Christopher Columbus*, ed. and trans. J. M. Cohen (Middlesex, U.K.: Penguin, 1969), 121.

63. Roberto Fernández Retamar, *Caliban and Other Essays* (Minneapolis: University of Minnesota Press, 1989), 8.

64. See Christina A. Sue and Tanya Golash-Boza, "'It Was Only a Joke': How Racial Humour Fuels Colour-Blind Ideologies in Mexico and Peru," *Ethnic and Racial Studies* 36, no. 10 (2013): 1584.

65. See Taylor, *The Archive and the Repertoire*, 95.

66. Grosfoguel, "The Structure of Knowledge in Westernized Universities," 87.

67. Walter D. Mignolo, *The Darker Side of the Renaissance* (Ann Arbor: University of Michigan Press, 1995), ix. Mignolo argues, "If the Spanish Empire declines in the modern/colonial period and Castilian became a second-class language in relation to languages of European modernity (French, English, and German), it was mainly because Castilian had lost its power as a knowledge-generating language. It became a language more suited for literary and cultural expressions" (ix).

68. Hannah Arendt writes, "Colonization took place in America and Australia, the two continents that, without a culture and history of their own, had fallen into the hands of Europeans." Arendt, *Origins of Totalitarianism*, 186.

69. Neither the history of colonialism nor the history of theoretical critiques of colonialism (post-, de-, anti-) has accounted for the copresence of Africans and indigenous peoples in the colonial Americas. Most historians view the "victimization of Africans and Indians as two entirely separate processes" instead of understanding racism as the leading ideology and mechanism of colonialism. Alan Gallay, "Indian Slavery in the Americas," Gilder Lerhman Institute of American History, https://www.gilderlehrman.org/history-by-era/origins-slavery/essays/indian-slavery-americas. See also Alan Gallay, ed., *Indian Slavery in Colonial America* (Lincoln: University of Nebraska Press, 2009); and Alan Gallay, *The Indian Slave Trade: The Rise of the English Empire in the American South, 1670–1717* (New Haven, CT: Yale University Press, 2002). For theories of race and post-, de-, and anticoloniality, scholars in Latin America have long turned to African and Indian scholars trained in the U.K. or France, and intellectuals from the Anglophone (Stuart Hall) or Francophone (Fanon, Césaire) or even Spanish (Roberto Fernández Retamar) Caribbean also trained in France and the U.K., to think through race and coloniality from the perspective of other, fundamentally different, instances of colonialism. Colonial metropoles in Britain and France played central roles in training theorists from their former colonies and disseminating their findings. Spain has played no such role. The particularities on ongoing coloniality in the Americas do not figure into the ways in which people like Arendt and Foucault thought about race as the ideological driver.

70. Juan López Intzín, "La insurgencia del Ch'ulel: Corazonar su potencial político y epistemológico descentrando la hegemonía del saber occidental," paper presented at the Hemispheric Institute of Performance and Politics Encuentro, New York, July 11–19, 2003.

71. Leda Martins, "Performances of Spiral Time," keynote address, Hemispheric Institute Encuentro, New York, July 2003, https://hemisphericinstitute.org/en/hidvl-presentations/hidvl-presentations1/enc2003-leda-martins1.html.

72. Rivera Cusicanqui, "Ch'ixinakax utxiwa," 96.

73. James Maffie, *Aztec Philosophy: Understanding a World in Motion* (Boulder: University Press of Colorado, 2014), 419.

74. "Para explicar los tiempos del zapatismo, [Eduardo] Galeano dijo que su reloj no era ni digital, ni análogo, ni mucho menos un "smartwatch"; su reloj era más como un reloj de arena: uno en el que se podía ver el tiempo transcurrido y tratar de entenderlo, pero en el que también podía verse el tiempo que viene." Sub

Galeano, Raúl Romero, "Los muros del capital, las grietas de la izquierda: El reloj de arena y el mundo organizado en fincas," *Subversiones: Agencia Autónoma de Comunicación*, April 13, 2017, http://subversiones.org/archivos/128547.

75. Rebecca Schneider, "Appearing to Others as Others Appear: Thoughts on Performance, the Polis, and Public Space," in *Performance in the Public Sphere*, ed. Ana Pais (Lisbon: Centro de Estudos de Teatro/FLUL and Performativa, 2018).

76. See chapter 6.

77. Tomson Highway, "The Place of the Indigenous Voice in the 21st Century," keynote address, Hemispheric Institute Encuentro, Montreal, 2014, http://hemisphericinstitute.org/hemi/en/enc14-keynote-lectures/item/2299-tomson-highway-the-place-of-the-Indigenous-voice-in-the-21st-century.

78. T. S. Eliot, "Burnt Norton," in *Collected Poems, 1909–1935* (New York: Faber and Faber, 1936), lines 1–10.

79. Gary Genosko and Scott Thompson use tense theory to explore the temporalities of the surveillance systems we inhabit, a present "tense fragmented and pulverized into all too fascinating bits" coexisting with the "future perfect" of utopian and dystopian visions and the rapidly developing (in the early 2000s) "political logics of preemption." Gary Genosko and Scott Thompson, "Tense Theory: The Temporality of Surveillance," in *Theorizing Surveillance: The Panopticon and Beyond*, ed. David Lyon (Cullompton, U.K.: Willan, 2006), 124.

80. Brian Massumi, *Ontopower* (Durham, NC: Duke University Press, 2016), 7.

81. Ricardo Dominguez, "#FearlessGestures: Disturbing Insecurity States Now," Modern Language Association panel, Rights under Repression, New York, January 6, 2018.

82. Alison Kodjak, "Separating Kids from Their Parents Can Lead to Long-Term Health Problems," *Morning Edition*, National Public Radio, June 20, 2018, https://www.npr.org/sections/health-shots/2018/06/20/621872722/separating-kids-from-their-parents-is-a-recipe-for-long-term-health-problems.

83. Dussel, *The Invention of the Americas*, 110.

84. See Rebecca Schneider, "Protest Now and Again," *TDR: The Drama Review* 54, no. 2 (2010): 7–11.

85. Schneider, "Protest Now and Again."

86. Homero Aridjis, "Migrants Ride a 'Train of Death' to Get to America and We're Ignoring the Root of the Problem," *Huffington Post*, September 7, 2014, https://www.huffpost.com/entry/migrants-train-of-death-america-_b_5568288.

87. Roque Planas, "The Mind-Blowing Fact about Immigration No One Mentions," *Huffington Post*, September 24, 2013, https://www.huffingtonpost.com/2013/09/24/americans-immigrating-mexico_n_3984078.html.

88. Century 21, https://www.century21.com/.

89. Google Dictionary, https://www.google.com/search?q=relentless&ie=utf-8&oe=utf-8&client=firefox-b-1.

90. Ruchir Sharma, "The Millionaires Are Fleeing. Maybe You Should, Too," *New York Times*, June 2, 2018, https://www.nytimes.com/2018/06/02/opinion/sunday/millionaires-fleeing-migration.html.

91. See Greg Grandin, *The End of the Myth: From the Frontier to the Border Wall in the Mind of America* (New York: Metropolitan, 2019).

92. J. Hillis Miller, "The Critic as Host," in *Modern Criticism and Theory: A Reader*, ed. David Lodge and Nigel Wood (London: Routledge, 2013), 404.

93. Jacques Derrida, "Derelictions of the Right to Justice," in *Negotiations: Interventions and Interviews, 1971–2001*, ed., trans., and with an introduction by Elizabeth Rottenberg (Stanford, CA: Stanford University Press, 2002), 133.

94. Migrants actually pay billions in taxes and receive very little back. See Melissa Cruz, "Yes, All Immigrants—Even Undocumented—Pay Billions in Taxes Each Year," American Immigration Council, April 16, 2018, http://immigrationimpact.com/2018/04/16/undocumented-immigrants-pay-taxes/.

95. Simpson, *Dancing on Our Turtle's Back*, 3.

96. Guillermo Gómez-Peña, *Ethno-techno: Writings on Performance, Activism, and Pedagogy*, ed. Elaine Peña (London: Routledge, 2005), 22.

97. Quijano, "Coloniality and Modernity/Rationality," 172.

98. Boaventura de Sousa Santos, *Epistemologies of the South: Justice against Epistemicide* (London: Routledge, 2016), 24.

99. Grosfoguel, "The Structure of Knowledge in Westernized Universities," 86. Quijano, in "Coloniality and Modernity/Rationality": "Repression fell, above all, over the modes of knowing, of producing knowledge, of producing perspectives, images and systems of images, symbols, modes of signification, over the resources, patterns, and instruments of formalized and objectivised expression, intellectual or visual" (169).

100. "The Requerimiento [Requirement] was written in 1510 by the Council of Castile to be read aloud as an ultimatum to conquered Indians in the Americas. It asserted the religious authority of the Roman Catholic pope over the entire earth, and the political authority of Spain over the Americas (except Brazil) from the 1493 papal bull that divided the western hemisphere between Spain and Portugal. It demanded that the conquered peoples accept Spanish rule and Christian preaching or risk subjugation, enslavement, and death. Often the Requerimiento was read in Latin to the Indians with no interpreters present, or even delivered from shipboard to an empty beach, revealing its prime purpose as self-justification for the Spanish invaders." Council of Castile, "Requerimiento 1510," National Humanities Center Resource Toolbox, 2006/2011, https://nationalhumanitiescenter.org/pds/amerbegin/contact/text7/requirement.pdf.

101. Fernando de Alva Ixtlilxochitl, *Obras Históricas*, vol. 2 (Mexico City: Oficina Tip. de la Secretaría de Fomento, 1891–92), 18, quoted in Miguel León-Portilla, *La Filosofía Náhuatl: Estudiada en sus Fuente* (Mexico City: Ediciones Especiales del Instituto Indigenista Interamericano, 1865), 74. See too Alfredo López Austin, *Educación Mexica: Antología de documentos Sahaguntinos* (Mexico: UNAM, 1985), 56, 62.

102. Gloria M. Delgado de Cantú, *Historia de México: El proceso de gestacíon de un pueblo*, vol. 1, 5th ed. (Mexico City: Pearson Educación de México, 2006), 220.

103. Fernando de Alva Ixtlilxochitl in León-Portilla, *La Filosofía Náhuatl*, 79.

104. Thanks to Odi González Jimenez and Omar Alejandro Dauhajre for this insight. Thanks also to Alan Durston for continuing to elaborate on the complex meanings of *yacha*, the root of *yachasun*, that can mean to know, to learn, to teach, and to reside, among other possibilities.

105. Francisco de Avila, *The Huarochirí Manuscript: A Testament of Ancient and Colonial Andean Religion*, ed. Frank Salomon (Austin: University of Texas Press, 1991), 41.

106. Simpson, *Dancing on Our Turtle's Back*.

107. Critical Art Ensemble, "Recombinant Theatre and Digital Resistance," *TDR: The Drama Review* 44, no. 4 (winter 2000): 157.

108. Michel Foucault, *Society Must Be Defended: Lectures at the College de France, 1975–1976*, trans. David Macey (New York: Picador, 2003), 6.

109. Foucault, *Society Must Be Defended*, 8.

110. Stefano Harney and Fred Moten, *The Undercommons: Fugitive Planning and Black Study* (New York: Minor Compositions, 2013).

111. Silvia Rivera Cusicanqui, in "The Potosí Principle: Another View of Totality" (*e-misférica* 11, no. 1 [2014], https://hemisphericinstitute.org/en/emisferica-11-1 -decolonial-gesture/11-1-essays/the-potosi-principle-another-view-of-totality.html), expresses her dislike for the term "decolonial," which she finds trendy, "boring," and "practically useless for action in the streets and for engaging with concrete indigenous struggles." She prefers "anticolonial" and "demolition" instead of "deconstruction" because "[she] think[s] it is more coherent to try to connect with the direct language of subalterns, rather than with the word-games of high-brow *afrancesado* intellectuals."

112. Terry Eagleton, *Materialism* (New Haven, CT: Yale University Press, 2016), 13.

113. Tara McPherson, *Feminist in a Software Lab: Difference + Design* (Cambridge, MA: Harvard University Press, 2018), 52.

114. Santos, *Epistemologies of the South*, 12, 11.

115. J. Halberstam, *The Queer Art of Failure* (Durham, NC: Duke University Press, 2011), 2.

116. Harney and Moten, *The Undercommons*, 38.

117. Arendt, *The Human Condition*, 223.

118. Rivera Cusicanqui elaborates in her essay "The Potosí Principle": "In the Andean region, we can see a different configuration of collective subjectivity, which we have termed as a *ch'ixi* subjectivity, located in the middle zone or *taypi* of the colonial confrontation, and which is marked by a particular tension between the individual 'I' and the collective 'we.' We speak of a collective self-fashioning [*autopoiesis*] that lives out of its own contradictions: a dialectic that does not culminate in a synthesis but lives in permanent movement, articulating the autochthonous with the alien in subversive and mutually contaminating ways."

119. Personal communication via email with Peter Kulchyski, January 25, 2019.

120. Allen J. Christenson, trans., *Popol Vuh: Sacred Book of the Quiché Maya People* (Hampshire, U.K.: O Books, 2003), 51–52.

121. Jean-Luc Nancy, *The Birth of Presence*, trans. Brian Holmes et al. (Stanford, CA: Stanford University Press, 1993), 9.

122. Nancy, *The Birth of Presence*, 10.

123. *Da-sein*, as defined by Heidegger, "is a being that does not simply occur among other beings. Rather, it is ontically distinguished by the fact that in its being this being is concerned *about* its very being." Martin Heidegger, *Being and Time*, trans. Joan Stambaugh (Albany: State University of New York Press, 1996), 10, emphasis in original.

124. Rivera Cusicanqui also writes of bilinguality as potentially decolonizing: "The possibility of a profound cultural reform in our society depends on the decolonization of our gestures and acts and the language with which we name the world. The reappropriation of bilingualism as a decolonizing practice will allow for the creation of a 'we' as producers of knowledge and interlocutors who can have discussions as equals with other centers of thought and currents in the academies of our region and also of the world" ("Ch'ixinakax utxiwa," 106).

125. See Juan López Intzín, "Epistemologies of the Heart," in *Resistant Strategies*, ed. Marcos Steuernagel and Diana Taylor (New York: HemiPress, 2020), https://hemisphericinstitute.org/resistantstrategies.

126. López Intzín, "Epistemologies of the Heart."

127. Christenson, *Popol Vuh*, 73.

128. Juan López Intzín, "La primera jornada Carlos Lenkersdorf. De lenguas, prácticas y otros mundos: La interpelación tojolabal a la modernidad," paper delivered at Centro de Estudios Latinoamericanos de la Facultad de Ciencias Políticas y Sociales-UNAM (Nacional University of Mexico), Mexico, May 9, 2012.

129. Juan López Intzín, interview with Diana Taylor, Hemispheric Institute, April 29, 2016, https://vimeo.com/164782063.

130. Juan López Intzín, "Ich'el ta muk': Insights from the Construction of Lekil kuxlejal: Towards a Visibilization of 'Other' Knowledges from the Matrix of the Tseltal Feel-Thinking and Feel-Knowing," in Steuernagel and Taylor, *Resistant Strategies*, https://resistantstrategies.tome.press/ichel-ta-muk-insights-from-the-construction-of-lekil-kuxlejal-towards-a-visibilization-of-other-knowledges-from-the-matrix-of-the-tseltal-feel-thinking-and-feel-k/, and an earlier version in "*Ich'el ta muk*': La trama en la construcción del Lekil kuxlejal. Hacia una visibilización de saberes 'otros' desde la matricialidad del sentipensar-sentisaber tseltal," in *Practicas Otras de Conocimiento(s): Entre crisis, entre guerras*, vol. 1 (San Cristóbal de Las Casas, Mexico: Cooperativa editorial Retos, 2015); Rivera Cusicanqui, "Ch'ixinakax utxiwa," 105.

131. "El stalel como modos de ser-estar-pensar-sentir, actuar y conocer-saber el mundo." Juan López Intzín, "El Ch'ulel multiverso e intersubjetividad en el stalel maya tseltal," in *Lengua, Cosmovisión, Intersubjetividad: Acercamientos a la obra de Carlos Lenkersdorf* (Mexico City: UNAM, 2015). For English and Spanish, see Juan López Intzín, "The Ch'ulel-Multiverse and Intersubjectivity in the Maya Tseltal Stalel" (trans. Marlène Ramírez-Cancio), in Steuernagel and Taylor, *Resistant Strategies*, https://resistantstrategies.tome.press/the-chulel-multiverse-and-intersubjectivity-in-the-maya-tseltal-stalel/.

132. "El ch'ulel es lo que vuelve sujeto a todo lo existente, hace que interactuemos de sujeto a sujeto." López Intzín, "El Ch'ulel multiverso e intersubjetividad en el stalel maya tseltal."

133. Steuernagel and Taylor, *Resistant Strategies*, https://hemisphericinstitute.org/resistantstrategies.

134. "Esta humanización de las 'cosas' no es otra cosa que el-re-cono-ci-mien-to a la coesencia y coexistencia del ch'ulel y que hay de darles ich'el-tamuk' (respeto y reconocimiento a su grandeza y dignidad)." López Intzín, "El Ch'ulel multiverso e intersubjetividad en el stalel maya tseltal."

135. Bruno Latour, *Facing Gaia: Six Lectures on the Political Theology of Nature*, Institute for Earthbound Studies, February 2013, http://www.earthboundpeople .com/wp-content/uploads/2015/02/Bruno-Latour-Gifford-Lectures-Facing-Gaia -in-the-Anthropocene-2013.pdf.

136. Taylor and Novak, *Dancing with the Zapatistas*, http://scalar.usc.edu/anvc /dancing-with-the-zapatistas/index.

137. N. Katherine Hayles, "The Cognitive Nonconscious: Enlarging the Mind of the Humanities," *Critical Inquiry* 42, no. 4 (2016): 783–808. Even more generalized in ch'ulel than in Hayles's division of the cognizers versus noncognizers: "I propose another distinction to replace human/nonhuman: cognizers versus noncognizers. On one side are humans and all other biological life forms, as well as many technical systems; on the other, material processes and inanimate objects" (799). She argues against rigid binaries: "To express more adequately the complexities and pervasiveness of these interactions, we should resist formulations that reify borders and create airtight categories. The better formulation, in my view, is not a binary at all but interpenetration, continual and pervasive interactions that flow through, within, and beyond the humans, nonhumans, cognizers, noncognizers, and material processes that make up our world" (801).

138. "In general, at all levels of life, not just at the level of nucleic acid molecules, a complexity, which serves a specific function . . . corresponds to an embodied knowledge, translated into the constructions of a system. The environment is a rich set of potential niches: each niche is a problem to be solved, to survive in the niche means to solve the problem, and the solution is the embodied knowledge, an algorithm of how to act in order to survive. Hayles, "The Cognitive Nonconscious," 789, quotes Ladislav Kováč, "Fundamental Principles of Cognitive Biology," *Evolution and Cognition* 6, no. 1 (2000): 59.

139. Hayles, "The Cognitive Nonconscious," 788.

140. Hayles, "The Cognitive Nonconscious," 799.

141. Hayles, "The Cognitive Nonconscious," 800.

142. Kováč quoted in Hayles, "The Cognitive Nonconscious," 790.

143. Hayles, "The Cognitive Nonconscious," 792.

144. See Andy Clark and David Chalmers, "Appendix: The Extended Mind," in Andy Clark, *Supersizing the Mind: Embodiment, Action, and Cognitive Extension* (Oxford: Oxford University Press, 2008), 220–32; Hanne De Jaegher and Ezequiel Di Paolo, "Participatory Sense-Making: An Enactive Approach to Social Cognition," *Phenomenology and the Cognitive Sciences* 6 (2007): 485–507; Thomas Fuchs and Hanne De Jaegher, "Enactive Intersubjectivity: Participatory Sense-Making and Mutual Incorporation," *Phenomenology and the Cognitive Sciences* 8 (2009): 465–86; Edwin Hutchins, *Cognition in the Wild* (Cambridge, MA: MIT Press, 1995); Yvonne Rogers, *A Brief Introduction to Distributed Cognition* (Brighton, U.K.: School of Cognitive and Computing Sciences, University of Sussex, 1997).

145. "Peripatetic School," Wikipedia, accessed October 7, 2019, https://en .wikipedia.org/wiki/Peripatetic_school.

146. Georges Bataille, in his short piece "The Big Toe" (1929) calls the toe "the most *human* part of the human body." In *Visions of Excess: Selected Writings*,

1927–1939, ed. Allan Stoekl, trans. Allan Stoekl with Carl R. Lovitt and Donald M. Leslie Jr. (Minneapolis: University of Minnesota Press, 1985), 20–23

147. William Hazlitt, "On Going a Journey," *New Monthly Magazine*, January 1822, https://sites.ualberta.ca/~dmiall/Travel/hazlitt.htm.

148. Antonin Artaud, letter to Jean Paulhan, August 15, 1935. Quoted in Luis Mario Schnieder, "Prologue," in *México y Viaje al pais de los tarahumara* (Mexico City: Fondo de Cultura Económica, 1984), 22.

149. Gilles Deleuze and Felix Guattari, *Anti-Oedipus: Capitalism and Schizophrenia*, trans. Helen R. Lane, Robert Hurley, and Mark Seem (Minneapolis: University of Minnesota Press, 1983).

150. Deleuze and Guattari, *Anti-Oedipus*, 9.

151. Frédéric Gros, *A Philosophy of Walking* (New York: Verso, 2014), 199.

152. Gros, *A Philosophy of Walking*, 200.

153. Gros, *A Philosophy of Walking*, 201.

154. French philosopher Frédéric Gros's *A Philosophy of Walking* offers other thoughts, including some by thinkers such as Rimbaud, Rousseau, Kant, Nietzsche, and Gandhi. Much of that book reflects on the "I" sometimes sharing solitude with others. At times walking is a form of flight, a "passing through" landscape and life (52). Company is an impediment, as walking establishes a dialogue between body and soul: "When I walk, I soon become two. My body and me" (56).

155. See the interviews with migrants in Diana Taylor et al., *Art, Migration, and Human Rights*.

156. See Taylor et al., *Art, Migration, and Human Rights*.

157. NEM pret NEN, "to live," NEHNEM means "to go along, to walk, to wander." Frances Karttunen, *An Analytical Dictionary of Náhuatl*, rev. ed. (Norman: University of Oklahoma Press, 1992). Thanks to Manuel R. Cuellar for this connection.

158. See Dussel, *The Invention of the Americas*, 184n17.

159. Elizabeth Hill Boone, *Stories in Red and Black: Pictorial Histories of the Aztecs and Mixtecs* (Austin: University of Texas Press, 2000), 50.

160. Boone, *Stories in Red and Black*, 120. A similar observation was made by Dana Leibsohn, "Primers for Memory: Cartographic Histories and Nahua Identity," in *Writing without Words: Alternative Literacies in Mesoamerica and the Andes*, ed. Elizabeth Hill Boone and Walter Mignolo (Durham, NC: Duke University Press, 1994). Cited in Boone, *Stories in Red and Black*.

Two Enacting Refusal

1. Carlos Monsivais, "'Somos borregos!' 'Nos llevan!' 'Bee!' 'Bee!' Un relato de ingratitudes y su consecuencia pictórica," Crónica de 1968-VI, June 14, 2016, http://www.mty.itesm.mx/dhcs/deptos/ri/ri-802/lecturas/nvas.lecs/1968-monsi/mc0290.htm. Also see Paco Ignacio Taibo II, *68* (Mexico City: Planeta, 1991), 68; and Elena Poniatowska, *Massacre in Mexico*, trans. Helen R. Lane (Columbia: University of Missouri Press, 1992), 46. A similar act, with a different political valence, occurred in 2014 when New York City police officers turned their backs on the large screen showing Mayor Bill de Blasio as he spoke at a funeral for slain officers. Dean Schabner, "Hundreds Turn Their Back on de Blasio at NYPD Officer's

Funeral," *ABC News*, December 27, 2014, https://abcnews.go.com/US/nypd-officers -turn-back-de-blasio-cops-funeral/story?id=27851746. The police snubbed de Blasio for accepting the legitimate claim by Black Lives Matter activists that the police killings of unarmed African Americans had to stop. See Jennifer Fermino, "Mayor de Blasio, in Candid Speech at CUNY Event, Returns to Controversial Topic Dealing with Race That Angered Police," *Daily News*, February 18, 2016, https://www .nydailynews.com/news/politics/de-blasio-returns-controversial-topic-angered -cops-article-1.2536870.

2. Hannah Arendt, *The Human Condition* (Chicago: University of Chicago Press, 1998), 178.

3. Arendt, *The Human Condition*, 179.

4. Louis Althusser, "Ideology and Ideological State Apparatus (Notes toward an Investigation," in *Lenin and Philosophy and Other Essays* (New York: Monthly Review Press, 2001), 118.

5. Félix Guattari, "The Place of the Signifier in the Institution," in *The Guattari Reader*, ed. Gary Genosko (Hoboken, NJ: Blackwell, 1996), 152.

6. Félix Guattari, *Chaosmosis: An Ethico-aesthetic Paradigm*, trans. Paul Bains and Julian Pefanis (Sydney: Power Institute, 1995), 9, emphasis added.

7. J. L. Austin, *How to Do Things with Words* (Cambridge, MA: Harvard University Press, 1962), 8, 12.

8. Austin, *How to Do Things with Words*, 54.

9. Andrew Parker and Eve Sedgwick, "Introduction," in *Performativity and Performance* (New York: Routledge, 1995), 9.

10. Parker and Sedgwick, "Introduction," 9.

11. Here I am inspired by Vilém Flusser's argument about gesture and affect in *Gesture*, trans. Nancy Ann Roth (Minneapolis: University of Minnesota Press, 1991), 1–9. He defines gesture: "Gestures are movements of the body that express an intention" but "for which there is no satisfactory casual explanation" (1)—that is, gestures are actions, not reactions. "Gestures," he argues, "express and articulate that which they symbolically represent," while "'affect' is the symbolic representation of states of mind through gestures" (4). I discuss this at length later in this book.

12. Mel Y. Chen, *Animacies: Biopolitics, Racial Mattering, and Queer Affect* (Durham, NC: Duke University Press, 2012), 2.

13. Manuel Castells, *Networks of Outrage and Hope: Social Movements in the Internet Age* (Cambridge: Polity, 2012), 134.

14. L. A. Kauffman, *How to Read a Protest: The Art of Organizing and Resistance* (Berkeley: University of California Press, 2018), 5–7.

15. Austin, *How to Do Things with Words*, 11. Article I.

16. Artistic and activist practices often disrupt performatives. Las Yeguas del Apocalysis (Mares of the Apocalypse), composed of Francisco Casas and Pedro Lemebel, two radical and brilliant gay performers in Chile, provides a good example. They were feared at literary and art exhibits, given their relish for scandal and crashing self-declared highbrow events. "They were not invited to the meeting of intellectuals with Patricio Aylwin (president of Chile from 1990–94) just before the elections of 1989, but they came anyway. They came onstage wearing

high heels and feathers and extended a banner that said 'homosexuals for change.' Upon coming down from the stage, Francisco Casas jumped on then senatorial candidate, Ricardo Lagos, and gave him a kiss on the mouth." (El escándalo era la constante de las "Yeguas." Para el encuentro de los intelectuales con Patricio Aylwin previo a las elecciones de 1989 no fueron convocadas pero llegaron igual. Subieron al escenario con tacos y plumas y extendieron un lienzo que decía "Homosexuales por el cambio." Al bajar del escenario, Francisco Casas se lanzó sobre el entonces candidato a senador Ricardo Lagos y le dio un beso en la boca.) "Las Yeguas del Apocalipsis," *Memoria Chilena*, accessed February 11, 2020, http://www .memoriachilena.cl/temas/dest.asp?id=pedrolemebel%281955-%29yeguas.

17. Michel de Certeau, *The Practice of Everyday Life*, trans. Steven F. Randall (Berkeley: University of California Press, 1984), 25–26.

18. I have already written about relajo as acts of spontaneous disruption that defy authority, rupturing (even for a moment) the configuration and limits of the group or community. "It is an act of devalorization, or what the late Mexican intellectual Jorge Portilla calls 'desolidarization' with dominant norms in order to create a different, joyously rebellious solidarity—that of the underdog. It is a 'negative' form of expression in that it's a declaration against, never for, a position. Yet, relajo proves non-threatening, because it is humorous and subversive in ways that allow for critical distancing rather than revolutionary challenge. It is an aside, not a frontal attack." Diana Taylor, *The Archive and the Repertoire: Performing Cultural Memory in the Americas* (Durham, NC: Duke University Press, 2003), 129. See also Jorge Portilla, *Fenomenología del relajo* (Mexico City: Fondo de Cultura Económica, 1986).

19. Benjamin Arditi, "Insurgencies Don't Have a Plan—They Are the Plan: Political Performatives and Vanishing Mediators," *e-misférica* 10, no. 2 (2013), http:// hemisphericinstitute.org/hemi/en/e-misferica-102/arditi.

20. Arditi, "Insurgencies Don't Have a Plan."

21. Monsivais, "'Somos borregos!'"

22. Rebecca Schneider, "Appearing to Others as Others Appear: Thoughts on Performance, the Polis, and Public Space," in *Performance in the Public Sphere*, ed. Ana Pais (Lisbon: Centro de Estudos de Teatro and Per Form Ativa), 35.

23. Sianne Ngai, *Ugly Feelings* (Cambridge, MA: Harvard University Press, 2005), 91.

24. Ngai, *Ugly Feelings*, 123.

25. Kevin Quashi, *The Sovereignty of Quiet: Beyond Resistance in Black Culture* (New Brunswick, NJ: Rutgers University Press, 2012), 3.

26. Erica Chenoweth and Maria J. Stephan, *Why Civil Resistance Works* (New York: Columbia University Press, 2012), 5.

27. "A las 18:50 horas, 'las campanas de la Catedral fueron lanzadas a vuelo, ignorándose los motivos,' informaron los agentes de la DGIPS, pero una nota del diario *Excélsior* afirmó que el sacerdote Jesús Pérez dio permiso a los estudiantes para que entraran al templo y subieran a tocar las campanas. Después (el religioso) 'encendió las luces del templo a petición de los estudiantes.'" Gustavo Castillo cites the report by the Dirección General de Investigaciones Políticas y Sociales (DGIPS), attached to Secretaria de Gobernación, then headed by Luis Echeverría Alvarez,

who became the next president of Mexico. See Gustavo Castillo, "A 40 Años: Persecución militar y desalojo del Zócalo," *La Jornada*, August 27, 2008, http://www.jornada.unam.mx/2008/08/27/index.php?section=politica&article=012n1pol.

28. For a more recent analysis of the role of the U.S. in Mexico and Central America, see Greg Grandin, *Empire's Workshop: Latin America, the United States, and the Rise of the New Imperialism Project* (New York: Owl, 2006).

29. The Zapatista movement, as I discuss in chapter 3, inspired antiglobalization movements such as those that converged at the wto meetings in Seattle in 1999.

30. Monsivais, "'Somos borregos!'"

31. "Burócratas del DDF [Departamento del Distrito Federal] (que) habían sido acarreados . . . al acto de desagravio, ante lo ominoso del evento, empezaron a corear '¡somos borregos!,' '¡somos acarreados!' El acto terminó con la intervención policiaca y del Ejército, con una nueva persecución por las calles del Centro Histórico." Castillo, "A 40 Años," cites the report by DGIPS. In 2004, Luis Echeverría Alvarez, former president of Mexico, was brought up on charges of crimes against humanity for the disappearance and extraofficial killings of students and activists during the 1970s Dirty War. "Mexico: Ex-President Charged in 'Dirty War' Killings," Human Rights Watch, July 22, 2004, https://www.hrw.org/news/2004/07/22/mexico-ex-president-charged-dirty-war-killings.

32. Taibo, *68*, 68.

33. Poniatowska, *Massacre in Mexico*, 46.

34. "His social satire is sometimes not subtle, as in *Cuentos Patrióticos* (Patriotic Tales), 1997, which refers to 1968 demonstrations in the Zócalo, Mexico City's main plaza. Where bureaucrats had rebelled by walking in a circle bleating like sheep, Alÿs led a flock of real sheep around a flagpole at the plaza's center." Barbara A. MacAdam, "Francis Alÿs: Architect of the Absurd," *ARTnews*, July 15, 2013, http://www.artnews.com/2013/07/15/architect-of-the-absurd/.

35. Katrin Wittneven, "The Paradox of Praxis Step by Step: Approaching Francis Alys," *DB Artmag*, September 19–October 27, 2004, http://www.db-artmag.com/archiv/2004/e/7/2/270.html.

36. Taylor, *The Archive and the Repertoire*.

37. Hayden White, "History as Fulfillment," in *Philosophy of History after Hayden White*, ed. Robert Doran (London: Bloomsbury Academic, 2013), 36.

38. Dwight Conquergood, *Cultural Struggles: Performance, Ethnography, Praxis*, ed. and with critical introduction by E. Patrick Johnson (Ann Arbor: University of Michigan Press, 2013), 21.

39. Conquergood, *Cultural Struggles*, 21.

40. Conquergood, *Cultural Struggles*, 19.

41. I agree with Mary Louise Pratt's understanding of these terms as bound up with the language of power, colonialism, and conquest: "Ethnographic texts are those in which European metropolitan subjects represent to themselves their others (usually their conquered others)" while she calls autoethnography "a text in which people undertake to describe themselves in ways that engage with representations others have of them" (Mary Louise Pratt, "Arts of the Contact Zones," in *Ways of Reading: An Anthology for Writers*, 6th ed., ed. David Bartholomae and Anthony Petrosky [New York: Bedford St. Martins, 2002], 608–9).

42. In *The Archive and the Repertoire*, I define scenarios as "an act of trans-fer, as a paradigm that is formulaic, portable, repeatable, and often banal because it leaves out complexity, reduces conflict to its stock elements, and encourages fantasies of participation" (54). "Simultaneously *set-up* and *action*, scenarios frame and activate social dramas. The set-up lays out the range of possibilities; all the elements are there: encounter, conflict, resolution, and dénouement, for example. These elements, of course, are in themselves the product of social economic, po-litical, and social structures that they, in turn, tend to reproduce. All scenarios have localized meaning, though many attempt to pass as universally valid. Actions and behaviors arising from the set-up might be predictable, a seemingly natural consequence of the assumptions, values, goals, power relations, presumed audi-ence, and epistemic grids established by the set-up itself. But they are, ultimately, flexible and open to change" (28).

43. Pierre Nora, quoted in Shoshana Felman, *The Juridical Unconscious: Trials and Traumas in the Twentieth Century* (Cambridge, MA: Harvard University Press), 110, Felman's translation. Originally in Pierre Nora, "Le Retour de l'événement," in *Faire de l'histoire: Nouveaux problèmes*, vol. 1, ed. Jacques Le Goff and Pierre Nora (Paris: Gallimard, 1974), 220, 223.

44. "Lo único que funciona es la memoria. La memoria colectiva. Incluso la más pequeña y triste memoria individual." Taibo, *68*, 68.

45. Francis Alÿs, "La multiplicación de los borregos" [The multiplication of sheep], in *Cuentos patrióticos* [Patriotic tales], video created in collaboration with Rafael Ortega, Mexico City, 1997, http://www.francisalys.com/cuentos-patrioticos/. While "The Multiplication of Sheep" is usually dated 1997, Alÿs communicated to me through an email sent by Cuauhtemoc Medina that it was actually performed in 1998, to commemorate the thirty-year anniversary of the student massacre: "La cosa es muy fácil: iba a ser para el aniversario de la matanza de estudiantes de Tlatelolco y los treinta años en aquel momento de la protesta de los burócra-tas. En realidad se presentó en el 98. Ocurre simultáneamente al Perro de Tres patas (Negrito) y la Revolución de la tortilla, que era esencialmente una tortilla haciendo una revolución en el cielo frente al monumento a Lázaro Cárdenas en el Eje Central" (email from Cuauhtemoc Medina received by Diana Taylor, Decem-ber 26, 2017).

46. Alÿs, "La multiplicación de los borregos."

47. Diana Taylor, *Performance* (Durham, NC: Duke University Press, 2016).

48. Natasha Marie Llorens and Attilia Fattori Franchini, "Works in the Exhib-ition: Francis Alys," in *Troubling Space: The Summer Session*, Zubludowicz Collec-tion, London, 2012, 9, http://www.zabludowiczcollection.com/uploads/files/ZCCO _TEXT_ARTWORK.pdf.

49. Arendt, *The Human Condition*, 179.

50. Judith Butler, *Notes toward a Performative Theory of Assembly* (Cambridge, MA: Harvard University Press, 2015), 58.

51. Andrea Noel, "Get Over It, Ex Mexican President Tells Parents of Miss-ing Students on US Caravan," *Vice News*, March 19, 2015, https://news.vice.com /article/get-over-it-ex-mexican-president-tells-parents-of-missing-students-on-us -caravan.

52. Richard Schechner, *Between Theater and Anthropology* (Philadelphia: University of Pennsylvania Press, 1985), 36.

53. Schneider, "Appearing to Others as Others Appear," 40.

Three Camino Largo

1. The five caracoles are La Realidad, Roberto Barrios, La Garrucha, Oventic, and Morelia. Zapatista Army of National Liberation, "Fechas y otras cosas para la escuelita Zapatista," *Enlace Zapatista*, March 17, 2013, http://enlacezapatista.ezln .org.mx/2013/03/17/fechas-y-otras-cosas-para-la-escuelita-zapatista/.

2. The reason the Zapatistas convened the CDN (national democratic convention) was to "discuss and agree on a civil, peaceful, popular, and national organization in the struggle for freedom and justice." They explicitly said they would not assume a protagonistic role in this organization: "The moment has come to tell everyone that we do not want and cannot take the place that some want us to take, the place from where emanate all opinions, all routes, all answers, all truths: we will not do it." They want to energize the national struggle and keep fighting for the same goals in their own way. Speaking in the name of "the voice of EZLN," the speaker asks those in attendance "that you not forget the differences that separate us and that—more often than not—pit us one against the other, that you set them aside for a moment, some days, some hours, enough minutes so you can discover the common enemy." Zapatista Army of National Liberation, "Fechas y otras cosas para la escuelita Zapatista," 55.

3. Zapatista Army of National Liberation, "Fechas y otras cosas para la escuelita Zapatista," 74.

4. Rosalva Bermudez-Ballin, trans., "San Andres Accords," Struggle Site, January 18, 1996, http://struggle.ws/mexico/ezln/san_andres.html.

5. Bermudez-Ballin, "San Andres Accords," 112.

6. Marta Molina, "And the Silence Became Poetry and Mexico Listened," trans. Julie Ann Ward, in *Dancing with the Zapatistas*, ed. Diana Taylor with Lorie Novak (Durham, NC: Duke University Press and HemiPress, 2015), http://scalar .usc.edu/anvc/dancing-with-the-zapatistas/marcha-7.

7. Subcomandande Marcos, "Malas y No Tan Malas Noticias," *Enlace Zapatista*, November 3, 2013, http://enlacezapatista.ezln.org.mx/2013/11/03/malas-y-no-tan -malas-noticias/.

8. Among the participants were Nora Cortiñas, president of the Association of Mothers of the Disappeared (Linea Fundadora), and Pablo Gonzáles Casanova, former head of UNAM, Mexico's autonomous university.

9. Art and Resistance, the course description read, "explores the many ways in which artists and activists use art (performance, mural paintings, graffiti, writing, music) to make a social intervention in the Americas. The theoretical part of the course remains in active conversation with the practice-based-research component of the course. Jesusa Rodríguez will lead an intensive one-week performance workshop that will culminate in a public action as part of the course. Jacques Servin of The Yes Men will also participate, offering a lecture and a lab. Lorie Novak will lead the digital media component of the course. Performances,

video screenings, guest lectures, and visits to FOMMA, Chiapas Media Project, a Zapatista community, and other activist projects will provide an additional dimension to the questions raised by the theoretical readings and discussions. Students will be encouraged to explore possibilities for practice-based research, develop their own sites of investigation, and share their work in a final presentation." See Hemispheric Institute of Performance and Politics, "Courses: 'Summer 2013: Art and Resistance,'" https://hemisphericinstitute.org/en/courses/summer-2013-intro-art-and-resistance-in-san-cristobal-de-las-casas-mexico.html.

10. Epistemicide, as I explore in chapter 1, was coined by Boaventura de Sousa Santos in *Epistemologies of the South: Justice against Epistemicide* (London: Routledge, 2016).

11. Jordan Bradley, "Poverty in Mexico," Borgen Project, August 10, 2013, http://borgenproject.org/poverty-in-mexico/.

12. Subcomandante Marcos, *Our Word Is Our Weapon: Selected Writings*, ed. Juana Ponce de León (New York: Seven Stories), 24.

13. Pan American Health Organization, "Health in the Americas, 2012 Edition," accessed January 28, 2020, https://www.paho.org/salud-en-las-americas-2012/index.php?option=com_docman&view=download&category_slug=hia-2012-country-chapters-22&alias=137-mexico-137&Itemid=231&lang=en.

14. In Diana Taylor, *Disappearing Acts: Spectacles of Gender and Nationalism in Argentina's "Dirty War"* (Durham, NC: Duke University Press, 1997), I define "percepticide" as self-blinding: "The triumph of the atrocity was that it forced people to look away—a gesture that undid their sense of personal and communal cohesion even as it seemed to bracket them from their volatile surroundings. Spectacles of violence rendered the population silent, deaf, and blind" (122). The performance was conceived and executed by Helaine Vosters in 2015.

15. See Diana Taylor et al., *Art, Migration, and Human Rights: A Collaborative Dossier by Artists, Scholars, and Activists on the Issue of Migration in Southern Mexico* (New York: HemiPress, 2015), http://chiapas2015.tome.press.

16. See Jorge Portilla, *La fenomenología del relajo* (Mexico City: Fondo de Cultura Económica, 1986).

17. Paul Westheim, *The Art of Ancient Mexico* (Garden City, NY: Doubleday Anchor, 1965), 107.

18. Marcos, *Our Word Is Our Weapon*, 24.

19. Marcos, *Our Word Is Our Weapon*, 6.

20. Westheim writes, "He must act to offset the danger; he must be alert, he must struggle and offer his own life on the sacrificial stone" (*Art of Ancient Mexico*, 107). While this might seems overly dramatic, Comandanta Ramona, like many other Zapatistas, clearly states that she does not expect to live and see the social justice she fights for.

21. Marcos, *Our Word Is Our Weapon*, 9.

22. Marcos, *Our Word Is Our Weapon*, 19.

23. See Michael Taussig's discussion of Marcos's unmasking in "The Disorganization of the 'Organization of Mimesis': The Subcomandante Marcos Unmasked," in *Defacement: Public Secrecy and the Labor of the Negative* (Stanford, CA: Stanford University Press, 1999).

24. John Emigh, *Masked Performance: The Play of Self and Other in Ritual and Theatre* (Philadelphia: University of Pennsylvania Press, 1996), xix.

25. Diana Taylor, "The Death of a Political 'I': The Subcomandante Is Dead, Long Live the Subcomandante!," in Taylor and Novak, *Dancing with the Zapatistas*, http://scalar.usc.edu/anvc/dancing-with-the-zapatistas/marcos -declares-himself-dead. To hear Marcos's final speech, go to "Entre la Luz y la Sombra: Últimas palabras del Subcomandante Marcos," Radio Zapatista, May 25, 2014, http://radiozapatista.org/?p=9766.

26. James Maffie, *Aztec Philosophy: Understanding a World in Motion* (Boulder: University Press of Colorado, 2014), 40.

27. Anne Marie Balsamo, "The Virtual Body in Cyberspace," quoted in Jill Lane, "Digital Zapatistas," *Drama Review* 47, no. 2 (summer 2013): 129–44.

28. "Subcomandante Marcos Reading: The Word and the Silence," YouTube, posted July 23, 2010, https://www.youtube.com/watch?v=FVgOfwhRSwo.

29. Jacques Attali, *Noise: The Political Economy of Music*, trans. Brian Massumi (Minneapolis: University of Minnesota Press, 1985), 6.

30. María Josefina Saldaña-Portillo, *The Revolutionary Imagination in the Americas and the Age of Development* (Durham, NC: Duke University Press, 2003), 193.

31. Saldaña-Portillo, *The Revolutionary Imagination in the Americas*, 192.

32. Saldaña-Portillo, *The Revolutionary Imagination in the Americas*.

33. Marcos, *Our Word Is Our Weapon*, 48.

34. Herman Bellinghausen, "Ramona Will Represent the EZLN at the National Indigenous Congress," Struggle Site, October 10, 1996, http://struggle.ws/mexico /ezln/san_andres.html.

35. Bellinghausen, "Ramona Will Represent the EZLN."

36. Bellinghausen, "Ramona Will Represent the EZLN."

37. Tyler Morgenstern, "Hacking the Border to Pieces: Technology, Poetics, and Protest at the Speed of Dreams," *Art Threat*, October 8, 2012, http://artthreat.net /2012/10/ricardo-dominguez-hacking-border/.

38. As I was writing this, Manuel Andrés López Obrador won the 2018 presidential elections, and the Zapatistas have asked that he act on his explicit support for indigenous communities in part by protecting their lands and sovereignty. However, Sup Galeano and Moisés held a press conference arguing that the new government would not really change much in Mexico: "El EZLN dice que el gobierno de López Obrador decepcionará y no cambiará al país," *Animal Político*, July 6, 2018, https://www.animalpolitico.com/2018/07/el-ezln-dice-que-el -gobierno-de-lopez-obrador-decepcionara-y-no-cambiara-al-pais/.

39. Jean Franco, *Cruel Modernity* (Durham, NC: Duke University Press, 2013), 8.

40. Diana Taylor and Jacques Servin, "Nosotros: An Interview with a Zapatista," trans. Gabriel Burgazzi Rodriguez and Oscar Lozano Pérez, in Taylor and Novak, *Dancing with the Zapatistas*, http://scalar.usc.edu/anvc/dancing-with-the -zapatistas/nosotros-an-interview-with-a-zapatista.

41. Paulo Freire, *Pedagogy of the Oppressed*, trans. Myra Bergman Ramos (New York: Bloomsbury, 2000), 81.

42. Silvia Rivera Cusicanqui, "Ch'ixinakax utxiwa: A Reflection on the Practices and Discourses of Decolonization," *South Atlantic Quarterly* 111 (winter 2012): 100.

43. Universities were built in Peru and Mexico in 1551, Bolivia in 1552, Santo Domingo in 1538, Bogotá in 1580, Quito in 1586. Dozens more were built in the following century. See "List of Colonial Universities in Hispanic America," Wikipedia, last edited January 5, 2020, https://en.wikipedia.org/wiki/List_of_colonial _universities_in_Hispanic_America.

44. Rivera Cusicanqui, "Ch'ixinakax utxiwa," 101.

45. Columbus's first letter spells out the colonialist position: "I had taken some Indians by force from the first island that I came to, in order that they might learn our language, and communicate to us what they knew respecting the country; which plan succeeded excellently, and was a great advantage to us, for in a short time, either by gestures and signs, or by words, we were enabled to understand each other." Columbus, "Excerpt from The First Voyage," in *Select Letters of Christopher Columbus with Other Original Documents Relating to His Four Voyages to the New World*, trans. and ed. R. J. Major (London: Hakluyt Society, 1847), https://www.gilderlehrman.org/sites/default/files/inline-pdfs/Columbus%20Letter%20Complete.doc.pdf.

46. I make this point in Diana Taylor, "Scenes of Cognition: Performance and Conquest," *Theatre Journal* 56, no. 3 (2004): 353–72.

47. Jesusa Rodríguez, "Pedagogy of Stones," in Taylor et al., *Art, Migration, and Human Rights*, http://chiapas2015.tome.press/chapter/collaborative-pedagogies/.

48. Rodríguez, "Pedagogy of Stones."

49. Walter F. Morris Jr., *A Textile Guide to the Highlands of Chiapas: Guía Textil de los Altos de Chiapas*, ed. Carol Karasik (Aspen, CO: Thrums), 2011.

50. James C. Scott, *Domination and the Arts of Resistance: Hidden Transcripts* (New Haven, CT: Yale University Press, 1990), 4–5.

51. "Present," Wikipedia, last edited August 8, 2019, https://en.wikipedia.org /wiki/Present.

52. Antonin Artaud, "Le Visage Humain, June 1947," in *Antonin Artaud: Works on Paper*, ed. Margit Rowell (New York: Museum of Modern Art, 1996), 94.

53. Gilles Deleuze and Felix Guattari, *A Thousand Plateaus: Capitalism and Schizophrenia*, trans. Brian Massumi (Minneapolis: University of Minnesota Press, 1987), 168.

54. See Lane, "Digital Zapatistas."

55. Carlos Monsivais, EZLN: *Documentos y Comunicados*, vol. 5: *"La marcha del color de la tierra" 2 de diciembre de 2000 / 4 de abril 2001* (Mexico City: Ediciones Era, 2003); Lane, "Digital Zapatistas."

56. For more images from Oventic, and a history of the murals, see Taylor and Novak, *Dancing with the Zapatistas*, http://scalar.usc.edu/anvc/dancing-with-the-zapatistas/index.

57. Subcomandante Marcos quoted in Monsivais, EZLN, 59.

58. Esther's speech is quoted in Monsivais, EZLN, 47.

59. Jason Beaubien, "How Diabetes Got to Be the No. 1 Killer in Mexico," *All Things Considered*, NPR, April 5, 2017, https://www.npr.org/sections/goatsandsoda /2017/04/05/522038318/how-diabetes-got-to-be-the-no-1-killer-in-mexico.

60. "Those who struggle together are brothers and sisters, regardless of the color of our skin or the language that we learned as children." Marcos, *Our Word Is Our Weapon*, 84.

61. Marcos, *Our Word Is Our Weapon*, 76.

62. This echoes Philip Abrams's observation that "the state is not the reality which stands behind the mask of political practice. It is itself the mask which prevents our seeing political practice for what it is." See Philip Abrams, "Notes on the Difficulty of Studying the State," *Journal of Historical Sociology* 1 (1988): 58.

63. In Taussig, *Defacement*, 239.

64. Taussig, *Defacement*, 246.

65. Emmanuel Levinas, "Exteriority and the Face," in *Totality and Infinity: An Essay on Exteriority,* trans. Alphonso Lingis (Dordrecht: Kluwer Academic, 1991), 197.

66. Michel de Certeau, *The Practice of Everyday Life*, trans. Steven Rendall (Berkeley: University of California Press, 1984), xix.

67. Achille Mbembe, "Necropolitics," trans. Libby Meintjes, *Popular Culture* 15, no. 1 (winter 2003): 11–40.

68. Enrique Dussel, *The Invention of the Americas: Eclipse of the Other and the Myth of Modernity*, trans. Michael D. Barber (New York: Continuum, 1995), 99.

69. Juan López Intzín, "Sp'ijilal O'tan: Saberes o Epistemologías del Corazón," Modern Language Association's Presidential Forum Address, New York, January 2018.

70. Deleuze and Guattari, *A Thousand Plateaus*, 16.

71. Roger Burbach, "Roots of Postmodern Rebellion in Chiapas," *New Left Review* 205 (1994): 113–24.

72. Maffie, *Aztec Philosophy*, 35.

73. John Holloway, *Change the World without Taking Power: The Meaning of Revolution Today* (London: Pluto, 2002), 8.

74. Taylor and Servin, "Nosotros."

75. Taylor and Servin, "Nosotros."

76. Santos, *Epistemologies of the South*, 12.

77. The Zapatista website *Enlace Zapatista* posted the following reflection on the snail when they decided to call their administrative centers "caracoles" in 2003: Dicen aquí que los más antiguos dicen que otros más anteriores dijeron que los más primeros de estas tierras tenían aprecio por la figura del caracol. Dicen que dicen que decían que el caracol representa el entrarse al corazón, que así le decían los más primeros al conocimiento. Y dicen que dicen que decían que el caracol también representa el salir del corazón para andar el mundo, que así llamaron los primeros a la vida. Y no sólo, dicen que dicen que decían que con el caracol se llamaba al colectivo para que la palabra fuera de uno a otro y naciera el acuerdo. Y también dicen que dicen que decían que el caracol era ayuda para que el oído escuchara incluso la palabra más lejana. Eso dicen que dicen que decía. Yo no sé. Yo camino contigo de la mano y te muestro lo que ve mi oído y escucha mi mirada. Y veo y escucho un caracol, el "pu'y," como le dicen en lengua acá. . . . *Así los "Caracoles" serán como puertas para entrarse a las comunidades y para que las comunidades salgan; como ventanas para vernos dentro y para que veamos fuera; como bocinas para sacar lejos nuestra palabra y para escuchar la del que lejos está.*

Pero sobre todo, para recordarnos que debemos velar y estar pendientes de la cabali-
dad de los mundos que pueblan el mundo.
"Chiapas: La Treceava Estela," *Enlace Zapatista*, July 21, 2003, https://
enlacezapatista.ezln.org.mx/2003/07/21/chiapas-la-treceava-estela-primera-parte
-un-caracol/. Also quoted in Juan López Intzín, "Epistemologies of the Heart," in
Resistant Strategies, ed. Marcos Steuernagel and Diana Taylor (Durham, NC: Duke
University Press and HemiPress, forthcoming, 2020), https://hemisphericinstitute
.org/resistantstrategies.

78. López Intzín, "Epistemologies of the Heart."

79. Westheim, *Art of Ancient Mexico*, 116.

80. Alexander Cockburn and Ken Silverstein, "Major U.S. Bank Urges Zapatista
Wipe-Out: 'A Litmus Test for Mexico's Stability,'" *Counterpunch* 2, no. 3 (1995).

81. Translated by the author from a video of the event. The same speech is cited
in José Gil and Isaín Mandujano, "Una década de caracoles," *Proceso*, August 25,
2013, 34–36.

82. Marcos, *Our Word Is Our Weapon*, 52.

83. Subcomandante Marcos, "Fourth Declaration of the Lacandon Jungle"
(1996), in Marcos, *Our Word Is Our Weapon*, 117.

84. Morgenstern, "Hacking the Border to Pieces."

85. Marcos, *Our Word Is Our Weapon*, 41.

86. Marcos, *Our Word Is Our Weapon*, 56.

87. Interview with Juana Cruz Jiménez, Chiapas, Mexico, July 25, 2017, Tzomé
Ixuk Mujeres Organizadas, https://migration.hemi.press/tzome-ixuk-mujeres
-organizadas/.

88. "Audience," Online Etymology Dictionary, https://www.etymonline.com
/word/audience.

89. "In order to understand food security, Zapatista students are frequently
taught hands-on agro-ecological techniques outside the classroom. This means
they learn how to apply sustainable farming techniques while participating in
the planting/harvesting of organic crops. This area of experiential and localized
education stresses the importance of working the land in order to attain the
skills needed to achieve food sovereignty for future generations. It also provides
an overview of how transgenic modifications and privatizations of seeds/plants/
life are deemed to be overt threats to, and blatant attacks upon, their culture."
Levi Gahman, "Mexico's Zapatista Movement May Offer Solutions to Neoliberal
Threats to Global Food Security," Truthdig, August 21, 2016, http://www.truthdig
.com/report/item/zapatista_movement_solutions_neoliberal_threat_food
_security_20160821.

90. "Poco a poco vamos aprendiendo de manera colectiva conjunta que el compartir, respetando nuestra diferencias, es lo que nos puede traer caminos posibles,
soluciones posibles a las enfermedades de individualización que el capitalismo nos
ha incrustado en el corazón" (my translation). Juan López Intzin, "Rediscovering
the Sacred and the End of Hydra Capitalism," invited lecture, Hemispheric Institute,
New York, April 14, 2016, https://vimeo.com/164639566, at time stamp 1:23. Also
in Steuernagel and Taylor, *Resistant Strategies*, https://hemisphericinstitute.org
/resistantstrategies/rediscovering-the-sacred-and-the-end-of-hydra-capitalism/.

91. Marcos, "Malas y No Tan Malas Noticias."

92. Viridiana Ríos, "Chiapas, peor que ayer," *Nexos*, January 2014, 26.

93. "Reconocimiento de los derechos a la educación, la vivienda, la salud, la tierra (a fuerza de discriminación, lo obvio, lo indiscutible, se vuelvo lo utópico)." Monsivais, *EZLN*, 34.

Four Making Presence

1. Testimony given during the trial against general Efraín Ríos Montt and Mauricio Rodríguez Sánchez.

2. Testimony of expert witness Jaime Romeo Valdez Estrada in Emi MacLean, Shawn Roberts, Matthew Eisenbrandt, Date Doyle, and Jo-Marie Burt, *Judging a Dictator: The Trial of Guatemala's Ríos Montt* (New York: Open Society Justice Initiative, 2013), 14, https://www.opensocietyfoundations.org/sites/default/files/judging-dicatator-trial-guatemala-rios-montt-11072013.pdf.

3. Ricardo Dominguez, "#FearlessGestures: Disturbing Insecurity States Now," panel presentation, Modern Language Association, New York, January 4–7, 2018.

4. MacLean et al., *Judging a Dictator*, 40.

5. MacLean et al., *Judging a Dictator*, 41.

6. Dennis Tedlock, *Rabinal Achi: A Mayan Drama of War and Sacrifice* (New York: Oxford University Press, 2003), 2.

7. See Diana Taylor, "Introduction to *Rabinal Achi* (*Man of Rabinal*)," in *Stages of Conflict: A Critical Anthology of Latin American Theater and Performance*, ed. Diana Taylor and Sarah J. Townsend (Ann Arbor: University of Michigan Press, 2008), 29.

8. On July 18, 1982, in Rabinal, Baja Verapaz, "the army abused and massacred 250 Mayan villagers (mostly elderly, women and children) after first bombarding the village from the air and with mortars. Soldiers raped and executed young girls and killed children by smashing them against the ground and throwing them into burning houses." "Guatemalan Genocide" cites the Recovery of Historical Memory project with the list of massacres on Wikipedia, last edited January 4, 2020, https://en.wikipedia.org/wiki/Guatemalan_genocide.

9. Interview by Diana Taylor with Don José León, the living memory and keeper of the script in Rabinal, Guatemala, January 2010.

10. "In testimony that stunned the courtroom and the nation, Hugo Ramiro Leonardo, a former soldier who served as a mechanic in an engineering brigade that worked in various military installations in the Ixil region during 1982 and 1983, testified via videoconference that Tito Arias, the nom de guerre of President Pérez Molina, who was at the time an official in charge of the military installation in a region of Nebaj, Quiché, ordered soldiers to burn and loot villages, and later to execute people as they fled to the mountains. In a public response, the president denied the accusations. Leonardo testified: 'As far as I could tell, the order was: "Indian seen, Indian dead"' (Indio visto, indio muerto)." Testimony of expert witness Jaime Romeo Valdez Estrada in MacLean et al., *Judging a Dictator*, 5, https://www.opensocietyfoundations.org/sites/default/files/judging-dicatator-trial-guatemala-rios-montt-11072013.pdf.

11. "According to a 1999 United Nations-mandated truth commission, more than 200,000 died or were forcibly disappeared during Guatemala's internal armed conflict, over 80% from Mayan indigenous populations with state security personnel and paramilitaries responsible for 93 percent of the violations. The commission identified over 600 massacres, and found that the state was responsible for systematic violence. The three-year period between 1981 and 1983 accounts for 81 percent of the violations reported by the truth commission related to the 36 year conflict—with nearly half (48%) of all reported violations occurring during 1982, the year in which Ríos Montt came to power." MacLean et al., *Judging a Dictator*, 1.

12. "This was the first conviction in the world of a former head of state for genocide in a domestic, rather than international, court." MacLean et al., *Judging a Dictator*, 3.

13. Anna-Claire Bevan, "US Film Could Help Nail Guatemala's Former Dictator Efraín Ríos Montt," *Guardian*, March 20, 2012, https://www.theguardian.com /global-development/poverty-matters/2012/mar/20/film-could-nail-guatemalan -dictator.

14. "No mostré el testimonio cuando lo hice. Yo nunca hablo ni doy información ni lo vuelvo didáctico, solo acciono. El trabajo tiene varias lecturas." Regina José Galindo, personal email correspondence with the author, July 16, 2014.

15. Nicholas Bourriaud, *Relational Aesthetics*, trans. Simon Pleasance and Fonza Woods, with Mathieu Copeland (Paris: Les presses du réel, 2002), 18.

16. Aristotle, *The Poetics of Aristotle*, trans. Stephen Halliwell (London: Duckworth, 1987), 41.

17. Sophocles, *Antigone*, in *The Harvard Classics*, vol. 8 (New York: P. F. Collier & Son, 1909).

18. Tedlock, *Rabinal Achi*, 31. The speeches of the two warriors parallel each other; one speaks, and the other repeats what he said and adds a new line; the first repeats that and adds another new line. "May Sky and Earth be with you / brave man / prisoner / captive. . . . Aren't you on the run, in the face of violence/in the face of war?" (30). They dance and Cawek responds: "I am brave / I am a man / so say your words, sir. 'What place did you flee in the face of violence / in the face of war?' So say your words, sir. / Am I brave? / Am I a man? / Would a man of valor just run away in the face of violence/in the face of war? Yet this is what your words say, sir" (31).

19. Methods such as reflective structured dialogue and others include active listening exercises to engage in conversations on difficult and divisive topics.

20. In *Cruel Modernity*, Jean Franco asks the compelling question, "Why, in Latin America, did the pressures of modernization and the lure of modernity lead states to kill?" (Durham, NC: Duke University Press, 2013, 2). Her book is an extensive study of the factors that contributed to the ways in which governments "marginalized indigenous and black peoples" and "created an environment in which cruelty was enabled in the name of national security" (2).

21. Kaitlin M. Murphy has a powerful reflection on this series of photographs: In July of 1997, Guatemalan photographer Daniel Hernández-Salazar, who documented the exhumations of mass graves for the Fundación de Antropología Forense (Guatemalan Foundation of Forensic Anthropology), was at a gravesite

where the remains of nine peasants were being painstakingly disinterred. A forensic anthropologist showed Hernández-Salazar a bullet-pierced shoulder blade that resembled a butterfly wing. Another set of dug-up scapulas brought to mind the wings of an angel, an image that haunted Hernández-Salazar in the following months [Steven Hoeslcher, "Angels of Memory: Photography and Haunting in Guatemala City," *GeoJournal* 73, no. 3 (2008): 207]. Covering the impact of the civil war in Guatemala had left Hernández-Salazar increasingly dissatisfied with what he felt was the inability of photojournalism to adequately portray the atrocity's magnitude. He reflected, "Years pass by. They pile up like pages in a book. Everything goes unpunished. I have to scream" (ibid.). Kaitlin M. Murphy, *Memory Mapping: Visuality, Affect, and Embodied Politics in the Americas* (New York: Fordham University Press, 2019), 2.

22. Regina José Galindo, *De Hecho Los Ángeles* (1999). When I asked her if she knew of Daniel Hernández-Salazar's angels, she replied, "Eso del angel es mi castigo. Por supuesto que no tenía nada que ver con lo de Daniel ni lo conocía. Te digo que me han molestado con eso fue una mala decisión de diseño de vestido. . . . Como verás nunca más mande a hacer vestidos." (That angel stuff was my punishment. Of course it had nothing to do with Daniel and I didn't even know him. I'm telling you people have bothered me with that but it was a bad dress-design decision. . . . As you'll see I never had any more dresses made.) Personal correspondence with the author, March 30, 2017.

23. Subcomandante Marcos, *Our Word Is Our Weapon: Selected Writings*, ed. Juana Ponce de León (New York: Seven Stories, 2001), 6.

24. Chantal Mouffe, *Agnostics: Thinking the World Politically* (London: Verso, 2013), xii.

25. Octavio Paz, "Máscaras Mexicanas," in *El laberinto de la soledad* (1950; reprint, Mexico City: Fondo de Cultura Económico, 2018), 48–50.

26. Mouffe, *Agnostics*, xii.

27. For a history of Guatemala up to 1954, see Greg Grandin, *The Blood of Guatemala: A History of Race and Nation* (Durham, NC: Duke University Press, 2000).

28. Bartolomé de Las Casas, *A Short Account of the Destruction of the Indies*, ed. and transl. Nigel Griffin (London: Penguin, 1992), 15.

29. Las Casas writes that to feed their dogs, the Spaniards "always have a ready supply of natives, chained and herded like so many calves on the hoof. These they kill and butcher as need arises" (*A Short Account of the Destruction of the Indies*, 125).

30. Hannah Arendt, *Origins of Totalitarianism* (New York: Harcourt, 1976), 192. Arendt is writing of the massacres of peoples on what she calls the "Dark Continent," and her explanation of racism is inadequate to the American context (racism directed at people who "had not created a human world" does not apply to the empires that existed in what is now Mexico, Guatemala, and Peru), but the observation that Europeans treated the conquered as inhuman remains on point.

31. Las Casas, *A Short Account of the Destruction of the Indies*, 126.

32. "Valladolid Debate" (1550–1551), Project Gutenberg, accessed March 28, 2017, http://central.gutenberg.org/articles/valladolid_debate.

33. Aníbal Quijano, "Coloniality and Modernity/Rationality," *Cultural Studies* 21, no. 2 (2007): 172.

34. Quijano, "Coloniality and Modernity/Rationality," 173.

35. Michael Taussig, *The Nervous System* (London: Routledge, 1992).

36. Diana Taylor, *The Archive and the Repertoire: Performing Cultural Memory in the Americas* (Durham, NC: Duke University Press, 2003).

37. Boaventura de Sousa Santos, *Epistemologies of the South: Justice against Epistemicide* (London: Routledge, 2016).

38. Franco, *Cruel Modernity*.

39. Michel Foucault, *Security, Territory, Population: Lectures at the College de France, 1977–78*, ed. Michel Senellart, trans. Graham Burchell (New York: Picador, 2007), 1.

40. Foucault, *Security, Territory, Population*.

41. These decrees about the treatment of populations, I believe, go beyond what Foucault recognizes as the "negative" use of "population" (epidemics resulting in depopulation and efforts at repopulation) that he cites as taking place before the eighteenth century (*Security, Territory, Population*, 66–67). Rather, the mechanisms of control of the general populations that he associates with biopower begin to take shape in the Americas in the sixteenth century—the formation of racial categories, humans who can be bought and sold, stripped of their names, kinships, religious practices, languages, to be relocated and worked to death. The stripping of political subjecthood of people considered populations to be managed, thus, I think happened before the shift Foucault writes of as happening in the eighteenth century: "The population no longer appears as a collection of subjects of right, as a collection of subject wills who must obey their sovereign's will through the intermediary of regulations, laws, edicts and so on. It will be considered as a set of processes to be managed" (70).

42. Wikipedia describes the Valladolid debates as the first debates to focus on human rights. "Valladolid Debate," Wikipedia, last edited December 17, 2019, https://en.wikipedia.org/wiki/Valladolid_debate. See too Rolena Adorno, "The Polemics of Possession: Spain on America, circa 1550," in *Empires of God: Religious Encounters in the Early Modern Atlantic*, ed. Linda Gregerson and Susan Juster (Philadelphia: University of Pennsylvania Press, 2013), *Project MUSE*, muse.jhu.edu /book/21911.

43. Foucault, *Security, Territory, Population*, 70.

44. Quijano, "Coloniality and Modernity/Rationality"; Pablo González Casanova, "Colonialismo Interno (Una Redefinición)," in *La teoria marxista hoy: Problemas y perspectivas*, ed. Atilio A. Boron, Javier Amadeo, and Sabrina Gonzalez (Buenos Aires: Conseja Latinoamericano de Ciencias Sociales, 2006).

45. Rigoberta Menchú, "Kidnapping and Death of Rigoberta's Mother," edited version of the chapter from *I, Rigoberta Menchú, an Indian Woman in Guatemala* (London: Verso, 1985).

46. Achille Mbembe, "Necropolitics," trans. Libby Meintjes, *Popular Culture* 15, no. 1 (2003): 14, emphasis in original.

47. The historical facts surrounding the crimes that left the 200,000 dead in Guatemala are gradually coming to light now that the archives of the dictatorship

have been recuperated. Kate Doyle, director of the National Security Archive Guatemala Project, and Kirsten Weld, in Weld's *Paper Cadavers: The Archives of the Dictatorship in Guatemala* (Durham, NC: Duke University Press, 2014), recount how stacks of yellowing and molding papers were found, abandoned, in an old warehouse that had served as a torture and detention center. Unlike the dictatorships in Argentina and Chile, the Guatemalan military did not even bother to destroy the evidence. Who, they calculated, would care?

48. "What Is the School of the Americas?," Will Miller Green Mountain Veterans For Peace, accessed January 20, 2020, https://wmgmvfp.wixsite.com/vermont/soa-watch.

49. Ronald Reagan, "Remarks in San Pedro Sula, Honduras, Following a Meeting with President Jose Efrain Rios Montt of Guatemala," Ronald Reagan Presidential Library and Museum, December 4, 1982, https://www.reaganlibrary.gov/research/speeches/120482f.

50. Grandin, *The Blood of Guatemala*, 11.

51. Central America has the highest murder rate of women in the world—El Salvador ranks first, and Guatemala third. Seven of the top ten countries on the list are in Latin America: "El Salvador heads the list with a rate of 8.9 homicides per 100,000 women in 2012, followed by Colombia with 6.3, Guatemala with 6.2, Russia with 5.3 and Brazil with 4.8. Mexico and Suriname are also in the top ten." Mimi Yagoub, "Why Does Latin America Have the World's Highest Female Murder Rates?," *InSight Crime*, February 11, 2016, http://www.insightcrime.org/news-analysis/why-does-latin-america-have-the-world-s-highest-female-murder-rates.

52. Regina José Galindo, "American Gold," *e-misférica* 8, no. 1 (2011), http://hemi.nyu.edu/hemi/fr/e-misferica-81/galindo.

53. Greg Grandin, *Empire's Workshop: Latin America, the United States, and the Rise of the New Imperialism* (New York: Owl, 2006).

54. Grandin, *Empire's Workshop*, 2.

55. Nadia Seremetakis, ed., *The Senses Still: Perception and Memory as Material Culture in Modernity* (Chicago: University of Chicago Press, 1994), 12. Quoted in André Lepecki, *Exhausting Dance: Performance and the Politics of Movement* (London: Routledge, 2006), 15.

56. Aristotle, *The Poetics of Aristotle*, 118.

57. Taylor, *The Archive and the Repertoire*, chapter 2.

58. Quijano, "Coloniality and Modernity/Rationality," 168.

59. Mbembe, "Necropolitics," 21.

60. Mbembe, "Necropolitics," 28–29, 40.

61. "We were already dead. We meant absolutely nothing." Comandante Ramona, in Marcos, *Our Word Is Our Weapon*, 6.

62. Emmanuel Levinas, "Exteriority and the Face," in *Totality and Infinity: An Essay on Exteriority*, trans. Alphonso Lingis (Dordrecht: Kluwer Academic, 1991), 197.

63. Hannah Arendt, *The Human Condition* (New York: Anchor, 1969), 178.

64. Grandin, *Empire's Workshop*, 1.

65. Grandin, *Empire's Workshop*, 2.

66. Grandin, *Empire's Workshop*, 2.

67. Carolyn Pedwell, "Empathy, Accuracy, and Transnational Politics," *Theory, Culture and Society*, December 22, 2014, http://www.theoryculturesociety.org/carolyn-pedwell-on-empathy-accuracy-and-transnational-politics/.

68. Frans de Waal, *The Age of Empathy: Nature's Lessons for a Kinder Society* (New York: Harmony, 2009), 79.

69. See Elizabeth Povinelli, *Economies of Abandonment: Social Belonging and Endurance in Late Liberalism* (Durham, NC: Duke University Press, 2011), on Ursula Le Guin's "The Ones Who Walk Away from Omelas." The child held naked and desperate in the broom closet seems to secure the happiness and well-being of Omelas. How do people, the townspeople of Omelas, and we, the readers, respond? Povinelli argues that "the ethical imperative is not to put oneself in the child's place, nor is it to experience the anxiety of potentially being put in her place. Le Guin's fiction rejects this ethics of liberal empathy. Instead, the ethical imperative is to know that your own good life is already in her broom closet, and as a result, either you must create a new organization of enfleshment by compromising on the goods to which you have grown accustomed (and grown accustomed to thinking of as 'yours' including the health of your body) or admit that the current organization of enfleshment is more important to you than her suffering" (4).

70. See M. Cikara, E. Bruneau, J. J. Van Bavel, and R. Saxe, "Their Pain Gives Us Pleasure: How Intergroup Dynamics Shape Empathic Failures and Counterempathic Responses," *Journal of Experimental Social Psychology* 55 (2014): 110–25, http://www.psych.nyu.edu/vanbavel/lab/documents/Cikara.etal.2014.JESP.pdf.

71. Rebecca Jennings, "Melania Trump Wears 'I Really Don't Care, Do U?' Jacket on Trip to Migrant Children," *Vox*, June 21, 2018, https://www.vox.com/2018/6/21/17489632/melania-trump-jacket-zara-i-really-dont-care-do-u.

72. Francisco Goldman, "Regina José Galindo," BOMB—*Artists in Conversation*, January 1, 2006, http://bombmagazine.org/article/2780/regina-jos-galindo.

73. "Cambiar el mundo o tener objetivos tan amplios y ambiguos quizas si sea demasiado para mis expectativas pero la injusticia y tratar de moficarla es una lucha para mi continua." (Changing the world or having very broad and ambiguous objectives is perhaps too much of an expectation for me but trying to modify injustices is a constant struggle for me.) Regina José Galindo, personal email to the author, September 4, 2014.

74. Ricardo Dominguez, "Poetry, Immigration and the FBI: The Transborder Immigrant Tool," interview by Leslie Nadir, *Hyperallergic*, July 2012, http://hyperallergic.com/54678/poetry-immigration-and-the-fbi-the-transborder-immigrant-tool/.

75. "Todas ellas con un proyecto de vida, familia, trabajo, sueños. Todas ellas fueron silenciadas, arrebatadas de las formas más violentas de esta tierra, en contra de su voluntad. Todas ellas fueron asesinadas en Guatemala. Lesionadas, humilladas, torturadas, asesinadas por la exclusiva razón de ser mujeres." "Presencia: Un proyecto de Regina José Galindo," *El Siglo*, March 2017, http://www.s21.gt/2017/03/presencia-proyecto-regina-jose-galindo/.

76. "Sus cuerpos dejaron de estar acá, pero ellas permanecen en las memorias, en sus vestidos, en sus objetos." Quimy De León, "Regina José Galindo: 'Quiero ponerme en los vestidos de las otras,'" *Prensa Comunitaria*, March 6, 2017, http://

www.prensacomunitaria.org/regina-jose-galindo-quiero-ponerme-en-los-vestidos
-de-las-otras/.

77. Regina José Galindo, telephone interview with the author, September 21,
2014.

Five Traumatic Memes

1. The Hemispheric Institute organized two events at New York University to
bring the case of the 43 to public awareness. The first, *When Governments Kill
Their Students* (December 10, 2014), was a performance, installation, and teach-
in (https://hemisphericinstitute.org/en/events/when-governments-kill-their
-students.html), and *Until We Find You: The Disappeared of Ayotzinapa* (2016)
was an exhibition of photographs taken by Emily Pederson, who accompanied
the families in the early aftermath of the September 26 attack, and a digital
publication by HemiPress by the same name (https://untilwefindyou.tome
.press/).

2. The nonbinding PPT, started in Bologna in 1979 to bring charges against governments for egregious crimes that their countries will never prosecute, has been
the only court to hold Mexico responsible to date.

3. "Forced disappearance: In international human rights law, a forced disappearance occurs when a person is secretly abducted or imprisoned by a state or
political organization or by a third party with the authorization, support, or acqui-
escence of a state or political organization, followed by a refusal to acknowledge
the person's fate and whereabouts, with the intent of placing the victim outside the
protection of the law." "Forced Disappearance," Wikipedia, accessed October 15,
2019, https://en.wikipedia.org/wiki/Forced_disappearance.

4. Richard Dawkins, *The Selfish Gene* (Oxford: Oxford University Press, 1976).

5. My thanks to David Konstan, my colleague and classicist on call, for helping
me identify the Greek roots.

6. Dawkins, *The Selfish Gene*, 192.

7. Dawkins, *The Selfish Gene*.

8. Dawkins, *The Selfish Gene*.

9. An Xiao Mina, *Memes to Movements: How the World's Most Viral Media Is
Changing Social Protest and Power* (Boston: Beacon, 2019), 6.

10. This builds on Richard Schechner's insight, "performance is never for the
first time," in *Between Theater and Anthropology* (Philadelphia: University of Pennsylvania Press, 1986), 36.

11. While mimesis, understood in its classical Greek meaning of *mimeisthai*
or "to imitate," belongs to the repertoire of embodied, reiterated practice, memes
often lack corporeality. They have different ways of entering our system. While
jokes may pass by word of mouth, ideas and symbols can seem to jump from brain
to brain. People commonly use words such as "contagion" or "virus" to describe
their transmission.

12. Schechner, *Between Theater and Anthropology*, 36.

13. Stephen Halliwell, *The Aesthetics of Mimesis: Ancient Texts and Modern
Problems* (Princeton, NJ: Princeton University Press, 2002), 6.

14. See David Konstan, "The Two Faces of *Mimesis*," review of S. Halliwell, *The Aesthetics of Mimesis: Ancient Texts and Modern Problems*, *Philosophical Quarterly* 54 (2004): 301–8.

15. The term "memesphere" was coined by Sergio Parra, *Cultiva tu Memesfera: Somos lo que nos Rodea* (Spain: Ediciones Arcopress, 2015).

16. The Wikipedia entry on memetics shows the widespread notion of a meme as "'hosted' in the minds of one or more individuals, and which can reproduce itself, thereby jumping from mind to mind. Thus what would otherwise be regarded as one individual influencing another to adopt a belief is seen as an idea-replicator reproducing itself in a new host." "Memetics," Wikipedia, accessed October 15, 2019, https://en.wikipedia.org/wiki/Memetics.

17. Mina, *Memes to Movements*, 6–7.

18. Mark A. Jordan, "What's in a Meme?," Richard Dawkins Foundation for Research and Science, February 4, 2014, https://richarddawkins.net/2014/02/whats-in-a-meme/.

19. See *Yuyanapac*, especially the photograph by Vera Lentz on the cover of the catalogue of a woman holding the photograph of her missing loved one. Art and Reconciliation, accessed February 11, 2020, https://artreconciliation.org/arts-and-reconciliation/case-studies/yuyanapaq/.

20. Diana Taylor, "Trauma as Durational Performance," *Villa Grimaldi*, 2016, http://villagrimaldi.typefold.com/.

21. Cathy Caruth, *Unclaimed Experience: Trauma, Narrative, and History* (Baltimore, MD: Johns Hopkins University Press, 1996), 1–2.

22. Here Aristotle's understanding of mimesis becomes pertinent in another way: "The pity and fear that move the audience are also 'embodied' in, built into, the dramatic construction itself" (quoted in Konstan, "The Two Faces of *Mimesis*," 161). The reason I experience pain in viewing this traumatic composition, as opposed to the pleasure afforded the viewer of pity and fear in the dramatic structure, is that this triad belongs to the real world. The young people represented in these photos are human beings who have been made to disappear.

23. Caruth, *Unclaimed Experience*, 5.

24. See José de Córdoba and Juan Montes, "'It's a Crisis of Civilization in Mexico.' 250,000 Dead. 37,400 Missing," *Wall Street Journal*, November 14, 2018, https://www.wsj.com/articles/its-a-crisis-of-civilization-in-mexico-250-000-dead-37-400-missing-1542213374. The "Movimiento Migrante Mesoamericano, a Central American non-profit that advocates for migrant rights in North America, claims that 70,000 to 120,000 Central American foreign migrants disappeared in Mexico between 2006 and 2012 ("Comunicado De La X Caravana")." The numbers cannot be accurately calculated due to faulty databases (4). Rafael Mora reports that "between 2007 and 2014 138,589 people were murdered in Mexico." Rafael Mora, "A Sub-national Analysis of Homicides and Disappearances in Mexico," Justice in Mexico Working Paper Series, vol. 14, no. 3 (February 2016), https://justiceinmexico.org/wp-content/uploads/2016/03/sub_national_analysis_of_homicides_and_disappearances_in_mexico_rafaelmora-final.pdf.

25. The *World Report* documented in 2015 that "Mexico's security forces have participated in widespread enforced disappearances since former President

Calderón (2006–2012) launched a war on drugs. Members of all security forces continue to carry out disappearances during President Enrique Peña Nieto administration, in some cases, collaborating directly with criminal groups." "Enforced Disappearances," in *World Report 2015: Mexico*, Human Rights Watch, 2015, https://www.hrw.org/world-report/2015/country-chapters/mexico.

26. Carlos Fazio, *Estado de emergencia: De la guerra de Calderón a la guerra de Peña Nieto* (Mexico City: Grijalbo, 2016).

27. Fazio, *Estado de emergencia*, 350.

28. See José Reveles, *Echale la culpa a la heroína: De Iguala a Chicago* (Mexico City: Grijalbo, 2016).

29. Fazio, *Estado de emergencia*.

30. Fazio, *Estado de emergencia*, 364.

31. Emmanuel Levinas, "Peace and Proximity," in *Basic Philosophical Writings*, ed. Adriaan T. Peperzak, Simon Critchley, and Robert Bernasconi (Bloomington: Indiana University Press, 1996), 169.

32. "'I've Had Enough,' Says Mexico Attorney General in Massacre Gaffe," *Reuters*, November 9, 2014, http://www.reuters.com/article/us-mexico-violence -idUSKBN0IT04D20141110.

33. Andrea Noel, "Get Over It, Ex Mexican President Tells Parents of Missing Students on US Caravan," *Vice News*, March 19, 2015.

34. The GIEI included Alejandro Valencia Villa, Ángela María Buitrago, Carlos Martin Beristaín, Claudia Paz y Paz Baile, and Francisco Cox Vial.

35. Grupo Internacional de Expertos Independientes, "Informe Ayotzinapa II," 2016, https://www.oas.org/es/cidh/actividades/giei/GIEI-InformeAyotzinapa2.pdf.

36. Anabel Hernández, interview on the release of her book, *La Verdadera Noche de Iguala*, on CNN: "Ejército 'Ordenó, Orquestó y Organizó' la Noche en la que Desaparecieron los 43: Anabel Hernández en CNN," *Arestigui Noticias*, November 28, 2016, http://aristeguinoticias.com/2811/mexico/ejercito-ordeno-orquesto-y -organizo-la-noche-en-la-que-desaparecieron-los-43-anabel-hernandez-en-cnn/.

37. Roberto González Villarreal, *Ayotzinapa: La rabia y la esperanza* (Mexico City: Editorial Terracotta, 2015), 140.

38. González Villarreal, *Ayotzinapa*, 143.

39. Achille Mbembe, "Necropolitics," trans. Libby Meintjes, *Popular Culture* 15, no. 1 (2003): 17.

40. Carlos Fazio claims that disappearance as a state political practice was ordered by Hitler on December 12, 1941, in a state document that called for the secret detention and disappearance of people (Nacht-und-Nebel-Erlass), *Estado de emergencia*, 361. The terms the Nazis used were "vanish" and *vernebelt*, or "transformed into mist." "Nacht und Nebel," Wikipedia, last edited December 28, 2019, https://en.wikipedia.org/wiki/Nacht_und_Nebel.

41. Hannah Arendt, *The Human Condition* (New York: Anchor, 1969), 178.

42. Diana Taylor, "El espectáculo de la memoria," *Teatro al sur* (Argentina), spring 2001.

43. Rivera Sun, "Remembering Argentina's Mothers of the Disappeared," *CounterPunch*, April 25, 2016, http://www.counterpunch.org/2016/04/25/remembering -argentinas-mothers-of-the-disappeared/.

44. "Comadres fue fundado en 1977; un período en que 'desapariciones' andaban a la orden del día en El Salvador. El grupo se estableció porque los familiares de personas 'desaparecidas' necesitaban compartir el dolor con compañeros y para juntar fuerzas. Hoy en día las mujeres de Comadres trabajan para esclarecer un gran número de 'desapariciones.'" "Bienvenidos," Comadres: Comité de Madres Mons. Romero, accessed February 11, 2020, http://comadres.org/main_espanol.html.

45. See Carlos Henriquez Consalvi's memoir, *Broadcasting the Civil War in El Salvador: A Memoir of Guerrilla Radio*, trans. Charles Leo Nagel and A. L. (Bill) Prince (Austin: University of Texas Press, 2010), first published in Spanish as *La terquedad del Izote: La historia de Radio Venceremos* (Mexico City: Editorial Diana, 2003). We interviewed with Henriquez Consalvi as part of the Hemispheric Institute's Ecologies of Migrant Care project, November 23, 2016 (https://migration.hemi.press/carlos-henriquez-consalvi/).

46. The description of how Comadres took form could have been quoted directly from the testimonies of the Madres de Plaza de Mayo: "Madres y familiares, luego de la masacre comenzaron la búsqueda de sus seres queridos, aquellos que no llegaron a casa. En la interminable búsqueda en hospitales, cárceles y morgues, las caras de aquellas mujeres se fueron reconociendo unas con otras, en su dolor se ayudaban, repartiéndose lugares con la esperanza de encontrar en el menor tiempo a sus familiares." Gloria Guzmán Orellana and Irantzu Mendia Azkue, *Mujeres con Memoria: Activistas del Movimiento de Derechos Humanos en El Salvador* (Bilboa, Spain: Editorial Hegoa, 2013), 34, http://publicaciones.hegoa.ehu.es/es/publications/292.

47. The U.S. backed the Salvadoran military to the tune of one million dollars a day during the Reagan era.

48. Interview with Sara Hernández, Mexico City, 2016.

49. Interview with COFAMIDE, San Salvador, November 23, 2016.

50. Interview with Sister María Isabel Arantes as part of the Ecologies of Migrant Care project (https://migration.hemi.press/hermana-maria-izabel-arantes/).

51. Interview with Marta Sánchez, San Cristóbal de las Casas, November 16, 2016.

52. The Misión Internacional de Observación de Derechos Humanos en la Frontera or the International Mission of Observers on Human Rights asked international observers to examine the conditions of migrants on the Guatemala-Mexico border during November 8–15, 2016.

53. The United Nations forum o Immigration posted the following account: "The summit was convened by the *Movimiento Migrante Mesoamericano* and the Italian *Carovani Migranti*, two NGOs which assist mothers and families of missing migrants in Central America and Italy, respectively. Associations representing families of the missing sent delegations to the Summit, including the Tunisian *Association Mères des Disparus*, the Algerian *Collectif de Familles des Harraga d'Annaba*, the Mauritanian *Association des Femmes Chefs de Famille*, the Salvadoran *Comité de Migrantes Desparecidos*, the Honduran *Comité de Familiares de Migrantes Desaparecidos del Progreso* and the Mexican *Red de Enlaces Nacionales*." "The Forgotten 'Migrant Caravan': Historic Launch of Global Movement of Fami-

lies of the Missing," IOM, November 6, 2018, https://www.iom.int/news/forgotten
-migrant-caravan-historic-launch-global-movement-families-missing.

54. See Paula Monaco Felipe, *Ayotzinapa: Horas Eternas* (Mexico City: Editorial B, 2016).

55. Arendt, *The Human Condition*, 180.

56. Trevor Paglen points to the "strange dialectics of secrecy and geography that take place under conditions of top-secret production" in "Goatsucker: Toward a Spatial Theory of State Secrecy," *Environment and Planning D: Society and Space* 28 (2010): 760, http://journals.sagepub.com/doi/abs/10.1068/d5308.

57. Interview with Liliana Felipe, Mexico City, January 2016.

58. Interview with Sister Valdette Willeman, November 2017.

Six We Have Always Been Queer

1. See María Elena Martínez, "Archives, Bodies, and Imagination: The Case of Juana Aguilar and Queer Approaches to History, Sexuality, and Politics," *Radical History*, no. 210 (fall 2014): 159–82, for segments from the archival accounts of the case. Sodomy, as Martha Few notes, included sexual acts with either men or women in this period and context. Martha Few, "'That Monster of Nature': Gender, Sexuality, and the Medicalization of a 'Hermaphrodite' in Late Colonial Guatemala," *Ethnohistory* 54, no. 1 (winter 2007): 169.

2. Jesusa Rodríguez, personal correspondence, May 25, 2014. "Nosotras acá seguimos en la larga historia de Juana La Larga y la verdad ha sido muy interesnate tratar el tema de la sexualidad que nunca habíamos abordado así directamente."

3. Jack Halberstam, *Trans*: A Quick and Quirky Account of Gender Variability* (Oakland: University of California Press, 2018), 84.

4. Narciso Esparragosa y Gallardo, "Hermafroditas," *La Gazeta de Guatemala* 8, no. 310, July 4, 1803, folio 269, https://archive.org/stream /lagazetadguate00betoguat#page/168/mode/2up. Spelling as in the original. Translations into English unless otherwise indicated.

5. Martha Few states that Esparragosa was "at the height of his career" when he took on the Aguilar case and "was arguably one of the leading physicians in Central America with a growing international reputation." Few, "'That Monster of Nature,'" 162.

6. Esparragosa y Gallardo, "Hermafroditas," 270.

7. Esparragosa y Gallardo, "Hermafroditas," 271.

8. "Al organo que acabo de describir han concedido las fisiologistas la propiedad de excitar la concupiscencia. . . . Ha contribuido mucho al reprehensible abuso que han comedito algunas mugeres con saciar caprichosamente su lascibia, defraudando lo que á los varones tiene concedido la naturaleza." Esparragosa y Gallardo, "Hermafroditas," 271.

9. Esparragosa y Gallardo, "Hermafroditas," 279.

10. Esparragosa y Gallardo, "Hermafroditas."

11. Few, "'That Monster of Nature,'" 161.

12. Esparragosa writes of the "obscena confricacion que se suele acostumbrar entre dos mugeres" in "Hermafroditas," 279.

13. Esparragosa y Gallardo, "Hermafroditas," 280.

14. Richard M. Bonnie, Anne M. Coughlin, John C. Jefferies Jr., and Peter W. Low, *Criminal Law* (Westbury, NY: Foundation, 1997), 251; "Impossibility Defense," Wikipedia, last edited January 1, 2020, https://en.wikipedia.org/wiki /Impossibility_defense. See also Colin Dayan, *The Law Is a White Dog: How Legal Rituals Make and Unmake Persons* (Princeton, NJ: Princeton University Press, 2011).

15. Few, "'That Monster of Nature,'" 173n1, says that criminal charges against Aguilar for "violat[ing] and talk[ing]" to a woman in what is now El Salvador date back to 1792.

16. Martínez, "Archives, Bodies, and Imagination," 161.

17. Jesusa Rodríguez, *Sor Juana en Almoloya*, Hemispheric Institute Digital Video Library, 1995, http://hemisphericinstitute.org/hemi/en/hidvl-profiles /elhabito-performances/item/40-habito-almoloya. For the text, see Jesusa Rodríguez, *Sor Juana in Prison: A Virtual Pageant Play*, in *Holy Terrors: Latin American Women Perform*, ed. Diana Taylor and Roselyn Costantino (Durham, NC: Duke University Press, 2003).

18. Rodríguez, *Sor Juana in Prison*.

19. Martínez, "Archives, Bodies, and Imagination," 163.

20. Michelle Lara Olmos, "Ni una más: Femicides in Mexico," Justice in Mexico, April 4, 2018, https://justiceinmexico.org/femicidesinmexico/.

21. See performance, "Jesusa Rodríguez and Liliana Felipe: Juana La Larga," Hemispheric Institute, June 23, 2014, http://hemisphericinstitute.org/hemi/en /enc14-performances/item/2330-enc14-performances-Rodríguez-felipe-juana.

22. By facial mask, I refer to the practice some artists have, such as Rodríguez, Denise Stoklos, or Jacques Servin of The Yes Men, to set their face in a fairly rigid masklike position to depict a character. Unlike facial expressions that reflect deep feelings and attitudes, such as the many Anna Deavere Smith draws on to perform numerous characters in her solo performances, the facial mask is only outward facing, put on like a mask. Like a mask, it accentuates one feature, and so it's given to essentialism and stereotyping. Rodríguez turned her back to the audience while donning this face, just as she would a mask. She has a repertoire of facial masks she has used for different personages—Mexican politicians mostly—and she changes them rapidly and constantly in her cabaret performances.

23. For an excellent discussion of racism in Mexico, see Federico Navarrete, *Alfabeto del racism mexicano* (Barcelona: Malpaso Ediciones, 2016); and Federico Navarrete, *México racista: Una denuncia* (Mexico City: Penguin Random House Grupo Editorial, 2016).

24. Christina A. Sue and Tanya Golash-Boza, "'It Was Only a Joke': How Racial Humour Fuels Colour-Blind Ideologies in Mexico and Peru," *Ethnic and Racial Studies* 36, no. 10 (2013): 1582.

25. Few, "'That Monster of Nature.'"

26. Octavio Paz, "Máscaras Mexicanas," in *El laberinto de la soledad* (1950; reprint, Mexico City: Fondo de Cultura Económico, 2018), 48.

27. Domingo F. Sarmiento, *Facundo*, 4th ed. (Paris: Librería Hachette y Cia, 1874), 22.

28. "Para los mexicanos la mujer es un ser obscuro, secreto y pasivo" (For Mexicans, woman is an obscure, secret, and passive being). Paz, "Máscaras Mexicanas," 40.

29. "La mujer es sólo un reflejo de la voluntad y querer masculinos." Paz, "Máscaras Mexicanas," 39.

30. Octavio Paz, "Los hijos de la Malinche," in *El laberinto de la soledad*, 73.

31. Anahi Rama and Lizbeth Diaz, "Violence against Women 'Pandemic' in Mexico," Reuters, March 7, 2014, http://www.reuters.com/article/2014/03/07/us -mexico-violence-women-idUSBREA2608F20140307.

32. Personal communication. Thanks to Annie Sansonetti for taking the time to walk me through some of the trans-related debates brought up by this chapter.

33. Lois Weaver, "The Long Table," Split Britches, accessed January 22, 2020, http://www.split-britches.com/longtable.

34. For the video of the Long Table discussion, see Lois Weaver, "Long Table: Representing Bodies and Experiences" [video], Hemispheric Institute, June 26, 2014, http://hemisphericinstitute.org/hemi/en/enc14-manifestos/item/2596 -longtable-representing-bodies-and-experiences.

35. Jack Halberstam, "You Are Triggering Me! The Neo-liberal Rhetoric of Harm, Danger and Trauma," *Bully Bloggers*, July 5, 2014, http://bullybloggers .wordpress.com/2014/07/05/you-are-triggering-me-the-neo-liberal-rhetoric-of -harm-danger-and-trauma/.

36. Halberstam, *Trans**, 84.

37. Jesusa Rodríguez, email to Jack Halberstam, July 9, 2014.

38. José Esteban Muñoz, *Cruising Utopia: The Then and There of Queer Futurity* (New York: New York University Press, 2009), 1.

39. "Muxe," Wikipedia, last edited February 1, 2020, https://en.wikipedia.org /wiki/Muxe.

40. See *Final Judgment*, in *Stages of Conflict: A Critical Anthology of Latin American Theater and Performance*, ed. Diana Taylor and Sarah J. Townsend (Ann Arbor: University of Michigan Press, 2008), 48–58; and Louise M. Burkhart, ed., *Aztecs on Stage: Religious Theater in Colonial Mexico* (Norman: University of Oklahoma Press, 2011), 68.

41. Guillermo Bonafil Batalla, *México Profundo: Reclaiming a Civilization*, trans. Philip A. Dennis (Austin: University of Texas Press, 1996), xvi–xvii.

42. See James Maffie, *Aztec Philosophy: Understanding a World in Motion* (Boulder: University Press of Colorado, 2014), especially "The Cosmos as Teotl's Artistic-Shamanistic Self-Transformation," 38–42.

43. Jesusa Rodríguez, in Diana Taylor, *Performance* (Durham, NC: Duke University Press, 2016).

44. To hear Tomson Highway's lecture, see "The Place of the Indigenous Voice in the 21st Century," keynote address presented at the Ninth Hemispheric Institute of Performance and Politics Encuentro, Montreal, June 21–28, 2014, http:// hemisphericinstitute.org/hemi/en/enc14-keynote-lectures/item/2299-tomson -highway-the-place-of-the-indigenous-voice-in-the-21st-century.

45. Anjali Arondekar, personal communication, March 30, 2015.

46. Sara Ahmed, *The Cultural Politics of Emotion* (New York: Routledge, 2004), 28.

47. Martínez, "Archives, Bodies, and Imagination," 174.

48. Hannah Gadsby, *Nanette* (Netflix, 2018).

49. Melena Ryzik, "Raging against Empty Laughter," *New York Times*, July 29, 2018, AR 1.

50. Lauren Berlant and Sianne Ngai, "Comedy Has Issues," *Critical Inquiry* 43 (winter 2017): 233.

51. Berlant and Ngai, "Comedy Has Issues."

52. Berlant and Ngai, "Comedy Has Issues," 235.

53. Ana Paulina Lee, a member of the Work Group, wrote when I asked her about the impromptu performance:

Prior to the Encuentro in Montreal, Alice Jim at Concordia curated an art show where the artist had this "it's a small world" fabric. The artist turned it into a fashion show and did a performance/fashion show. The fashion show was obviously a parody of the stereotypes. The artist is based in Montreal so she had all the clothes from the show. We used the clothes and decided to turn the Long Table with Jesusa into a runway—sort of an appropriation of the racial stereotypes, performing a mockery of yellowface in response to Jesusa's performance of yellowface. I would call it a circumoceanic performance, building on [Joseph] Roach [*Cities of the Dead: Circum-Atlantic Performance* (Columbia University Press, 1996)] a performance of yellowface that is also citation and substitution. The performance was a way for us to do something immediate, confront the humiliating representation, but the experience of incorporating it and seeing the audience seeing us as a stereotype made me feel very vulnerable. I might as well have been naked. Then, I saw Marlene and your expression and I gained strength to keep going but the most shocking part was that no one really saw us. After we talked about it and realized, We didn't interrupt anything. The conversation at the Long Table continued like it does after a burp. I wish we performed as a burp! That would have been great.

Personal correspondence, July 28, 2018.

54. Lee, personal correspondence.

55. Ahmed, *The Cultural Politics of Emotion*, 29.

56. Susan Stryker, "My Words to Victor Frankenstein above the Village of Chamounix: Performing Transgender Rage," GLQ 1 (1994): 249. Thanks to Annie Sansonetti for this suggestion.

57. Halberstam, *Trans**, 87.

58. Michel Foucault, *The Government of Self and Others: Lectures at the College de France, 1982–1983* (New York: Picador, 2010), 68.

Seven Tortuous Routes

Earlier versions of sections of this chapter appeared in Marianne Hirsch and Nancy K. Miller, eds., *Rites of Return: Diaspora Poetics and the Politics of Memory* (New York: Columbia University Press, 2011), and Elspeth H. Brown and Thy Phu, eds., *Feeling Photography* (Durham, NC: Duke University Press, 2014).

1. "Valech Report," Wikipedia, last edited December 29, 2019, https://en.wikipedia.org/wiki/Valech_Report.

2. Roland Barthes, *Camera Lucida: Reflections on Photography*, trans. Richard Howard (New York: Hill and Wang, 2010), 40.

3. For a list of the spaces taken over by the Pinochet military dictatorship, see "Recinto CNI—Avenida Republica 517: Santiago—Region Metropolitana," Memoria Viva, accessed February 11, 2020, http://www.memoriaviva.com/Centros /00Metropolitana/Recinto_CNI_republica_517.htm.

4. Teresa Meade writes that Villa Grimaldi was the "only 'memorial' of torture in Latin America" when it was built in 1995. Now Parque de la Memoria and ESMA in Buenos Aires also function as memorials. Teresa Meade, "Holding the Junta Accountable: Chile's 'Sitios de Memoria' and the History of Torture, Disappearance, and Death," *Radical History Review* 79 (2001): 123–39, https://muse.jhu.edu /journals/radical_history_review/v079/79.1meade.html.

5. For general information on Plan Condor, see "Operation Condor," Wikipedia, last edited February 3, 2020, https://en.wikipedia.org/wiki/Operation_Condor.

6. Audiotape, Villa Grimaldi visit, 2010.

7. See Vittorio Gallese, "The 'Shared Manifold' Hypothesis: From Mirror Neurons to Empathy," *Journal of Consciousness Studies* 8, no. 5–7 (2001): 33–50.

8. See Michael J. Lazzara, *Chile in Transition: The Poetics and Politics of Memory* (Gainesville: University Press of Florida, 2006), for an excellent analysis of Pedro Matta's tour and Villa Grimaldi.

9. Pedro Alejandro Matta, "A Walk through a 20th Century Torture Center: Villa Grimaldi, Santiago de Chile: A Visitor's Guide" (self-published brochure, 2000), 13.

10. Ricardo Dominguez, "#FearlessGestures: Disturbing Insecurity States Now," panel presentation, Rights under Repression, Modern Language Association, New York, January 6, 2018.

11. Marcial Godoy-Anativia, "The Body as Sanctuary Space: Towards a Somatic Topography of Torture" (unpublished manuscript, 1997).

12. See Vittorio Gallese, "Intentional Attunement: The Mirror Neuron System and Its Role in Interpersonal Relations," accessed January 23, 2020, https://www .academia.edu/2207384/Intentional_attunement.

13. See Thomas A. Abercrombie, *Pathways of Memory and Power: Ethnography and History among an Andean People* (Madison: University of Wisconsin Press, 1998).

14. Diana Taylor, *Disappearing Acts: Spectacles of Gender and Nationalism in Argentina's "Dirty War"* (Durham, NC: Duke University Press, 1997).

15. Fredric Jameson, *Signatures of the Visible* (New York: Routledge, 1992), 54.

16. See Ayşe Gül Altınay, María José Contreras, Marianne Hirsch, Jean Howard, Banu Karaca, and Alisa Solomon, eds., *Women Mobilizing Memory* (New York: Columbia University Press, 2019).

17. See my interview with her in the digital book, Diana Taylor, *Villa Grimaldi*, "This Is Not the Place," 2016, http://villagrimaldi.typefold.com/.

18. Charlotte Delbo, *Days and Memory*, trans. R. Lamont (Evanston, IL: Northwestern University Press, 1990).

19. Thanks to Liliana Felipe, whose sister was disappeared by the Argentine military, for this insight. Videotaped interview, July 2014, Mexico City, MVI_8596.

20. Villa Grimaldi: Corporación Parque por la Paz, http://www.museovillagrimaldi .info/virtual/villa.html.

21. Now that Bachelet's second term is over and Piñera has once more come into power, there is a renewed attack on memory sites. The minister of culture, Mauricio Rojas, was fired after creating a public firestorm by declaring that the Museo de la Memoria was "a montage [whose] purpose, undoubtedly achieved, is to shock the spectator, leave him astonished, to prevent him from reasoning." "Chile Culture Minister under Fire for Criticizing Memory Museum," TeleSur, August 12, 2018, https://www.telesurenglish.net/news/Chile -Culture-Minister-Under-Fire-For-Criticizing-Memory-Museum-20180812 -0006.html. See also "Chile Minister Resigns over Human Rights Museum Row," *BBC News*, August 14, 2018, https://www.bbc.com/news/world-latin-america -45177884.

22. Guillermo Calderón's 2010 play, *Villa*, depicts three female characters, all called Alejandra, sitting around a table with a model of Villa Grimaldi on it, to decide its fate. Their options—rebuild the former torture site, build a museum, or create a memory park—were being fiercely debated by survivors and human rights activists at the time Villa Grimaldi was recuperated.

Eight Dead Capital

1. This is the opening line of Oswald de Andrade, "The Cannibalist Manifesto," *Third Text* 13, no. 46 (1999): 92–95.

2. Cesare Lombroso, the nineteenth-century Italian criminologist and physician, is considered the "father" of criminology.

3. The script, *Bom Retiro 958 metros*, was written by Joca Reiners Terron in collaboration with Teatro da Vertigem, 2012.

4. W. J. T. Mitchell, quoted by Jane Bennett, *Vibrant Matter: A Political Ecology of Things* (Durham, NC: Duke University Press, 2010), 2.

5. Bill Brown, ed., *Things* (Chicago: University of Chicago Press, 2004), 5.

6. Bennett, *Vibrant Matter*, 6.

7. Guy Debord, *The Society of the Spectacle* (Detroit: Black and Red, 1983), 49.

8. Antonin Artaud, letter to Jean Paulhan, August 15, 1935. Quoted in Luis Mario Schnieder, "Prologue," in *México y Viaje al pais de los tarahumara* (Mexico City: Fondo de Cultura Económica, 1984), 22.

9. As I argued in chapter 1, the term *peripatetic*, from the ancient Greek word περιπατητικός (*peripatêtikos*), which means "of walking" or "given to walking about," denotes a methodology of learning through walking, a practice associated with Aristotle's walking in circles around the outside edge of the grove as he spoke with his students, who literally followed him.

10. The list of characters places the Red Dress as a character alongside the Consumer.

11. Bertolt Brecht, *Brecht on Theatre: The Development of an Aesthetic*, ed. and trans. John Willett (New York: Hill and Wang, 1964), section 35, 190.

12. Antonin Artaud, "Preface: The Theatre and Culture," in *The Theater and Its Double* (New York: Grove, 1958).

13. Étienne Balibar, *Politics and the Other Scene*, trans. Christine Jones, James Swenson, and Chris Turner (London: Verso, 2002), 12.

14. Deleuze and Guattari describe "desiring-machines" as endlessly interconnected, as "binary machines, obeying a binary law or set of rules governing associations: one machine is always coupled with another. The productive synthesis, the production of production, is inherently connective in nature: "and . . ." "and then . . ." Gilles Deleuze and Felix Guattari, *Anti-Oedipus: Capitalism and Schizophrenia*, trans. Robert Hurley, Mark Seem, and Helen R. Lane (Minneapolis: University of Minnesota Press, 1983), 5.

15. Rebecca Schneider, "It Seems as If . . . I Am Dead: Zombie Capitalism and Theatrical Labor," *Drama Review* 56 (winter 2012): 156. See Karl Marx, *Capital*, where he writes that capital is only alive when it is working: "The inversion of the relation between dead and living labour, between value and the forces that create value, mirrors itself in the consciousness of capitalist." Karl Marx, *Capital*, vol. 1: *A Critique of Political Economy*, trans. Samuel Moore and Edward Aveling (New York: Dover, 2011), 217.

16. "We make no distinction between man and nature: the human essence of nature and the natural essence of man become one within nature in the form of production or industry, just as they do within the life of man as a species." Deleuze and Guattari, *Anti-Oedipus*, 4.

17. See introduction. *Ninguneo* means making a somebody a nobody.

18. See Greg Grandin, "This Mass Grave Isn't the Mass Grave You Have Been Looking For," *The Nation*, November 17, 2014; and Jeremy Adelman, *Sovereignty in the Iberian Atlantic* (Princeton, NJ: Princeton University Press, 2006).

19. Sven Beckert, *Empire of Cotton: A Global History* (New York: Vintage, 2014), 36.

20. The dybbuk is originally a malevolent, clinging character from Jewish mythology.

21. "Las traducciones que se hacen de este concepto tienden a ser místicas, religiosas: algunos lo usan como alma, y el concepto de alma proviene directamente de una cultura católica, por ahí es de donde jalan el significado de almas o espíritus, o incluso consciencia. Pero digamos que 'chulel' se refiere a la vida que todo tiene. Es esa presencia que constituye y completa todas las cosas que existen en este universo y que por eso mismo tienen su importancia, su grandeza. Como constituyen este universo, forman parte de nosotros, no podemos negarlo. Eso es el 'chulel.'" Diana Taylor and Jacques Servin, "Nosotros: An Interview with a Zapatista," trans. Gabriel Burgazzi Rodriguez and Oscar Lozano Pérez, in *Dancing with the Zapatistas*, ed. Diana Taylor with Lorie Novak (Durham, NC: Duke University Press and HemiPress, 2015), http://scalar.usc.edu/anvc/dancing-with-the -zapatistas/nosotros-an-interview-with-a-zapatista.

22. "In general, at all levels of life, not just at the level of nucleic acid molecules, a complexity, which serves a specific function . . . corresponds to an embodied knowledge, translated into the constructions of a system." N. Katherine Hayles, "The Cognitive Nonconscious: Enlarging the Mind of the Humanities," *Critical Inquiry* 42, no. 4 (2016): 789; quoting Ladislav Kováč, "Fundamental Principles of Cognitive Biology," *Evolution and Cognition* 6, no. 1 (2000): 59.

23. Terry Eagleton, *Materialism* (New Haven, CT: Yale University Press, 2016), 12.

24. Eagleton, *Materialism*, 13.

25. Guy Debord, *The Society of the Spectacle* (Detroit: Black and Red, 1983), chapter 1, unit 4.

26. Roland Barthes, *Camera Lucida*, trans. Richard Howard (New York: Hill and Wang, 1981), 59.

27. Debord, *The Society of the Spectacle*, 28.

28. Martin Jay, *Downcast Eyes* (Berkeley: University of California Press, 1993).

29. People in wheelchairs, Araújo tells me later, are carried down.

30. This theatre, which operated from 1960 until 2004 under the name of TAIB (Theatre of Israeli Brazilian Art), was part of a Jewish cultural center known as Casa do Povo, which was a stronghold of the resistance to the dictatorship and is still functioning today. Like the rest of the center, the theatre had fallen into disrepair, and *Bom Retiro 958 metros* was part of an attempt to reactivate the space and its history.

31. Interesting to note here that the enormous corruption scandal (known as the Carwash Operation) surrounding Petrobras, a state-owned petroleum company, brought down the government of President Dilma Rousseff and opened the way to the soft coup d'etat by right-wing forces. Paulo Sotero, "Petrobras Scandal: Brazilian Political Corruption Scandal," *Encyclopaedia Britannica*, April 10, 2018, https://www.britannica.com/event/Petrobras-scandal.

32. James Maffie, *Aztec Philosophy: Understanding a World in Motion* (Boulder: University Press of Colorado, 2014), 42.

33. Quoted in Shoshana Zuboff, "You Are Now Remotely Controlled," *New York Times*, January 24, 2020, https://www.nytimes.com/2020/01/24/opinion/surveillance-capitalism.html. See also https://twitter.com/GlumBird/status/1210733770510225408.

34. Zuboff, "You Are Now Remotely Controlled."

35. Zuboff, "You Are Now Remotely Controlled."

36. Eagleton, *Materialism*, 8.

37. Teatro da Vertigem, *Patronato 999 metros*, Festival Santiago a Mil, Santiago de Chile, 2015.

38. Boaventura de Sousa Santos, *Epistemologies of the South: Justice against Epistemicide* (London: Routledge, 2016), 26.

39. "The vision of the motherfathers, ancestors to the Mayas, came all at once, so that they saw perfectly, they knew everything under the sky whenever they sighted the four sides, the four corners in the sky on the earth." "The Gods [fearing their power] blinded their creations, as the face of a mirror is breathed upon. Their vision flickered. Now it was only when they looked nearby that things were clear." Dennis Tedlock, *Breath on the Mirror: Mythic Voices and Visions of the Living Maya* (San Francisco: Harper, 1993), 9.

Nine The Decision Dilemma

An earlier and much shorter version of this piece appeared in Diana Taylor, *Performance* (Durham, NC: Duke University Press, 2016).

1. The Yes Men describe themselves as follows: "The Yes Men work with progressive orgs to help fight neoliberal policies through humor and trickery." "Who Are We?," The Yes Men, accessed January 27, 2020, https://www.theyesmen.org/.

2. "Impersonate," Online Etymology Dictionary, https://www.etymonline.com/word/impersonate.

3. "Impersonate," Online Etymology Dictionary.

4. Jacques Rancière, "Aesthetic Separation, Aesthetic Continuity," in *The Emancipated Spectator* (London: Verso, 2009), 62.

5. Samuel Taylor Coleridge, *The Collected Works of Samuel Taylor Coleridge: Biographia Literaria* (Princeton, NJ: Princeton University Press, 1983), chapter 14.

6. "Legal dictionary," *The Free Dictionary*, http://legal-dictionary.thefreedictionary.com/agreement.

7. Clearly some attempts at definition are coming from the legal system, such as the "Definitions; generally" section of the U.S. Code 21/321 (Legal Information Institute, Cornell Law School, https://www.law.cornell.edu/uscode/text/21/321). Nonetheless, many terms, such as "hate speech" and "crimes," remain elusive.

8. Welles apologized for the "War of the Worlds" broadcast. CriticalPast, "George Orson Welles Apologizes for His Broadcast of the War of the Worlds: HD Stock Footage," YouTube, posted May 30, 2014, https://www.youtube.com/watch?v=IfBdm5MItew.

9. "Sophie Calle's 'The Address Book,' an Excerpt," *New Yorker*, October 8, 2012, http://www.newyorker.com/books/page-turner/sophie-calles-the-address-book-an-excerpt.

10. See "Libel," Legal Information Institute, Cornell Law School, https://www.law.cornell.edu/wex/libel.

11. "Agreement," Business Dictionary, http://www.businessdictionary.com/definition/agreement.html.

12. I outline the many challenges of defining performance in Diana Taylor, *Performance* (Durham, NC: Duke University Press, 2016).

13. See Maria Teresa Marrero, "Public Art, Performance Art, and the Politics of Site," in *Negotiating Performance: Gender, Sexuality, and Theatricality in Latin/o America*, ed. Diana Taylor and Juan Villegas (Durham, NC: Duke University Press, 1994), 111.

14. Augusto Boal, *Theatre of the Oppressed*, trans. Charles A. McBride and Maria-Odilia Leal McBride (New York: Theatre Communications Group, 1985), 144.

15. "Impersonation," Free Dictionary, http://legal-dictionary.thefreedictionary.com/Impersonation.

16. June 25, 1948, ch. 645, 62 Stat. 742; Pub. L. 103-322, title XXXIII, § 330016(1) (H), September 13, 1994, 108 Stat. 2147, https://www.law.cornell.edu/uscode/text/18/912.

17. "New York Consolidated Laws, Penal Law, PEN § 190.25 Criminal Impersonation in the Second Degree," FindLaw, http://codes.lp.findlaw.com/nycode/PEN/THREE/K/190/190.25#sthash.3YcoLANi.dpuf.

18. "Corporation," Online Etymology Dictionary, http://www.etymonline.com/index.php?term=corporation.

19. Thanks to David Shorter for this observation.

20. Kate Cox, "How Corporations Got the Same Rights as People (but Don't Ever Go to Jail)," *Consumerist*, September 12, 2014, https://consumerist.com/2014/09/12/how-corporations-got-the-same-rights-as-people-but-dont-ever-go-to-jail/.

21. Cox, "How Corporations Got the Same Rights."

22. Richard M. Bonnie, Anne M. Coughlin, John C. Jefferies Jr., and Peter W. Low, *Criminal Law* (Westbury, NY: Foundation, 1997), 251. "Impossibility Defense," Wikipedia, last edited January 1, 2020, https://en.wikipedia.org/wiki /Impossibility_defense. I discuss this defense in chapter 6.

23. "Restrictions on Genetically Modified Organisms: Mexico," Library of Congress, June 9, 2015, http://www.loc.gov/law/help/restrictions-on-gmos/mexico.php.

24. See the pro-GMO report by Graham Brookes and Peter Barfoot, "GM Crops: Global Social-Economic and Environmental Impacts, 1996–2011" (Dorchester: PG Economics, 2013), which acknowledges that the study was partially funded by Monsanto. There are many more, but it's important to note as Jill Richardson does that Monsanto funds research, endows chairs, and interferes with research at top universities in the U.S. ("Stanford's 'Spin' on Organics Allegedly Tainted by Biotechnology Funding," Cornucopia Institute, September 12, 2012, http://www .cornucopia.org/2012/09/stanfords-spin-on-organics-allegedly-tainted-by -biotechnology-funding/). This funding of U.S. universities is common practice, as is the revolving door policy whereby officials from corporations serve as administrators at universities and vice versa. Naomi Oreskes and Erik M. Conway, in *Merchants of Doubt* (New York: Bloomsbury, 2010), explain how the tobacco industry kept regulation at bay, and customers hooked, long after it was known that smoking causes cancers by hiring scientists to muddy the picture by producing doubt. The same, Oreskes says, has been done by Exxon in the climate debate catastrophe: Naomi Oreskes, "Exxon's Climate Concealment," *New York Times*, October 10, 2015, A21. The same has also happened with other industries.

25. A Greenpeace document stated: "Under the Convention on Biological Diversity (CBD) adopted in 1992, the 190 ratifying countries agreed on the importance of establishing adequate safety measures for the environment and human health to address the possible risks posed by GMOs (genetically modified organisms). Intense negotiations started in 1995 and resulted in the adoption of the final text of the Cartagena Protocol on Biosafety (thereafter referred to as the Biosafety Protocol or BSP) in 2000." "Greenpeace Supports the Cartagena Protocol on Biosafety" (Amsterdam: Greenpeace International, February 2004). See also "The Cartagena Protocol on Biosafety," Convention on Biological Diversity, accessed January 28, 2020, https://bch.cbd.int/protocol/.

26. The Yes Men, accessed April 14, 2015, http://theyesmen.org/.

27. Andy Bichlbaum [Jacques Servin], "Identity Correction," in *Beautiful Trouble: A Toolbox for Revolution*, ed. Andrew Boyd and David Oswald Mitchell (New York: O/R, 2012), 60. *Beautiful Trouble* is also available online, http://explore .beautifultrouble.org/#-1:00000.

28. Carrie Lambert-Beatty, "Make-Believe: Parafiction and Plausibility," *October* 129 (summer 2009): 54.

29. Lambert-Beatty, "Make-Believe." Lambert-Beatty adds, "Unlike historical fiction's fact-based but imagined worlds, in parafiction real and/or imaginary personages and stories intersect with the world as it is being lived. Post-simulacral, parafictional strategies are oriented less toward the disappearance of the real than

toward the pragmatics of trust. Simply put, with various degrees of success, for various durations, and for various purposes, these fictions are experienced as fact" (54).

30. For the fake Dow Chemical announcement on the BBC, see Yes Men, "Bhopal Disaster," YouTube, posted January 2, 2007, http://www.youtube.com/watch?v=liwlvbro9ei; and for the Chamber of Commerce hoax, "The Yes Men Pull Off Prank Claiming US Chamber of Commerce Had Changed Its Stance on Climate Change," *Democracy Now!*, October 20, 2009, http://www.democracynow.org/2009/10/20/yes_men_pull_off_prank_claiming.

31. See Yes Men, "Bhopal Disaster."

32. For the video of the BBC coverage of Dow Chemical accepting responsibility for the Bhopal disaster, see Yes Men, "Bhopal Disaster."

33. "In February 2012, it was widely reported in the 2012 Stratfor email leak that Dow Chemical Company hired private intelligence firm Stratfor to monitor the Yes Men." The source for this is listed as "Stratfor Was Dow's Bhopal Spy: WikiLeaks," *Times of India*, February 28, 2012. "Yes Men," Wikipedia, last edited December 17, 2019, https://en.wikipedia.org/wiki/The_Yes_Men#Dow_Chemical.

34. "Chamber of Commerce v. Servin," Electronic Frontier Foundation, accessed October 2, 2015, https://www.eff.org/cases/chamber-commerce-v-servin.

35. "Chamber of Commerce v. Servin." In *Campbell v. Acuff-Rose Music Inc.*, the Supreme Court recognized parody to be fair use, even when it is done for profit.

36. The Yes Men's film *The Yes Men Are Revolting* shows their impersonation of the Chamber of Commerce and its aftermath: Andy Bichlbaum, Mike Bonanno, and Laura Nix, dirs., *The Yes Men Are Revolting* (New York: The Orchard, 2014).

37. "Chamber of Commerce v. Servin: Complaint," Electronic Frontier Foundation, accessed October 2, 2015, https://www.eff.org/node/56749.

38. Stephen Halliwell, *The Aesthetics of Mimesis* (Princeton, NJ: Princeton University Press, 2002), 20.

39. Zoë Schlanger, "Monsanto Is About to Disappear. Everything Will Stay Exactly the Same," *Quartz*, June 5, 2018, https://qz.com/1297749/the-end-of-the-monsanto-brand-bayer-pharmaceuticals-is-dropping-the-name-monsanto/.

40. Cox, "How Corporations Got the Same Rights."

41. See Resistencia Creativa, http://resistenciacreativadf.blogspot.com/.

42. For the full announcement on the fake website, see "Mexico Grants Monsanto Approval to Plant Large-Scale GM Corn Fields," Monsanto, August 14, 2013, http://monsantoglobal.com.yeslab.org/mexico-grants-mexico-approval-to.html.

43. See the Yes Lab website for a full description of the digital action (http://yeslab.org/monsanto).

44. The Yes Men do not seek to perpetuate a lie, unlike the case in which a man lied about receiving the Medal of Honor ("United States v. Alvarez," Legal Information Institute, Cornell Law School, https://www.law.cornell.edu/supremecourt/text/11-210). The point, rather, is to reveal the lie perpetrated on the public by corporations such as Dow Chemical and Monsanto.

45. To read the leaked letter, see Yes Men, "Leaked Letter from Monsanto to Mexican Government," Yes Lab, August 14, 2013, http://yeslab.org/monsanto-leak.

46. Yes Men, "Leaked Letter."

47. Victor Turner, *From Ritual to Theatre: The Human Seriousness of Play* (New York: Performing Arts Journal, 1982), 10.

48. Richard Schechner, *The Future of Ritual: Writings on Culture and Performance* (London: Routledge, 1993), 27.

49. Bertolt Brecht, *Brecht on Theatre: The Development of an Aesthetic*, ed. and trans. John Willett (New York: Hill and Wang, 1964), 192.

50. Brecht, *Brecht on Theatre*, 193.

51. See J. L. Austin, *How to Do Things with Words* (Cambridge, MA: Harvard University Press, 1962); and Judith Butler, *Excitable Speech: A Politics of the Performative* (New York: Routledge, 1997). Thanks to Anurima Banerji for pointing out this connection.

52. Thanks to Grace McLaughlin for her research assistance tracking down the cases and to Professor Amy Adler (NYU Law) for her help with this essay.

53. Harvey A. Silverglate, David French, and Greg Lukianoff, *FIRE's Guide to Free Speech on Campus* (Philadelphia: Foundation for Individual Rights in Education, 2012), includes a chapter on academic freedom, which it defines "as a general recognition that the academy must be free to research, teach, and debate ideas without censorship or outside interference." It notes that "however fuzzy its definition or uncertain its actual legal application [it] is still a powerful concept, crucial to our understanding of the university as a true marketplace of ideas" (1510).

54. Silverglate, French, and Lukianoff, *FIRE's Guide to Free Speech on Campus*.

55. Quoted in Victor Luckerstan, "Can You Go to Jail for Impersonating Someone Online?," *Time*, January 22, 2013, http://business.time.com/2013/01/22/can-you -go-to-jail-for-impersonating-someone-online/.

56. John Leland, "Top Court Champions Freedom to Annoy," *New York Times*, May 13, 2014, http://www.nytimes.com/2014/05/14/nyregion/top-court-champions -freedom-to-annoy.html?smid=pl-share&_r=1.

57. See Kaye Spector, "Mexico Bans GMO Corn, Effective Immediately," EcoWatch, October 16, 2013, https://www.ecowatch.com/mexico-bans-gmo-corn -effective-immediately-1881801967.html; and "Juez da sentencia histórica: Ordena a Sagarpa y Semarnat frenar entrega de permisos para el maíz transgénico," *SinEmbargo*, October 10, 2013, http://www.sinembargo.mx/10-10-2013/781011. For more information about the situation in Mexico in regard to Monsanto, and the activists who are working to keep the transnational corporation out, see "Análisis de Coyuntura Octubre 2013," Fundación Semillas de Vida, October 2013, http:// www.semillasdevida.org.mx/index.php/component/content/article/91-categ -analisis-de-coyuntura-2013/145-10-13.

58. Angélica Enciso L., "Firme, la suspensión de permisos para cultivo de maíz transgénico," *La Jornada*, December 24, 2013, http://www.jornada.unam.mx/2013 /12/24/politica/020n1pol.

59. See Don Quiñones, "Mexican Judge Departs from Script, Turns Monsanto's Mexican Dream into Legal Nightmare," *Wolf Street*, September 1, 2014, http:// wolfstreet.com/2014/09/01/mexican-judge-departs-from-script-turns-monsantos -mexican-dream-into-legal-nightmare/.

60. Jesusa Rodríguez, personal communication, August 3, 2018.

61. Nathan Bomey, "Monsanto Shedding Name: Bayer Acquisition Leads to Change for Environmental Lightning Rod," *USA Today*, June 4, 2018, https://www.usatoday.com/story/money/2018/06/04/monsanto-bayer-name/668418002/.

62. Thanks to Mary Notari, the original YES MA'AM, and Jacques Servin for conferring this title on me.

Epilogue

1. See Ecologies of Migrant Care, https://migration.hemi.press.

2. Leonila Vasquez, interview, August 13, 2017, Ecologies of Migrant Care, accessed January 27, 2020, https://migration.hemi.press/leonila-vasquez/.

3. See Oscar Martínez, *The Beast: Riding the Rails and Dodging Narcos on the Migrant Trail*, trans. Daniela Maria Ugaz and John Washington (London: Verso, 2013).

4. "The word 'empathy' is used in many ways, but here I am adopting its most common meaning, which corresponds to what eighteenth-century philosophers such as Adam Smith called 'sympathy.' It refers to the process of experiencing the world as others do, or at least as you think they do. To empathize with someone is to put yourself in her shoes, to feel her pain." Paul Bloom, "Against Empathy," *Boston Review*, September 10, 2014, http://bostonreview.net/forum/paul-bloom-against-empathy.

5. Frans de Waal, *The Age of Empathy: Nature's Lessons for a Kinder Society* (New York: Harmony, 2009), 80.

Bibliography

Abercrombie, Thomas A. *Pathways of Memory and Power: Ethnography and History among an Andean People*. Madison: University of Wisconsin Press, 1998.

Abrams, Philip. "Notes on the Difficulty of Studying the State." *Journal of Historical Sociology* 1, no. 1 (1988): 58–89.

Adelman, Jeremy. *Sovereignty in the Iberian Atlantic*. Princeton, NJ: Princeton University Press, 2006.

"Afro-Mexicans." Wikipedia. Last edited January 4, 2020. https://en.wikipedia.org /wiki/Afro-Mexicans.

Ahmed, Sara. *The Cultural Politics of Emotion*. New York: Routledge, 2004.

Alfred, Charlotte. "These 10 Countries Have the World's Highest Murder Rates." *Huffington Post*, April 10, 2014. http://www.huffingtonpost.com/2014/04/10 /worlds-highest-murder-rates_n_5125188.html.

Althusser, Louis. "Ideology and Ideological State Apparatus (Notes toward an Investigation)." In *Lenin and Philosophy and Other Essays*, translated by Ben Brewster, 85–126. New York: Monthly Review Press, 2001.

Alÿs, Francis. *Cuentos patrióticos* [Patriotic tales]. In collaboration with Rafael Ortega. Mexico City, 1997. Video. http://www.francisalys.com/cuentos -patrioticos/.

"Análisis de Coyuntura Octubre 2013." Fundación Semillas de Vida, October 2013. http://www.semillasdevida.org.mx/index.php/component/content/article/91 -categ-analisis-de-coyuntura-2013/145-10-13.

Andrade, Oswald de. "The Cannibalist Manifesto." *Third Text* 13, no. 46 (1999): 92–95.

Arditi, Benjamin. "Insurgencies Don't Have a Plan—They Are the Plan: Political Performatives and Vanishing Mediators." *e-misférica* 10, no. 2 (2013). http:// hemisphericinstitute.org/hemi/en/e-misferica-102/arditi.

Arendt, Hannah. *The Human Condition*. New York: Doubleday Anchor, 1959.

Arendt, Hannah. *The Origins of Totalitarianism*. New York: Harcourt, 1976.

Aridjis, Homero. "Migrants Ride a 'Train of Death' to Get to America and We're Ignoring the Root of the Problem." *Huffington Post*, September 7, 2014. https://www.huffpost.com/entry/migrants-train-of-death-america-_b _5568288.

Aristotle. *The Poetics of Aristotle*. Translated with commentary by Stephen Halliwell. London: Duckworth, 1987.

Artaud, Antonin. "Le Visage Humain, June 1947." In *Antonin Artaud: Works on Paper*, edited by Margit Rowell, 94–97. New York: Museum of Modern Art, 1996.

Artaud, Antonin. "Preface: The Theater and Culture." In *The Theater and Its Double*. New York: Grove Press, 1958.

Attali, Jacques. *Noise: The Political Economy of Music*. Translated by Brian Massumi. Minneapolis: University of Minnesota Press, 1985.

Austin, J. L. *How to Do Things with Words*. Cambridge, MA: Harvard University Press, 1975.

Avila, Francisco de. *The Huarochirí Manuscript: A Testament of Ancient and Colonial Andean Religion*. Translated by Frank Salomon and George L. Urioste. Austin: University of Texas Press, 1991.

Azoulay, Ariella. "Unlearning Human Rights." Panel presentation. Modern Language Association, New York, January 4–7, 2018.

Balibar, Étienne. *Politics and the Other Scene*. Translated by Christine Jones, James Swenson, and Chris Turner. London: Verso, 2002.

Barten, Laura. "In Their DNA: Finding El Salvador's Missing Children." *Forensic Magazine*, April 12, 2013. http://www.forensicmag.com/article/2013/04/their-dna-finding-el-salvador's-missing-children.

Barthes, Roland. *Camera Lucida*. Translated by Richard Howard. New York: Hill and Wang, 1981.

Bataille, Georges. "The Big Toe." In *Visions of Excess: Selected Writings, 1927–1939*, edited by Allan Stoekl, translated by Allan Stoekl with Carl R. Lovitt and Donald M. Leslie Jr., 20–23. Minneapolis: University of Minnesota Press, 1985.

Beaubien, Jason. "How Diabetes Got to Be the No. 1 Killer in Mexico." *All Things Considered*, NPR, April 5, 2017. https://www.npr.org/sections/goatsandsoda/2017/04/05/522038318/how-diabetes-got-to-be-the-no-1-killer-in-mexico.

Beckert, Sven. *Empire of Cotton: A Global History*. New York: Vintage, 2014.

Bellinghausen, Herman. "Ramona Will Represent the EZLN at the National Indigenous Congress." Struggle Site, October 10, 1996. http://struggle.ws/mexico/ezln/san_andres.html.

Bennett, Herman L. *Africans in Colonial Mexico: Absolutism, Christianity, and Afro-Creole Consciousness, 1570–1640*. Bloomington: Indiana University Press, 2003.

Bennett, Jane. *Vibrant Matter: A Political Ecology of Things*. Durham, NC: Duke University Press, 2009.

Benzoni, Girolamo. *Historia del Nuevo Mundo*. Madrid: Alianza, 1989.

Berlant, Lauren, and Sianne Ngai. "Comedy Has Issues." *Critical Inquiry* 43, no. 2 (winter 2017): 233–49.

Bermudez-Ballin, Rosalva, trans. "San Andres Accords." Struggle Site, January 18, 1996. http://struggle.ws/mexico/ezln/san_andres.html.

Bevan, Anna-Claire. "US Film Could Help Nail Guatemala's Former Dictator Efraín Ríos Montt." *Guardian*, March 20, 2012. https://www.theguardian

.com/global-development/poverty-matters/2012/mar/20/film-could-nail
-guatemalan-dictator.

Bichlbaum, Andy, Mike Bonanno, and Laura Nix, dirs. *The Yes Men Are Revolting.*
New York: The Orchard, 2014.

"Bienvenidos." Comadres: Comité de Madres Mons. Romero. Accessed February 11, 2020. http://comadres.org/main_espanol.html.

Boal, Augusto. *Games for Actors and Non-actors*, 2nd ed. Translated by Adrian Jackson. London: Routledge, 2002.

Boal, Augusto. *Theatre of the Oppressed.* Translated by Charles A. McBride and Maria-Odilia Leal McBride. New York: Theatre Communications Group, 1985.

Bomey, Nathan. "Monsanto Shedding Name: Bayer Acquisition Leads to Change for Environmental Lightning Rod." *USA Today*, June 4, 2018. https://www
.usatoday.com/story/money/2018/06/04/monsanto-bayer-name/668418002/.

Bonfil Batalla, Guillermo. *México Profundo: Reclaiming a Civilization.* Translated by Philip A. Dennis. Austin: University of Texas Press, 1996.

Bonnie, Richard J., Anne M. Coughlin, John C. Jefferies Jr., and Peter W. Low. *Criminal Law.* Westbury, NY: Foundation, 1997.

Boone, Elizabeth Hill. *Stories in Red and Black: Pictorial Histories of the Aztecs and Mixtecs.* Austin: University of Texas Press, 2000.

Bourriaud, Nicolas. *Relational Aesthetics.* Translated by Simon Pleasance and Fonza Woods with Mathieu Copeland. Paris: Les presses du réel, 2002.

Boyd, Andrew, and David Oswald Mitchell, eds. *Beautiful Trouble: A Toolbox for Revolution.* New York: OR, 2012. https://beautifultrouble.org.

Bradley, Jordan. "Poverty in Mexico." Borgen Project, August 10, 2013. http://
borgenproject.org/poverty-in-mexico/.

Brecht, Bertolt. "A Short Organum for the Theatre." In *Brecht on Theatre: The Development of an Aesthetic*, edited and translated by John Willett, 179–205. New York: Hill and Wang, 1964.

Brooke-Hitching, Edward. *The Phantom Atlas: The Greatest Myths, Lies, and Blunders on Maps.* London: Simon and Schuster, 2016.

Brookes, Graham, and Peter Barfoot. "GM Crops: Global Socio-economic and Environmental Impacts 1996–2011." Dorchester: PG Economics, 2013.

Brown, Bill. "Thing Theory." In *Things*, edited by Bill Brown, 1–16. Chicago: University of Chicago Press, 2004.

Burbach, Roger. "Roots of the Postmodern Rebellion in Chiapas." *New Left Review* 205 (1994): 113–24.

Butler, Judith. *Excitable Speech: A Politics of the Performative.* New York: Routledge, 1997.

Butler, Judith. *Notes toward a Performative Theory of Assembly.* Cambridge, MA: Harvard University Press, 2015.

Caballos, Esteban Mira. "Indios americanos en el Reino de Castilla, 1492–1550." *Temas Americanistas* 14 (1998): 1–24. https://institucional.us.es
/tamericanistas/uploads/revista/14/MIRA-CABALLOS.pdf.

Caruth, Cathy. *Unclaimed Experience: Trauma, Narrative, and History.* Baltimore, MD: Johns Hopkins University Press, 1996.

Castells, Manuel. *Networks of Outrage and Hope: Social Movements in the Internet Age*. Cambridge: Polity, 2012.

Castillo, Gustavo. "A 40 Años: Persecución militar y desalojo del Zócalo." *La Jornada*, August 27, 2008. http://www.jornada.unam.mx/2008/08/27/index .php?section=politica&article=012n1pol.

Castro, Rafa Fernandez de. "Mexico 'Discovers' 1.4 Million Black Mexicans—They Just Had to Ask." Fusion TV, December 15, 2015. https://fusion.tv/story/245192 /mexico-discovers-1-4-million-black-mexicans-they-just-had-to-ask/.

Césaire, Aimé. *A Tempest*. Translated by Richard Miller. New York: Theatre Communications Group, 2002.

"Chamber of Commerce v. Servin." Electronic Frontier Foundation. Accessed October 2, 2015. https://www.eff.org/cases/chamber-commerce-v-servin.

"Chamber of Commerce v. Servin: Complaint." Electronic Frontier Foundation. Accessed October 2, 2015. https://www.eff.org/node/56749.

Chen, Mel Y. *Animacies: Biopolitics, Racial Mattering, and Queer Affect*. Durham, NC: Duke University Press, 2012.

Chenoweth, Erica, and Maria J. Stephan. *Why Civil Resistance Works*. New York: Columbia University Press, 2012.

"Chile Culture Minister under Fire for Criticizing Memory Museum." TeleSur, August 12, 2018. https://www.telesurenglish.net/news/Chile-Culture-Minister -Under-Fire-For-Criticizing-Memory-Museum-20180812-0006.html.

Christenson, Allen J., trans. *Popol Vuh: The Sacred Book of the Quiché Maya People*. Hampshire, U.K.: O Books, 2003. http://www.mesoweb.com /publications/Christenson/PopolVuh.pdf.

Cikara, M., E. Bruneau, J. J. Van Bavel, and R. Saxe. "Their Pain Gives Us Pleasure: How Intergroup Dynamics Shape Empathic Failures and Counter-empathic Responses." *Journal of Experimental Social Psychology* 55 (2014): 110–25.

Clark, Andy, and David Chalmers. "Appendix: The Extended Mind." In Andy Clark, *Supersizing the Mind: Embodiment, Action, and Cognitive Extension*, 220–32. New York: Oxford University Press, 2008.

Cockburn, Alexander, and Ken Silverstein. "Major U.S. Bank Urges Zapatista Wipe-Out: 'A Litmus Test for Mexico's Stability.'" *CounterPunch*, February 1, 1995.

Coleridge, Samuel Taylor. *The Collected Works of Samuel Taylor Coleridge: Biographia Literaria*. Edited by James Engell and W. Jackson Bate. Princeton, NJ: Princeton University Press, 1983.

Columbus, Christopher. "Excerpt from the First Voyage." In *Select Letters of Christopher Columbus with Other Original Documents Relating to His Four Voyages to the New World*, translated and edited by R. J. Major, 1–17. London: Hakluyt Society, 1847. https://www.gilderlehrman.org/sites/default /files/inline-pdfs/Columbus%20Letter%20Complete.doc.pdf.

Columbus, Christopher. *The Four Voyages of Christopher Columbus*. Edited and translated by J. M. Cohen. Middlesex, U.K.: Penguin, 1969.

Conquergood, Dwight. *Cultural Struggles: Performance, Ethnography, Praxis*. Edited and with a critical introduction by E. Patrick Johnson. Ann Arbor: University of Michigan Press, 2013.

Consalvi, Carlos Henriquez. *Broadcasting the Civil War in El Salvador: A Memoir of Guerrilla Radio*. Translated by Charles Leo Nagel and A. L. (Bill) Prince. Austin: University of Texas Press, 2010. (First published in Spanish as *La terquedad del Izote: La historia de Radio Venceremos*. Mexico City: Editorial Diana, 2003.)

Cope, R. Douglas. *The Limits of Racial Domination: Plebeian Society in Colonial Mexico City, 1660–1720*. Madison: University of Wisconsin Press, 1994.

Cox, Kate. "How Corporations Got the Same Rights as People (But Don't Ever Go to Jail)." *Consumerist*, September 12, 2014. https://consumerist.com/2014/09/12/how-corporations-got-the-same-rights-as-people-but-dont-ever-go-to-jail/.

CriticalPast. "George Orson Welles Apologizes for His Broadcast of The War of the Worlds: HD Stock Footage." YouTube, posted May 30, 2014. https://www.youtube.com/watch?v=IfBdm5MItew.

Cruz, Melissa. "Yes, All Immigrants—Even Undocumented—Pay Billions in Taxes Each Year." Immigration Impact: A Project of the American Immigration Council, April 16, 2018. http://immigrationimpact.com/2018/04/16/undocumented-immigrants-pay-taxes/.

Dawkins, Richard. *The Selfish Gene*. Oxford: Oxford University Press, 1989.

Dayan, Colin. *The Law Is a White Dog: How Legal Rituals Make and Unmake Persons*. Princeton, NJ: Princeton University Press, 2011.

Debord, Guy. *The Society of the Spectacle*. Detroit: Black and Red, 1983.

de Certeau, Michel. *The Practice of Everyday Life*. Translated by Steven F. Rendall. Berkeley: University of California Press, 1984.

Deloria, Barbara, Kristen Foehner, and Sam Scinta, eds. *Spirit and Reason: A Vine Deloria, Jr., Reader*. Golden, CO: Fulcrum, 1999.

De Jaegher, Hanne, and Ezequiel Di Paolo. "Participatory Sense-Making: An Enactive Approach to Social Cognition." *Phenomenology and the Cognitive Sciences* 6 (2007): 485–507.

Delbo, Charlotte. *Days and Memory*. Translated by Rosette Lamont. Evanston, IL: Northwestern University Press, 1990.

De León, Quimy. "Regina José Galindo: 'Quiero ponerme en los vestidos de las otras.'" *Prensa Comunitaria*, March 6, 2017. http://www.prensacomunitaria.org/regina-jose-galindo-quiero-ponerme-en-los-vestidos-de-las-otras/.

Deleuze, Gilles, and Felix Guattari. *Anti-Oedipus: Capitalism and Schizophrenia*. Translated by Robert Hurley, Mark Seem, and Helen R. Lane. Minneapolis: University of Minnesota Press, 1983.

Deleuze, Gilles, and Felix Guattari. *A Thousand Plateaus: Capitalism and Schizophrenia*. Translated by Brian Massumi. Minneapolis: University of Minnesota Press, 1987.

Delgado de Cantú, Gloria M. *Historia de México: El proceso de gestacíon de un pueblo*, vol 1. Mexico City: Pearson Educación de México, 2006.

Derrida, Jacques. "Derelictions of the Right to Justice." In *Negotiations: Interventions and Interviews, 1971–2001*, edited, translated, and with an introduction by Elizabeth Rottenberg, 133–44. Stanford, CA: Stanford University Press, 2002.

de Waal, Frans. *The Age of Empathy: Nature's Lessons for a Kinder Society*. New York: Harmony, 2009.

Dominguez, Ricardo. "#FearlessGestures: Disturbing Insecurity States Now." Panel presentation, Modern Language Association, New York, January 4–7, 2018.

Dominguez, Ricardo. "Poetry, Immigration and the FBI: The Transborder Immigrant Tool." Interview by Leslie Nadir. *Hyperallergic*, July 23, 2012. http://hyperallergic.com/54678/poetry-immigration-and-the-fbi-the-transborder-immigrant-tool/.

Dussel, Enrique. *The Invention of the Americas: Eclipse of the Other and the Myth of Modernity*. New York: Continuum, 1995.

Eagleton, Terry. *Materialism*. New Haven, CT: Yale University Press, 2016.

"Ejército 'ordenó, orquestó y organizó' la noche en la que desaparecieron los 43: Anabel Hernández en CNN." *Arestigui Noticias*, November 28, 2016. http://aristeguinoticias.com/2811/mexico/ejercito-ordeno-orquesto-y-organizo-la-noche-en-la-que-desaparecieron-los-43-anabel-hernandez-en-cnn/.

Ejército Zapatista de Liberación Nacional. "Comunicado de Prensa del Subcomandante Marcos." *Chiapas*, May 28, 1994. https://www.bibliotecas.tv/chiapas/may94/28may94.html.

"El EZLN dice que el gobierno de López Obrador decepcionará y no cambiará al país." *Animal Político*, July 6, 2018. https://www.animalpolitico.com/2018/07/el-ezln-dice-que-el-gobierno-de-lopez-obrador-decepcionara-y-no-cambiara-al-pais/.

Eliot, T. S. "Burnt Norton." In *Collected Poems, 1909–1935*. New York: Faber and Faber, 1936. http://www.davidgorman.com/4Quartets/1-norton.htm.

Elliott, Allison. "Caste Systems in India." Postcolonial Studies, Emory University, 1997. https://scholarblogs.emory.edu/postcolonialstudies/2014/06/20/caste-system-in-india/.

Emigh, John. *Masked Performance: The Play of Self and Other in Ritual and Theatre*. Philadelphia: University of Pennsylvania Press, 1996.

Enisco L., Angélica. "Firme, la suspensión de permisos para cultivo de maíz transgénico." *La Jornada*, December 24, 2013. http://www.jornada.unam.mx/2013/12/24/politica/020n1pol.

"Entre la Luz y la Sombra: Últimas palabras del Subcomandante Marcos." Radio Zapatista, May 25, 2014. http://radiozapatista.org/?p=9766.

Esparragosa y Gallardo, Narciso. "Hermafroditas." *La Gazeta de Guatemala*, July 4, 1803. https://archive.org/stream/lagazetadguateoobeteguat#page/168/mode/2up.

"False Personation: Officer or Employee of the United States, 18 U.S.C. § 912 (1994). Legal Information Institute, Cornell Law School. https://www.law.cornell.edu/uscode/text/18/912.

Fanon, Frantz. *Black Skin, White Masks*. Translated by Charles Lam Markmann. New York: Grove, 1967.

Fazio, Carlos. *Estado de emergencia: De la guerra de Calderón a la guerra de Peña Nieto*. Mexico City: Grijalbo, 2016.

Felman, Shoshana. *The Juridical Unconscious: Trials and Traumas in the Twentieth Century*. Cambridge, MA: Harvard University Press, 2002.

Fermino, Jennifer. "Mayor de Blasio, in Candid Speech at CUNY Event, Returns to Controversial Topic Dealing with Race That Angered Police." *Daily News*, February 18, 2016. https://www.nydailynews.com/news/politics/de-blasio -returns-controversial-topic-angered-cops-article-1.2536870.

Fernández de Oviedo, Gonzalo. *Historia general y natural de las Indias*, vol. 4. Madrid: Atlas, 1992.

Fernández-Santamaria, J. "Juan Ginés de Sepúlveda on the Nature of the American Indians." *The Americas* 31, no. 4 (1975): 434–51. doi:10.2307/980012.

Few, Martha. "'That Monster of Nature': Gender, Sexuality, and the Medicalization of a 'Hermaphrodite' in Late Colonial Guatemala." *Ethnohistory* 54, no. 1 (2007): 159–76.

Final Judgement. In *Aztecs on Stage: Religious Theater in Colonial Mexico*, edited by Louise M. Burkhart and translated from the Nahuatl by Louise M. Burkhart, Barry D. Sell, and Stafford Poole. Norman: University of Oklahoma Press, 2011.

Final Judgement. In *Stages of Conflict: A Critical Anthology of Latin American Theater and Performance*, edited by Diana Taylor and Sarah J. Townsend, 48–58. Ann Arbor: University of Michigan Press, 2008.

Flores, Chantal. "These Relatives of Mexico's Disappeared Are Combing the Desert Looking for Bodies." *Vice News*, December 11, 2015. https://news .vice.com/article/these-relatives-of-mexicos-disappeared-are-combing-the -desert-looking-for-bodies.

Flusser, Vilém. *Gestures*. Translated by Nancy Ann Roth. Minneapolis: University of Minnesota Press, 2014.

Foucault, Michel. *The Government of Self and Others: Lectures at the College de France, 1982–1983*. Edited by Frédéric Gros and translated by Graham Burchell. New York: Picador, 2010.

Foucault, Michel. *Security, Territory, Population: Lectures at the Collège de France 1977–1978*. Edited by Michel Senellart and translated by Graham Burchell. New York: Picador, 2007.

Foucault, Michel. *Society Must Be Defended: Lectures at the Collège de France, 1975–76*. Translated by David Macey. New York: Picador, 2003.

Fox, Jonathan. "Mexico's Indigenous Population." *Cultural Survival* 23, no. 1 (1999). https://www.culturalsurvival.org/publications/cultural-survival -quarterly/mexicos-indigenous-population.

Franco, Jean. *Cruel Modernity*. Durham, NC: Duke University Press, 2013.

Freire, Paulo. *Pedagogy of the Oppressed*. Translated by Myra Bergman Ramos. New York: Bloomsbury, 2000.

"From Cable to the White House, the Mainstreaming of White Nationalism." Southern Poverty Law Center, August 24, 2018. https://www.splcenter.org /news/2018/08/24/weekend-read-cable-white-house-mainstreaming-white -nationalism.

Fuchs, Thomas, and Hanne De Jaegher. "Enactive Intersubjectivity: Participatory Sense-Making and Mutual Incorporation." *Phenomenology and the Cognitive Sciences* 8 (2009): 465–86.

Gadsby, Hannah. *Nanette*. Netflix, 2018.

Gahman, Levi. "Mexico's Zapatista Movement May Offer Solutions to Neoliberal Threats to Global Food Security." *Truthdig*, August 21, 2016. http://www .truthdig.com/report/item/zapatista_movement_solutions_neoliberal _threat_food_security_20160821.

Galindo, Regina José. "American Gold." *e-misférica* 8, no. 1 (2011). http://hemi.nyu .edu/hemi/fr/e-misferica-81/galindo.

Gallay, Allan, ed. *Indian Slavery in Colonial America*. Lincoln: University of Nebraska Press, 2009.

Gallay, Allan. "Indian Slavery in the Americas." Gilder Lehrman Institute of American History. Accessed October 2, 2019. https://www.gilderlehrman .org/history-by-era/origins-slavery/essays/indian-slavery-americas.

Gallay, Allan. *The Indian Slave Trade: The Rise of the English Empire in the American South, 1670–1717*. New Haven, CT: Yale University Press, 2002.

Gallese, Vittorio. "Intentional Attunement: The Mirror Neuron System and Its Role in Interpersonal Relations." Accessed January 23, 2020. https://www .academia.edu/2207384/Intentional_attunement.

Gallese, Vittorio. "The 'Shared Manifold' Hypothesis: From Mirror Neurons to Empathy." *Journal of Consciousness Studies* 8, no. 5–7 (2001): 33–50.

Genosko, Gary, and Scott Thompson. "Tense Theory: The Temporality of Surveillance." In *Theorizing Surveillance: The Panopticon and Beyond*, edited by David Lyon, 123–38. Cullompton, U.K.: Willan, 2006.

Gil, José, and Isaín Mandujano. "Una década de caracoles." *Proceso*, August 25, 2013.

Gill, Lesley. *The School of the Americas: Military Training and Political Violence in the Americas*. Durham, NC: Duke University Press, 2004.

Gillingham, Paul. "Preface." In *Dictablanda: Politics, Work, and Culture in Mexico, 1938–1968*, edited by Paul Gillingham and Benjamin T. Smith, vii–xiv. Durham, NC: Duke University Press, 2014.

Godoy-Anativia, Marcial. "The Body as Sanctuary Space: Towards a Somatic Topography of Torture." Unpublished manuscript, 1997.

Goldman, Francisco. "Regina José Galindo." Translated by Ezra Fitz and Francisco Goldman. *BOMB—Artists in Conversation*, January 1, 2006. http:// bombmagazine.org/article/2780/regina-jos-galindo.

Gómez-Peña, Guillermo. *Ethno-techno: Writings on Performance, Activism, and Pedagogy*. New York: Routledge, 2005.

González Casanova, Pablo. "Colonialismo Interno (Una Redefinición)." In *La teoria marxista hoy: Problemas y perspectivas*, edited by Atilio A. Boron, Javier Amadeo, and Sabrina Gonzalez, 409–34. Buenos Aires: Conseja Latinoamericano de Ciencias Sociales, 2006.

González Villarreal, Roberto. *Ayotzinapa: La rabia y la esperanza*. Mexico: Editorial Terracotta, 2015.

Grandin, Greg. *The Blood of Guatemala: A History of Race and Nation*. Durham, NC: Duke University Press, 2000.

Grandin, Greg. *Empire's Workshop: Latin America, the United States, and the Rise of the New Imperialism Project*. New York: Owl, 2006.

Grandin, Greg. *The End of the Myth: From the Frontier to the Border Wall in the Mind of America*. New York: Metropolitan, 2019.

Grandin, Greg. "This Mass Grave Isn't the Mass Grave You Have Been Looking For." *The Nation*, November 17, 2014. https://www.thenation.com/article/mass-grave-isnt-mass-grave-you-have-been-looking/.

Gregerson, Linda, and Susan Juster, eds. *Empires of God: Religious Encounters in the Early Modern Atlantic*. Philadelphia: University of Pennsylvania Press, 2013.

Gros, Frédéric. *A Philosophy of Walking*. New York: Verso, 2014.

Grosfoguel, Ramón. "The Structure of Knowledge in Westernized Universities." *Human Architecture: Journal of the Sociology of Self-Knowledge* 11, no. 1 (2013): 73–90. https://scholarworks.umb.edu/humanarchitecture/vol11/iss1/8/.

Grupo Internacional de Expertos Independientes. "Informe." 2015. http://prensagieiayotzi.wixsite.com/giei-ayotzinapa/informe-.

Grupo Internacional de Expertos Independientes. "Informe Ayotzinapa II." 2016. https://www.oas.org/es/cidh/actividades/giei/GIEI-InformeAyotzinapa2.pdf.

"Guatemalan Genocide." Wikipedia. Last edited January 4, 2020. https://en.wikipedia.org/wiki/Guatemalan_genocide.

Guattari, Félix. *Chaosmosis: An Ethico-aesthetic Paradigm*. Translated by Paul Bains and Julian Pefanis. Sydney: Power Institute, 1995.

Guattari, Félix. "The Place of the Signifier in the Institution." In *The Guattari Reader*, edited by Gary Genosko, 148–57. London: Blackwell, 1996.

Guzmán Orellana, Gloria, and Irantzu Mendia Azkue. *Mujeres con memoria: Activistas del movimiento de derechos humanos en El Salvador*. Bilboa Spain: Hegoa, 2013. http://publicaciones.hegoa.ehu.es/es/publications/292.

Halberstam, Jack. *The Queer Art of Failure*. Durham, NC: Duke University Press, 2011.

Halberstam, Jack. *Trans*: A Quick and Quirky Account of Gender Variability*. Oakland: University of California Press, 2018.

Halberstam, Jack. "You Are Triggering Me! The Neo-liberal Rhetoric of Harm, Danger and Trauma." *Bully Bloggers*, July 5, 2014. http://bullybloggers.wordpress.com/2014/07/05/you-are-triggering-me-the-neo-liberal-rhetoric-of-harm-danger-and-trauma/.

Halliwell, Stephen. *The Aesthetics of Mimesis: Ancient Texts and Modern Problems*. Princeton, NJ: Princeton University Press, 2002.

Harney, Stefano, and Fred Moten. *The Undercommons: Fugitive Planning and Black Study*. New York: Minor Compositions, 2013.

Hayles, N. Katherine. "The Cognitive Nonconscious: Enlarging the Mind of the Humanities." *Critical Inquiry* 42, no. 4 (2016): 783–808.

Hazlitt, William. "On Going a Journey." *New Monthly Magazine*, January 1822. https://sites.ualberta.ca/~dmiall/Travel/hazlitt.htm.

Heidegger, Martin. *Being and Time*. Translated by Joan Stambaugh. New York: State University of New York Press, 1996.

Hemispheric Institute of Performance and Politics. "Courses: 'Summer 2013: Art and Resistance.'" https://hemisphericinstitute.org/en/courses/summer-2013-intro-art-and-resistance-in-san-cristobal-de-las-casas-mexico.html.

Hemispheric Institute of Performance and Politics. "Vision Statement." http://hemisphericinstitute.org/hemi/.

Highway, Tomson. "The Place of the Indigenous Voice in the 21st Century." Keynote address presented at the Ninth Hemispheric Institute of Performance and Politics Encuentro, Montreal, June 21–28, 2014. http://hemisphericinstitute .org/hemi/en/enc14-keynote-lectures/item/2299-tomson-highway-the-place -of-the-indigenous-voice-in-the-21st-century.

Hoeslcher, Steven. "Angels of Memory: Photography and Haunting in Guatemala City." *GeoJournal* 73, no. 3 (2008): 195–217.

Holloway, John. *Change the World without Taking Power: The Meaning of Revolution Today*. London: Pluto, 2002.

Hutchins, Edwin. *Cognition in the Wild*. Cambridge, MA: MIT Press, 1996.

"Impossibility Defense." Wikipedia. Last edited January 1, 2020. https://en .wikipedia.org/wiki/Impossibility_defense.

"'I've Had Enough,' Says Mexico Attorney General in Massacre Gaffe." Reuters, November 9, 2014. http://www.reuters.com/article/us-mexico-violence -idUSKBN0IT04D20141110.

Jackson, Robert H. *Race, Caste, and Status: Indians in Colonial Spanish America*. Albuquerque: University of New Mexico Press, 1999.

Jameson, Fredric. *Signatures of the Visible*. New York: Routledge, 1992.

Jay, Martin. *Downcast Eyes*. Berkeley: University of California Press, 1993.

Jennings, Rebecca. "Melania Trump Wears 'I Really Don't Care, Do U?' Jacket on Trip to Migrant Children." *Vox*, June 21, 2018. https://www.vox.com/2018/6 /21/17489632/melania-trump-jacket-zara-i-really-dont-care-do-u.

Jordan, Mark A. "What's in a Meme?" Richard Dawkins Foundation for Research and Science, February 4, 2014. https://richarddawkins.net/2014/02/whats-in -a-meme/.

"Juez da sentencia histórica: Ordena a Sagarpa y Semarnat frenar entrega de permisos para el maíz transgénico." SinEmbargo, October 10, 2013. http://www .sinembargo.mx/10-10-2013/781011.

Karttunen, Frances. *An Analytical Dictionary of Nahuatl*, rev. ed. Norman: University of Oklahoma Press, 1992.

Kauffman, L. A. *How to Read a Protest: The Art of Organizing and Resistance*. Berkeley: University of California Press, 2018.

Kim, Won-Ho. "Korean-Latin American Relations: Trends and Prospects." *Asian Journal of Latin American Studies* 1 (1998). http://www.ajlas.org /AJLASArticles/1998Vol11SpecialIssue/Won-Ho%20Kim%20Korean-Latin%20 American%20Relations%20Trends%20and%20Prospects.pdf.

Kodjack, Alison. "Seperating Kids from Their Parents Can Lead to Long-Term Health Problems." *National Public Radio*, June 20, 2018. https://www.npr.org/sections /health-shots/2018/06/20/621872722/separating-kids-from-their-parents-is-a -recipe-for-long-term-health-problems.

Konstan, David. "The Two Faces of *Mimesis*." Review of *The Aesthetics of Mimesis: Ancient Texts and Modern Problems* by Stephen Halliwell. *Philosophical Quarterly* 54 (2004): 301–8.

Lambert-Beatty, Carrie. "Make-Believe: Parafiction and Plausibility." *October* 129 (2009): 51–84.

Lane, Jill. "Digital Zapatistas." *TDR: The Drama Review* 47, no. 2 (2003): 129–44.

Las Casas, Bartolomé de. *An Account, Much Abbreviated, of the Destruction of the Indies with Related Texts*. Edited by Franklin W. Knight and translated by Andrew Hurley. Indianapolis: Hackett, 2003.

Las Casas, Bartolomé de. *A Short Account of the Destruction of the Indies*. Edited and translated by Nigel Griffin. London: Penguin, 1992.

Latour, Bruno. *Facing Gaia: Six Lectures on the Political Theology of Nature*. Institute for Earthbound Studies, February 2013. http://www.earthboundpeople .com/wp-content/uploads/2015/02/Bruno-Latour-Gifford-Lectures-Facing -Gaia-in-the-Anthropocene-2013.pdf.

Lazzara, Michael J. *Chile in Transition: The Poetics and Politics of Memory*. Gainesville: University Press of Florida, 2006.

Leland, John. "Top Court Champions Freedom to Annoy." *New York Times*, May 13, 2014. http://www.nytimes.com/2014/05/14/nyregion/top-court -champions-freedom-to-annoy.html?smid=pl-share&_r=1.

Lemebel, Pedro. "Las Yeguas del Apocalipsis." Memoria Chilena: Biblioteca Nacional de Chile. http://www.memoriachilena.cl/602/w3-article-96708 .html.

Lentz, Vera. "Ayacucho 1984." *Yuyanapaq: To Remember* [exhibition]. Art and Reconciliation. Accessed January 28, 2020. https://artreconciliation.org/arts -and-reconciliation/case-studies/yuyanapaq/.

León-Portilla, Miguel. *La Filosofía Náhuatl: Estudiada en sus Fuente*. Mexico City: Ediciones Especiales del Instituto Indigenista Interamericano, 1865.

Lepecki, André. *Exhausting Dance: Performance and the Politics of Movement*. New York: Routledge, 2006.

Levinas, Emmanuel. "Exteriority and the Face." *Totality and Infinity: An Essay on Exteriority*. Translated by Alphonso Lingis, 187–240. Dordrecht: Kluwer Academic, 1991.

Levinas, Emmanuel. "Peace and Proximity." In *Emmanuel Levinas: Basic Philosophical Writings*, edited by Adriaan T. Peperzak, Simon Critchley, and Robert Bernasconi, 161–70. Bloomington: Indiana University Press, 1996.

Linares, Federico Navarrete. *Los Pueblos Indígenas de México: Pueblos Indígenas del México Contemporáneo*. Mexico City: Comisión Nacional Para el Desarrollo de los Pueblos Indígenas, 2008. https://www.gob.mx/cms /uploads/attachment/file/255517/monografia_nacional_pueblos_indigenas _mexico.pdf.

"List of Colonial Universities in Hispanic America." Wikipedia. Last edited January 5, 2020. https://en.wikipedia.org/wiki/List_of_colonial_universities_in _Hispanic_America.

Llorens, Natasha Marie, and Attilia Fattori Franchini. "Works in the Exhibition: Francis Alys." In *Troubling Space: The Summer Sessions*. Zabludowicz Collection, London, 2012. https://cdn.zabludowiczcollection.com/files/ZCCO _TEXT_ARTWORK.pdf?mtime=20150316165921.

López Austin, Alfredo. *Educación Mexica: Antología de documentos Sahaguntinos*. Mexico: UNAM, 1985.

López de Gómara, Francisco. *Historia General de las Indias*, vol. 1. Barcelona: Orbis, 1985.

López Intzín, Juan. "El Ch'ulel multiverso e intersubjetividad en el stalel maya tseltal." In *Lengua, Cosmovision, Intersubjetividad: Acercamientos a la obra de Carlos Lenkersdorf*. Mexico City: UNAM, 2015.

López Intzín, Juan. "El Ch'ulel: Una representación de la interdependencia e intersubjetividad." Paper presented at La Primera Jornada Carlos Lenkersdorf. De lenguas, prácticas y otros mundos. La interpelación tojolabal a la modernidad, Centro de Estudios Latinoamericanos, National Autonomous University of Mexico, Mexico City, May 9, 2012.

López Intzín, Juan. "Epistemologies of the Heart." In *Resistant Strategies*, edited by Marcos Steuernagel and Diana Taylor. Durham, NC: Duke University Press and HemiPress, forthcoming, 2020. https://hemisphericinstitute.org /resistantstrategies.

López Intzín, Juan. "*Ich'el ta muk'*: La trama en la construcción del *Lekil kuxlejal*. Hacia una hermeneusis intercultural o visibilización de saberes desde la matricialidad del sentipensar-sentisaber tseltal." In *Practicas Otras de Conocimiento(s): Entre crisis, entre guerras*, vol. 1, 181–98. San Cristóbal de Las Casas, Mexico: Cooperativa Editorial Retos, 2015.

López Intzín, Juan. "La insurgencia del Ch'ulel: Corazonar su potencial político y epistemológico descentrando la hegemonía del saber occidental." Paper presented at the Hemispheric Institute of Performance and Politics Encuentro, New York, July 11–19, 2003.

López Intzín, Juan. "Rediscovering the Sacred and the End of Hydra Capitalism." Invited lecture, Hemispheric Institute of Performance and Politics, New York, April 14, 2016. https://vimeo.com/164639566.

López Intzín, Juan. "Sp'ijilal O'tan: Saberes o Epistemologías del Corazón." Modern Language Association's Presidential Forum Address, New York, January 2018.

Luckerstan, Victor. "Can You Go to Jail for Impersonating Someone Online?" *Time*, January 22, 2013. http://business.time.com/2013/01/22/can-you-go-to -jail-for-impersonating-someone-online/.

MacAdam, Barbara A. "Francis Alÿs: Architect of the Absurd." *ARTnews*, July 15, 2013. http://www.artnews.com/2013/07/15/architect-of-the-absurd/.

MacLean, Emi, Shawn Roberts, Matthew Eisenbrandt, Kate Doyle, and Jo-Marie Burt. *Judging a Dictator: The Trial of Guatemala's Ríos Montt*. New York: Open Society Justice Initiative, 2013. https://www.opensocietyfoundations.org /sites/default/files/judging-dicatator-trial-guatemala-rios-montt-11072013.pdf.

Maffie, James. *Aztec Philosophy: Understanding a World in Motion*. Boulder: University Press of Colorado, 2014.

Manning, Erin. *The Minor Gesture*. Durham, NC: Duke University Press, 2016.

Marrero, Maria Teresa. "Public Art, Performance Art, and the Politics of Site." In *Negotiating Performance: Gender, Sexuality, and Theatricality in Latin/o America*, edited by Diana Taylor and Juan Villegas, 102–20. Durham, NC: Duke University Press, 1994.

Martínez, María Elena. "Archives, Bodies, and Imagination: The Case of Juana Aguilar and Queer Approaches to History, Sexuality, and Politics." *Radical History* 120 (2014): 159–82.

Martinez, Oscar. *The Beast: Riding the Rails and Dodging Narcos on the Migrant Trail*. Translated by Daniela Maria Ugaz and John Washington. London: Verso, 2013.

Martins, Leda. "Performances of Spiral Time." Keynote address presented at the Tenth Hemispheric Institute of Performance and Politics Encuentro, New York, July 2003. https://hemisphericinstitute.org/en/hidvl-presentations/hidvl-presentations1/enc2003-leda-martins1.html.

Marx, Karl. *Capital*, vol. 1: *A Critique of Political Economy*. Translated by Samuel Moore and Edward Aveling. New York: Dover, 2011.

Massumi, Brian. *Ontopower*. Durham, NC: Duke University Press, 2016.

Matta, Pedro Alejandro. "A Walk through a 20th Century Torture Center: Villa Grimaldi, Santiago de Chile: A Visitor's Guide." Self-published brochure, 2000.

Mbembe, Achille. "Necropolitics." Translated by Libby Meintjes. *Popular Culture* 15, no. 1 (2003): 11–40.

McPherson, Tara. *Feminist in a Software Lab: Difference + Design*. Cambridge, MA: Harvard University Press, 2018.

Meade, Teresa. "Holding the Junta Accountable: Chile's 'Sitios de Memoria' and the History of Torture, Disappearance, and Death." *Radical History Review* 79 (2001): 123–39.

"Memetics." Wikipedia. Accessed October 15, 2019. https://en.wikipedia.org/wiki/Memetics.

Menchú, Rigoberta. *I, Rigoberta Menchú, an Indian Woman in Guatemala*. London: Verso, 1985.

"Mexican Government on Trial for Crimes against Humanity: New York, September 25–26 2015." International Tribunal of Conscience. Accessed January 13, 2020. https://nlginternational.org/2015/09/mexican-government-on-trial-for-crimes-against-humanity/.

"Mexico: Ex-President Charged in 'Dirty War' Killings." Human Rights Watch, July 22, 2004. https://www.hrw.org/news/2004/07/22/mexico-ex-president-charged-dirty-war-killings.

"Mexico Grants Monsanto Approval to Plant Large-Scale GM Corn Fields." Monsanto, August 14, 2013. http://monsantoglobal.com.yeslab.org/mexico-grants-mexico-approval-to.html.

"Mexico Murder Rate Reaches Record High." *Al Jazeera*, June 22, 2017. https://www.aljazeera.com/news/2017/06/mexico-murder-rate-reaches-record-high-170622052056456.html?xif=.

"Mexico: Murders of Women Rise Sharply as Drug War Intensifies." *Guardian*, December 14, 2017. https://www.theguardian.com/world/2017/dec/14/mexico-murders-women-rise-sharply-drug-war-intensifies.

Michaud, Stephen. "Identifying Argentina's Disappeared." *New York Times*, December 27, 1987. https://www.nytimes.com/1987/12/27/magazine/identifying-argentina-s-disappeared.html.

Mignolo, Walter D. *The Darker Side of the Renaissance*. Ann Arbor: University of Michigan Press, 1995.

Miller, J. Hillis. "The Critic as Host." In *Modern Criticism and Theory: A Reader*, edited by David Lodge and Nigel Wood, 402–9. London: Routledge, 1988.

Molina, Marta. "And the Silence Became Poetry and Mexico Listened." Translated by Julie Ann Ward. In *Dancing with the Zapatistas*, edited by Diana Taylor with Lorie Novak. Durham, NC: Duke University Press and HemiPress, 2015. http://scalar.usc.edu/anvc/dancing-with-the-zapatistas/marcha-7.

Mónaco Felipe, Paula. *Ayotzinapa: Horas Eternas*. Mexico City: Ediciones B, 2016.

Monsivais, Carlos. EZLN: *Documentos y Comunicados*, vol. 5: *"La marcha del color de la tierra" 2 de diciembre de 2000 / 4 de abril 2001*. Mexico City: Ediciones Era, 2003.

Monsivais, Carlos. "'Somos borregos!' 'Nos llevan!' 'Bee!' 'Bee!': Un relato de ingratitudes y su consecuencia pictórica (Crónica de 1968-VI)." *Crónica*. Accessed January 13, 2020. https://www.mty.itesm.mx/dhcs/deptos/ri/ri-802/lecturas/nvas.lecs/1968-monsi/mc0290.htm.

Mora, Rafael. "A Sub-national Analysis of Homicides and Disappearances in Mexico." *Justice in Mexico Working Paper Series*, vol. 14, no. 3 (February 2016): 1–28. https://justiceinmexico.org/wp-content/uploads/2016/03/sub_national_analysis_of_homicides_and_disappearances_in_mexico_rafaelmora-final.pdf.

Morgenstern, Tyler. "Hacking the Border to Pieces: Technology, Poetics, and Protest at the Speed of Dreams." *Art Threat*, October 8, 2012.

Morris, Walter F., Jr. *A Textile Guide to the Highlands of Chiapas: Guía Textil de los Altos de Chiapas*. Edited by Carol Karasik. Aspen, CO: Thrums, 2011.

Mouffe, Chantal. *Agonistics: Thinking the World Politically*. London: Verso, 2013.

Muñoz, José Esteban. *Cruising Utopia: The Then and There of Queer Futurity*. New York: New York University Press, 2009.

Murphy, Kaitlyn M. *Memory Mapping: Visuality, Affect, and Embodied Politics in the Americas*. New York: Fordham University Press, 2018.

"Muxe." Wikipedia. Last edited February 1, 2020. https://en.wikipedia.org/wiki/Muxe.

"Nacht und Nebel." Wikipedia. Last edited December 28, 2019. https://en.wikipedia.org/wiki/Nacht_und_Nebel.

Nancy, Jean-Luc. *Being Singular Plural*. Translated by Robert Richardson and Anne O'Byrne. Stanford, CA: Stanford University Press, 2000.

Nancy, Jean-Luc. *The Birth of Presence*. Translated by Brian Holmes et al. Stanford, CA: Stanford University Press, 1993.

Navarrete, Federico. *Alfabeto del racism mexicano*. Barcelona: Malpaso Ediciones, 2016.

Navarrete, Federico. *México racista: Una denuncia*. Mexico City: Penguin Random House Grupo Editorial, 2016.

"New York Consolidated Laws, Penal Law, PEN § 190.25 Criminal Impersonation in the Second Degree." FindLaw. http://codes.lp.findlaw.com/nycode/PEN/THREE/K/190/190.25#sthash.3YcoLANi.dpuf.

Ngai, Sianne. *Ugly Feelings*. Cambridge, MA: Harvard University Press, 2005.

Noel, Andrea. "Get Over It, Ex Mexican President Tells Parents of Missing Students on US Caravan." *Vice News*, March 19, 2015. https://news.vice.com/article/get-over-it-ex-mexican-president-tells-parents-of-missing-students-on-us-caravan.

"Operation Condor." Wikipedia. Last edited February 3, 2020. https://en.wikipedia .org/wiki/Operation_Condor.

Oreskes, Naomi. "Exxon's Climate Concealment." *New York Times*, October 9, 2015, A21.

Oreskes, Naomi, and Erik M. Conway. *Merchants of Doubt: How a Handful of Scientists Obscured the Truth on Issues from Tobacco Smoke to Global Warming*. New York: Bloomsbury, 2010.

Paglen, Anthony. *European Encounters with the New World*. New Haven, CT: Yale University Press, 1993.

Paglen, Trevor. "Goatsucker: Toward a Spatial Theory of State Secrecy." *Environment and Planning D: Society and Space* 28 (2010): 759–71.

Pan American Health Organization. "Health in the Americas, 2012 Edition." Accessed January 28, 2020. https://www.paho.org/salud-en-las-americas-2012 /index.php?option=com_docman&view=download&category_slug=hia -2012-country-chapters-22&alias=137-mexico-137&Itemid=231&lang=en.

Parker, Andrew, and Eve Kosofsky Sedgwick. "Introduction." In *Performativity and Performance*, edited by Andrew Parker and Eve Kosofsky Sedgwick, 1–18. New York: Routledge, 1995.

Parra, Sergio. *Cultiva tu memesfera: Somos lo que nos rodea*. Spain: Ediciones Arcopress, 2015.

Paz, Octavio. "Máscaras Mexicanas." In *El laberinto de la soledad*. 1950; reprint, Mexico City: Fondo de Cultura Económico, 2018.

Pedwell, Carolyn. "Empathy, Accuracy and Transnational Politics." *Theory, Culture and Society*, December 22, 2014. http://www.theoryculturesociety .org/carolyn-pedwell-on-empathy-accuracy-and-transnational -politics/.

Planas, Roque. "The Mind-Blowing Fact about Immigration No One Mentions." *Huffington Post*, September 24, 2013. https://www.huffingtonpost.com/2013 /09/24/americans-immigrating-mexico_n_3984078.html.

Poniatowska, Elena. *Massacre in Mexico*. Translated by Helen R. Lane. Columbia: University of Missouri Press, 1992.

Portilla, Jorge. *Fenomenología del relajo*. Mexico City: Fondo de Cultura Económica, 1984.

Povinelli, Elizabeth. *Economies of Abandonment: Social Belonging and Endurance in Late Liberalism*. Durham, NC: Duke University Press, 2011.

Pratt, Mary Louise. "Arts of the Contact Zones." In *Ways of Reading: An Anthology for Writers*, 6th ed., edited by David Bartholomae and Anthony Petrosky, 608–9. New York: Bedford St. Martins, 2002.

"Presencia: Un proyecto de Regina José Galindo." *El Siglo*, March 9, 2017. https:// elsiglo.com.gt/2017/03/09/presencia-proyecto-regina-jose-galindo/.

"Present." Wikipedia. Last edited August 8, 2019. https://en.wikipedia.org/wiki /Present.

Quashi, Kevin. *The Sovereignty of Quiet: Beyond Resistance in Black Culture*. New Brunswick, NJ: Rutgers University Press, 2012.

Quijano, Aníbal. "Coloniality and Modernity/Rationality." *Cultural Studies* 21, no. 2–3 (2007): 168–78.

Quijano, Aníbal. "¡Qué tal Raza!" *América Latina en movimiento*, September 19, 2000. https://www.alainet.org/es/active/929.

Quijano, Aníbal, and Immanuel Wallerstein. "Americanity as a Concept, or the Americas in the Modern World-System." *International Social Science Journal* 134 (1992): 549–57.

Quiñones, Don. "Mexican Judge Departs from Script, Turns Monsanto's Mexican Dream into Legal Nightmare." *Wolf Street*, September 1, 2014. http://wolfstreet.com/2014/09/01/mexican-judge-departs-from-script-turns-monsantos-mexican-dream-into-legal-nightmare/.

Rama, Anahi, and Lizbeth Diaz. "Violence against Women 'Pandemic' in Mexico." *Reuters*, March 7, 2014. http://www.reuters.com/article/2014/03/07/us-mexico-violence-women-idUSBREA2608F20140307.

Rancière, Jacques. *The Emancipated Spectator*. London: Verso, 2009.

Reagan, Ronald. "Remarks in San Pedro Sula, Honduras, Following a Meeting with President Jose Efrain Rios Montt of Guatemala." December 4, 1982. https://www.reaganlibrary.gov/research/speeches/120482f.

"Recinto CNI—Avenida Republica 517: Santiago—Region Metropolitana." Memoria Viva. https://www.memoriaviva.com/Centros/00Metropolitana/Recinto_CNI_republica_517.htm.

"Restrictions on Genetically Modified Organisms: Mexico." Library of Congress, June 9, 2015. http://www.loc.gov/law/help/restrictions-on-gmos/mexico.php.

Retamar, Roberto Fernández. *Caliban and Other Essays*. Minneapolis: University of Minnesota Press, 1989.

Reveles, José. *Échale la culpa a la heroína: De Iguala a Chicago*. Mexico City: Vintage Español, 2015.

Ríos, Viridiana. "Chiapas, peor que ayer." *Nexos*, January 1, 2014. http://www.nexos.com.mx/?p=15676.

Rivera Cusicanqui, Silvia. "Ch'ixinakax utxiwa: A Reflection on the Practices and Discourses of Decolonization." *South Atlantic Quarterly* 111 (winter 2012): 95–109.

Rivera Cusicanqui, Silvia. "The Potosí Principle: Another View of Totality." *e-misférica* 11, no. 1 (2014). http://hemisphericinstitute.org/hemi/en/emisferica-111-decolonial-gesture/e111-essay-the-potosi-principle-another-view-of-totality.

Rivera Cusicanqui, Silvia. *Sociología de la imagen: Miradas ch'ixi desde la historia andina*. Buenos Aires: Tinta limón, 2015.

Rodríguez, Jesusa. "Pedagogy of Stones." In *Art, Migration, and Human Rights: A Collaborative Dossier by Artists, Scholars, and Activists on the Issue of Migration in Southern Mexico*, edited by Diana Taylor et al. New York: HemiPress, 2015. https://chiapas2015.tome.press/chapter/collaborative-pedagogies/.

Rodríguez, Jesusa. *Sor Juana en Almoloya*. Hemispheric Institute Digital Video Library, 1995. http://hemisphericinstitute.org/hemi/en/hidvl-profiles/elhabito-performances/item/40-habito-almoloya.

Rodríguez, Jesusa. *Sor Juana in Prison: A Virtual Pageant Play*. In *Holy Terrors: Latin American Women Perform*, edited by Diana Taylor and Roselyn Costantino, 211–26. Durham, NC: Duke University Press, 2003.

Rogers, Yvonne. *A Brief Introduction to Distributed Cognition*. Brighton, U.K.: School of Cognitive and Computing Sciences, University of Sussex, 1997.

Romero, Raúl. "Los muros del capital, las grietas de la izquierda: El reloj de arena y el mundo organizado en fincas." Subversiones: Agencia Autónoma de Comunicación, April 13, 2017. https://subversiones.org/archivos/128547.

Ryzik, Melena. "Raging against Empty Laughter." *New York Times*, July 29, 2018, AR-1.

Saldaña-Portillo, María Josefina. *The Revolutionary Imagination in the Americas and the Age of Development*. Durham, NC: Duke University Press, 2003.

Santos, Boaventura de Sousa. *Epistemologies of the South: Justice against Epistemicide*. London: Routledge, 2016.

Sarmiento, Domingo Faustino. *Facundo*. Buenos Aires: Biblioteca Argentina, 1921. http://www.gutenberg.org/files/33267/33267-h/33267-h.htm.

Schabner, Dean. "Hundreds Turn Their Back on de Blasio at NYPD Officer's Funeral." *ABC News*, December 7, 2010. https://abcnews.go.com/US/nypd-officers-turn-back-de-blasio-cops-funeral/story?id=27851746.

Schechner, Richard. *Between Theater and Anthropology*. Philadelphia: University of Pennsylvania Press, 1985.

Schechner, Richard. *The Future of Ritual: Writings on Culture and Performance*. London: Routledge, 1993.

Schlanger, Zoë. "Monsanto Is About to Disappear. Everything Will Stay Exactly the Same." *Quartz*, June 5, 2018. https://qz.com/1297749/the-end-of-the-monsanto-brand-bayer-pharmaceuticals-is-dropping-the-name-monsanto/.

Schneider, Luis Mario. Foreword to *Mexico y Viaje al Pais de los Tarahumaras*, by Antonin Artaud, 7–97. Mexico City: Fondo de Cultura Económica, 1984.

Schneider, Rebecca. "Appearing to Others as Others Appear: Thoughts on Performance, the Polis, and Public Space." In *Performance in the Public Sphere*, edited by Ana Pais. Lisbon: Centro de Estudos de Teatro/FLUL and Performativa, 2018.

Schneider, Rebecca. "It Seems as If . . . I Am Dead: Zombie Capitalism and Theatrical Labor." *TDR: The Drama Review* 56, no. 24 (2012): 150–62.

Schneider, Rebecca. "Protest Now and Again." *Drama Review* 54, no. 2 (2010): 7–11.

Scott, James C. *Domination and the Arts of Resistance: Hidden Transcripts*. New Haven, CT: Yale University Press, 1990.

Sepúlveda, Juan Ginés de. "Democrates Alter, or, On the Just Causes for War against the Indians." 1544. Columbia University Sources of Medieval History. Accessed January 1, 2020. http://www.columbia.edu/acis/ets/CCREAD/sepulved.htm.

Sharma, Ruchir. "The Millionaires Are Fleeing. Maybe You Should, Too." *New York Times*, June 2, 2018. https://www.nytimes.com/2018/06/02/opinion/sunday/millionaires-fleeing-migration.html.

Shear, Michael D., and Maggie Haberman. "Trump Defends Initial Remarks on Charlottesville; Again Blames 'Both Sides.'" *New York Times*, August 15, 2017. https://www.nytimes.com/2017/08/15/us/politics/trump-press -conference-charlottesville.html.

Silva, Denise Ferreira da. *Toward a Global Idea of Race*. Minneapolis: University of Minnesota Press, 2007.

Silverglate, Harvey A., David French, and Greg Lukianoff. *FIRE's Guide to Free Speech on Campus*. Philadelphia: Foundation for Individual Rights in Education, 2012. https://www.thefire.org/fire-guides/fires-guide-to-free-speech -on-campus-3/read-online/.

Simpson, Leanne Betasamosake. *Dancing on Our Turtle's Back: Stories of Nishnaabeg Re-creation, Resurgence, and a New Emergence*. Winnipeg: ARP, 2011.

Slaughter, Jane. "In Push for Education Reforms, Mexican Government Kills Teachers in the Street." *Labor Notes*, June 28, 2016. http://www.labornotes .org/2016/06/push-education-reforms-mexican-government-kills-teachers -street.

Smith, Linda Tuhiwai. *Decolonizing Methodologies: Research and Indigenous Peoples*, 2nd ed. London: Zed, 2012.

Solon, Olivia. "Richard Dawkins on the Internet's Hijacking of the Word 'Meme.'" *Wired*, June 20, 2013. http://www.wired.co.uk/article/richard-dawkins -memes.

Sommer, Doris. *Cultural Agency in the Americas*. Durham, NC: Duke University Press, 2006.

"Sophie Calle's 'The Address Book,' an Excerpt." *New Yorker*, October 8, 2012. http://www.newyorker.com/books/page-turner/sophie-calles-the-address -book-an-excerpt.

Sophocles. *Antigone*. In *The Harvard Classics*, vol. 8. New York: P. F. Collier & Son, 1909. https://www.ohio.k12.ky.us/userfiles/1153/Classes/7790/antigone.pdf.

Sotero, Paulo. "Petrobras Scandal: Brazilian Political Corruption Scandal." *Encyclopaedia Britannica*, April 10, 2018. https://www.britannica.com/event /Petrobras-scandal.

Spector, Kaye. "Mexico Bans GMO Corn, Effective Immediately." EcoWatch, October 16, 2013. https://www.ecowatch.com/mexico-bans-gmo-corn-effective -immediately-1881801967.html.

Spivak, Gayatri. "Scattered Speculations on the Subaltern and the Popular." In *An Aesthetic Education in the Era of Globalization*, 429–42. Cambridge, MA: Harvard University Press, 2012.

"Stanford's 'Spin' on Organics Allegedly Tainted by Biotechnology Funding." Cornucopia Institute, September 12, 2012. http://www.cornucopia.org/2012/09 /stanfords-spin-on-organics-allegedly-tainted-by-biotechnology-funding/.

Stannard, David E. *American Holocaust: The Conquest of the New World*. New York: Oxford University Press, 1992.

Steuernagel, Marcos, and Diana Taylor, eds. *Resistant Strategies*. New York: Hemi-Press, forthcoming, 2020.

"Stratfor Was Dow's Bhopal Spy: Wikileaks." *Times of India*, February 28, 2012. http://timesofindia.indiatimes.com/india/Stratfor-was-Dows-Bhopal-spy -WikiLeaks/articleshow/12062587.cms.

Stryker, Susan. "My Words to Victor Frankenstein above the Village of Chamounix: Performing Transgender Rage." GLQ: *A Journal of Lesbian and Gay Studies* 1, no. 3 (1994): 237–54.

Subcomandante Marcos. "Malas y No Tan Malas Noticias." *Enlace Zapatista*, November 3, 2013. http://enlacezapatista.ezln.org.mx/2013/11/03/malas-y-no -tan-malas-noticias/.

Subcomandante Marcos. *Our Word Is Our Weapon: Selected Writings*. Edited by Juana Ponce de León. New York: Seven Stories, 2001.

"Subcomandante Marcos Reading: The Word and the Silence." YouTube, posted July 23, 2010. https://www.youtube.com/watch?v=FVgOfwhRSwo.

Sue, Christina A., and Tanya Golash-Boza. "'It Was Only a Joke': How Racial Humour Fuels Colour-Blind Ideologies in Mexico and Peru." *Ethnic and Racial Studies* 36, no. 10 (2013): 1582–98.

Sun, Rivera. "Remembering Argentina's Mothers of the Disappeared." *CounterPunch*, April 25, 2016. http://www.counterpunch.org/2016/04/25 /remembering-argentinas-mothers-of-the-disappeared/.

Taibo, Paco Ignacio, II. *68*. Mexico City: Planeta, 1991.

Taussig, Michael. *Defacement: Public Secrecy and the Labor of the Negative*. Stanford, CA: Stanford University Press, 1999.

Taussig, Michael. *The Nervous System*. London: Routledge, 1992.

Taylor, Diana. *The Archive and the Repertoire: Performing Cultural Memory in the Americas*. Durham, NC: Duke University Press, 2003.

Taylor, Diana. "Dancing with the Zapatistas." In *Dancing with the Zapatistas*, edited by Diana Taylor with Lorie Novak. Durham, NC: Duke University Press and HemiPress, 2015. http://scalar.usc.edu/anvc/dancing-with-the -zapatistas/zapatistas.

Taylor, Diana. "The Death of a Political 'I': The Subcomandante Is Dead, Long Live the Subcomandante!" In *Dancing with the Zapatistas*, edited by Diana Taylor and Lorie Novak. Durham, NC: Duke University Press and HemiPress, 2015. http://scalar.usc.edu/anvc/dancing-with-the-zapatistas/marcos -declares-himself-dead.

Taylor, Diana. *Disappearing Acts: Spectacles of Gender and Nationalism in Argentina's "Dirty War."* Durham, NC: Duke University Press, 1997.

Taylor, Diana. "El Espectáculo de la Memoria: Trauma, Performance y Política." *Teatro al Sur* 15 (2000): 33–40.

Taylor, Diana. "Introduction to *Rabinal Achi* (*Man of Rabinal*)." In *Stages of Conflict: A Critical Anthology of Latin American Theater and Performance*, edited by Diana Taylor and Sarah J. Townsend, 29–33. Ann Arbor: University of Michigan Press, 2008.

Taylor, Diana. *Performance*. Durham, NC: Duke University Press, 2016.

Taylor, Diana. "Scenes of Cognition: Performance and Conquest." *Theatre Journal* 56, no. 3 (2004): 353–72.

Taylor, Diana. "This Is Not the Place." *Villa Grimaldi*. 2013. http://villagrimaldi
.typefold.com/chapter/3-1-this-is-not-the-place/.

Taylor, Diana. "Trauma as Durational Performance." *Villa Grimaldi*, 2016. http://
villagrimaldi.typefold.com/chapter/1-2-trauma-as-durational-performance/.

Taylor, Diana, and Jacques Servin. "Nosotros: An Interview with a Zapatista."
Transcribed and translated by Gabriel Burgazzi Rodriguez and Oscar
Lozano Pérez. In *Dancing with the Zapatistas*, edited by Diana Taylor
and Lorie Novak. Durham, NC: Duke University Press and HemiPress,
2015. http://scalar.usc.edu/anvc/dancing-with-the-zapatistas/nosotros-an
-interview-with-a-zapatista.

Taylor, Diana, et al. *Art, Migration, and Human Rights: A Collaborative Dossier
by Artists, Scholars, and Activists on the Issue of Migration in Southern
Mexico*. New York: HemiPress, 2015. http://chiapas2015.tome.press.

Tedlock, Dennis. *Breath on the Mirror: Mythic Voices and Visions of the Living
Maya*. San Francisco: Harper, 1993.

Tedlock, Dennis. *Rabinal Achi: A Mayan Drama of War and Sacrifice*. Oxford:
Oxford University Press, 2003.

Turner, Victor. *From Ritual to Theatre: The Human Seriousness of Play*. New York:
Performing Arts Journal, 1982.

"21 U.S. Code § 321. Definitions; Generally." Legal Information Institute, Cornell
Law School. https://www.law.cornell.edu/uscode/text/21/321.

"United States v. Alvarez." Legal Information Institute, Cornell Law School.
https://www.law.cornell.edu/supremecourt/text/11-210.

"Valech Report." Wikipedia. Last edited December 29, 2019. https://en.wikipedia
.org/wiki/Valech_Report.

Valenzuela, José Manuel, ed. *Juvencido: Ayotzinapa y las vidas precarias en
América Latina y España*. Barcelona: Ned Ediciones, 2015.

"Valladolid Debate" (1550–1551). Project Gutenberg. Accessed March 28, 2017.
http://central.gutenberg.org/articles/valladolid_debate.

"Valladolid Debate." Wikipedia. Last edited December 17, 2019. https://en
.wikipedia.org/wiki/Valladolid_debate.

Valle-Inclán, Ramón del. *Luces de Bohemia*. 1920. Wikisource. https://es
.wikisource.org/wiki/Luces_de_bohemia:Escena_duod%C3%A9cima.

Vinson, Ben, III. "Fading from Memory: Historiographical Reflections on the
Afro-Mexican Presence." *Review of Black Political Economy* 33, no. 1 (2005):
59–72.

Weaver, Lois. "The Long Table." Split Britches. Accessed January 22, 2020. http://
www.split-britches.com/longtable.

Weaver, Lois. "Long Table Etiquette." Long Table, http://hemisphericinstitute.org
/images/_PDF/long-table-etiquette.pdf.

Weaver, Lois. "Long Table: Representing Bodies and Experiences" [video]. Hemispheric Institute, June 26, 2014. http://hemisphericinstitute.org/hemi/en/enc14
-manifestos/item/2596-longtable-representing-bodies-and-experiences.

Weheliye, Alexander G. *Habeas Viscus: Racializing Assemblages, Biopolitics, and
Black Feminist Theories of the Human*. Durham, NC: Duke University
Press, 2014.

Weld, Kristen. *Paper Cadavers: The Archives of Dictatorship in Guatemala*. Durham, NC: Duke University Press, 2014.

Westheim, Paul. *The Art of Ancient Mexico*. Garden City, NY: Doubleday Anchor, 1965.

"What Is the soa?" Will Miller Green Mountain Veterans For Peace, accessed January 20, 2020. https://wmgmvfp.wixsite.com/vermont/soa-watch.

White, Hayden. "History as Fulfillment." In *Philosophy of History after Hayden White*, edited by Robert Doran, 35–46. London: Bloomsbury Academic, 2013.

Wittneven, Katrin. "The Paradox of Praxis Step by Step: Approaching Francis Alÿs." *DB Artmag*, September 19–October 27, 2004. https://fliphtml5.com/xrgx/hlnw/basic.

World Report 2015: Mexico. Human Rights Watch, 2015. https://www.hrw.org/world-report/2015/country-chapters/mexico.

Yagoub, Mimi. "Why Does Latin America Have the World's Highest Female Murder Rates?" *InSight Crime*, February 11, 2016. http://www.insightcrime.org/news-analysis/why-does-latin-america-have-the-world-s-highest-female-murder-rates.

Yes Men. "Bhopal Disaster." YouTube, posted January 2, 2007. https://www.youtube.com/watch?v=LiWlvBro9eI.

"The Yes Men: Dow Chemical." Wikipedia. Last edited December 17, 2019. https://en.wikipedia.org/wiki/The_Yes_Men#Dow_Chemical.

Yes Men. "Leaked Letter from Monsanto to Mexican Government." Yes Lab, August 14, 2013. http://yeslab.org/monsanto-leak.

Yes Men. "Monsanto and the Carnival of Corn." Yes Lab, August 14, 2013. http://yeslab.org/monsanto.

"The Yes Men Pull Off Prank Claiming US Chamber of Commerce Had Changed Its Stance on Climate Change." *Democracy Now!*, October 20, 2009. http://www.democracynow.org/2009/10/20/yes_men_pull_off_prank_claiming.

Zapatista Army of National Liberation. "Fechas y otras cosas para la escuelita zapatista." *Enlace Zapatista*, March 17, 2013. http://enlacezapatista.ezln.org.mx/2013/03/17/fechas-y-otras-cosas-para-la-escuelita-zapatista/.

Index

Dow Chemical, 233–34. *See also* Monsanto Corporation; Servin, Jacques; Yes Men, The

Doyle, Kate, 278–79n47

drug cartels, 62, 127, 134, 136

Duarte viuda de Ramírez, Della, 146

Dunn, Christopher, 242

durational performance, 88, 133, 152, 176, 188, 229; Mothers of the Plaza de Mayo and, 152; Zapatistas and, 77, 88

Dussel, Enrique, 12, 16

Ecologies of Migrant Care, 3, 246–47, 252nn5–7, 254n23, 284n45, 284n50, 297nn1–2

Eliot, T. S., 21

El Salvador, 2, 132, 143, 144–47, 279n51, 284n44, 286n15; traumatic meme in, 132, 146–47

embodied cognition, 9–10, 263n138

empathy, 122, 183, 185, 248, 297n4; Povinelli on, 280n69

Encuentro, Chile, 199

Encuentro, Montreal, x, 68, 153–54, 163–64, 166, 169, 171–72, 199, 243; Halberstam on, 154; Long Table and, 170, 172, 174; Rodríguez and Felipe's performance of *Juana la Larga* and, 154; town hall meeting and, 163–64

Encuentro, Rio de Janeiro, x

epistemicide, 23, 25, 76, 115; Santos on, 24

epistemologies of the heart, 32–36, 95, 262n125, 273–74nn77–78; enhearting and, xi, 33, 35; mind-heart and, 3; rebellious heart and, 35

Esparragosa y Gallardo, Narciso, 154, 158–59

Esther, Comandanta, 90

Europe, 4, 8, 70, 223, 234, 258n68, 277n30; Europeans, 7, 12, 13, 15–19, 113–16, 120, 156, 210, 255n29, 256n42; languages, 258n67; writings, 85. *See also* Arendt, Hannah; maps

Felipe, Liliana, 150, 153–54, 156–65, 167–71, 286n21

femicide, 118, 123, 126, 162; Galindo on, 126; Mexico and, 162

First Amendment, 242

footprints, 65–66; Mesoamerican maps and writings and, 42, 43

Foucault, Michel, 257n48

Fox, Vicente, 64, 139

France, 18, 109, 118–19, 258n69

Franco, Jean, 78, 115, 276n20

free labor, 15

Freudian phallus, 160

Galindo, Regina José, 107, 109; aloneness and, 122; "already dead" character and, 112; *Carguen con sus muertos/Carry Your Dead*, 119; Daniel Hernández-Salazar's angels and, 277n22; dead space and, 121; difference between artists and activists and, 125; *Earth*, 106, 109–11, 112, 119, 123–25; historical violence and, 112; *Infiltrado/Infiltrated*, 125; intervention and, 126, 280n73; mute victim/witness and, 110; performance for the camera and, 123; poetry and, 111; *Presencia*, 215; soft/hard power and, 118; spectatorship and, 126; testimony and, 276n14; tragedy and, 125; *Who Can Erase the Traces?*, 125; withholding reference and, 124

Gallay, Alan, 256n46, 258n69

genetically modified organisms (GMO), 230

Genosko, Gary, 259n79

Gerardi, Bishop Juan, 111

gesture, 94, 101, 141, 199; aggression and, 173; animatives and, 48; Brecht on, 247; codes and, 49; collectivity and, 74; defiance and, 53; Dominguez on, 249; empathy and, 247–48; emptiness and, 51, 247; epistemic potentialities and, 33; ethics of care and, 245; identification and, 11; injustice and, 4; Las Patronas and, 248; meetings and, 65; memes and, 129; militancy and, 5; militarism and, 92; minimalism and, 124; negative performatives and, 48; physical attack and, 163; political interventions and, 47; reciprocation and, 66; responsibility and, 248; silence and, 53; small moves and, 247; translation and, 7; world-making and, 198

Ginés de Sepulvida, Juan, 114

Godoy-Anativia, Marcial, xii, 3, 251n2, 289n11

Gómez-Peña, Guillermo, 10, 24, 123, 254n21; *I AM*, 10

González Casanova, Pablo, 116

González Villarreal, Roberto, 139

Grandin, Greg, xii, 117
Guatemala, 2, 39, 41, 124, 126, 132, 156; Antigone and, 111; appearance in, 121; disappearance in, 119; Galindo and, 109, 125; genocide in, 275n8; Guatemala-Mexico border, 72, 251–52n4, 284n52; *Guatemala: Nunca Más* (Guatemala: Never Again), 111; Hernández-Salazar and, 111, 276–77n21; human exploitation and, 118; indigenous people in, 115; Jacobo Árbenz and, 117; land expropriation, 117; Menchú and, 116; militarism in, 117; military dictatorship and, 107, 278–79n47; *Rabinal Achi* and, 108, 275n9; racism in, 277n30; Ríos Montt and, 107, 124, 275n1, 275n10, 276n11; traumatic memes in, 147; violence and, 117, 119; women in, 215, 279n51
Guattari, Félix, 40, 47, 61, 85, 95, 208, 225, 291n14, 291n16

Halberstam, Jack, 28–29, 35, 154, 173; low theory and, 28
Hall, Stuart, 17–18, 258n69
Haraway, Donna, 35
Harney, Stefano, xi–xii, 26, 28, 35
Hayles, N. Katherine, 36–37, 213, 263n137
Heidegger, Martin, 31, 261n123
Hemispheric Institute of Politics and Performance, x, 2, 79, 119, 229, 240, 243
Hernández, Sara, 146
Hernández-Salazar, Daniel, 111, 276–77n21
Highway, Tomson, 21, 169, 171, 287n44
Holloway, John, 35, 78
Honduras, 1–3, 143, 152, 252n7, 256n46
Huarochirí Manuscript, 25
humor, 75, 97, 157–58, 162–63, 166, 169–71, 209, 223, 234, 236, 252n7, 266n18; Halberstam on, 166; The Yes Men on, 292n1

Ibarra de Piedra, Rosario, 146
identity correction, 231, 235, 243
Immigration and Customs Enforcement (ICE), 15
impersonation, 157, 226–29, 239, 242; legal definitions of, 233; online vs. on the street, 240; The Yes Men and, 295n36
intersex people, 153

Kant, Immanuel, 12, 18
Karam, Jesús Murillo, 138

knowledge, xi–xii, 25–30, 37, 80–81, 223, 241, 244; archive and, xii, 201; being and, 33–34; colonization and, 25, 37; cosmovision and, 102; embodiment and, 263n138; experiential engagement with others and, 57; geographies and, 18; indigeneity and, 36, 115; interrelationality and, 30; isolated silos of, 9; mind-heart and, 33–34, 35; multiplicity and, 33–34; plurality and, 26; responsibility and, 5; *saberes* and, 34; self-knowledge and, 58; situated knowledge and, 10, 35, 95; snails and, 97; subject/object of, 115; thingliness and, 79; universal and, 35; walking and talking and, 38; Western educational systems and, 24, 26, 224; Zapatistas and, 83
Kováč, Ladislav, 36

La Bestia, 3, 204, 246
La Malinche, 7, 75, 161, 253n13
Lambert-Beatty, Carrie, 233, 294–95n29
Las Casas, Bartolomé de, 15, 113–15, 117, 277n29
Las Patronas, 246–48
Las Yeguas del Apocalysis, 265n16
Latour, Bruno, 35, 262
laughter, 50, 113, 157, 165, 170; Berlant and Ngai on, 171
Levinas, Emmanuel, 138
Long Table, 170, 172, 174
López, Xuno (Juan López Intzin), xi–xii, 32, 33–36, 95, 102, 249–50, 262n129
López Austin, Alfredo, 25
Lukianoff, Greg, 241, 296n53

Maffie, James, 20, 75, 95
maps, 42, 43, 177
Maribel, Capitán Insurgente, 74
Martinez, Daniel, 228
Martínez, María Elena, 153, 156, 159, 285n1
Martins, Leda, xii, 20, 258n71
Marx, Karl, 208, 291n15; Schneider on, 208
masks, 74–75, 108–9, 286n22; impersonation and, 239; Mexico and, 75; Zapatistas and, 85, 92, 94, 97, 101
Massumi, Brian, 94
Matta, Pedro, 176, 179, 199–200. *See also* Villa Grimaldi
Maya: animation in all things and, 212; city-state polities, 16; civilization, xi, 19,

35, 70, 84, 87, 89, 113, 117, 257n15; corn and, 107; court drama and, 108; education and, 25; epistemologies of the heart and, xi, 95; glyphs and, 97; Guatemala's internal armed conflict and, 276n11; highlands and, 40, 68–69, 71, 90, 110; Maya Ixil and, 107–8; motherfather ancestors and, 292n32; Popol Vuh and, 32–34; snails and, 97; technology and, 86; Toniná and, 72; worldview, 94–95, 97

Mbembe, Achille, 13, 121

McPherson, Tara, 27

memes, 64, 122, 129–34, 136, 141–43, 145–52, 245; memesphere and, 282n15; trauma and, 152

memorials, 151, 186, 289n4

memory, 9, 18, 25, 58, 62, 65, 95, 126, 206, 275n9, 290nn21–22; industry and, 203; Mobilizing Memory working group, 199; Villa Grimaldi and, 175, 177, 179, 186–92, 194, 196–97, 198, 201

Menchú, Rigoberta, 116–17, 253n9

Mendieta, Ana, 123

mestizo, 25, 29–30, 74, 87, 111, 148, 170

Mexican Spanish, 6

Mexico, ix–x, 1, 5, 7–8, 22, 30, 40, 58, 68, 84, 91–92, 118, 147, 177, 204, 240, 243, 244; African slaves in, 15; Afro-Mexicans and, 17, 168; Art and Resistance course in, 229; borders and, 2; Central American migrants in, 41; Chiapas, 70–71, 229; Chileans in, 175; civil servants and social justice in, 53; Codex Mexico (Codice México), 236–37; crime in, 134, 136; "Dirty War" in, 54; disappearance in, 134; femicide and, 162, 164; genetically modified corn in, 230, 236, 243; Guerrero, 136; Huichol/Wixáritar people of, 37; indigenous communities and populations in, 70, 103, 168; Institutional Revolutionary Party in, 46; Las Patronas in, 245; Los 43 in, 62, 127, 134, 136, 139, 152; masks in, 75; mediums of invasion and resistance in, 101; *mestizaje* and, 158; Mexican imaginary and, 56; *mexicanos al grito de guerra* and, 92; migrant shelters in, 3, 11, 22; Movimiento de Migrantes Mesoamericanos in, 148; National Biosecurity Commission of, 230; *ninguneo* and, 160–61; nonhumans and, 161; Oventic, 69; protest and, 51;

queerness and, 167; racist jokes and, 172; *relajo* in, 50; Rodríguez and, 153, 244; San Cristóbal de las Casas in, 148; social justice and, 152; student movement of 1968 in, 53, 136; Tepoztlán, 6; Tlateloco massacre and, 65; trans women in, 156, 164; traumatic meme in, 64, 145–46; U.S.-Mexico border, 122; Zapatistas and, 54, 77–78, 92, 98–99; zigzag movement and meandering in, 39; Zócalo in, 45, 55

Mignolo, Walter D., 30

migration, 34–35, 42, 91, 147; Central America and, 25; Chiapas and, 84

mimesis, 129–31, 183, 185, 235, 281n11. *See also* Aristotle; memes

Monsanto Corporation, 294n24, 295n39, 295nn42–45, 296n57; Chiapas and, 39; confidentiality and, 238; *corporare* and, 229; digital action against, 242; genetically modified corn in Mexico and, 39, 95, 229, 230, 236–37, 243; impersonation and, 235, 238; legality and, 229; mask of, 239; Mexico and, 296n59; military entities and, 241; New York University and, 243; parody and, 228; pig's mask and, 242; status of a legal person and, 226. *See also* Yes Men, The

Monsivais, Carlos, 51, 103

Moten, Fred, xi–xii, 26, 28, 35

mothers, 128–29, 131–32, 133, 140, 142–43, 150, 151–52

Mothers of the Plaza de Mayo, 46, 128, 131–32, 140, 142–45, 152, 188, 197, 247, 284n46

Mouffe, Chantal, 112

movements and, 144–45, 148–49

Movimiento de Migrantes Mesoamericanos, 148

Mourning Mothers of Khavaran, 143

Muñoz, José Esteban, 179

Murillo Karam, Jesús, 138

Murphy, Kaitlin M., 276–77n21

Museum of Memory and Human Rights, 192

mutual recognition, 4, 9, 35, 62, 90, 95–96, 248

NAFTA (North American Free Trade Agreement), 73, 78, 97

Nahuatl, xi–xii, 6

Nancy, Jean-Luc, 10, 31, 123, 253n17

necropolitics, 19, 23, 95, 121, 138, 143, 149, 186; necro-art and resistance and, 12

neoliberalism, 99–100, 103, 118, 172, 253–54n20

New York University, x, 4, 229–30, 241–44

Ngai, Sianne, 52, 171

Ngũgĩ wa Thiong'o, 27

ninguneo, 138, 160, 167, 173, 210, 291n17

Nixon, Richard, 122

Novak, Lorie, xii, 175, 230, 232, 237, 269n9

Oedipus, 109, 113

Oventic, 69, 76–77, 83, 85, 87, 104, 269n1, 272n56; anniversary party in, 68. *See also* Zapatistas

Parker, Andrew, 47

pedagogy of stones, 81. *See also* Rodríguez, Jesusa

Peña Nieto, Enrique, 138, 282–83n25

percepticide, 71, 80, 189, 270n14

Pérez Molina, Otto Fernando, 118

performance for camera, 123

performatives, 47–51, 52, 63, 94, 265n16; Parker and Sedgwick on, 47. *See also* animatives; Austin, J. L.

peripatetic, 38–40, 204, 207, 263n145, 290n9

Permanent People's Tribunal (PPT), 1, 127, 251n1

Philosophy of Walking, A (Gros), 264n154

Piñera, Sebastián, 196

Pinochet, Augusto, 143, 175, 179, 184, 189, 191, 196, 198, 201, 289n3

Plan Condor, 180, 289n5

Plato, 71; Arendt on, 29

poetry: Aristotle on, 109; Galindo and, 109, 111

Poniatowska, Elena, 56

Popol Wuj (or Vuh), 32–34

Portilla, Jorge, 50, 72, 266n18

postdisciplinarity, 27–28

Povinelli, Elizabeth, 280n69

practice-based research, 78, 83, 269n9

presenciar, 185, 194; *acompañar* and, 194

¡Presente!: accompaniment and, 89; attitude of, 19; authority's roll call and, 52; bilinguality and, 5; care and, 245; context of, 4; copresence and, 248; defiance and, 19, 44; difference and, 19, 21, 25, 31, 61, 71, 166, 182; embodied and

political aspects of, 9; empathetic gesture and, 247; encounters and, 109; feeling ridiculous and, 90; Galindo and, 126; gesture and, 247; *hacer presencia* and, 31, 45, 47; history and, 58; holding out one's hand and, 249; impersonation and, 228; indigenous thought and, 28; injustice and, 4; invitation and, 1, 44; isolation and, 106; knowing and, 24; learning and, 29; Madres de Plaza de Mayo and, 140; memes and, 133; memory and, 58; methodology and, 5; names and, 128; para-presente, 19; performance research/research as performance and, 29; political contestation and, 52; present tense and, 19; recognition and, 47; refusal and, 46; reiterative power and, 19; relational act and, 25; responsibility and, 249; self-reflective subjectivity and, 11; the shout and, 141; singular and plural and, 10; solidarity and, 46; Villa Grimaldi and, 184; vulnerability and, 90; walking and talking with others and, 25; witnessing and, 128

production, 26, 29, 162, 223, 291n14, 291n16; capitalism and, 96; culture and, 25; death and, 213; knowledge and, xi, 25, 30, 38; theatre and, 154

Quashi, Kevin, 53

queerness, 5, 9, 11, 20–21, 27, 84, 153, 163–67, 169–74, 210

Rabinal Achí, 108–9, 111–12, 118, 276n18

racism, 16, 51, 78, 113, 116, 118, 158, 171–72, 210, 256n46, 258n69; Arendt on, 277n30; in Mexico, 286n23

Ramona, Comandanta, 75, 95, 112, 270n20

Rancière, Jacques, 227

Reagan, Ronald, 117

recognition, xii, 139, 241, 296n53; coloniality and, 24; indigenous people and, 121; individuation and, 24; "I/we" and, 10; Maya civilization and, 68; misrecognition and, 63, 165; mutual recognition, 4, 9, 35, 62, 85–86, 90, 95–96, 248; nonrecognition and, 77, 94–95; self-recognition and, 115; situated heart and, 35; spaces of, 47, 52; spectatorship and, 123; truth and, 113; value and, 35; Villa Grimaldi and, 39; visibility and, 150

repertoire, xii, 11, 149, 281n11
Retamar, Roberto Fernández, 18, 258n69
Rettig Report, 198
Reverend Billy (aka Bill Talen), 227
Ríos Montt, Efraín, 107, 124, 275n1
Rivera Cusicanqui, Silvia, xi–xii, 1, 7–8, 20, 30–31, 33–36, 79, 112, 169
Rodríguez, Jesusa, xii, 5, 39, 70, 72–73, 79, 80, 83, 71, 226, 243–44; Art and Resistance course and, 229, 236, 269–70n9; drawing by, 73, 98; environmental activism and, 226; Felipe and, 153, 163, 165, 167–68; humor and, 169–70; Juana Aguilar and, 171; *Juana la Larga* (Long Juana), 153–62, 168; Long Table and, 165–66; masks and, 286n22; pedagogy of stones, 81–83

saberes, 11, 26, 34, 36, 95, 262n131; *conocer* and, 34, 36, 262n131; Intzín on, 262n130
sacred drums, 37
Saldaña-Portillo, María Josefina, 76
San Andrés Accords, 68
Sánchez, Marta, 148
San Cristóbal de las Casas, 69, 148, 236
Sansonetti, Annie, 163, 287n23, 288n56
Santos, Boaventura de Sousa, 24, 115, 224; monocultures, 24. *See also* epistemicide
Sarmiento, Domingo, 160
Saturday Mothers, 132
Schechner, Richard, 65, 239; not/not me/"I" and, 10, 11–12
Schneider, Rebecca, xi–xii, 21, 52, 208, 291n15
School of the Americas, 117–18, 201
Scott, James C., 84
Sedgwick, Eve, 47
Seremetakis, Nadia, 119
Servin, Jacques, 30, 39, 239–40, 243–44, 252n7; as Andy Bichlbaum of The Yes Men, 230–31; Art and Resistance course and, 236, 269–70n9; Dow impersonation and, 233–34; environmental activism and, 226; as Judge Finisterra on the BBC, 223; masks and, 286n22; U.S. Chamber of Commerce's lawsuit and, 234–36
Shakespeare, William, 18
Shaw, Peggy, 165, 174
silence, 19, 49, 54, 81, 109; Chile and, 184; femicide and, 126; memory and, 194; Mexico's "Dirty War" and, 54; Quashi

on, 53; survivors and, 197; Long Table and, 165; torture and, 189; traumatic memes and, 152; Zapatistas and, 69, 72, 74, 76–77
Silva, Denise Ferreira da, 12, 254n25
singularity, 10, 170; plurality and, 10
Solalinde, Father Alejandro, 1
space of appearance, 10, 23, 46, 53, 61, 63–64, 121, 142, 150, 170; Arendt on, 253n18; death and, 112, 128, 141; disappearance and, 47, 141, 197, 215; exchange and, 153; norms of appearance, 52; politics and protest and, 62
spectatorship, 218
Spivak, Gayatri, 4
stepped fret, 73, 97
Stryker, Susan, 173, 288n56

Taibo, Paco Ignacio, II, 55
Taussig, Michael, 115, 270n23
Teatro da Vertigem, 39, 203–6, 209–11, 213, 217, 222, 224; *Bom Retiro 958 metros* and, 203, 290n3, 292n30; *Patronato 999 metros* and, 292n37
tense theory, 259n79
terror, 119, 138, 147, 188, 208–11, 215, 246; individualization and, 194; Mbembe on, 121; Taussig on, 115
terrorism, 146–47, 150; Villa Grimaldi and, 196
testimony, 56, 109, 117–18, 123, 124, 150, 175, 184, 194, 275nn1–2, 275n10
thingification, 35, 210, 220
Thompson, Scott, 259n79
Tiananmen Mothers, 143
torture, 39, 62, 116–17, 119, 126–27, 137–40, 143, 146, 175–202, 278n47, 289n4, 290n22; witnessing and, 189, 199. *See also* memory; Villa Grimaldi
tourism, 23, 71, 190
transgender people, 3, 9, 11, 19–20, 27, 33, 153–54, 156, 163–74, 287n23; *muxe* or *muxhe* and, 167
translation, 6–7, 158, 165, 199; mistranslations and, 8, 165
trauma, 9, 20–21, 133, 140, 175, 184–85, 187–88, 190; activism and, 189; as durational performance, 176; Halberstam on, 166
Trump, Donald, 3, 49–50, 241; administration of, 119

Trump, Melania, 112, 133, 248
Turner, Victor, 239

undercommons, 28, 35
United States, 7, 28, 40, 55, 119, 127, 149;
    interventions in Latin America and, 54,
    122; Mexico and, 22, 39, 252n7; migrants
    and, 39, 42

Valech Report, 143, 175, 198
Victoria 82, 107
Villa Grimaldi, 39, 175–77, 179–80, 182,
    184, 187–91, 194, 196–201, 290n22; Pedro
    Matta's guided visit of, 176–77; survivors
    of, 175, 179–80, 185, 188, 194, 197–98,
    290n22; Taylor's first visit to, 192;
    Taylor's second visit to, 176
Vinson, Ben, III, 17, 255–56n40, 257n58
violence, 54–55, 111, 138, 174, 183, 191;
    against students, 136; against women,
    108–9, 124, 156–58, 161–62, 164, 172–73,
    210; anonymity and, 75; archive and,
    181; biopower and, 112; Chile and, 201;
    cosmology and, 95; criminality and,
    125, 181, 190; death and, 140; Descartes's
    ego cognito and, 254n26; disappearance
    and, 132–33, 215; economics and, 182;
    environment and, 9, 110; Galindo on,
    122; Guatemala and, 117, 119, 276n11;
    humor and, 163; indigenous people and,
    124; "I/not I" and, 12; linguistic and
    regional separation and, 19; memory
    and, 188, 198; Mexico and, 78; migrants
    and, 22; migration and, 13; migration
    in Chiapas and, 72; monocultures and,
    26; neoliberal government and, 92, 118;
    nonrecognition and, 94; percepticide
    and, 222; Pinochet and, 201; police
    and, 45; poverty and, 214; preemptive
    strikes and, 21; privatization of, 23, 214;
    Rabinal Achi and, 276n18; racism and,
    172; shared experience and, 169; slavery
    and, 210; spectacles and, 270n14; state
    and, 4, 11, 62, 64, 134, 151; survivors and,
    175; thingification and, 220; traumatic
    memes and, 129; Western classification
    and, 159; witnesses and, 121–22; youth
    movements and, 53; *Yuyanapac*
    (I remember) exhibition and, 132;
    Zapatistas and, 94–95, 122

walking and talking, xi, 2–5, 25–26, 30, 33,
    35, 38, 40
walking theory and, 9, 38–44. *See also*
    ¡Presente!
Wallerstein, Immanuel, 16
Weaver, Lois, 164
Weheliye, Alexander G., 13
Welles, Orson, 227
Westheim, Paul, 73
White, Hayden, 57
Willeman, Sister Valdette, 152
witnessing, 4, 9, 46, 124,
Wixáritar people of Central Mexico (the
    Huichol), 37

Yates, Pamela, 108
Yes Men, The, 39, 230–31, 243, 252n7,
    292n1; Art and Resistance course and,
    269–70n9; Dow impersonation and,
    233; environmental activism and, 226;
    facts and, 233; fake websites and, 233–36;
    hoax and, 237; lies and, 295n44; masks
    and, 286n22; performance/performative
    and, 240; U.S. Chamber of Commerce
    impersonation and, 233–34, 242, 295n36;
    U.S. Chamber of Commerce's lawsuit
    and, 234–36; Yes Ma'am and, 244

Zaleta, Marroquin, 243
Zapatistas, 28–29, 80, 87, 93, 102, 168, 222,
    245, 254n21; alternative democratic
    government and, 78, 98, 269n2; an-
    niversary party and, 68, 101; anonymity
    and, 74; "another world is possible" and,
    54; armed declaration of war and, 54, 92;
    authority and, 89; *camino largo* (long
    road) toward autonomy and, 68; *cara-
    coles* (autonomous municipalities) and,
    68; Che Guevara store and, 70; Chiapas
    and, 100; civil society and, 121–22; Co-
    mandanta Esther and, 90; Comandanta
    Ramona and, 270n20; connectivity and,
    95; durational performance and, 88;
    education and, 70–71; equality and, 90;
    escuelita (little school) and, 69; immo-
    bile Indian and, 94; indigenous popula-
    tions and, 70, 72–73, 90, 92; leadership
    and, 99; March for Dignity and, 103;
    masks and, 74–75, 84, 86, 94; Meso-
    american system of equivalences and, 95;

328   Index

Mexico's "bad" government and, 68; mutual recognition and, 95–96; murals and, 85; NAFTA (North American Free Trade Agreement) and, 73; Oventic and, 69, 77; *para no dejar de ser* (so as not to cease being) and, 36, 37; patience and, 88; practice-based research and, 83; rebel territory and, 69; refusal and, 48; resistance and, 91; silence and, 74, 76; silent march and, 69; slow, spiraling motion and, 39; snails and, 68, 97; social justice movements and, 100; stillness in presence and, 88; temporality and, 20, 100; unlearning and, 89; unmaking the world, 203; vulnerability and, 78; zigzag movement, 68, 77, 95

Zedillo, Ernesto, 68, 77, 93

Zócalo protests, 45, 53, 59

www.ingramcontent.com/pod-product-compliance
Lightning Source LLC
Chambersburg PA
CBHW051209170526
45166CB00005B/1818